CURRICULUM DEVELOPMENT
A Guide to Practice

Sixth Edition

Jon Wiles
University of North Florida at Jacksonville

Joseph Bondi
University of South Florida at Tampa

Upper Saddle River, New Jersey
Columbus, Ohio

Library of Congress Cataloging-in-Publication Data
Wiles, Jon.
    Curriculum development: a guide to practice / Jon Wiles, Joseph Bondi.—6th ed.
       p. cm.
    Includes bibliographical references and indexes.
    ISBN 0-13-089347-1
    1. Curriculum planning—United States. 2. Education—United States—Curricula. I.
Bondi, Joseph. II. Title.

LB2806.15.W55 2002
375′.001—dc21

                                    2001030618

Vice President and Publisher: Jeffery W. Johnston
Editor: Debra A. Stollenwerk
Editorial Assistant: Mary Morrill
Production Editor: Linda Hillis Bayma
Production Coordination: Ann Mohan, WordCrafters Editorial Services, Inc.
Design Coordinator: Diane C. Lorenzo
Cover Designer: Rod Harris
Production Manager: Pamela D. Bennett
Director of Marketing: Kevin Flanagan
Marketing Manager: Krista Groshong
Marketing Coordinator: Barbara Koontz

This book was set in Bembo by Carlisle Communications, Ltd. It was printed and bound by R.R. Donnelley
& Sons Company. The cover was printed by The Lehigh Press, Inc.

Pearson Education Ltd., *London*
Pearson Education Australia Pty. Limited, *Sydney*
Pearson Education Singapore Ptd. Ltd.
Pearson Education North Asia Ltd., *Hong Kong*
Pearson Education Canada, Ltd., *Toronto*
Pearson Educación de Mexico, S.A. de C.V.
Pearson Education—Japan, *Tokyo*
Pearson Education Malaysia Pte. Ltd.
Pearson Education, *Upper Saddle River, New Jersey*

Merrill
Prentice Hall

10 9 8 7 6 5 4 3 2

ISBN 0-13-089347-1

Jon Wiles

Joseph Bondi

ABOUT THE AUTHORS

Jon Wiles is a professor of education at the University of North Florida at Jacksonville and Joseph Bondi is a professor of education at the University of South Florida at Tampa. Both received their doctoral degrees from the University of Florida and they have served in various educational roles—as teachers, school and college administrators, and researchers. Their consulting firm of Wiles, Bondi, and Associates has conducted practice in forty states and ten foreign countries.

In addition to *Curriculum Development: A Guide to Practice,* Sixth Edition, Jon Wiles and Joseph Bondi have coauthored a number of other education books, including *Curriculum Planning: A New Approach* (1974), *Supervision: A Guide to Practice,* Fifth Edition (Merrill/Prentice Hall, 2000), *The New American Middle School: Educating Preadolescents in an Era of Change* (Merrill/Prentice Hall, 2001), *Practical Politics for School Administrators* (1981), *Principles of School Administration* (1983), and *The School Board Primer* (1985).

PREFACE

New instructional technologies, in particular the Internet, are changing the face of American education. Still less than one decade old, this new instructional resource is redefining the field of curriculum in a number of ways. Determining the scope and sequence of planned learning experiences, for example, has become difficult. Establishing criteria for the selection of organized learning presently has little focus. Historical precedents have little or no value in guiding curriculum leaders on many occasions. In short, this specialty area of educational leadership is in transition.

New to This Edition

The sixth edition of this text deviates from previous editions by focusing on the future of education rather than historical precedent. Chapters 1 and 6 address the impact of the new technologies on curriculum development in schools and provide educational leaders with new paradigms for understanding the changes that are occurring as we enter the twenty-first century.

In the past several years, teaching and learning in schools have shifted from the traditional construct of the teacher as the center of learning to a new model focused on the student as the critical ingredient in the classroom. This shift has major implications for both learning theory and instruction. We believe that this change also may be viewed as an opportunity to fulfill the century-old goal of progressive education to individualize instruction for all students.

In this edition we present curriculum development as a process of selecting from many options available to planners. In Chapter 6, eight curriculum designs are proffered that may shape future Internet-assisted lessons. The "new textbook" is discussed, and sample lessons are provided.

Also new in this edition are updates on model schools in the United States, links to the latest resources relating to curriculum development, new readings, and updated learning activities at the conclusion of each chapter.

Acknowledgments

We are grateful to the following reviewers for their helpful suggestions in the development of this manuscript: Muhammad Betz, Southeastern Oklahoma State University; Bonnie M. Beyer, University of Michigan, Dearborn; Carrine Bishop, Jackson State University; Cynthia G. Kruger, University of Massachusetts, Dartmouth; and Kay W. Terry, Western Kentucky University. We also remain indebted to our editor, Debbie Stollenwerk, for her helpful assistance in the renewal of this long-running text.

Jon Wiles

Joseph Bondi

≈ ≈

DISCOVER THE COMPANION WEBSITE ACCOMPANYING THIS BOOK

The Prentice Hall Companion Website: A Virtual Learning Environment

Technology is a constantly growing and changing aspect of our field that is creating a need for content and resources. To address this emerging need, Prentice Hall has developed an online learning environment for students and professors alike—Companion Websites—to support our textbooks.

In creating a Companion Website, our goal is to build on and enhance what the textbook already offers. For this reason, the content for each user-friendly website is organized by topic and provides the professor and student with a variety of meaningful resources. Common features of a Companion Website include:

For the Professor—

Every Companion Website integrates **Syllabus Manager™**, an online syllabus creation and management utility.

- **Syllabus Manager™** provides you, the instructor, with an easy, step-by-step process to create and revise syllabi, with direct links into Companion Website and other online content without having to learn HTML.
- Students may log on to your syllabus during any study session. All they need to know is the web address for the Companion Website and the password you've assigned to your syllabus.

≈ ≈

- After you have created a syllabus using **Syllabus Manager**™, students may enter the syllabus for their course section from any point in the Companion Website. The
- Clicking on a date, the student is shown the list of activities for the assignment. The activities for each assignment are linked directly to actual content, saving time for students.
- Adding assignments consists of clicking on the desired due date, then filling in the details of the assignment—name of the assignment, instructions, and whether it is a one-time or repeating assignment.
- In addition, links to other activities can be created easily. If the activity is online, a URL can be entered in the space provided, and it will be linked automatically in the final syllabus.
- Your completed syllabus is hosted on our servers, allowing convenient updates from any computer on the Internet. Changes you make to your syllabus are immediately available to your students at their next logon.

For the Student—

- **Topic Overviews**—outline key concepts in topic areas
- **Web Links**—a wide range of websites that provide useful and current information related to each topic area
- **Lesson Plans**—links to lesson plans for appropriate topic areas
- **Projects on the Web**—links to projects and activities on the web for appropriate topic areas
- **Education Resources**—links to schools, online journals, government sites, departments of education, professional organizations, regional information, and more
- **Electronic Bluebook**—send homework or essays directly to your instructor's email with this paperless form
- **Message Board**—serves as a virtual bulletin board to post—or respond to—questions or comments to/from a national audience
- **Chat**—real-time chat with anyone who is using the text anywhere in the country—ideal for discussion and study groups, class projects, etc.

To take advantage of these and other resources, please visit the *Curriculum Development: A Guide to Practice,* Sixth Edition, Companion Website at

www.prenhall.com/wiles

~ ~

RELATED TITLES FROM MERRILL EDUCATION

David G. Armstrong and Tom V. Savage
Teaching in the Secondary School: An Introduction, 5th Edition
ISBN: 0-13-028766-0

Traci Bliss and Joan Mazur
K–12 Teachers in the Midst of Reform: Common Thread Cases
ISBN: 0-13-937327-6

Joseph F. Callahan, Leonard H. Clark, and Richard D. Kellough
Teaching in Middle and Secondary Schools, 7th Edition
ISBN: 0-13-029285-0

Judy Eby, Adrienne Herrell, and Jim Hicks
Reflective Planning, Teaching, and Evaluation: K–12, 3rd Edition
ISBN: 0-13-029296-6

David Jacobsen, Paul Eggen, and Donald Kauchak
Methods for Teaching: Promoting Student Learning, 6th Edition
ISBN: 0-13-030898-6

Richard D. Kellough and Patricia Roberts
A Resource Guide for Elementary School Teaching: Planning for Competence, 5th Edition
ISBN: 0-13-027844-0

~ ~

BRIEF CONTENTS

CONTENTS

Chapter 5
Curriculum Management Planning   131

PART III
INSTRUCTIONAL CONCERNS   173

Chapter 6
Instruction in a Technological Era   175

Chapter 7
Elementary School Programs and Issues   215

PART I

THE CHANGING NATURE OF CURRICULUM

chapter 1

CURRICULUM IN AN AGE OF TECHNOLOGY

For nearly a century the study of curriculum has been largely historical and reconstructive in nature. Educators have used the ideas, great writings, model programs, and significant social events shaping public education as the lens for understanding present conditions and even for projecting foreseeable futures in education. In a single decade, all of that has changed! As we begin life in the twenty-first century, what has transpired during the past two hundred years in schools is no longer a certain or reliable guide to what is happening or may soon happen. Professional educators need new frameworks for the study of education and particularly for the field of curriculum. Our old views are now handicapping us in adjusting to the new age of technology.

The last decade of the twentieth century witnessed what 1960s futurist Kenneth Boulding[1] termed a "systems break." Boulding defined these breaks as the dissolution of patterns of linear thinking or statistical series related to the activities of humankind. Such breaks, he stated, would divide human history into separate parts and introduce new eras for humankind. In the extreme form, such breaks would create what Alvin Toffler called "future shock," in which conventional thinking would be reduced to a kind of thoughtful uncertainty.[2] A colleague of Boulding's in the 1960s, Kenneth Clark, noted that under such extreme conditions, prediction would become the most accurate indicator of future events. "Clark's Law" noted that "when a distinguished elder stated that something was possible, he would be almost certainly right. When the same elder stated that something was impossible, he would be very probably wrong."[3]

This is the apparent condition of education today, only we are lacking even the wise elders and their predictions about what comes next. Educators are being swept along by events not of their making, and in many cases, the feeling is most uncomfortable.

The single catalyst of the 1990s that changed everything in education was the Internet. This wonderful knowledge tool, both scary in its scale and exciting in its possibilities, has completely altered traditional conceptions of schooling, teaching, and learning. This edition of *Curriculum Development: A Guide to Practice* is dedicated to an exploration of the effects of these changing conditions. While new paradigms have not yet fully emerged to structure our thinking about these changes, we will attempt to present some of the challenging assumptions that are beginning to guide our thinking about curriculum in this new learning age. For many seasoned educators, these thoughts will be disturbing, even unbelievable. For those preparing for educational leadership over the next quarter century, these thoughts may open new intellectual avenues for conceptualizing what education may become.

Rather than beginning this text with a review of the historical factors that have shaped the evolution of curriculum study, as in our previous five editions, we choose instead to address the meaning of the new technologies head-on. These technological factors represent nothing less than a new "criterion" for curricular decision making. We are only now beginning to grasp the meaning of a world where learning is "24/7"—accessible to everyone on a twenty-four hour, seven-days-a-week basis. The traditional institution of the school is now only a "shell casing," a shadow of what it was a hundred years ago, or even a decade ago. Text has become hypertext, and time, space, media, and students, the critical variables in any curriculum, have taken on new forms.

We once saw a sign posted in a school that read, "If the finger points to the problem, the educator will study the finger." To date, this has been the most common response by curriculum theorists in reacting to these new and interactive technologies. Our current expenditures on technology in schools in the United States is about $7 billion a year,[4] and the haphazard pursuit of technology in many school districts is distorting budgets, disrupting instruction, and unbalancing the curricula that children are experiencing in the classroom. Curriculum development has become political, defined by David Easton as "the authoritative allocation of scarce resources."[5] For many districts, the new technologies are a financial swamp characterized by a bewildering set of choices with high stakes, a series of trade-offs for cost benefit.

Yet, despite the scale and importance of these new learning technologies, educators are addressing technological change in piecemeal fashion, seeing technology as an end rather than as a means. Technology has become almost hypnotic for educators, and the forces of change are sweeping us along with "Gold Rush" fervor without pausing for rational considerations such as cost/benefit ratios. The press of new events, substantive and relentless, is daily rolling up the traditional and historical structures of education. New school options such as proprietary education, home schooling, virtual education, and even nonschooling are challenging every aspect of schooling, education, and training. We are, simply put, living future shock.

In this context of massive and substantive change, what is the meaning of traditional curriculum reference points such as the Old Deluder Satan Act, John Dewey's lab school, the Civil Rights Act of 1964, or Goals 2000? Surely these former "essentials" are rapidly migrating from the "need to know" to the "nice to know" category. Just as today's schoolchildren quickly become bored with a teacher whose perception is fixed in the past, today's educational leadership students studying curriculum yearn to face forward to the future that is now enveloping us. These future leaders need perspective to understand the scale of change. They need new paradigms for organizing thinking about such change. They need adaptive organizational skills for the "shock" that is upon us. While the second half of the twentieth century was often a roller coaster of adjustment and change, those times will pale in comparison with what is on the immediate horizon.

In 1997 the National School Boards Association predicted that "there will be as much change in the next three decades in America as there was in the last three centuries."[6] KMPG in their 1999 publication "At the Gateway of the Knowledge Economy," acknowledged that the pace of change had accelerated beyond our expectations, and that "technology had become the driver of change as well as the enabler of change in America."[7] Bill Gates, founder of Microsoft, when told that the government was going to force the breakup of his world-class company in May 2000, responded:

> We're just at the beginning of this revolution. Even in the next ten years, we'll do more to change society than we've done in the past twenty-five years.[8]

The statistics come to us in staccato fashion. In 1997 60 percent of homes with children had some kind of computers. Eleven million Internet users were under age 15.[9] The number of web sites increased from 300,000 to 2.3 million between 1996 and 1998. By July 2000 there were approximately 10 million available web sites.[10] By 2002 the number of non-English speakers, using the Internet will outnumber the English speakers, and there will be more Chinese users than English users by 2005.[11] What do these figures mean for schools? For teaching and learning? For life on this planet during the next twenty-five years?

These sources, and so many others like them, seem to be indicating that one era has passed and another has arrived. A "systems break," an event that has yet to be fully understood, has occurred and will continue to change education forever. We need, in the words of Joseph Murphy, a new scaffolding upon which to construct education in this new century.[12] A fundamental and irreversible change in the meaning of the term curriculum has happened, and we are now in a critical period of adjustment in education.

The response of professional educators to these significant changes has been guarded. Overwhelmed by the ever-expanding scope of the new knowledge base, we have broken it down to focus on isolated learnings. Testing has become our escape hatch from having to address these conditions. Education leaders have failed to address the meaning of the new technologies because of a real fear that we've lost control of what we do. We have continued to do the "same old thing" when we know that such behavior is certainly dysfunctional and detrimental to the students in our care. The old curriculum questions—What is worth knowing?, How do we learn?, or What is essential?—must be revisited and redefined by curriculum workers. The field of curriculum is the essential element in this renewal process, and public education will fail or adapt to technological changes according to the response of curriculum leadership in our schools.

A SCENARIO

"St. Johns Schools Plan Home Link: Computer-Like Devices to Be Distributed" read the headlines of a local paper in November 1999. One of Florida's most technologically advanced school systems was moving to break out of the paper-and-pencil age, to shed the expensive textbook adoptions, and to overcome the basic economic inequities that surround computer ownership and Internet usage. The news release heralded a planned $20 million program to provide each schoolchild with a wireless "pointing device" that would allow the child to access learning over the district's server around the clock.[13]

This cutting-edge effort immediately found support from industry that recognized the possibility for a new market and, perhaps, an opportunity to supply thousands of districts with software curricula. A school population fifteen times larger than the entire military at the height of the Vietnam War does not go unnoticed; it is a super-market by any business standard.

In this local plan, the district would place antennae on school building roofs and "beam" education to anyone holding a receiver. The wireless devices possess a battery life of eight hours, allowing even children with no electricity in their homes to become fully educated. This district would become a lighthouse for hundreds of other districts wanting to become a part of the new age of technology.

In some ways this scenario, which was being carried out as this text was written, sheds light on the role of curriculum workers and public education in this technological age. Curriculum is a field that analyzes, designs, implements, and evaluates the development of school programs. Because most people in the field of curriculum have traditionally been novices in the area of technology, the professional perspective has value in this age of transition to a high-tech future. Curriculum workers ask questions, compare and contrast options, check means–ends connections, and are the evaluative and assessing part of the school team. They represent a kind of intellectual filter on the mindless pursuit of technological capacity in schools.

In the Florida scenario, the curriculum person might want to know why this district is going to take such a risky step to implement new technologies. For a district with a $100 million budget, $20 million is a heavy bet under any circumstances. That same curriculum person might want to know what is actually being purchased in the process. In an age when cell towers are being taken down to make way for microwave and satellite-download technologies (or handheld cell phone/computers), this proposed technology appears already obsolete. Aren't there other cheaper and more effective technologies? Twenty million dollars, in a district with 20,000 students, equals $1,000 per student or $28,000 per classroom just to implement the technology. What, if any, is the cost–benefit ratio of this venture?

The curriculum person should also have concerns about traditional questions of substance in the new curriculum. Like a television station, someone will have to staff, select, organize, and distribute the new learnings. If the district plans to contract for such distribution from software companies such as Oracle or CCC, wouldn't the district fall into the old Gillette syndrome (they give you the razor and then sell you the blades)? Orin Klapp once observed that in education fine lines separate the hero, villain, and fool.[14]

Also, the traditional but very real question of deciding what will be taught and how these learnings will be delivered to students is relevant. What defines this new curriculum (scope)? How will the new learnings be organized (sequence)? How will we decide what will be studied (criteria)? How will these decisions be made (decision-making process)? These aren't new questions, but they are the stuff of any curriculum development effort.

Finally, important policy dimensions are relevant to this new technological change. Will fewer teachers be needed because of these devices? Are we going to differentiate staffing? Are we prepared to invest 5 to 10 percent of our budget training teachers to use, contribute to, and fix these devices the way industry would? Do we need to keep building $35 million high schools and spending significant portions of our school budgets on busing students?

Most disturbing is the distinct possibility that the Florida district, like others, has totally missed the "meaning" of the new interactive technologies for learning. By insisting on a control mechanism (the home server with passive receivers used by students to access), it appears that all possibilities for nonlinear and creative learning are being abandoned. In reality, how is this idea any different from the use of an educational television station, an item that exists in most school districts with receivers already present in most classrooms and 96 percent of all U.S. homes?

In short, what are the details of this exotic plan? Can this effort possibly succeed without a needs assessment, specifications, goal targets, and evaluation/validation criteria? Has this idea already been attempted? Is the idea even worth trying? What are the odds that this venture will be successful? Is this district mesmerized by industry "glitter"? When we look more closely, perhaps curriculum theory and a historical understanding of schooling still has value in this age of technology.

These are the kind of questions educators with curriculum training should be asking about technology on a daily basis. Curriculum leaders need to become informed, and they need to understand that just because the new technologies are interesting, they aren't necessarily useful. As we in education begin to lose enthusiasm for the endless gadgets, we can begin to focus on what these new tools can do for children in the classroom. This is our starting point for the study of curriculum in the twenty-first century.

THE SIGNIFICANCE OF THIS CHANGE

In these early years of the twenty-first century, educators seem incapable of grasping the significance of what is happening to their world. They must soon wake up or lose their ability to manage this change. Nothing short of the purpose of educating is at stake. Doing nothing is not a choice for us. Doing the wrong thing has implications for the 53 million public school students that we serve. We must move quickly to start serious discussions about what is happening. As the novelty of moving information around wears off, schools have a window of opportunity to try to answer the question, What do these new tools mean for students?

The primary truth that will guide such inquiry is that the center of learning has shifted from the teacher to the student. Schools that assume a knowledge-mastery curriculum led by a knowledgeable teacher are doomed to obsolescence. Only when school leaders and teachers acknowledge that the monopoly of learning has been broken forever can we begin to define the new role of schooling.

It is instructive to view this basic change in our societal educating process in terms of three lenses: (1) the impact of this change, (2) the new perspectives, and (3) the operational decisions we must make.

Impact

We are now living in a world in which the future has, at best, a five-year horizon. It is, quite literally, impossible to know what kind of world our children will experience as adults, or to predict or even imagine their career patterns as adults. The fantasy of 1950s Dick Tracy wristwatches and spy satellites has been overrun by wearable technology and web sites such as Terraserver, a website featuring spy satellite photos. In the near future people will use the Internet (not personal computers) to store information, and people will be able to access and link multiple personal web sites from a variety of devices such as cell phones, computers, and television sets. In a word, the new technologies will soon be tailored to the individual needs of users.

This "digital convergence," which integrates computers, communication, and consumer electronics, means that everyday life will become richer and more fulfilling for those fortunate enough to have access to these assets. As Gagné observed, "learning is limited by what the learner perceives."[15] In the old world (pre-1995) learners received knowledge through the perceptions of other people. In the post-1995 world, learners can have their own perceptions of knowledge. Learning has been fundamentally transformed by this ability to access knowledge and perceive it subjectively.

In the United States and more acutely in the rest of the world, we are approaching a crisis of "digital divide." Some people have access to new technology and new opportunities for growing, while others are still dependent on the older system for their enlightenment. For example, 69 percent of all U.S. households in which someone holds a bachelor's degree have computers and 45 percent have Internet access. In households in which people hold less than a high school diploma, the numbers fall to 16 percent and 14 percent, respectively.[16]

People with access to the new hardware, such as electronic books, pocket-sized personal computers, and personal computer tablets, will exit the world of collected knowledge, written knowledge, and stored knowledge and enter a global village of knowledge exchange. For these people, acquiring knowledge will give way to using knowledge, and the learning process will be accessible at home, at school, in the community, or in the car.

The sudden and iconoclastic nature of this change in information access has stupefied and befuddled educators. The old game is over. But, in response to this change educators have studied the technology rather than the implications of the new technology. They are, in essence, studying the finger instead of the problem to which the finger is pointing.

New Perspectives

Alvin Toffler, who has consistently projected the future for thirty years, once observed: "The illiterate of the year 2000 will not be the individual who cannot read and write, but the one who cannot learn, unlearn, and relearn."[17] Our historic understanding of becoming educated as being the recipient of unusual information is completely obsolete in this new technological era. Training will have a five-year shelf life in the twenty-first century, and knowledge will be constantly redefined and reinterpreted. The key buzz words of the 1990s, postmodernism and constructivism, have been activated.

For the new learner, the ability to access endless variations of inert knowledge, or tailored information, means that learning is both an internal and subjective process. While educators in public school settings now could provide a totally individualized learning experience for each of the 53 million students in school, it is unrealistic to think that they will succeed. Rather, it is more probable that the learners will begin to seek out their own access points (home schooling, charter schools, virtual schools) according to their own interests. The fate of "organized learning," long the basis of all cultural and social renewal, is no longer certain. The many "publics" (i.e., diversity of political, ethnic, and cultural influences) that emerged in U.S. schools during the last forty years of the twentieth century will likely demand the creation of curricula to reflect their own realities—a postmodern state of affairs, for sure.

Individual learners will certainly be attracted to the new associate and relational learning proffered by the interactive technologies. These technologies will create seductive learning environments, such as the earlier video games for children in the 1980s and 1990s. Individuals will learn by doing, by interacting, using multiple senses (not just hearing and seeing), and they will receive feedback to refine and understand and to build new knowledge in association with previous personal understandings. The advanced technologies will assist in visualization, model building, data analysis, and a host of higher-level learning skills.

The newest computers being developed likely will be able to adjust to the learning preferences of each learner using "aptitude by treatment interaction" (ATI) procedures. Personal learning preferences such as cognitive tempo, field dependence, focal attention, bandwidth, visualization, and holistic information will be read by the computer using the student's eyes as the guide; the student will be quickly "typed," and the delivery will be adjusted to the preferences. These rich hypermedia environments will undoubtedly produce smarter learners who can use and apply their education in more creative ways. Learners will be superior, albeit detached, citizens of the twenty-first century.[18]

Not fully explored yet is the effect of these delivery media and environments on the development of intelligence and human brains. If, as we understand, learning itself changes the structure of the brain, and that structure determines how the brain organizes itself for future learning, then our conceptions of intelligence and appropriate behavior become vastly important constructs for the application of these new technological media. Intelligence may be redefined in terms of an individual's flexibility, synthesizing capacity, and ability to create novel responses. Brain research will focus on rewiring (the plastic brain), new relationships and capacity (the spatial brain), and change (the emotional brain).[19]

What about teaching and learning? Is there a spot in this new era for the traditional classroom teacher, the mainstay of public education in the United States for three hundred years? Will learning theory, learning strategies, and learning tactics remain the same with the application of these new interactive media? Or, will behaviorism in schools (i.e., emphasis on tests, grades, high structure and control) give way to a new and different learning construct that might allow teachers to be rewarded for their human qualities rather than a mechanistic assessment of the outcome performances of their students?

Already, there is a strong movement in the United States toward a new form of differentiated staffing using labels such as "lead teacher" and "teacher mentor." James McKenzie, in his technological "Teacher Vanguard," explained how he looks for and selects new teachers who possess "nerve" or daring, raw talent, an eagerness to learn, and respect and empathy for other teachers in this time of change.[20] Such selection, of course, raises the possibilities of using Jung's personality indicators (see the Myers-Briggs or David Keirsey's work) to find new-age teachers.[21]

The fate of such technological pioneers in the classrooms will depend heavily on the support systems established by the school systems, including hardware, infrastructures, software, technical support, maintenance, telecommunication access, and most important, training. Without these essential kinds of assistance, in massive applications, the best and the brightest of teachers will be seduced by industry. Who could blame these new-age teachers for leaving a dying social institution?

In regard to the act of learning itself, it seems obvious that behaviorism and the highly structured classrooms of the past are being pushed off the stage as a new learner-centered (constructivist) philosophy is established. Heavily dependent on our understanding of thinking, memory, brain development, and personal learning preferences (motivation), this new philosophy will lead educators to new learning theory and instructional strategies appropriate to the technological era.

The following fourteen principles of student-centered learning, developed by a task force of the American Psychology Association in 1995, will guide the development of such a new learning approach:

1. The learning of complex subject matter is most effective when it is an intentional process of constructing meaning from information and experience.

2. The successful learner, over time and with the support of instructional guidance, can create meaningful, coherent representations of knowledge.
3. The successful learner can link new information with existing information in meaningful ways.
4. The successful learner can create and use a repertoire of thinking and reasoning strategies to achieve complex learning goals.
5. Higher order strategies for selecting and monitoring mental operations facilitate creative and critical thinking.
6. Learning is influenced by environmental factors, including culture, technology, and instructional practices.
7. What and how much is learned is influenced by the learner's motivation. The motivation to learn, in turn, is influenced by the individual's emotional state, interest and goals, and habits of thinking.
8. The learner's creativity, higher order thinking, and natural curiosity all contribute to motivation to learn. Intrinsic motivation is stimulated by tasks of optimal novelty and difficulty, relevant to personal interests, and providing for personal choice and control.
9. Acquisition of complex knowledge and skills requires extended learner effort and guided practice. Without the learner's motivation to learn, the willingness to exert this effort is unlikely without coercion.
10. As individuals develop, there are different opportunities and constraints for learning. Learning is most effective when differential development within and across physical, intellectual, emotional, and social domains is taken into account.
11. Learning is influenced by social interaction, interpersonal relations, and communication with others.
12. Learners have different strategies, approaches, and capabilities for learning that are a function of prior experience and heredity.
13. Learning is most effective when differences in the learner's linguistic, cultural, and social backgrounds are taken into account.
14. Setting appropriate high and challenging standards and assessing the learner as well as the learning process, are integral parts of the learning process.[22]

Operational Decisions

Clearly, time is of the essence for curriculum leaders to help education define its role in a time of such significant change. It is not at all certain that public schools can make the transition to the new learning age that has arrived so abruptly.

Like most institutions in our society, schools are heavily invested in past capital expenditures. School buildings, teachers on continuing contract, library holdings, stadiums, school sites, and so forth, suggest the status quo rather than change. For example, how do traditional school buildings and teaching units (80 percent of all educational costs) fit with the new electronic access of learning?

It will be particularly difficult for schools to accept the notion of a learner-centered curriculum. Schools, like churches, have experienced centuries of special privilege and a monopoly on learning. Public schools have had fiscal support from society, growing at a rate of 6 percent a year for as long as anyone can remember. The paternal, judging, and controlling aspects of the educational "business" won't fall away easily.[23]

The truth is, the relationship of schools to technological change in our society has been deficient from the beginning of the computer movement. Educators have lacked insight into the meaning of these learning instruments, and we have failed to educate ourselves about the trends that drive technological change. We are presently secondhand consumers of technology who have distorted both our budgets and our mission in pursuit of a high-tech image. Public schools are not yet making a successful transition to the new information age, and we must change dramatically if we are to do so.

The Internet has actually been in our society since 1969 when the military created ARPAnet (Advanced Research Project Agency network) to link military sites during the Vietnam War. This net was transformed in 1986 to the National Science Foundation net (NSFnet) linking six supercomputers for the space program. It was finally determined by Congress to be a commercial network (the World Wide Web or www) on April 30, 1995. Browsers and search engines provided popular access to this resource in the late 1990s, and schools followed the commercial applications.

Looking back, the reaction of schools to these learning tools (the finger, not the problem) was to be a consumer and purchase these expensive items without any meaningful vision. Districts first bought demo products (Commodore, Texas Instruments, and Apple, to name a few) before settling on the Apple IIe as the workhorse for the classroom. Apple Computers, the first with sound educational software and a teacher-friendly format, also had attractive games for students. By the early 1990s many districts had entire labs of Apples for skill development; the most advanced districts moved to connected computers or networks (i.e., local area networks (LANs) and wide area networks (WANs) by the late 1990s.

When the new Internet began to feature rich multimedia learning resources accessible by anyone, anytime, schools did not respond to the possibilities for a different kind of learning. Rather, the wealthy districts purchased high-speed machines with modems and discovered the additional cost of phone lines in schools. The nonlinear formats puzzled school leaders who had no familiarity with creating curriculum from such varied resources. Time, space, media, and learners were no longer "contained" in the traditional dependence format of the classroom. Suddenly, curriculum development was more like an interdisciplinary unit, pulling sources from everywhere into a nebulous conceptual mass; the Internet was akin to throwing all of the library books onto the floor and then searching for a title.

A brief era followed during which public schools purchased commercial software or produced CD-ROMs in-house in an attempt to bring order to the chaos of limitless and random knowledge on the Internet. In many districts the fear of pornographic material simply masked a greater fear of loss of control over both the students and the process of learning.

Today, perhaps as many as 20 percent of all school districts, such as the St. Johns district in Florida, are beginning to experiment with alternative forms of teaching and learning. The other school districts continue to pursue the latest equipment or are at rest in financial exhaustion from the futility of always having to purchase a faster or more complex model of computer. Some are still hoping that "these things will pass," a highly unlikely scenario.

Bill Gates, the new symbol of U.S. technological genius, feels certain that the next generation of software from Microsoft (BizTech and Visual Studio) will take us to an even higher plane of learning. The latest technology will create applications for the user; digital convergence, the integration of computers, communication, and consumer electronics, will be fully achieved at this level. Cross this observation with the newest line of IBM's "wearable technology," and we get a peek at the future (but only as far as 2005).

So, what decisions can curriculum leaders make that will help schools and districts transition from nineteenth-century to the twenty-first-century learning formats? How can we learn to cope with these "disruptive" technologies that provide simpler, cheaper, and more user-friendly ways of learning? The answer to these two questions may determine our longevity in the teaching–learning business. Surely, schools cannot expect an indefinite governmental subsidy just because they are the country's largest and most stable institution.

Of true interest to us is the growing importance of philosophy in solving this paradox of intellectual poverty amidst technological plenty. The field of curriculum was born out of philosophical questions in the early part of the twentieth century; these same questions will be the basis for our response to the technological changes of the twenty-first century. In order for schools to extricate themselves from the vise of too-rapid change, they will have to identify or redefine their basic purpose.

Centuries of defining education as "knowing" must give way to a newer and more relevant purpose of helping individuals use knowledge. This will be, as previously observed, most difficult since schools are virtual monuments to knowledge acquisition and behaviorism. Classroom organization, teacher behavior, record keeping, and all of the other practices found in schools are all geared toward the control of outcome as measured by "knowing." We believe that, soon, students and parents and even teachers will no longer submit to such control mechanisms when they have viable options for learning through the new technologies. Schools and districts, directed by curriculum leadership, must soon begin altering their mission, even in the face of legal mandates by state legislatures for ever-increasing control of the learning process.

In the new learning environment of schools, students will be the focus of all efforts. The learner will be active, not passive. The learner will be allowed to make choices and will have to become more responsible for learning. In addition, the curriculum will have to be redesigned for student access and use. These statements, and others like them, suggest a new process of educating in which learning is "individualized," or constructed, for the person being educated. In a country where we keep track of billions of credit card transactions, we now have the tools to make a century-old dream of meeting the needs of each student a reality.

To start the transition, districts should consider the beginning operational decision of leaving behind the "stand alone" personal computer and its software and beginning to invest exclusively in connectivity. Learning in the twenty-first century cannot be contained in a lab, serviced by a company such as CCC or Oracle, placed on district servers, or reduced to a set of appropriate CD-ROMs. With the Internet, we have an instrument that can touch anything, anywhere on earth, instantly, at our fingertips. More important, our students have this same instrument at home. Connectivity may be a control issue for schools, but it also means empowerment for districts and for teachers interested in developing meaningful curricula for our students.

A second operational decision within our control is to begin to integrate technology throughout the curriculum. We can do this only if we allow our teachers and our students a true participative role in the process. Entrepreneurship may be the key to gaining such participation quickly. For years schools have shamelessly used teachers for various tasks without adequate compensation. If school leaders find it distasteful to pay lead teachers to redesign the curriculum for the twenty-first century, they should rest assured that industry will not have a problem with such compensation. This fact may redefine what is meant by schools being "businesslike" in the twenty-first century.

A third operational decision schools can make is to begin investing in the training necessary to make this transition to the twenty-first century successful. In the new era of learning, change will always be technical before it is intellectual. We must make all teachers comfortable with technology, and we must allow teachers to unilaterally use technology to enhance the curriculum. This will mean a loss of control but a gain in strength for schools. Education presently invests less than one-half of 1 percent of its budget on training, while some industries invest up to 10 percent of their budgets in responding to change. Failure to make this decision would ensure the failure of school as a twenty-first century institution.

Making these preliminary operational decisions will not necessarily guarantee a successful transition to the new learning age. But these three decisions, if activated, will start to refocus the efforts of curriculum workers from "means" to "ends." We can assume that there will be an endless stream of new computers and learning technologies in the future, but we can only react to them in a meaningful way if we have criteria for their selection and application. Begin by asking how these tools will help your teachers or students. Ask, What skills will our students need in the foreseeable future of information exchange? Ask, How can schools contribute to the ability of teachers and students to cope with technological change?

While these three operational decisions will start schools and districts on their way to changing, a much more difficult level of change waits beyond these early steps. In the future all schools will need to redefine what they do. This will be a freewheeling process in which all things will be called into question. Do we need these expensive school buildings in an information-access age? Do we need textbooks? Do we need to purchase so many school buses? Do we need the same kind of stand-up, subject-certified teacher? Can we learn to share resources with other social institutions? Can we establish a new learning relationship with parents? Can we agree on what information students should possess as the basis for future learning? Can we develop nonstandard evaluation standards? Can we use our fiscal resources in better ways to help students learn?

These are not idle questions, nor are they novel ones. Curriculum leaders have been asking these questions, and more, throughout the last century. They are precisely the kind of questions that we should be asking in regard to the new role of technology in schools. The questions no longer are internal or the basis of only school decision making; they have implications for business, government, and families. Such decisions will be public decisions, and the process will often be a rocky one for school leaders.

The critical concern in all of this is whether school and district leaders will allow classroom teachers to emerge as our new instructional leaders. We believe this single decision is key to any substantial process of transition, and one that all public schools must make in the coming decade. The past century has witnessed a major underestimation of teacher abilities by a paternal system that perhaps saw teachers as a threat to external control of learning. In our work with teacher leaders, we have come to realize the intelligence, dedication, and technical skill possessed by some of our best teachers.[24] We believe that if schools are to transition to a new form of twenty-first-century learning in a timely fashion, the largest and most significant decision must be to let our best teachers lead this transition. Classroom teachers are probably the only ones who can bring these new technologies into our schools and make them work.

We can also expect that teachers will be fearful. They too fear a loss of control in their classrooms. They may fear losing their jobs to technology as is happening in other walks of life. Rewards for their leadership must be significant and extrinsic. The "vanguard" must be put in touch with each other and protected from group norms and peer pressure when they begin to "bust the rate."* School leaders must remember that what constitutes the teaching place (virtual and otherwise) and the teacher (differentiated by skill and pay) is up for grabs. We should all expect that schools will not look like they do now when the transition is complete.

Other roles must change as well for schools to operate successfully in the new technological age. As schools make the transition, the following new roles will be expected of other leaders:

Administrative Leaders
1. Must take the initiative in designing or selecting new structures for organization, communication, and instructional redesign.

Busting the rate is a business term that refers to when an employee performs at a rate higher than peers. Such employees are generally the subject of peer pressure.

2. Must demand that assessment be made for technological spending along the lines suggested in this chapter. Cost–benefit analyses should be based exclusively on instructional goals.
3. Must begin thinking about a time of nonpermanence in education. Just as portable buildings became a fixture in school construction, leasing should become a fixture in technological applications.
4. Must force an investment in technological training. Hardware should be considered a means, not an end. The true need is for a savvy workforce that can adjust and adapt.

Curriculum Leaders

1. Must acknowledge a constructivist future in classroom learning. Any prolonged attempt to standardize learning will promote unfavorable comparisons among schools and encourage individuals to seek viable options beyond the schools.
2. Must see technology primarily as a means for greater connectivity. The possibilities for enrichment should be stressed to teachers at the classroom level.
3. Must begin to redefine student outcomes in terms of knowledge use, not knowledge mastery. In the future, students may have to unlearn much of what they thought they knew to be true.
4. Must follow lead teachers (and students) who are the true pioneers in this change process. Schools have people who are knowledgeable about the new technologies, but most don't hold leadership titles.

Instructional Leaders

1. Must identify the new teacher. Recruitment of these persons will be easier than retraining those who don't match the profile.
2. Must find the resources to pay these technological leaders for their creativity and competence.
3. Must understand that teachers learn best from each other. Learning is a social process, and "show and tell" strategies work best in education.
4. Must begin to use technology to train teachers about technology. Business now conducts 60 percent of all training through technology.

Human Services Leaders

1. Must help teachers to understand human differences, learning preferences, disabilities, and uniqueness. These understandings will highlight the importance of a technology curriculum that can individualize instruction.
2. Must encourage the creation of learner-centered environments in schools. In the future, schools cannot resemble the factory image of the nineteenth century.
3. Must facilitate the identification of the teacher "vanguard" by looking for flexible and inquiring individuals who are curious about technology.
4. Must attempt to increase awareness of brain research. With technology, schools will build the next generation.

SUMMARY

This chapter discussed the new and dominating force in modern curriculum development. In this sixth edition, we see the new learning technologies as the most important variable impacting schools today. Traditional and historical orientations to the field of curriculum must be seen in the context of these novel and massive changes occurring in our schools.

A revolution in teaching and learning is occurring. Schools, as highly structured, behavioristic, and controlling institutions, are endangered by the introduction of new interactive learning technologies. The centuries-old monopoly of learning by schools is clearly being uncoupled by these new media. Schools must change or become the dying relics of another age. Whether our country's largest social institution can make the transition to a new era is uncertain. Curriculum leadership and teacher involvement are critical to a successful passage.

Curriculum leaders and others serving in administrative, instructional, and human services leadership roles must force school "systems" to confront the changes that are occurring. We believe the most important task before us is to redefine the mission of today's school or see the current school population siphoned off by more responsive and accessible media for learning.

SUGGESTED LEARNING ACTIVITIES

1. Create a list of the forces that seem to be driving schools toward a technological future. Can you rank-order these items?

2. What concerns do you have about the evolution of U.S. schools into a third stage of development characterized by postmodernism and technology?

NOTES

1. Kenneth Boulding, *The Meaning of the Twentieth Century* (New York: Harper and Row, 1964).
2. Alvin Toffler, *Future Shock* (New York: Random House, 1970).
3. As cited in Boulding, *The Meaning of the Twentieth Century,* p. 30.
4. EnGuage, NCREL Conference on Technology, "Technology Use in Schools," Atlanta, Georgia, June 2000.
5. David Easton, *A Systems Analysis of Political Life* (New York: Wiley and Sons, 1965).
6. National School Boards Association, Washington, D.C., Position paper 1997.
7. As cited in KMPG, "At the Gateway of the Knowledge Economy," (White paper), July 1999.
8. Bill Gates in "Next Phase of Internet Will Be More Personal," Associated Press syndicated, June 6, 2000.
9. Dan Tapscott, *Growing Up Digital: the Rise of the Net Generation* (New York: McGraw-Hill, 1997).
10. IDC's Internet Commerce Market Model, http://glreach.com/globstats, July 2000.
11. Anick Jesdanum, Associated Press, "U.S. Rules the Internet—But Not for Long," June 25, 2000.
12. Joseph Murphy, AASA-School Administrator, "Core Strategies for Reforming Schools," http://www.aasa.org, December 1999.
13. Marge Maraghy, "St. Johns Schools Plan Home Link," *Florida Times Union,* November 11, 1999.

14. Orin Klapp, *Heroes, Villains, and Fools* (Englewood Cliffs, NJ: Prentice Hall, 1962).

15. Robert Gagné, *Instructional Technology Foundations* (Hillsdale, NJ: LEA, 1987), p. 316.

16. "1999 Internet Use," White House Press Release, April 17, 2000.

17. Alvin Toffler, *Powershift: Knowledge, Wealth and Violence at the Edge of the 21st Century* (New York: Bantam, 1990).

18. White paper by Jon Wiles and David Tai, "Designing Instruction for a New Century," NSTD Conference, Orlando, Florida, March 1999.

19. S. I. Greenspan, *The Growth of the Mind and the Endangered Origins of Intelligence* (Reading, MA: Addison-Wesley, 1997).

20. James McKenzie, "Creating the Vanguard: Identifying and Growing the Pioneers," http://www.fromnowon.org/eschool/cadre.html, February 24, 1999.

21. For example, see David Keirsey, *Please Understand Me II: Temperament, Character, Intelligence* (Del Mar, CA: Prometheus, 1998); see also Isabel Myers, *Introduction to Type* (Swarthmore, PA: 1970).

22. American Psychological Association, "Learner-Centered Psychological Principles," http://www.apa.org/lcp2/edlcptest.html, May 18, 2000.

23. For a great discussion of this problem, see Ivan Illich, *Deschooling Society* (New York: Harper and Row, 1971).

24. Author Jon Wiles serves as co-director of LearningWebs, Inc., a nonprofit Florida corporation (http://www.learnweb.org). The study of Florida's elite League of Teachers, "Some of Our Best Teachers," found a highly competent group of teachers available for leadership roles in the transition to the twenty-first century.

ADDITIONAL READING

Berman, S. "The World Is the Limit in the Virtual High School." *Educational Leadership* 55, 3 (November 1997): 52–54.

Debenham, J. "Computers, Schools and Families: A Radical Vision for Public Schools." *THE Journal* 22, 1 (February 1994): 58–61.

Early, Margaret J., and Kenneth J. Rehage. *Issues in Curriculum: A Selection of Chapters from Past NSSE Yearbooks.* Chicago: University of Chicago Press, 1999.

Foshay, Arthur Wellesley. *The Curriculum: Purpose, Substance, Practice.* New York: Teachers College Press, 2000.

Fund, J. "Politics, Economics, and Education in the 21st Century." *Imprimis* 27, 5 (May 1998).

Glanz, Jeffrey, and Linda S. Behar-Horenstein. *Paradigm Debates in Curriculum and Supervision: Modern and Postmodern Perspectives.* Westport, CT: Greenwood, 2000.

Healy, Jane. *Endangered Minds.* New York: Touchstone, 1990.

Keating, Michele, Mary Wood-Piazza, and Jon Wiles. *Learning Webs: Curriculum Journeys on the Internet.* Unpublished manuscript.

Kotulak, Robert. *Inside the Brain.* Kansas City, MO: Andrews McMeel, 1996.

McNeil, John D. *Curriculum: A Comprehensive Introduction.* New York: John Wiley & Sons, 1999.

Mohnson, B. "Stretching Bodies and Minds through Technology." *Educational Leadership* 55, 3 (November 1997): 46–48.

Walsh, Paddy. *Curriculum.* New York: Continuum International, 2000.

WEB SITES

American Psychological Association—Learner-centered psychological principles: http://www.apa. org/ed/lcp.html

CEO Forum on Education and Technology: http://www.ceoforum.org

Computer Strategies Assessment: http://www.compstrategies.com/staffdevelopment/index.html

Curriculum assessment and instruction: http://www.ncrel.org/info/curriculum/

National education standards for teachers: http://cnets.iste.org/index3.html

Office of Education Technology: http://www.ed.gov/Technology

chapter **2**

CURRICULUM IN THE NEW ERA

For those not in professional education, the term *curriculum* is usually associated with a document such as a syllabus, teacher's guide, or textbook. But, for professional educators, the word *curriculum* is usually more broadly defined. It may include a set of global intentions, perhaps a formal plan or organizational structure, and any one of a number of delivery media. Above all, curriculum leaders are concerned with purpose in educational programs, and the clarification of a program's purpose is always an essential prerequisite to any sound curriculum development. The element of choice is present in every curriculum decision, and those choices always reflect values.

In the opening chapter, we used the example of an innovative technology program in a school district to illustrate the absence of such global conceptions. In many ways, the failure of the field of curriculum development to go beyond a mechanical and piecemeal approach to program development results from the absence of a large vision. In the new technology age, such vision must be present before leaders confront the overwhelming number of choices and options.

Curriculum development is a process whereby the choices of designing a learning experience for students are made and then activated through a set of coordinated activities. Curriculum development, for the professional, is a logical process that begins with clear goals and proceeds in an "if–then" manner until finished. In other words, the process of curriculum development is deductive in nature, resulting in finer and finer actions to accomplish the intended purpose of the curriculum.

Curriculum development usually begins with a set of questions that initially reveal value preferences and then later undergird planning efforts and program evaluation. When formalized, these value preferences are referred to as *educational philosophies* or *learning theories*. Examples of such questions might be, What learner outcome do we wish to promote? or, How will the students actually learn? To begin curriculum work without such clarification and structure is to invite an incomplete or inconsistent product.

For the curriculum development process to be logical, boundaries for inclusion or exclusion must be established. These boundaries are usually determined through a process of developing goals, objectives, or desired outcomes that provide both structure and direction to efforts. Sometimes, however, forces external to education introduce variables that cannot be predicted or controlled, thus introducing an illogical element into the curriculum development process. In the United States, political, economic, and social forces disrupt and redirect curriculum development efforts. Because of such influences, being consistent is a major concern of workers in the field.

The assessment of curricula is always subjective since the plan always reflects preferences and values. However, curriculum development as a process is neutral and can be judged by its efficiency. The critical question for curriculum developers is, Does the program developed serve our intentions? Although considerable controversy surrounds the purposes of many curricula, the *process* of curriculum development is fairly standard and has long been widely accepted.

A traditional way of thinking about curriculum development is to use a model or an analogy. Like an architect who cannot design a home until certain information about style (ranch, colonial, modern) and function (number of bedrooms, special rooms) is known, curriculum planners can't design a technology program or a new social studies program until they know the purpose and the intended outcome. Over time, the field of curriculum has focused on a cyclical model to guide the process of development: analysis, design, implementation, and evaluation. If followed, this model provides a rational and deductive way of creating school programs from inception to assessment. We will return to the model later in this chapter.

Given these observations, curriculum development activities in a school setting can be both purposeful and process oriented. The primary purpose of all curriculum development efforts in schools is the improvement of learning for students.

THE EVOLUTION OF SCHOOLING—THREE ERAS

A sense of history is very important for persons entering curriculum leadership. The American education system is unique in the modern world, and without a historical perspective, many contemporary practices might seem odd or even illogical. A historical perspective may also prove valuable in keeping the curriculum development efforts focused on long-term goals as opposed to events of the moment.

We divide the history of education in the United States into three eras: the evolutionary era, the modern era, and the postmodern era. The first era describes education as it evolved into a unique world form. The second era reflects most of the twentieth-century period. The third era, or postmodern era, describes current events.

The Evolutionary Era

This history begins only twenty-seven years after the landing on Plymouth Rock, when the settlers established a regulatory act to govern their first "grammar" school (1635). Early European settlers came to America to escape religious persecution, and they pursued their religious beliefs with vigor. Martin Luther had taught that the Bible must be read to ward off the work of the devil, and so the first known regulation, the Old Deluder Satan Act (1647), established schools for that purpose.[1]

A second purpose for education in America, established quite early, was to develop a "literate citizen" capable of participating in acts of governance for the common good. Benjamin Franklin, for instance, spoke often of the "rise of the common man" and the need for strong citizen participation. The concept of a "participatory democracy" rationalized many early schools in America.

Finally, a third idea about schools in the colonies was that they were useful for promoting the common good and for bringing about desired changes in society. Following the War of 1812, for instance, schools were expected to teach about our national identity and emerging beliefs.

As civilization spread in the colonial areas and beyond, forming schools went hand-in-hand with the development of communities. Usually, such schools were of minimal duration (several years at most), were taught in a one-room schoolhouse erected by the community, and focused on basic literacy skills. Quite early, these "American" schools took on characteristics that were unlike European schools of that era.

Horace Mann (1796–1859) is forever linked to early education efforts in this nation and is often called the "Father of the American Public School." Mann, a legislator and U.S. congressman from Massachusetts, was instrumental in passing early laws governing education in his home state. He helped establish the first teacher-training institution in 1839 and later served as the first commissioner of education in Massachusetts. He advocated schooling that was universal, free, and nonsectarian. After a visit to Prussia in 1843, Mann returned to the United States to establish a "graded school ladder" concept and helped gain support for the first tax-supported elementary schools in 1850.

As early as 1779, Thomas Jefferson was advocating free schools for the children of colonists. This proposal was in stark contrast to the prevailing European practice in which "dual tracks" of free and private education were maintained. A Free Public School Society was formed around 1800 in New York City and educated over 600,000 pupils in its fifty-year history.

Indicative of the early social functions of education in America was the provision of the Northwest Ordinance (1787), which mandated that all townships in new states set aside land for schools as a precondition for becoming recognized communities.

Paralleling the establishment of this popular education system in the elementary grades was an unrelated system of higher education dating from the establishment of Harvard College in 1636. The higher education system, unlike the public elementary system, was private and exclusive. The conception of education at this level was focused solely on producing learned men and leaders for the emerging nation. This distinction between the two systems is very important to understand because, even as we enter the twenty-first century, various philosophies compete in our society to define education. The roots of these differences were present from the beginning of our nation.

Private education in the early colonies produced judges, legislators, and persons in other leadership roles. Upon finishing the elementary years, these students would secure a tutor or attend an academy to prepare for college. This private "bridge" to leadership roles in American society existed for most of the eighteenth and nineteenth centuries. Eventually, laws to support secondary schools with taxes (1821) and the establishment of public land-grant colleges and universities (1862) began to break this private schooling domination. Public taxation for secondary schools became universal in the United States following the historic Kalamazoo Case, an 1872 Michigan Supreme Court case.

Thus, after two centuries, a solid educational system consisting of both public and private elements had been established in the United States and was being supported by citizens. With the exception of the turmoil surrounding the Civil War, the development of schools was an ever-expanding process leading to the establishment of this nation's strongest institution. The purpose of the American school was clearly literacy and knowledge acquisition, but with signs of some social utility mixed in.

The final stage for completing the universal school ladder in the United States came during the 1890s when a number of national committees met to organize and coordinate both the subjects taught and the levels of schooling. By far the best-known of these committees was the prestigious Committee of Ten, headed by President Charles Eliot of Harvard University. Working in 1892 and 1893, this committee sought to coordinate the secondary education programs of the states by establishing college entrance requirements. The committee recommended a standard set of high school courses, and a parallel committee established a "unit" measure for each course taken. Thereafter, students were awarded unit credits (Carnegie units) for each course with a set number required for graduation and college entrance.

Thus, by the end of the nineteenth century, students could attend tax-supported free public schools for up to twelve years and study a highly standardized curriculum at the secondary level despite the fact that education is a "state right" according to the U.S. Constitution (a residual right by omission). As the twentieth century began, a traditional and standard form of education was in place.

The Modern Era

In the late eighteenth and early nineteenth centuries, new ideas about children and learning were emerging in Europe. The traditional wisdom of that era viewed children as incomplete adults who needed to be shaped into preferred forms. Several European educators challenged those traditional views and became early advocates for working with the young in different ways.

Jean-Jacques Rousseau (1712–1778) was one of the earliest writers to see children as unfolding and malleable. Writing in his book *Émile* (1762), Rousseau argued that children were innately good (not evil) and called for a controlled environment in which positive growth could occur naturally. Rousseau believed that learning was most successful when education began with the student's interests.

Another early child advocate was Johann Pestalozzi (1746–1827), who advocated a "learning by doing" approach to education. In his book *Leonard and Gertrude* (1781), Pestalozzi described the behavior of children at his school in Yverdon, Switzerland, an early laboratory school. This educator is known for addressing the growth of the whole child in learning: the head, the heart, and the hands.

A third widely read European of this era, Friedrich Froebel (1782–1852) has been credited with establishing the early kindergarten *(Kleinkinderschaftig)* and having an important impact on later American education. Froebel, who had studied with Pestalozzi, spoke of the natural development in children and developed "readiness" materials to help each child move along in his or her early growth.

Finally, the German educator Johann Herbart (1776–1841) influenced the thoughts of U.S. educators, but with a different philosophical orientation. Unlike Rousseau, Pestalozzi, and Froebel, Herbart believed that schools should be highly structured and should prepare future citizens of the social-political community by shaping their minds. He felt that teachers could "build" the minds of children from the outside using subject matter as building blocks and delivering information through systematic lesson plans. Education for Herbart was a social mission rather than a matter of individual growth in pupils, and his methodology stressed concentration and mental immersion to accomplish the mission.

The effect of these European ideas was to suggest that education might be more than recitation and the "pounding in" of predetermined subject matter. Instead of focusing on what the teacher taught, each of these Europeans looked at the child and the methodology as critical. In doing so, their ideas introduced the concept of choice in educational decision making and launched some of the earliest debates about the what, who, and how of planning for learning.

Also affecting the first curriculum debates in this nation was Charles Darwin (1809–1882), the naturalist, who drew together the works of many others to suggest his theory of natural evolution in living things. As the official naturalist on the *Beagle* during its scientific expedition (1831–1836), Darwin documented that different surroundings tend to produce different outcomes in the growth of plants and animals (*On the Origin of Species,* 1859). Although educators did not directly apply Darwin's theory to education, his ideas were certainly in the minds of many educators who first began to explore the possibility that environment influenced learning.

At a centennial celebration in Philadelphia in 1876, many of the ideas just mentioned were showcased for American educators and soon took root in their writings. From that time on, more than one conception of education existed in the United States, and modern educational theory competed with traditional beliefs about education.

During this period of early diversity, knowledge became the focus of traditional educators. Francis Parker, for example, began a unification process in 1883 to define subject areas. An early survey of teaching practices by Joseph Mayer Rice (1892) found the public school curriculum to be "meandering" and disorganized. In that same year, Eliot's Committee of Ten began advocating five common content areas (his "windows on the soul") to serve as college entrance prerequisites for all students regardless of their home state. These notions of a "general education" quickly shaped all public schooling and were based on a "like students and single purpose" rationale. Traditionalists saw all children progressing through a fixed, sequential curriculum with progress marked by a ladder of grade levels.

In sharp contrast to these traditionalists' views of education, new or progressive educators at the turn of the century were building on the European ideas of the previous century. These educators saw each child as unique and sought to broaden the purpose of education to include both social and personal development. John Dewey (1859–1952) is usually credited with bridging this gap from an older and more traditional definition of education to the newer and distinctly American definition of education.

Dewey built on those earlier European thoughts to advocate a new and very active definition of education for children. Seeing the mind as something to be developed (not filled or shaped), Dewey suggested taking old principles of learning and demonstrating practical applications as defined by the experiences of the learner. The goal of education, according to Dewey, was to both organize and activate knowledge. But, said Dewey, the learner rather than the teacher is the source of such organization. Each individual, he proposed, must find ideas that work in practical experience and see these ideas as truth.

Dewey's credibility as a writer and theorist came as he applied his theories at the University of Chicago Lab School (1896–1904). Here, children learned by doing. Dewey later advocated the need for citizens in a democracy to find the truths of participation during the school years by living in a democratic institution. His book *Democracy and Education* (1916) is a classic statement of this belief.

Dewey's influence around the beginning of the twentieth century is hard to overstate. Many of his students at the University of Chicago, such as Harold Rugg (*The Child-Centered School,* 1928) and George Counts (*Dare the School Create a New Social Order,* 1932) became major advocates of the progressive ideas. The formation of the Progressive Education Association (PEA) in 1919 led to many publications and applications of Dewey's theory.

If a single year could be selected for when the true differences of the approaches to education in the United States became evident, it would probably be 1918. In that year, another conception for secondary education was proposed,

The Seven Cardinal Principles by the Commission on the Reorganization of Secondary Education, and the first text on curriculum was produced (Franklin Bobbitt, *The Curriculum,* 1918). The American way of educating was unfolding, and the field of curriculum was emerging as a subspecialty of professional education.

Decisions about whether the school should teach a body of knowledge, help develop the individual student, or promote social programs and priorities could not be made in a decentralized education system. In reality, American education programs simply evolved during these formative years. The pattern of schooling that emerged from a historical model of scholarship was superimposed on a coarse and dynamic culture, which was then influenced by the advent of psychology and human development research. The result was a mixed bag at best.

The Commission on the Reorganization of Secondary Education was formed in 1913 and met for five years to resolve some of the problems. The committee debated the three conceptions (academic, personal, and social) and the emerging multitude of philosophies and learning theories. In 1918 this committee produced what stands as the definitive statement on the purpose of American education, The Seven Cardinal Principles. These directions for American educational planning are still referred to regularly by educational curriculum workers:

1. Health.
2. Command of fundamental processes.
3. Worthy home membership.
4. Vocation.
5. Citizenship.
6. Worthy use of leisure time.
7. Ethical character.

Curriculum, as a specialized area of study in professional education, emerged from a growing need to study, order, arrange, and otherwise rationalize the changing forms of American education. To gather the many visions, clarify the intentions, organize schooling structures, implement programs, and assess the success of curricula in meeting goals required a new field of study.

As the twentieth century began, American education was in transition from a classical system practiced for centuries in Europe and in the United States to a more expedient form of schooling that served broader purposes. Among the accomplishments by 1900 were the following:

- Schooling was a state responsibility rather than a church role.
- Public education was seen as a social need, not a charity.
- Education was a right of citizens, not a privilege.
- Taxes could be used to support education through secondary levels.
- Education was compulsory for all children in all states.
- Control of education was established at the state level.
- Subjects were a constant in educational planning for learning.

☐   Human development was perceived as evolutionary.
☐   Schools could be used to promote social unity.
☐   Education could be used for social regeneration.

Among the realities for new curriculum theorists by the time of Bobbitt's first text was an awareness of humanistic thought, an emerging awareness of human development, and the beginning of mechanistic (behavioral) processes used to engineer curriculum development. These forces and others both broadened the horizons of early planners and presented those planners with a large number of choices in defining education.

The growth of the modern education system in the United States from the beginning of the twentieth century until the late twentieth century reflects these early trends. Schools grew in number; curricula diversified; and social forces such as wars, depressions, and the integration of our society modified the basic forms of the American school. A timeline of many of these important events is found in Figure 2.1.

The Postmodern Era

Schools during the modern era of American education operated under some unspoken assumptions that characterized our society. It was assumed, for example, that all Americans held the same values—those of white, Anglo-Saxon protestants. It was accepted that schools were the place of learning, and that only schools could "certify" an education. It was acknowledged that the purpose of becoming educated was "knowing" and that the process of education required a knowledgeable teacher to be successful. In sporadic fashion, all of these assumptions undergirding a modern and traditional education system began to break down in the United States during the forty-year period from 1960 to 2000.

The signs of decay and change first appeared during the Civil Rights period in the late 1960s and early 1970s. The concept of *e plurbus unum* (of many, one) was deemed inapplicable to some populations. Blacks, Hispanics, women, gays, and other populations were forced to use law and demonstration to establish their place in U.S. society. This discovery of "many publics" (i.e., various groups advocating for their interests) and multiculturalism was accelerated during the protests following the Vietnam era. By the end of the 1980s, America as a "salad bowl" had become America as a layer cake, and in many communities schools became the battleground for the promotion of values. In the 1990s this would lead to a postmodern stance by some curriculum theorists.

The idea that schools were "the learning place" soon came under attack as their biases toward certain populations were revealed. In particular, Ivan Illich's 1971 book *Deschooling Society* portrayed schools as simple extensions of a capitalist system needing to control and select its agents. Popular books by Kohl, Heardon, and others painted less-than-flattering portraits of the American schoolroom.

Coupled with this unveiling of the "real school," was an accountability movement born out of financial need. As the inflation of the 1970s and 1980s ate

400 B.C.	Height of Greek influence when ideas of tutorial learning and elite leadership training were first formalized
400 A.D.	Height of the Roman Empire that modeled a far more popular "citizenship model" education system
800	Beginning of "Dark Ages" during which civilization declined and knowledge was preserved by individual scholarship and early monastic libraries
1200	Beginning of the enlightenment during which civilization reemerged. Early universities founded in France, Italy, Spain, and England
1456	First books printed by printing presses—dispersion of knowledge to masses begins
1492	Columbus finds the Americas
1500	First Latin grammar schools in England
1536	First classical secondary school (Gymnasium) established in Germany
1620	Plymouth Colony, Massachusetts, established
1635	Boston Latin grammar schools founded
1636	Harvard University founded
1647	In Massachusetts the Old Deluder Satan Act compels establishment of schools when fifty households are present in a community
1650	First tax support for schools in Massachusetts
1751	Benjamin Franklin establishes the first academy (secondary school)
1779	Thomas Jefferson proposes a "free school" for Virginian men and women for up to three years
1787	Northwest Ordinance passed, which established provisions for territories to becomes states, including mandatory school sites in townships
1789	Constitution of the United States adopted
1805	New York Free School society established to educate 500,000 pupils without expense
1821	Boston English Classical School established. First tax-supported secondary school.
1852	First compulsory school laws passed in Massachusetts by Horace Mann
1862	Morrill Land Grant Act establishes land for public universities in all states (engineering, military science, and agriculture)
1872	State Supreme Court in Michigan upholds tax support for secondary schools
1883	Francis Parker establishes the first subject matter groupings as an early form of Curriculum
1892	First comprehensive study of American education by Joseph M. Rice
1892	Charles Eliot, president of Harvard University, forms the Committee of Ten
1896	John Dewey opens the University of Chicago Laboratory School to demonstrate alternative teaching methods
1904	First comprehensive physiological studies of school children in New York by G. Stanley Hall

FIGURE 2.1   Timeline of Events in the Growth of the Modern Education System

Source: Jon Wiles, *Curriculum Essentials* (Boston: Allyn & Bacon, 1999, pp. 2–4. Used by permission).

1905	First mental measurement scales on intelligence published by Alfred Binet
1909	First junior high school established
1918	Franklin Bobbitt publishes the first text in Curriculum
1918	Commission on the Reorganization of Secondary Education publishes The Seven Cardinal Principles
1919	Progressive Education Association founded
1932	The Eight Year Study begins (1932–1940)
1938	The Educational Policies Commission publishes its four-point objectives for education—The Purposes of Education in American Democracy
1946	Congress passes the G.I. Bill to further the education of veterans
1954	U.S. Supreme Court rules in Brown v. Topeka that public schools must racially integrate previously "separate but equal" schools
1957	Russia launches Sputnik satellite, beginning both a space and an education race
1958	U.S. Congress passes the National Defense Education Act, initiating serious federal funding of public education
1964	Civil Rights Act passed by Congress
1965	The Elementary and Secondary Education Act (ESEA) passes, bringing "titled" programs to public schools
1972	Title IX amendment to the ESEA outlaws discrimination on the basis of sex
1975	Public Law 94-142 provides federally guaranteed rights for all handicapped children in public schools
1979	U.S. Department of Education established
1985	Commercial availability of personal computers in United States

FIGURE 2.1   *Continued*

into school budgets, the cry for outcome-based education and, in the 1990s, "test results" eroded general support for schools as the sole agent of an education. Training and education were distinguished, and alternative forms of "school" were invented and even legislated.

Finally, the notion that a knowledgeable teacher was required for the schooling process to be successful fell away with the advent of the personal computer, a drill master far superior to an individual classroom teacher when it comes to drill-type instruction. The richness and variety of the Internet completely discounted student dependence on a teacher or other single source of learning.

And so, as the twentieth century drew to a close, the purpose and rationale of education, and even the method of becoming educated, was in chaos. Postmodern theorists urged the oppressed and enlightened to throw off the shackles of the public school and create their own "curriculum" with personal relevance based on their own values. Giroux and Aronowitz, in their 1991 text *Postmodern Education,* advised "curriculum's function is to name and privilege particular histories and experiences. In its current dominant form, it does so in such a way as to marginalize or silence the voices of subordinate groups."[2]

Interactive technology advocates, such as Apple's Wozeinek and Microsoft's Gates, didn't attack schools, but simply went around them. Learning was no longer a monopoly; it was no longer place-bound. It was accessible seven days a week and twenty-four hours a day, and it was nonlinear. With these conditions pressing schools, American education began a new and exciting, albeit confusing, era in the twenty-first century.

DEFINING CURRICULUM

We can understand a lot of what curriculum is, and is not, by its semantics. People in the field of curriculum spend a lot of energy arguing about the definition of the word. The word *curriculum* has been in existence since about 1820, although the first professional use of the word in America came about a century later. The Latin word *currere* means "to run" or "to run the course." With time, the traditional definition of school curriculum meant the course of study.

Most noneducators think of curriculum and curriculum development in terms of this traditional definition, equating the term with a course of study or a text—those items that establish the course. Some highly traditional educators think of curriculum in these terms as well, although to do so requires a very narrow definition of education:

> The curriculum should consist of permanent studies—the rules of grammar, reading, rhetoric and logic, and mathematics (for the elementary and secondary school), and the greatest books of the western world (beginning at the secondary level of schooling).[3]

> The curriculum must consist essentially of disciplined study in five great areas: (1) command of mother tongue and the systematic study of grammar, literature, and writing, (2) mathematics, (3) sciences, (4) history, (5) foreign languages.[4]

> The curriculum should consist entirely of knowledge which comes from the disciplines. . . . Education should be conceived as a guided recapitulation of the process of inquiry which gave rise to the fruitful bodies of organized knowledge comprising the established disciplines.[5]

> The curriculum is a systematic group of courses or sequence of subjects required for graduation or certification in a major field of study.[6]

> The curriculum is such permanent subjects as grammar, reading, logic, rhetoric, mathematics, and the greatest books of the western world that embody essential knowledge.[7]

The definition of curriculum as a product, or as a completely contained experience, proved unsatisfactory to many educators involved in the development of school programs. Very early in this century, the enormous growth in knowledge meant that "knowing" could no longer be contained in print form only. With the dissemination of such knowledge through technical means, identifying what constitutes essential knowledge became difficult.

In addition, the composition of schools in this period changed considerably. The population of the secondary school grew from 200,000 students in the 1890s to nearly five million students by 1924. Schooling was no longer the preserve of a small elite who would attend college; it was now a universal experience. In some cases, skills of citizenship took precedence over classical knowledge acquisition, and new courses had to be devised for learners.

As new courses were added to the curriculum, and as the differences among individual learners became more obvious to teachers and administrators, the definition of the curriculum began to stretch. Specialists in the field began to differentiate among various kinds of curricula: planned and unplanned (the hidden curriculum) and technical and practical learnings. Bobbitt, for example, writing in 1924, stated:

> The curriculum may be defined in two ways: (1) it is the range of experiences, both indirect and direct, concerned in unfolding the abilities of the individual, or (2) it is a series of consciously directed training experiences that the schools use for completing and perfecting the individual.[8]

Following this theme, Hollis Caswell and Doak Campbell in 1935 wrote of the socializing function of the schooling experience. The curriculum, they said, "is composed of all of the experiences children have under the guidance of the school."[9] Other writers continued this theme of seeing curriculum as an experience (process) rather than a product.

> A sequence of potential experiences is developed by the school for the purpose of disciplining children and youth in group ways of thinking and acting. This set of experiences is referred to as the curriculum.[10]

> The curriculum is now generally considered to be all of the experiences that learners have under the auspices of the school.[11]

> Curriculum is all of the experiences that individual learners have in a program of education whose purpose is to achieve broad goals and related specific objectives, which is planned in terms of a framework of theory and research or past or present professional practices.[12]

By the mid–1950s, it became increasingly evident that schools had a tremendous influence on students' lives. Some of those influences were structured; others were due to the congregation of youth. It was recognized that students also had experiences not planned by the school. During this period, definitions were dominated by those aspects of the curriculum that were planned, as opposed to simply the content or general experiences of students.

> The curriculum is all of the learning of students which is planned by and directed by the school to attain its educational goals.[13]

> A curriculum is a plan for learning.[14]

> We define curriculum as a plan for providing sets of learning opportunities to achieve broad goals and related specific objectives for an identifiable population served by a single school center.[15]

> A curriculum [is] usually thought of as a course of study or plan for what is to be taught in an educational institution.[16]

Beginning in the 1960s and continuing into the new century, there has been concern for the performance of educational programs. This focus, often referred to as *accountability* in schools, has pushed the definition of the curriculum toward an emphasis on ends or outcomes:

> Curriculum is concerned not with what students will do in the learning situation, but with what they will learn as a consequence of what they do. Curriculum is concerned with results.[17]

> [Curriculum is] the planned and guided learning experiences and intended outcomes, formulated through systematic reconstruction of knowledge and experience, under the auspices of the school, for the learners' continuous and willful growth in personal-social competence.[18]

In the mid-1990s, the concept of an evolving and nonplanned set of experiences for children emerged under the label of "postmodern":

> A new sense of educational order will emerge as well as new relations between teachers and students, culminating in a new concept of curriculum. The linear, sequential, easily quantifiable ordering system dominating education today could give way to a more complex, pluralistic, unpredictable system or network. Such a complex network will, like life itself, always be in transition, in process.[19]

> In closed societies, the elite's values are superimposed on the people. Education, as a practice of freedom, rejects the notion that knowledge is extended or transferred to students as if they were objects.[20]

> As we move into the 21st Century, we find ourselves no longer constrained by modernist images of purpose and history. Elements of discontinuity, rapture, and difference (chaos) provide alternative sets of referents by which to understand modernity as well as to challenge and modify it. The term *post-modern* is a rejection of grand narratives and any form of totalizing thought. It embraces diversity and locality. It creates a world where individuals must make their way, where knowledge is consistently changing, and where meaning is no longer anchored in history.[21]

We see the curriculum as a desired goal or set of values that can be activated through a development process culminating in experiences for students. The degree to which those experiences are a true representation of the envisioned goal or goals is a direct function of the effectiveness of the curriculum development efforts. The purpose of any such design is the option of the group engaged in such development.

Although the definition of curriculum has been altered in response to social forces and expectations for the school, the process of curriculum development has remained constant. Through analysis, design, implementation, and evaluation, curriculum developers set goals, plan experiences, select content, and assess outcomes of school programs. These constant processes have contributed to the emergence of structure in curriculum planning.

STRUCTURE IN CURRICULUM PLANNING

Definitions of curriculum and visions for the purpose of education have been expansive during the past century, but the structure of curriculum development has remained a filling-in process. The principles that exist in the field of curriculum have evolved more from practice than from logic or enlightenment. As a result, the theory of curriculum has followed the practice found in school environments.

The focus of most curricular principles is specific rather than global. As Daniel Tanner and Laurel Tanner noted,

> In the absence of a holistic conception of curriculum, the focus is on piecemeal and mechanical functions . . . the main thrust in curriculum development and reform over the years has been directed at microcurricular problems to the neglect of macrocurricular problems.[22]

Principles of curriculum have evolved as core procedures rather than theoretical guidelines. The cause for this evolution of principles is a combination of the absence of systematic thinking about curriculum planning; the vulnerability of curriculum planning to social, political, technical, and economic forces; and the constantly changing priorities of education in the United States.

Because of this situation, identification of curricular principles is difficult. Hilda Taba described the almost unmanageable condition of curriculum approaches in this way:

> Decisions leading to change in curriculum organization have been made largely by pressure, by hunches, or in terms of expediency instead of being based on clear-cut theoretical considerations or tested knowledge. The scope of curriculum has been extended vastly without an adequate consideration of the consequence of this extension on sequence or cumulative learning. . . . The fact that these perplexities underlying curriculum change have not been studied adequately may account for the proliferation of approaches to curriculum making.[23]

Prior to the major curriculum reforms in the late 1950s and early 1960s, most curriculum development in school settings was oriented toward producing content packages. In developing courses of study, curriculum specialists sought to refine school programs by redesigning essential topic areas and updating older programs on a scheduled basis. This rather static role for curriculum practitioners in the field resulted in the evolution of both theoretical constructs for developing curriculum and operational procedures that changed little over time.

An early observation by Dewey that "the fundamental factors in the educational process are (1) the learner, (2) the society, and (3) organized subject matter"[24] set the stage for defining curriculum parameters. These themes were echoed in 1926 by Dewey's former student, Harold Rugg, who wrote, "There are, indeed, three critical factors in the educational process: the child, contemporary American society, and standing between them, the school."[25] Another student of Dewey's, Boyd Bode, renewed this theme of three parts in 1931 when he observed, "The difference in curriculum stems from three points of view: (1) the standpoint of the subject matter specialists, (2) the standpoint of the practical man, and (3) the interests of the learner."[26]

By 1945 these three general concerns were finding acceptance in most curriculum literature. Taba, for instance, discussed the three sources of data in curriculum planning as (1) the study of society, (2) studies of learners, and (3) studies of subject matter content.[27] By the early 1960s Taba had further refined the study of society to mean "cultural demands . . . a reflection of the changing social milieu of the school."[28]

Gaining acceptance as a fourth important planning base for curriculum in the mid-1950s and early 1960s was the study of learning itself. Studies from various schools of psychology and the advent of sophisticated technology in school settings raised new possibilities and choices for educators who were planning programs.

These four major areas of concern for curriculum planners, known as the foundations or "bases" of planning, remain the basis of most analysis, design, implementation, and evaluation of school programs today. These vital areas of concern are addressed later in this chapter.

The importance of these planning bases as organizers for thinking about the development of educational programs is best summarized by Taba, a curriculum specialist concerned with the development aspects of curriculum:

> Semantics aside, these variations in the conception of the function of education are not idle or theoretical arguments. They have definite concrete implications for the shape of educational programs, especially the curriculum. . . . If one believes that the chief function of education is to transmit the perennial truths, one cannot but strive toward a uniform curriculum and teaching. Efforts to develop thinking take a different shape depending on whether the major function of education is seen as fostering creative thinking and problem solving or as following the rational forms of thinking established in our classical tradition. As such, differences in these concepts naturally determine what are considered the "essentials" and what are the dispensable frills in education.[29]

Paralleling the conceptual mapping out of the field of curriculum concerns was the evolution of operational procedures. Early curriculum development focused on subject content, which was a mechanical and rather simple operational technique developed in the 1920s and which continued as the dominant operational concern until the early 1960s. Writing in the 1926 National Society for the Study of Education Yearbook, Rugg outlined the operational tasks of curriculum development as a three-step process: (1) determine the fundamental objectives, (2) select activities and other materials of instruction, and (3) discover the most effective organization and placement of this instruction.[30]

By 1950 the technique of "inventory, organize, and present" had reached refinement in Ralph Tyler's widely read four-step analysis:

1. What educational purposes shall the school seek to attain?
2. What educational experiences can be provided that are likely to attain those purposes?

3. How can these educational experiences be effectively organized?
4. How can we determine whether these purposes are being attained?[31]

By addressing the assessment of curriculum development, Tyler introduced the concept of the curriculum development cycle whereby evaluation led to a reconsideration of purpose. Such a cycle in schools illuminated the comprehensiveness of the planning activity and later gave birth to refinements such as systems analysis and taxonomies of learning. Tyler's four-step model also rekindled a fifty-year-old effort to develop manageable behavioral objectives in education.[32]

The ordering of the development procedure also encouraged a mechanistic approach to curriculum development. Such approaches, long practiced in schools, are thoroughly represented in curriculum literature through various definitions:

> Curriculum development . . . is basically a plan of structuring the environment to coordinate in an orderly manner the elements of time, space, materials, equipment and personnel.[33]

> The function of curriculum development is to research, design, and engineer the working relationships of the curricular elements that will be employed during the instructional phase in order to achieve desired outcomes.[34]

Perhaps the most refined version of Tyler's procedure for developing school curriculum was outlined by Taba in 1962. Seven major steps of curriculum development were identified:

1. Diagnosis of needs.
2. Formulation of objectives.
3. Selection of content.
4. Organization of content.
5. Selection of learning experiences.
6. Organization of learning experiences.
7. Determination of what to evaluate and means of doing it.

Within each step, Taba provided substeps, which identified criteria for action. For example, in the selection of learning experiences, it is important that the curriculum developer consider the following:

1. Validity and significance of content.
2. Consistency with social reality.
3. Balance of breadth and depth of experiences.
4. Provision for a wide range of objectives.
5. Learnability-adaptability of the experience to life of student.
6. Appropriateness to needs and interests of learners.[35]

More modern lists of these steps differ from Taba's in that they present curriculum as a more comprehensive process, which may or may not be tied to a content product. In the following example, for instance, Kathryn Feyereisen presents curriculum development as a problem-solving action chain:

1. Identification of the problem.
2. Diagnosis of the problem.
3. Search for alternative solutions.
4. Selection of the best solution.
5. Ratification of the solution by the organization.
6. Authorization of the solution.
7. Use of the solution on a trial basis.
8. Preparation for adoption of the solution.
9. Adoption of the solution.
10. Direction and guidance of staff.
11. Evaluation of effectiveness.[36]

The broader focus of the Feyereisen description reflects a growing concern in curriculum development with planning for change in school environments from a macroperspective. Curriculum development is increasingly a process with systemic concerns.

Other examples of the basic structure of the curriculum cycle could be provided at this point, but it should be clear that a regular review process developed and was widely practiced in American schools between 1920 and 1960. This process reflected the historical dominance of subject matter content as the focus of curriculum renewal:

> Certainly, a review of the plans made and implemented today and yesterday leaves no doubt that the dominant assumption of past curriculum planning has been the goal of subject matter mastery through a subject curriculum, almost inextricably tied to a closed school and graded school ladder, to a marking system that rewards successful achievement of fixed content and penalizes unsuccessful achievement, to an instructional organization based on fixed classes in the subjects and a timetable for them.[37]

Progress in the so-called substantive dimension of curriculum development continues today. Since the early 1970s curriculum specialists have employed systems thinking in school planning efforts. Such comprehensive planning efforts have allowed curriculum leaders to engineer program improvement in new and efficient ways. The process of curriculum development, from the inception of an idea to the final assessment of the reconstruction effort, is becoming a highly skilled area of curriculum leadership.

In sharp contrast, the visionary or theoretical dimension of curriculum work has progressed little in half a century. Despite an increased knowledge base, growing understanding of human development, sophistication in the use of technology, and an emerging focus on teaching and learning, curriculum models remain primitive and traditional. If Rip Van Winkle woke up in America after a long sleep, he would at least recognize schools. In the beginning of the twenty-first century, theoretical dimensions of curriculum development remain suppressed by a dependence on economic sponsorship, political conservatism, and the failure of educators to gain consensus for any significant change in the schooling process.

Moreover, the introduction of the new interactive technologies, using the Internet as a focal point, make much of the above irrelevant. Curriculum developers will be hard-pressed to even catalog, let along control, select, and order, the new information available to learners. Real-time delivery, anytime delivery, and nonlinear delivery of information to the learner via the Internet will not easily fit this historical construct. New paradigms and new models will be needed if curriculum development as a process in schools is to survive the "rush" of the technological age.

FOUNDATIONS OF CURRICULUM PLANNING

In the evolution of curriculum as a professional focus in education, four major planning areas have dominated thinking about schools. To these four areas, we advocate adding a fifth, technology:

1. Social forces in society.
2. Treatment of knowledge.
3. Human growth and development.
4. Learning as a process.
5. Technology.

These areas, called the *foundations of curriculum,* organize information for planners and help us to see patterns in the "who, what, when, and why" of public education.

Social Forces

The United States will likely enter a major period of transformation in the years 2001–2010. Changes in the composition of our population, dramatic changes in the power of our economy, new and powerful technologies, and a different kind of world order all portend changes for schools. In the lifetime of our grandparents, the United States transitioned from an agrarian society to an industrial society. Work became mechanized, the population became urban and mobile, and the role of an individual in society was redefined. Today, with the transformation to a postindustrial society dominated by technology and global interdependence, the nation is once again redefining itself.

In advanced countries, the relationship between education and such change is dynamic and interdependent. To the degree that education "programs" all children for a society that no longer exists, such education is dysfunctional to that society. By the same token, if a changing society insists that schooling retain traditional forms in the face of massive changes, it may well doom itself to obsolescence and decline. As we progress in the first years of the twenty-first century, curriculum planners must seek to understand the true nature of social and technical changes so that they can build these changes into the schooling process. How communication affects the changing social structure of our country is one of many such social forces.

At the beginning of the twentieth century, communication was primitive by today's standards. There was a great dependence, of course, on the printed page. The telegraph existed, the telephone was in the infant stages of development, and motion pictures were a promising medium. Mass communication, however, was both scarce and inefficient. Any communication, such as the result of a presidential election, took considerable time to disseminate. Within a fifty-year period, three mass communication devices appeared that altered this pattern: (1) radio, (2) television, and (3) computers.

Radio was the first communication medium to broaden the scope of the organized knowledge that had previously been in the domain of schools and print documents. Large amounts of information could be distributed quickly and, by early in the century, could even be broadcast to other countries.

> The effect of radio on the expansion of nonrelated and nonapplied knowledge is analogous to the distribution of seed by a grass spreader, creating in effect a "carpet of knowledge" by cultivating a lawn so thick that single blades became indistinguishable. Said simply, knowledge on the radio was both equal and without value. Perspectives of knowledge under such conditions can be clouded; conjecture can be misinterpreted as fact.[38]

Television, another means by which we gained information, was even more influential in one respect. Beaming into 96 percent of all homes an average of six and one-half hours daily by 1970, this medium influenced the values and standards of U.S. society. Speaking in his classic book *Crisis in the Classroom,* Charles Silberman observed:

> Television has taken over the mythic role in our culture; soap operas, situation comedies, Westerns, melodramas, et al., are folk stories or myths that convey or reinforce the values of the society. . . . The trouble is that television does not enable its audience to see things the way they really are. On the contrary, while more current and realistic than schools, television nonetheless presents a partial and, in important ways, distorted view of contemporary society.[39]

By the late 1970s, concern for controlling the impact of television, particularly as a medium affecting the thoughts and perceptions of children, was intense. Congressional hearings, campaigns by parent–teacher organizations, and criticism by members of the television industry were common.[40] A line from a widely acclaimed movie, *Network,* summarized the impact of television as a communication medium:

> This tube can make or break presidents, popes, prime ministers. This tube is the most awesome goddamned force in the whole godless world. And woe is us if it ever falls into the hands of the wrong people.[41]

In the late 1990s, manufacturers presented "lock-out chips" to parents as one option for controlling youths' viewing of television.

A third communication innovation of the twentieth century that has had a major effect on both society and schools was the computer. The initial impact of the computer was more subtle than that of radio or television because of its mystique and inaccessibility. But, the final implications of computer usage via the Internet are that it will become much more powerful than either radio or television.

> Fifty years ago the comical product of the "madcap" scientists' nocturnal devisements, today computer science is as much a part of our lives as our favorite breakfast cereal, and with every day that passes encroaches ever so more fitfully into the domain of human life, human decisions, and human behavior.
>
> Partly akin to the television in its mechanical wizardry, whereas the television indoctrinates, the computer coerces us into action through its assumed infallibility in making decisions and plotting paths of action necessary to our living in comfort. While the computer habituates the pinnacle of man's intellectual genius, it is likewise the jailer who holds the key to our intellectual freedom. With his piece-by-piece orientation to information and knowledge application, man is, quite simply, presented with an unchallengeable opponent in the computer. The variance in speed in processing knowledge posits man in the impossible position of receiving computation as *fait accompli* from the computerized savant. In creating the computer, man has performed the heretofore-thought-impossible task of devising a being superior to himself in intellectual capacity, a being who can theoretically "outthink" all men combined, a being who in fact is a god.[42]

In terms of data processing and the generation of cross-referenced knowledge systems delivered at lightning speed and in multiple media, the computer age has presented a momentous challenge to society and school planners. In one decade, we have grown accustomed to satellite-transmitted instantaneous relays, home videocams, direct-dial networked telecommunication (cell phones), through-the-wall cable transmission, and facsimile capacities. We are no longer surprised by wearable technology and tens of millions of unique web sites. The advanced world and segments of the Third World are awash in technology that is significantly impacting our conceptions of school.

Only one century ago, schooling was almost exclusively a knowledge-focused activity. Students and teachers interacted to master essentials such as Virgil's *Aeneid* and Xenophon's *Anabasis,* orthography, and Latin prose. Events in the late 1990s and the early years of the twenty-first century, social changes and technological access, have called this kind of curriculum and learning into question. Steven Wozniak, cofounder of Apple Computer, stated the case in the following manner twenty years ago:

> It's healthy to learn basic concepts such as arithmetic and logic, but there is just no point in having to solve the problems over and over again every day. It's a waste of time. . . . machines can do that stuff and leave us to think about more important things . . . personal computers are going to free people from the mundane things . . . they will allow people's minds to work at a higher level.[43]

Today, because of communication capability advances—radical advances in a very short period of time—some fundamental issues about schooling have been revived. If, for instance, knowledge is being generated, disseminated, and delivered at a pace beyond our capacity to absorb it, what is the point in organizing schools around the mastery of essential data? If there is too much to be known today, what essential knowledge should all of our citizens possess? If radio, television, and personal computers can disseminate fundamental information about the society in which we live, at a fraction of the cost of the schooling process, what, if any, should be the new role of the formal educating system?

In the United States, adapting to the changing social patterns and their implications for schooling is perhaps even more challenging than adapting to technology. A complex web of family-work-government programs and mobility have altered the type of student seen in public schools and the role of the school for that pupil. Beginning in the 1960s when Great Society programs rewarded single-parent family patterns, the United States has seen the emergence of a new, nonnuclear family. Such families combine persons with different names and origins into a loose economic network dependent on constant economic and social support from agencies. Such new families move and reconstitute themselves often, which disrupts school continuity. They can require large sums to accommodate their special needs.

One of the major characteristics of this new society is a shrinking population of children and a rapidly growing body of older citizens. In the year 2000 one in nine children qualified for special education programs, and new trends such as children born with drug dependence make these already expensive students a challenging task for educators. These children of "new" families and the growing population of older citizens will make demands and expect services from public schools in the next decade.

School planners looking at the future during the first decade of the twenty-first century can only guess at what additional changes will occur in social institutions and structures. In the late 1990s the obvious trends included the following:

- Expanded social services to provide for the growing needs of students in schools.
- Longer school days and school years to accommodate the child-care demands of working parents.
- Better and more sophisticated information networks to monitor student mobility and school progress.
- Increased communication between business and education to prepare a workforce that will be suited to a service economy and postindustrial society.

To those decade-old needs, the first years of the twenty-first century call for us to focus our full attention on the following:

- The power of new technologies on learning.
- A major reallocation of educational resources.

- ☐   The difference between education and training.
- ☐   The connectivity of information in schools.

Treatment of Knowledge

The kinds of social changes outlined in the previous section have had a major effect on the treatment of knowledge in curriculum planning. Not only has knowledge become more plentiful and more widely disseminated because of technological advances, but also the shifting social currents in the United States have acted to redefine the utility of knowledge in everyday life. Since all knowledge contains value when applied, knowledge can no longer be treated as a value-free commodity or "good in itself." Increasingly, the public is interested in what is being taught in school and how that information is being conveyed to students. (Note, for example, the controversy surrounding the 500th anniversary of the landing of Columbus in America.) Curriculum planners in the 1990s wrestled with the selection, organization, relevance, presentation, and evaluation of knowledge in schools. Curriculum leaders of the twenty-first century will have a much more difficult task in dealing with knowledge.

Arno Bellack, writing forty years ago during the early curriculum reforms, outlined the planner's dilemma:

> In current debates about what should be taught in schools, the "conventional wisdom" long honored in pedagogical circles about the nature of knowledge and the role of knowledge in the curriculum is being called into question. The enemy of conventional wisdom, Professor Galbraith (the originator of that felicitous term) tells us, is the march of events. The fatal blow comes when conventional ideas fail to deal with new conditions and problems to which obsolescence has made them inapplicable. The march of events in the world at large that is placing new demands on the schools, and in the world of scholarship that is making new knowledge in great quantities, is forcing us to reexamine our ideas about the nature of knowledge and its place in the instructional program.[44]

The scope of information available to scholars, and to schoolchildren, has been immense for fifty years. Estimates of the rate at which organized knowledge doubled its volume ranged from every seven years in the mid-1960s to every two years by the mid-1970s. In the first years of the new century, such estimates seem laughable. The 5 million new web sites created in the first six months of the year 2000 tell us that knowledge is no longer controlled or quantifiable. Traditional curriculum tasks such as reviewing and updating subject content have become unmanageable.

Related to the problems of scope and volume of organized knowledge is one of organization. Cases of knowledge overload are plentiful, conjuring visions of a nation choking on the proliferation of its own wisdom:

> The American crisis, and particularly in terms of its schools, seems clearly to be related to an inability to act. It is not that we do not will action but that we are unable to act, unable to organize our knowledge or put existing knowledge to use.

The intellectual machinery of our society no longer works or we no longer know how to make it work.[45]

Educational planners, in general, have ignored the glut of data that relates to traditional school subjects or have dealt with it as minutia in testing programs. There have been some serious efforts to confront the problem of knowledge overload by focusing on the structure of information rather than on information itself. One of the best-known leaders of this reorganization movement was Jerome Bruner. Bruner rationalized the shift away from the mastery of essential data to the study of representative data structures in this way:

> Teachers ask me about the "new curricula" as though they were some special magic potion. They are nothing of the sort. The new curricula are based on the fact that knowledge has an internal connectedness, a meaningfulness, and that for facts to be appreciated and understood and remembered, they must be fitted into that internal meaningful context.[46]

Another response (1970s) related to the reorganization of knowledge sources for the school curriculum was the advent of "new" fields of knowledge created from crossing standard disciplines of study. Knowledge in the sciences, such as biochemistry, and in the social sciences, such as demography, gave rise to new structures of organization. The incorporation and management of such new areas posed difficult problems for school planners owing to the compactness of traditional knowledge organizations.

With the dramatic increase in the volume of knowledge, and the corresponding questions of how to organize it meaningfully, came even more pressing inquiries about the purpose of knowledge in organized learning. Although challenges to the knowledge-based curriculum weren't novel, the regularity with which educators questioned the traditional motif of educating in public schools during the 1980s and 1990s was surprising. Defining education in a new way called for a different definition of learning. In the 1960s, Earl Kelley wrote:

> The only man who is educated is the man who has learned how to learn; the man who has learned how to adapt and change; the man who has realized that no knowledge is secure, that only the process of seeking knowledge gives the basis for security.[47]

Futurist Alvin Toffler, in assessing the onrush of the knowledge explosion as it related to the role of schooling, observed:

> Instead of assuming that every subject taught today is taught for a reason, we should begin from the reverse premise: nothing should be included in the required curriculum unless it can be strongly justified in terms of the future. If this means scrapping a substantial part of the formal curriculum, so be it.[48]

By the early 1990s the delivery of knowledge direct-to-the-learner was increasing dramatically. Bypassing the traditional schooling format were new interactive video networks and a host of personal computers with sophisticated software capability. By the late 1990s the Internet was pumping unlimited knowledge into U.S. homes without order or reason. At home, many students learned music, art, languages, geography, and other topics of choice, thus breaking the monopoly of schools over knowledge and its delivery. The competition for students from virtual schools and proprietary schools increased dramatically. The traditional educational system was beginning to dissolve.

The reaction of educational planners to the problem of knowledge organization was to emphasize the identification of goals and objectives for education, which would serve as guidelines for content selection. This was followed quickly by intensive testing for information acquisition in select areas such as basic skills. The new buzzword of the 1990s was "standards," and this orientation placed knowledge in a new and different role in educational planning, organization, scope, and sequence variables.[49]

Another consideration for educational planners that related to treatments of knowledge was the way in which individual learners reacted to information. In particular, research efforts studying the effects of attitude, emotion, and feelings toward learning (affect), and the process of information manipulation, storage, and retrieval (cognition), linked reception and retention of learning with readiness and attitudes toward learning. The question of form of knowledge thus became a concern. ATI research and brain development literature, discussed in Chapter 1, illustrate the sophistication of activity in this area.

Closely related to the relationship of affect and knowledge were two other concerns of educational planners: language usage and the medium of delivery. When curriculum planners attempted to bring knowledge to the schools, they had to deal with school populations that represented many cultures. Planners were confronted with both nonstandard English and a problem in basic communication.

A final area that affected the planning of knowledge use in schools was the advent of serious forecasting of the future. As educators reviewed past use of knowledge and studied the present knowledge explosion, the wisdom of continuing with a content-dominated curriculum was questioned. After all, facts, by definition, were phenomena of the past and present rather than of the future. In some respects, traditional knowledge placed blinders on our ability to escape the pull of the present and open our minds to the real possibilities of the future. The call for creative, nonlinear thinking presented an interesting challenge.

The Internet and the development of search engines and browsers accelerated this concern to unimagined levels in the last years of the twentieth century. If creativity amounts to making unusual associations, then any student in the Internet age can be considered creative given the many possible combinations of knowledge. Nonlinear learning is an area that all curriculum persons will have to master in the early years of this new century.

In summary, the questions raised in assessing organized knowledge as a planning foundation are significant: What is to be taught? What should be the role of organized knowledge? What is the relative importance of knowledge bodies? What is the correct organization of information? What is the best form for bringing knowledge to students? How is all of this changed by the instantaneous and global access of information by any learner without teacher assistance? All of these questions must now be addressed by educational planners.

Human Growth and Development

A third foundational consideration important to educational planners has been the growing body of information related to human development. These data have been critical in such regular school activities as placement and retention, counseling, and planning curricular content and activities. Knowledge about human development has also provided the impetus for the development of a host of new school programs: early childhood education, special education, compensatory education, and middle school education. Perhaps most important, our understandings about patterns of growth and development have caused educators to perceive formal educational planning from the perspective of the individual student.

In the twenty-first century, our understanding of human differences will be critical to rationalizing a totally individual learning plan for each student. It will also form the basis for teaching and learning strategies, as well as the selection of appropriate learning technologies.

Contributions to our understanding of human development were gradual throughout the twentieth century. As information about human development accumulated, various schools of thought emerged in an effort to organize the data. These interpretations of our knowledge about human growth provide the basis for the differences in educators' learning theories. Such differences can most clearly be understood in relation to several basic issues related to human development.

One issue revolves around the question of what constitutes normal development. Because of records kept over an extended time on the physical maturation of schoolchildren, educators are now fairly able to predict ranges of growth for chronological age. It appears, in general, that children in the United States are achieving physical maturation at an ever-earlier age. Such findings are attributed to better health and nutritional care during childhood.

Our knowledge of intellectual, social, and emotional development during the school-age years is considerably less precise. However, organized inquiry has developed significant studies that guide our present decision making about development-related factors in these areas.

In the area of intelligence, considerable documentation exists regarding student performance on intelligence-measuring devices such as the Stanford–Binet Scale. Little concrete evidence exists, however, to support hypotheses about intellect or intellectual capacity. What we currently operate with are models of how people are believed to develop and normal ranges of development in the capacity to think.

Without question, the dominant model in this area is one developed by Swiss educator Jean Piaget nearly sixty-five years ago. Piaget hypothesized four distinct but chronologically successive models of intelligence: (1) sensorimotor, (2) preoperational, (3) concretely operational, and (4) formal operational. Piaget's model of continual and progressive change in the structure of behavior and thought in children has assisted educators in preparing intellectual experiences in schools.[50]

In the areas of social and emotional growth of students, even less precise data about human development exist. Classic studies such as Project Talent,[51] Growing Up in River City,[52] and the Coleman Report[53] provided long-term studies of particular populations. Data related to emotional development have been compiled by the National Institutes of Mental Health but are on abnormal populations. For educational planners, the question of what constitutes "normal" growth is largely unresolved as we begin the new century, particularly in areas such as creativity.[54]

Another issue relating to human development is whether such growth can be or should be controlled or accelerated. Primary research with infants and children by White and associates[55] suggests that development can indeed be accelerated through both experience and environment.[56] The work of behaviorist B. F. Skinner,[57] on the other hand, is conclusive in its demonstration that behavior can be shaped. These two options leave the curriculum developer with significant value decisions about both the anticipated outcome of an education and the more mechanical aspects of planning learning experiences.

Two final human development issues are indicative of the many planning considerations facing curriculum developers. First, we have the mind-boggling question of the ultimate human being that we might create, since human development is somewhat malleable. For instance, medical research in the 1980s and 1990s demonstrated an amazing capacity to change gene pools, transplant organs, and apply chemistry to alter behavior. Diet and direct stimulation seem capable of emphasizing one human behavior over another. Studies in mind control and extrasensory perception promise that "directing" human intelligence is within the domain of formal schooling. The notion that a computer could "program" the human brain for learning is not far-fetched.

Even more curious is our growing understanding of emotion and affective growth. Work with individuals of different personality styles and preferences may offer schools the possibility of selecting instructional strategies to match the emotions and perceptions of the learner.[58]

Issues such as defining normal growth, promoting preferred kinds of growth, and giving emphasis to certain types of cognitive and affective growth make the study of human development, or human engineering, a necessary foundation for curriculum planning in the twenty-first century.

Learning as a Process

New understandings of human development, new perspectives of the role of knowledge in learning, and new technologies useful to the schooling process have resulted in a variety of learning approaches becoming fashionable and acceptable in schools. Specifically, school planners must begin to incorporate the following facts into their designs of educational programs: (1) the biological basis of development can be altered; (2) physical maturation can be retarded or accelerated through diet and stimulation; (3) intellectual growth can be stimulated and directed, and even programmed; (4) cultural influences on learning can be controlled or encouraged; and (5) technology is capable of teaching students in new and productive ways. These "new realities" suggest that schools can promote multiple types of learning in the classroom and therefore facilitate different types of learning environments in schools. Learning theory will become a more important part of curriculum work in the near future.

At the level of philosophy, a topic to be treated more fully in the following chapter, educators differ considerably regarding the type of development that schools should promote. Three major approaches to learning have evolved: (1) a behavioral approach, (2) an approach incorporating drive theories, and (3) an environmental approach. These basic approaches to learning have numerous identifiable subtheories; an abbreviated discussion is presented here to indicate the range of learning theory that exists among school planners.

The behavioral approach is characterized by an external perspective of the learning process, viewing learning as a product of teacher behavior. Under this approach to learning, educational planners and teachers who deliver such plans study the student to ascertain existing patterns of behavior and then structure specific learning experiences to encourage desired patterns of behavior.

Armed with terms such as conditioning (repetitive response), reinforcement (strengthening behavior through supportive action), extinction (withdrawing reinforcement), and transfer (connecting behavior with response), the behavioral learning theorist seeks to shape the student to a predetermined form. Common school practices under this learning approach are fixed curricula, didactic (question–answer) formats, and programmed progression through materials. Perhaps the most interesting and controversial use of this learning approach in schools today is the practice of behavior modification.

Behavior modification is a simple cause–effect programming of observable behavior. The procedure uses a four-step technique: (1) identifying the problem, (2) recording baseline data, (3) installing a system to alter behavior, and (4) evaluating the new condition. As an external system of behavior control, behavior modification is not concerned with the attitudes or motivations of students under such a system, but rather with the results of the modification system. According to this learning approach, behavior that is rewarded will continue; behavior that goes unrewarded will be extinguished.

A second learning theory is the need-structured approach, which is concerned with the needs and drives of students and seeks to use such natural motivational energy to promote learning. Teachers often analyze and use the interests and needs of students as instructional vehicles when following this approach.

Key terms used with the needs/drive approach are readiness, identification, imitation, and modeling. Taking a cue from Freudian psychology, this theory orders the curriculum to coordinate with developmental readiness. Students learn through the pursuit of unfulfilled needs, often modeling the behaviors of others or developing predictable identification patterns.

Drive theories rely heavily on findings of human growth and development in planning curricular activities. This set of theories is dependent on student growth in planning school experiences.

The environmental approach to learning is concerned with the restructuring of the learning environment or of students' perceptions so that they may be free to develop. Unlike the static definition of growth presented by the behavioral approach or the dependent theories of need-structured approaches, the environmental approach is dynamic in nature. It acknowledges human diversity, believes in human potential, and promotes both uniqueness and creativity in individuals.

The basis of the environmental approach is the belief that behavior is a function of perception and that human perceptions are the result of both experiences and understandings. When students have positive experiences that are self-enhancing, their perception and understanding of themselves and the world around them are altered. These new perceptions, in turn, allow for additional growth experiences. Student potential for development under this learning approach is limitless.

These three primary approaches to the structuring of learning in schools, which might be labeled *push, pull,* and *restructure,* are very different in their assumptions about people and possibilities for human development. They differ, for instance, in their beliefs about human potential, in their vantage points in describing learning (external versus internal), and in their beliefs about the source of academic motivation.

To select any one of these approaches to learning means that basic classroom considerations such as the design of learning spaces, the choice of materials, and the roles of participants will have a distinct form. The learning theory of the planner is crucial to decision making and projection. As such, learning as a process represents a strong fourth planning foundation (see Figure 2.2).

Technology

Technology, while still unfolding, is a fifth foundational area for curriculum planning in the twenty-first century. The pervasiveness of this influence, which is far more than just a social force, is changing each of the other four foundations for planning. Our society is being transformed by computers. Knowledge bases are exploding and

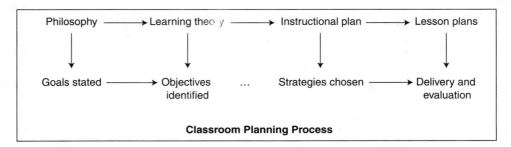

FIGURE 2.2   Classroom Planning as a Subset of Curriculum Planning

have become totally unmanageable in schools. Students are developing intellectually along new and nonlinear lines. Learning theory has entered into new territory, and students and machines combine to use all of the senses in learning.

The impact of technology on the physical structure of the school, on its mission, on its use of humans as teachers, and on its curriculum and learning theory is only now coming into some focus. The next decade promises to be a challenging and exciting time for curriculum personnel.

The area of educational foundations is highly complex. It is an effort to bring order to a rapidly changing world that has an increasing number of relevant variables. Throughout the treatment of foundations of curriculum planning, there is an element of choice: which input to select, which data to validate, which decisions to make.

Ultimately, the choices and decisions related to the selection, activation, and evaluation of educational designs are normative matters. Before educational planners can be effective and consistent in their work, they must understand their personal belief systems and formulate a philosophy of education that complements that system. The following chapter introduces some established philosophies of education and assists you in determining your priorities for schools.

ISSUES AND IMPEDIMENTS

Obviously, many choices face those who plan American educational programs, and from these choices come major issues reflecting bedrock values. The scope of our school programs, their purpose and organization, the focus of their delivery, and many other questions remain largely unanswered. Contrast the following list of questions compiled by Thomas Briggs in 1926 with those being asked today:

1. What are the desired ends of education?
2. What is the good life?
3. To what extent shall education modify the character and actions of future citizens?
4. For what ends are the schools responsible?
5. What subject areas are most vital in attaining these ends?
6. What should be the content of these subject arrangements?
7. How should the material be organized?
8. What is the responsibility of each level of schooling?
9. What is the relative importance of each course of study?
10. How much time should be allotted for each subject?
11. How long should education be continued at public expense?
12. What is the optimum length of the school day? School year?
13. What is the optimum work load for each pupil?
14. What are the most probable future needs of the pupil?[59]

Questions such as these, then and now, encourage debate, inquiry, and experimentation in schools. Curriculum, as a field of inquiry, has developed in an effort to study such issues and translate what is learned into viable school programs. In the new age of technology in schools, it is vital that curriculum personnel continue in this role of questioner.

While the answers to such questions should be made by appointed officials in a centralized or nationalized system of education, the unique decentralization of the U.S. education model presents abnormal impediments that include the following:

- ☐   The absence of clear goals.
- ☐   The unpredictable entry of power sources from outside.
- ☐   A consistent dependence on money as the moving force.
- ☐   Structural line and staff relationships in the district.
- ☐   The absence of "systems" thinking in problem solving.
- ☐   An operational orientation to the present rather than the future.
- ☐   Decentralized decision making and policy implementation.
- ☐   The absence of evaluative feedback in policy renewal.
- ☐   An incomplete linkage to vital research.
- ☐   Inadequate training and understaffing of personnel.
- ☐   Administrative turnover.

At the school district level, at which most practice is conducted, regular barriers to the improvement of school programs exist:

1. An inadequate theory of implementation, which includes too little time for teachers to plan for and learn new skills and practices.
2. District tendencies toward faddism and quick-fix solutions.
3. Lack of sustained central office support and follow-through.
4. Underfunding of projects, or trying to do too much with too little support.
5. Attempts to manage the projects from the central office instead of developing school leadership and capacity.
6. Lack of technical assistance and other forms of intensive staff development.
7. Lack of awareness of the limitations of teacher and school administrator knowledge about how to implement the project.
8. The turnover of teachers in each school.
9. Too many competing demands or overload.
10. Failure to address the incompatibility between project requirements and existing organizational policies and structures.
11. Failure to understand and take into account site-specific differences among schools.
12. Failure to clarify and negotiate the role of relationships and partnerships.[60]

The type of role assumed by the curriculum planner in making such decisions, under such conditions, is an issue itself. The extreme positions on this question of role are reflected in the following statements:

Curriculum planning lies at the heart of educational planning—dealing with the definition of educational ends and the engineering of means for achieving them.[61]

Curriculum theory should be a subordinate of total educational theory.[62]

Arguments about which of these role definitions is most suitable for curriculum workers are complex. Those who believe in an assisting technical role argue that curriculum theory and practice have traditionally been far apart. So-called blue sky curriculum designs rarely achieve fruitful application in the real world of schools. If curriculum developers are to be useful, so the argument goes, they must meet the real needs of education. This can be done best by maintaining a tractive or static orientation, being specific in operations, and serving where needed.

Arguments that hold that curriculum developers should provide leadership by being both dynamic and intellectual and by achieving a global orientation to education are multiple. Bruce Joyce provides the strongest argument against the traditional posture:

> In the past, educational planners have been technically weak (unable often to clarify ends or engineer means) and morally or technically unable to bring about a humanistic revolution in education . . . curriculum workers have defined themselves as helpers, not leaders, letting the community and teachers make decisions and then assisting in the implementation of those decisions.
>
> By focusing on schools and teachers in schools, curriculum is being forced to operate within the parameters of the institution . . . by far the most paralyzing effect of the assumptive world in which the curriculum specialist lives is that it tends to filter out all ideas which might improve education but which fit awkwardly into the school pattern.[63]

Those calling for an active role for the curriculum specialist argue that, because of the traditional orientation, the field of curriculum has continued to speak the language of sequence, prerequisites, academic achievement, and mastery. Learning theories that do not fit the existing school program, or are not seen as feasible in terms of current teacher practices, are neglected.

The perception of a curriculum specialist as a thinker, designer, leader, and projectionist goes back to the writings of Dewey, Counts, and other progressives of the early twentieth century. Counts, for instance, observed that "the goals of education must be determined by philosophical and analytical concepts of the good life."[64] Among those perceiving curriculum development as a dynamic operation, there is a great fear that the gravitational pull of bureaucracy in education has won out. With each consolidation of schools, with each new piece of legislation, with each new regulation, the school becomes more closed to change, more self-perpetuating, and more product oriented.

We believe that the visionary aspects of curriculum development are essential to a rational process of improving school programs. We see curriculum development as a process of promoting desired change through purposeful activities, which produce a condition in which environmental variables are controlled and behavior is directional. When these things occur, quality programs can be designed, implemented, and evaluated by educational leaders.

As with the role of the curriculum specialist, the mission or end sought by those acting in a program development capacity is not always certain. The open nature of public schools, the diversity of value structures in the United States, the press of socioeconomic conditions, and the inability of educators to control change all contribute to a certain amount of murkiness in school planning.

To a degree greater than most educational planners like to admit, change occurs in school settings in spite of planning. James MacDonald summarized the difficulty in this manner:

> The development of the curriculum in the American public schools has been primarily an accident. A description of what curriculum exists is essentially a political and/or ethical document rather than a scientific or technical one. It is a statement which indicates the outcomes of a very complex interaction of groups, pressures, and events which are most often sociopolitical in motivation and which result in decisions about what ought to be.[65]

SUMMARY

A curriculum is a plan for learning. All such plans contain a vision of what should be, as well as a structure that translates those visions into experiences for learning. Curriculum development, then, is a process that organizes the learning act along the line of value preferences.

Because of the decentralized nature of American education, the role of curriculum workers in interpreting values and arranging learning experiences is extremely important. Considerable difference exists in curriculum definitions, which indicates varied perceptions of the responsibilities of school programming.

Although the question, What will schools do? is unanswered in the first years of this new century, the process by which curriculum is developed is highly defined. We see curriculum development as a deductive process following the historic cycle of analysis, design, implementation, and evaluation.

In the second half of the twentieth century, curriculum planners moved to assimilate and organize extensive data related to the development of school programs. Key issues about the purpose of school programs led to the collection and ordering of such data in four areas: social forces, treatment of knowledge, human growth and development, and the process of learning. To these four areas, we added a fifth, technology. In the future, planners face an increasing number of choices about what schools can be.

SUGGESTED LEARNING ACTIVITIES

1. Develop a time line of major events that have influenced education and altered the definition of the term *curriculum*.
2. Identify some ways in which curriculum workers analyze, design, implement, and evaluate school programs.
3. After reading this chapter, write your own definition of curriculum. Which words suggest an active role? A passive role?
4. What major changes in the foundation areas have occurred in the past decade?

What implications do they have for schools in a postmodern age?
5. Looking ahead one decade, what additional changes can schools anticipate?
6. How would you respond to the postmodern position that history can no longer guide us in planning school programs?

7. Outline the events that have taken American education into a "postmodern" era.
8. Compare the assumptions of a "modern" era of curriculum development with those of a "postmodern" era. What has really changed?

NOTES

1. The Old Deluder Satan Act was one of the first regulatory acts passed by the colonists in the 1640s.
2. Paolo Freire, *Education for Critical Consciousness* (New York: Continuum, 1973).
3. Robert M. Hutchins, *The Higher Learning in America* (New Haven, CT: Yale University Press, 1936), p. 82.
4. Arthur Bestor, *The Restoration of Learning* (New York: Alfred A. Knopf, 1956), pp. 48–49.
5. Phillip H. Phenix, "The Disciplines as Curriculum Content," in A. Harry Passow, ed., *Curriculum Crossroads* (New York: Teachers College Press, 1962), p. 64.
6. Peter F. Oliva, *Developing the Curriculum* (New York: Longman, 1988), p. 6.
7. Colin Marsh and George Willis, *Curriculum Alternative Approaches: Ongoing Issues* (Upper Saddle River, NJ: Prentice Hall, 1995).
8. Franklin Bobbitt, *How to Make a Curriculum* (New York: Houghton Mifflin, 1924), p. 10.
9. Hollis L. Caswell and Doak S. Campbell, *Curriculum Development* (New York: American Book Company, 1935), p. 66.
10. B. Othanel Smith, William O. Stanley, and J. Harlen Shores, *Fundamentals of Curriculum Development* (New York: Harcourt Brace Jovanovich, 1957), p. 3.
11. Ronald Doll, *Curriculum Improvement,* 2nd ed. (Boston: Allyn and Bacon, 1970).
12. Ralph W. Tyler, "The Curriculum Then and Now," in *Proceedings of the 1956 Conference on Testing Problems* (Princeton, NJ: Educational Testing Service, 1957), p. 79.
13. Hilda Taba, *Curriculum Development: Theory and Practice* (New York: Harcourt Brace Jovanovich, 1962), p. 11.

14. J. Galen Saylor and William M. Alexander, *Curriculum Planning for Schools* (New York: Holt, Rinehart & Winston, 1974), p. 6.
15. Mauritz Johnson, "Appropriate Research Directions in Curriculum and Instruction," *Curriculum Theory Network* 6 (Winter 1970–71): 25.
16. John McNeil, *Curriculum: A Comprehensive Introduction,* 3rd ed. (New York: Macmillan, 1985).
17. Daniel Tanner and Laurel Tanner, *Curriculum Development: Theory into Practice,* 3rd ed. (New York: Macmillan, 1995), p. 67.
18. Tanner and Tanner, *Curriculum Development: Theory into Practice,* Preface.
19. William Doll, Jr., *A Post Modern Perspective on Curriculum* (New York: Teachers College Press, 1993), p. 3.
20. P. Freire, *Education for a Critical Consciousness* (New York: Seabury Press, 1973), p. 96.
21. S. Aronowitz and H. Giroux, *Postmodern Education* (Westport, CT: Greenwood, 1991).
22. Tanner and Tanner, *Curriculum Development: Theory into Practice,* p. 68.
23. Taba, *Curriculum Development: Theory and Practice,* p. 9.
24. John Dewey, *The Child and the Curriculum* (Chicago: University of Chicago Press, 1902), p. 4.
25. Harold Rugg, *Curriculum-Making: Past and Present,* 26th Yearbook, Part I, National Society for the Study of Education (Chicago: University of Chicago Press, 1926), p. 22.
26. Boyd H. Bode, "Education at the Crossroads," *Progressive Education* 8 (1931): 543–544.
27. Hilda Taba, "General Techniques of Curriculum Planning," *American Education in the Postwar*

Period, 44th Yearbook, Part I, National Society for the Study of Education (Chicago: University of Chicago Press, 1945), p. 58.

28. Taba, *Curriculum Development: Theory and Practice,* p. 10.

29. Taba, *Curriculum Development: Theory and Practice,* p. 30.

30. Rugg, *Curriculum-Making: Past and Present,* p. 22.

31. Ralph W. Tyler, *Basic Principles of Curriculum and Instruction* (Chicago: University of Chicago Press, 1949).

32. Robert F. Mager, *Goal Analysis* (Belmont, CA: Fearon, 1972).

33. Kathryn Feyereisen, A. John Fiorino, and Arlene T. Nowak, *Supervision and Curriculum Renewal: A Systems Approach* (New York: Appleton-Century-Crofts, 1970), p. 204.

34. A. Dean Hauenstein, *Curriculum Planning for Behavioral Development* (Worthington, OH: Charles A. Jones, 1975), p. 6.

35. Taba, *Curriculum Development: Theory and Practice,* p. 12.

36. Feyereisen et al., *Supervision and Curriculum Renewal,* p. 61.

37. William M. Alexander, "Curriculum Planning as It Should Be," address to Association for Supervision and Curriculum Development Conference, Chicago, October 29, 1971.

38. Jon Wiles and John Reed, "Quest: Education for a Technocratic Existence" (Unpublished manuscript, 1975), p. 58.

39. Charles Silberman, *Crisis in the Classroom* (New York: Random House, 1970), pp. 33–34.

40. For an unusual historical perspective of this problem, see *The National Elementary Principal* 56, 3 (January/February 1977).

41. Paddy Chayefsky, *Network,* released by United Artists, 1977.

42. Wiles and Reed, "Quest," pp. 61–62.

43. Mike Malone, "Getting Personal," *Apple Magazine* 2, 1 (1981).

44. Arno A. Bellack, "Conceptions of Knowledge: Their Significance for Curriculum," in William Jenkins, ed., *The Nature of Knowledge: Implications for the Education of Teachers* (Milwaukee: University of Wisconsin-Milwaukee, 1962), p. 42.

45. Charles Reich, "The Greening of America," *New Yorker* (September 26, 1970): 43–44.

46. Jerome S. Bruner, "Structures in Learning," *NEA Journal* 52 (March 1963): 26.

47. Earl C. Kelley, *Education for What Is Real* (New York: Harper, 1947).

48. Alvin Toffler, *Future Shock* (New York: Random House, 1970).

49. Feyereisen et al., *Supervision and Curriculum Renewal,* p. 138.

50. Jean Piaget, *The Language and Thought of a Child* (New York: Doubleday, 1959).

51. John C. Flanagan, *The Identification, Development, and Utilization of Human Talents: The American High School Student,* Cooperative Research Project No. 635 (Pittsburgh, PA: University of Pittsburgh, 1964).

52. Robert J. Havighurst et al., *Growing Up in River City* (New York: John Wiley & Sons, 1962).

53. Frederick Mosteller and Daniel P. Moynihan, eds., *On Equalization of Educational Opportunity* (New York: Vintage Books, 1972).

54. Jon Wiles and Joseph Bondi, "The Care and Cultivation of Creativity," *Early Years* 12, 1 (August/September 1981): 34–37, 46, 108.

55. Burton L. White, *Experience and Environment: Major Influences on the Development of the Young* (Englewood Cliffs, NJ: Prentice Hall, 1973).

56. "Baby Research Comes of Age," *Psychology Today* 21, 5 (May 1987): 46–48.

57. B. F. Skinner, *Beyond Freedom and Dignity* (New York: Bantam/Vintage Books, 1972).

58. Lawrence Kohlberg and Rochelle Mayer, "Development as an Aim of Education," *Harvard Educational Review* 42 (November 1972): 452–453.

59. Thomas H. Briggs, *Curriculum Problems* (New York: Macmillan, 1926).

60. Bruce Joyce, ed., "Changing School Culture through Staff Development," *Association for Supervision and Curriculum Development 1990 Yearbook* (Alexandria, VA: ASCD, 1990), p. 7.

61. Bruce Joyce, "The Curriculum Worker of the Future," *The Curriculum: Retrospect and Prospect,* 71st Yearbook, Part I, National Society for the Study of Education (Chicago: University of Chicago Press, 1971), p. 307.

62. George Beauchamp, *Curriculum Theory* (Willamette, OR: Kagg Press, 1968).

63. Joyce, "The Curriculum Worker of the Future," p. 64.

64. Robert J. Schaefer, "Retrospect and Prospect," *The Curriculum: Retrospect and Prospect,* 71st Yearbook, National Society for the Study of Education (Chicago: University of Chicago Press, 1971), p. 10.

65. James MacDonald, "Curriculum Development in Relation to Social and Intellectual Systems," *The Curriculum: Retrospect and Prospect,* 71st Yearbook, National Society for the Study of Education (Chicago: University of Chicago Press, 1971), p. 95.

ADDITIONAL READING

Aronowitz, S., and H. Giroux. *Education Still Under Siege.* Westport, CT: Greenwood, 1993.

Bobbitt, Franklin. *The Curriculum.* Boston: Houghton Mifflin, 1918.

Caswell, Hollis, and Doak S. Campbell. *Curriculum Development.* New York: American Book Company, 1935.

Dewey, John. *Democracy and Education.* New York: Macmillan, 1916.

Doll, Ronald. *Curriculum Improvement: Decision-Making and Process,* 9th ed. Needham Heights, MA: Allyn and Bacon, 1996.

Hass, G., and F. Parkay. *Curriculum Planning: A Contemporary Approach.* Needham Heights, MA: Allyn and Bacon, 1999.

Jones, B., and R. Maloy. *Schools for an Information Age.* Westport, CT: Greenwood, 1996.

Keating, Michele, Jon Wiles, and Mary Piazza. *LearningWebs: Curriculum Journeys on the Internet.* Upper Saddle River, NJ: Merrill/Prentice Hall, 2001.

Leicester, Mal et al. *Classroom Issues: Practice, Pedagogy, and Curriculum.* New York: Falmer Press, 1999.

McCulloch, Gary et al. *The Politics of Professionalism: Teachers and the Curriculum.* New York: Continuum International, 2000.

National Society for the Study of Education. *The Curriculum: Retrospect and Prospect.* Chicago: NSSE, 1971.

Quike, John. *A Curriculum for Life: Schools for a Democratic Learning Society.* New York: Open University Press, 1999.

Sears, J. *Teaching and Thinking about Curriculum.* New York: Teachers College Press, 1990.

Taba, Hilda. *Curriculum Development: Theory and Practice.* New York: Harcourt Brace Jovanovich, 1962.

Tanner, Daniel. *History of School Curriculum.* New York: Macmillan, 1989.

Tanner, Laurel, ed. *Critical Issues in Curriculum.* Chicago: National Society for the Study of Education, 1988.

Toffler, Alvin. *Powershift: Knowledge, Wealth and Violence at the Eve of the 21st Century.* New York: Bantam Books, 1990.

PART II

THE ESSENTIAL ELEMENTS OF CURRICULUM

chapter 3

THE ROLE OF PHILOSOPHY IN CURRICULUM PLANNING

At the heart of purposeful activity in curriculum development is an educational philosophy that assists in answering value-laden questions and making decisions from among the many choices. For John Dewey, America's most famous educator, a philosophy was a general theory of educating. One of Dewey's students, Boyd Bode, saw a philosophy as "a source of reflective consideration." Ralph Tyler, a leader in curriculum throughout much of the twentieth century, likened philosophy to "a screen for selecting educational objectives."

Philosophies can, therefore, serve curriculum leaders in many ways. They can help to

- ☐ suggest purpose in education;
- ☐ clarify objectives and learning activities in school;
- ☐ define the roles of persons working in schools; and
- ☐ guide the selection of learning strategies and tactics in the classroom.

A philosophy is essential to any meaningful curriculum development effort. This is especially true as we enter the age of Internet-assisted curricula.

In arriving at an educational philosophy, curriculum specialists are forced to consider value-laden choices. In this age of rapidly changing ideas of how to define and operate a school, decisions made in defining the scope of curriculum will directly impact the substance and structure of educational programs. Curriculum specialists who are aware of their own beliefs about education and learning will make better everyday decisions.

The need for curriculum workers to hold a philosophy of education became increasingly obvious in the second half of the twentieth century as the rate of change in education accelerated. Public education witnessed wave after wave of innovation, reform, new themes, and other general signals of dissatisfaction with the status quo. Indicative of the seriousness of calls for reformation of public schools is the following statement issued by the President's Advisory Commission on Science:

> When school was short, and merely a supplement to the main activities of growing up, the form mattered little. But school has expanded to fill time that other activities once occupied, without substituting for them. . . . Every society must somehow solve the problem of transforming children into adults, for its very survival depends on that solution. In every society there is established some kind of institutional setting within which the transformation is to occur, in directions predicated by societal goals and values. . . . In our view, the institutional framework for maturation in the United States is in need of serious examination. The school system, as it now exists, offers an incomplete context for the accomplishment of many important facets of maturation.[1]

Another example of this dissatisfaction with the status quo is found in the following statement by John Gatto, the Year 2000 Teacher of the Year in New York state:

> Public education teaches a covert curriculum whether teachers realize it or not. This curriculum consists of confusion, class position, indifference, emotional dependence, intellectual dependency, and provisional self-esteem.
>
> Gatto observed that this docile and obedient population, perfect for the factory or the army, was exactly what the Prussians had in mind when America adopted their educational system 200 years ago.[2]

Although many are calling for change in public education today, there is no strong mandate for the direction of such change in the United States. In the absence of centralized public planning and policy formation, local school boards rely on input from pressure groups, expert opinion, and various forces in the societal flow. Often, decisions about school programs are made in an isolated, piecemeal fashion without serious consideration of the pattern of decision making. When goals are unclear, when there is no public consensus about what schools should accomplish, when there are value-laden decisions, or when curriculum specialists are unable to articulate positions on controversial issues clearly, schools slip into the all-too-common pattern of reactive thinking and action. Currently, schools are being pushed along by technology and legislative mandates to test.

The absence of direction often results in a curriculum that includes nearly everything but accomplishes little. Given the public nature of American education, the dynamic nature of public school decision-making forums, and the dependence of school boards and superintendents on curriculum specialists for direction, the beliefs and values of the curriculum leader must be clear.

THE SEARCH FOR A PHILOSOPHICAL ATTITUDE

Although there has been a steady interest in educational philosophies for over a century in the United States, the use of such an orientation in program planning has been severely limited in the public education system. With the exception of the "progressive schools" of the 1930s, the "alternative" schools of the early 1970s, and the magnet and charter schools and home schooling of the 1990s, few American education programs have emerged that reflect strong philosophical understanding and commitment. As Robert M. McClure noted:

> With depressing few exceptions, curriculum design until the 1950s was a process of layering society's new knowledge on top of a hodgepodge accumulation of old knowledge and arranging for feeding it, in prescribed time units, to students who may or may not have found it relevant to their own lives.[3]

The dependence of school leaders on public acquiescence for the development of school programs explains, in large part, the absence of philosophical consistency and the standardization of school programs over time. Without public demand for or approval of change, often interpreted in the public forum as no opposition, elected school leaders have failed to press for more distinct school programs.

Equally, the mandate of public education to serve all learners has acted to restrict the specification of educational ends and the development of tailored programs. The concept of school as the assimilator of diverse cultures, from the turn of the century until the mid-1960s, contributed to the general nature of public school education.

Another factor in the absence of educational specificity in programs has been the lack of strong curriculum leadership at state and local levels. With the exception of university-based theorists, few curriculum specialists have had the understanding of philosophy, the clarity of vision, and the technical skills to direct school programs toward consistently meaningful activity. Although this condition is rapidly improving because of the greatly increased number of persons trained in curriculum development, the presence of a highly skilled curriculum leader often separates the successful school district from the mediocre school district.

The development of a clear and consistent set of beliefs about the purpose of education requires considerable thought, for there is much information to consider and strong arguments for the many philosophical positions that have developed. Perhaps the most important is Galen Saylor and William M. Alexander's observation that schooling is always a "moral enterprise":

> A society establishes and supports schools for certain purposes; it seeks to achieve certain ends or attain desired outcomes. Efforts of adults to direct the experiences of young people in a formal institution such as the school constitute preferences for certain human ends and values.

> Schooling is a moral venture, one that necessitates choosing values among innumerable possibilities. These choices constitute the starting point in curriculum planning.[4]

To illustrate the diversity of beliefs about the purpose of formal education and approaches to educating, consider the two following statements by Robert Hutchins and A. S. Neill. These statements are representative of two established educational philosophies: *perennialism* and *existentialism*. First, Hutchins:

> The ideal education is not an ad hoc education, not an education directed to immediate needs; it is not a specialized education, or a preprofessional education; it is not a utilitarian education. It is an education calculated to develop the mind.
>
> I have old-fashioned prejudices in favor of the three R's and the liberal arts, in favor of trying to understand the greatest works that the human race has produced. I believe that these are permanent necessities, the intellectual tools that are needed to understand the ideas and ideals of our world.[5]

Now, Neill:

> Well, we set out to make a school in which we should allow children to be themselves. In order to do this, we had to renounce all discipline, all direction, all suggestion, all moral training. . . . All it required was what we had—a complete belief in the child as a good, not evil being. For almost forty years, this belief in the goodness of the child has never wavered; it rather has become a final faith. My view is that a child is innately wise and realistic. If left to himself without adult suggestions of any kind, he will develop as far as he is capable of developing.[6]

Such differences of opinion about the purpose and means of educating are extreme, but they illustrate the range of choices to be made by curriculum planners. These statements also indicate the trends of education that various philosophies favor. The perennialists, who favor a highly controlled curriculum, much structure, strict discipline, and uniform treatment for students, can easily identify with trends such as back-to-the-basics and accountability. The existentialists, who see a non-school environment for personal growth, an environment with highly individualized activities and low degrees of formal structure, can identify with alternative programs, student rights movements, the new technologies, and other nonstandard choices.

CRITICAL QUESTIONS TO BE ANSWERED

Each curriculum planner must face and answer some difficult questions about the purpose and organization of schooling. The answers to such questions are critical to school planning and establish the criteria for future decision making and action. As Saylor and Alexander stated the condition, it is one of defining responsibility:

> In selecting the basic goals which the school should seek to serve from among the sum total of ends for which people strive the curriculum planner faces the major

issue: In the total process of human development what parts or aspects should the school accept responsibility for guiding?[7]

Daniel Tanner and Laurel Tanner observed that three major ends for schooling have been suggested repeatedly in the past:

> Throughout the twentieth century educational opinion and practice have been sharply divided as to whether the dominant source and influence for curriculum development should be the body of organized scholarship (the specialties and divisions of academic knowledge), the learner (the immature developing being), or society (contemporary adult life).[8]

The decision of the curriculum leader to relate to the knowledge bases of the past, the social concerns of the present, or the future needs of society is critical. Among other things, this decision will determine whether the role of the curriculum specialist is to restructure or only to refine the existing system of education.

Most often, curriculum development in schools is a mechanical, static function because the content base is accepted as the main criterion for curriculum work:

> In the absence of reflective consideration of what constitutes the good man leading the good life in the good society, the curriculum tends to be regarded as a mechanical means of developing the necessary skills of young people in conformance with the pervading demands of the larger social scene. Under such circumstances, the school does not need to bring into question the existing social situation, nor does it need to enable pupils to examine through reflective thinking possible alternative solutions to social problems. Instead, the school is merely expected to do the bidding of whatever powers and forces are most dominant in the larger society at any given time.[9]

If, however, the curriculum planner accepts the needs of learners as a criterion for planning school programs, as was done in the early childhood and middle school programs of the 1970s or special education "inclusion" of the 1990s, the purpose of the formal education program is altered. The same is true if the purpose of schools is seen as social reform or improving society. In accepting an alteration of the traditional criteria for developing school programs, curriculum developers "cross over" into an advocacy role for change as they attempt to restructure the existing curriculum. The effectiveness of such a position in curriculum work is often determined by the clarity of the new objectives to be achieved. In the first decade of the twenty-first century, the Internet proffers options never before imagined including the "virtual school."

A number of primary questions override the value choices of all major educational philosophies: What is the purpose of education? What kind of citizens and what kind of society do we want? What methods of instruction or classroom organization must we provide to produce these desired ends?

McNeil poses eight questions that are useful in developing the philosophical assumptions needed to screen educational objectives:

1. Is the purpose of school to change, adapt to, or accept the social order?
2. What can a school do better than any other agency or institution?
3. What objectives should be common to all?
4. Should objectives stress cooperation or competition?
5. Should objectives deal with controversial issues, or only those things for which there is established knowledge?
6. Should attitudes be taught? Fundamental skills? Problem-solving strategies?
7. Should teachers emphasize subject matter or try to create behavior outside of school?
8. Should objectives be based on the needs of the local community? Society in general? Expressed needs of students?[10]

THE STRUGGLE TO BE A DECISIVE LEADER

Few educators would deny the importance of a philosophy in directing activity, but few school districts or teachers relish discussions on the topic. Even well-known educators have confessed a dislike for such discourse:

> It is well to rid oneself of this business of "aims of education." Discussions on this subject are among the dullest and most fruitless of human pursuits.[11]

> A sense of distasteful weariness overtakes me whenever I hear someone discussing educational goals and philosophy.[12]

In the past, part of the problem with discussing educational philosophies in earnest has been the pervasiveness of the subject-dominated curriculum in American schools. This problem has been further compounded by "expert opinion" on the topic by college professors who are products of the system and therefore possess a monumental conflict of interest in rendering an opinion. In school districts in which inquiry into the purpose of educating has been quickly followed by retrenchment of the subject-matter curriculum, philosophical discussions have produced little payoff. But, when inquiry into educational purpose is honest, open, and leads to meaningful change, philosophical discussions are among the most exciting endeavors.

Charles Silberman, in his book *Crisis in the Classroom,* expressed the meaning of philosophical understandings for the learning programs of the school:

> What educators must realize, moreover, is that how they teach and how they act may be more important than what they teach. The way we do things, that is to say, shapes values more directly and more effectively than the way we talk about them. Certainly administrative procedures like automatic promotion, homogeneous grouping, racial segregation, or selective admission to higher education affect "citizenship education" more profoundly than does the social studies curriculum. And children are taught a host of lessons about values, ethics, morality, character, and conduct every day of the week, less by the conduct of the curriculum than by the way schools are

organized, the ways teachers and parents behave, the way they talk to children and each other, the kinds of behavior they approve or reward and the kinds they disapprove and punish. These lessons are far more powerful than verbalizations that accompany them and that they frequently controvert.[13]

Two major benefits can be derived from an exploration of philosophical attitudes. First, major problem areas and inconsistencies in the school program can be identified:

> Many contemporary educational principles and practices are something of a hodge-podge rooted in premises about the nature of man and his relationship with his physical-social environment that frequently are incompatible with one another.[14]

Second, areas of common ground among those responsible for educational leadership can be discovered. Common values that overlap individual beliefs form the most fertile ground for curricular collaboration and the development of successful projects and programs.

Before curriculum specialists can work with parents, teachers, administrators, and other educators to explore educational values, they must examine their own attitudes. During this process, the curriculum worker is seeking to identify a value structure that can organize and relate the many aspects of planning.

To clarify the values and beliefs that will tie together curriculum organization, instructional procedures, learning roles, materials selection, and other components of school planning, curriculum leaders must identify themes that seem true to them. Although this process may be time consuming, the investment is necessary. In order to be both decisive and effective in their roles, curriculum leaders must combat the urge to ignore the value implications of the job or reduce all arguments to "thoughtful uncertainty." The press of technology threatens any curriculum leadership unwilling to take a stand.

DETERMINANTS OF AN EDUCATIONAL PHILOSOPHY

Major philosophies of life and education have traditionally been defined by three criteria: What is good? What is true? What is real? Individual perceptions of goodness, truth, and reality differ considerably, and an analysis of these questions reveals unique patterns of response. When such responses are categorized and labeled, they become formal philosophies.

In the language of philosophy, the study of goodness is referred to as *axiology*, truth as *epistemology*, and reality as *ontology*. Axiological questions deal primarily with values; in a school context, philosophical arguments are concerned with the ultimate source of values to be taught. Questions of an epistemological nature in a school context are directed toward the media of learning or the best means of seeking truth. Ontological questions, in search of reality, are most often concerned with the substance of learning, or content of study. Thus, the standard philosophical inquiries concerning goodness, truth, and reality are translated into questions concerning the source, medium, and form of learning in a school environment.

These queries are not simple, for there are many ways to select ideas, translate them into instructional patterns, and package them into curriculum programs. Those possibilities are forever increasing as our knowledge of the world becomes more sophisticated. Essential questions arise, questions that must be answered prior to planning learning experiences for students. Should schools exist? What should be taught? What is the role of the teacher and the student? How does the school deal with change?

FIVE EDUCATIONAL PHILOSOPHIES

There are many educational philosophies, but for the sake of simplicity, it is possible to extract five distinct ones: (1) perennialism, (2) idealism, (3) realism, (4) experimentalism, and (5) existentialism. Collectively, these philosophies represent a broad spectrum of thought about what schools should be and do. Educators holding these philosophies would create very different schools. In the following sections, each of these standard philosophies is discussed in terms of its posture on axiological, epistemological, and ontological questions.

The five standard philosophies are compared in Table 3.1 in terms of attitudes on significant questions.

Perennialism

The most conservative, traditional, or inflexible of the five philosophies is *perennialism*, a philosophy drawing heavily from classical definitions of education. Perennialists believe that education, like human nature, is a constant. Because the distinguishing characteristic of humans is the ability to reason, education should focus on developing rationality. Education, for the perennialist, is a preparation for life, and students should be taught the world's permanencies through structured study.

For the perennialist, reality is a world of reason. Such truths are revealed to us through study and some through divine acts. Goodness is to be found in rationality itself. Perennialists favor a curriculum of subjects and doctrine taught through highly disciplined drill and behavior control. Schools, for the perennialist, exist primarily to reveal reason by teaching eternal truths. The teacher interprets and tells. The student is a passive recipient. Because truth is eternal, all change in the immediate school environment is largely superficial.

Idealism

Idealism is a philosophy that espouses the refined wisdom of men and women. Reality is seen as a world within a person's mind. Truth is to be found in the consistency of ideas. Goodness is an ideal state, something to strive to attain.

TABLE 3.1 Five Major Educational Philosophies

	Perennialism	Idealism	Realism	Experimentalism	Existentialism
Reality Ontology	A world of reason and God	A world of the mind	A world of things	A world of experience	A world of existing
Truth (Knowledge) Epistemology	Reason and revelation	Consistency of ideas	Correspondence and sensation (as we see it)	What works, What is	Personal, subjective choice
Goodness Axiology	Rationality	Imitation of ideal self, person to be emulated	Laws of nature	The public test	Freedom
Teaching Reality	Disciplinary subjects and doctrine	Subjects of the mind—literary, philosophical, religious	Subjects of physical world—math, science	Subject matter of social experiences—social studies	Subject matter of choice—art, ethics, philosophy
Teaching Truth	Discipline of the mind via drill	Teaching ideas via lecture, discussion	Teaching for mastery, of information—demonstrate, recite	Problem solving, project method	Arousing personal responses—questioning
Teaching Goodness (Values)	Disciplining behavior (to reason)	Imitating heroes and other exemplars	Training in rules of conduct	Making group decisions in light of consequences	Awakening self to responsibility
Why Schools Exist	To reveal reason and God's will	To sharpen the mind and intellectual processes	To reveal the order of the world and universe	To discover and expand the society we live in to share experiences	To aid children in knowing themselves and their place in society
What Should Be Taught	External truths	Wisdom of the ages	Laws of physical reality	Group inquiry into social problems and social sciences, method and subject together	Unregimented topic areas
Role of the Teacher	Interprets, tells	Reports, person to be emulated	Displays, imparts knowledge	Aids, consultant	Questions, assists student in personal journey
Role of the Student	Passive reception	Receives, memorizes	Manipulates, passive participation	Active participation, contributes	Determines own rules
School's Attitude Toward Change	Truth is eternal, no real change	Truth to be preserved, antichange	Always moving toward perfection, orderly change	Change is ever present, a process	Change is necessary at all times

Idealists favor schools that teach subjects of the mind, such as are found in most public school classrooms. Teachers, for the idealist, would be models of ideal behavior.

For idealists, the schools' function is to sharpen intellectual processes, to present the wisdom of the ages, and to present models of behavior that are exemplary. Students in such schools would have a somewhat passive role, receiving and memorizing the reporting of the teacher. Change in the school program would generally be considered an intrusion on the orderly process of educating.

Realism

For the *realist,* the world is as it is, and the job of schools is to teach students about the world. Goodness, for the realist, is found in the laws of nature and the order of the physical world. Truth is the simple correspondences of observation.

The realist favors a school dominated by subjects of the here-and-now world, such as math and science. Students would be taught factual information for mastery. The teacher would impart knowledge of this reality to students or display such reality for observation and study. Classrooms would be highly ordered and disciplined, like nature, and the students would be passive participants in the study of things. Changes in school would be perceived as a natural evolution toward a perfection of order.

Experimentalism

For the *experimentalist,* the world is an ever-changing place. Reality is what is actually experienced. Truth is what presently functions. Goodness is what is accepted by public test. Unlike the perennialist, idealist, and realist, the experimentalist openly accepts change and continually seeks to discover new ways to expand and improve society.

The experimentalist favors a school with heavy emphasis on social subjects and experiences. Learning would occur through a problem-solving or inquiry format. Teachers would aid learners or consult with learners who would be actively involved in discovering and experiencing the world in which they live. Such an educational program, which focuses on value development, would factor in group consequences.

Existentialism

The *existentialist* sees the world in terms of personal subjectivity; goodness, truth, and reality are individually defined. Reality is a world of existing, truth subjectively chosen, and goodness a matter of freedom.

For existentialists, schools, if they existed at all, would be places that assisted students in knowing themselves and learning their place in society. If subject matter existed, it would be a matter of interpretation such as the arts, ethics, or philosophy. Teacher–student interaction would center around assisting students in their personal learning journeys. Change in school environments would be embraced as both a natural and necessary phenomenon. Nonschooling and an individually determined curriculum would be a possibility.

PHILOSOPHY PREFERENCE ASSESSMENT

Because schools are complex places with many forces vying for prominence, few educators hold a pure version of any of these philosophies. These schools of thought have evolved as distinctive forms of philosophy following the examination of beliefs on pertinent issues. When an educator chooses not to adopt a single philosophy, or blends philosophies, or selectively applies educational philosophies in practice, he or she is said to hold an *eclectic* position. Most classrooms and public schools come closest to an eclectic stance, applying philosophical preferences as conditions demand.

Whatever the educator's philosophy or beliefs about schools—and each of the five philosophies presented here is a legitimate belief—it is critical that these values be clarified and understood in terms of their implications. To this end, you can participate in a self-assessment (see Figure 3.1) that has been developed to show preferences on value-laden educational questions.

What Is Your Philosophy?

The test question numbers from Figure 3.1 that relate to the five standard philosophies of education are as follows:

1. Perennialist:	6,	8,	10,	13,	15,	31,	34,	37
2. Idealist:	9,	11,	19,	21,	24,	27,	29,	33
3. Realist:	4,	7,	12,	20,	22,	23,	26,	28
4. Experimentalist:	2,	3,	14,	17,	25,	35,	39,	40
5. Existentialist:	1,	5,	16,	18,	30,	32,	36,	38

Scoring Steps
1. For each set (for example, the eight perennialist questions), add the value of the answers given. In a single set of numbers, the total should fall between 8 (all ones) and 40 (all fives).
2. Divide the total score for each set by 5 (example: 40 4 5 5 8).
3. Plot the scores on the graph shown in Figure 3.2.

Interpretation of Scoring. Having scored and plotted your responses on the grid provided, you now have a profile of your own beliefs about schools. It can be noted that some patterns are common and, therefore, subject to interpretation. The pattern already on the grid in Figure 3.2, for instance, is a composite response by over 5,000 students, both graduate and undergraduate, at five universities.

Pattern 1. If your profile on the response grid is basically flat, reflecting approximately the same score for each set of questions, an inability to discriminate in terms of preference is indicated. See Figure 3.3.

Directions: For each item below, respond according to the strength of your belief, scoring the item on a scale of 1 through 5. A one (1) indicates strong disagreement, a five (5) strong agreement. Use a separate sheet of paper.

1. Ideal teachers are constant questioners.
2. Schools exist for societal improvement.
3. Teaching should center around the inquiry technique.
4. Demonstration and recitation are essential components for learning.
5. Students should always be permitted to determine their own rules in the educational process.
6. Reality is spiritual and rational.
7. Curriculum should be based on the laws of natural science.
8. The teacher should be a strong authority figure in the classroom.
9. The student is a receiver of knowledge.
10. Ideal teachers interpret knowledge.
11. Lecture-discussion is the most effective teaching technique.
12. Institutions should seek avenues toward self-improvement through an orderly process.
13. Schools are obligated to teach moral truths.
14. School programs should focus on social problems and issues.
15. Institutions exist to preserve and strengthen spiritual and social values.
16. Subjective opinion reveals truth.
17. Teachers are seen as facilitators of learning.
18. Schools should be educational "smorgasbords."
19. Memorization is the key to process skills.
20. Reality consists of objects.
21. Schools exist to foster the intellectual process.
22. Schools foster an orderly means for change.
23. There are essential skills everyone must learn.
24. Teaching by subject area is the most effective approach.
25. Students should play an active part in program design and evaluation.
26. A functioning member of society follows rules of conduct.
27. Reality is rational.
28. Schools should reflect the society they serve.
29. The teacher should set an example for the students.
30. The most effective learning does not take place in a highly structured, strictly disciplined environment.
31. The curriculum should be based on unchanging spiritual truths.
32. The most effective learning is nonstructured.
33. Truth is a constant expressed through ideas.
34. Drill and factual knowledge are important components of any learning environment.
35. Societal consensus determines morality.
36. Knowledge is gained primarily through the senses.
37. There are essential pieces of knowledge that everyone should know.
38. The school exists to facilitate self-awareness.
39. Change is an ever-present process.
40. Truths are best taught through the inquiry process.

FIGURE 3.1   Philosophy Preference Assessment

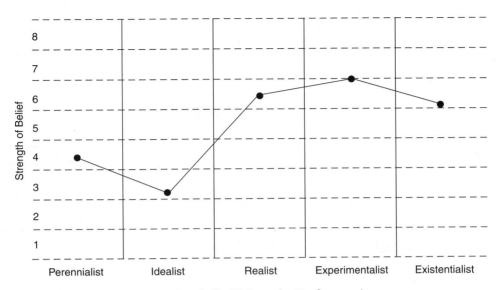

FIGURE 3.2   Composite Graph for Philosophy Preference Assessment

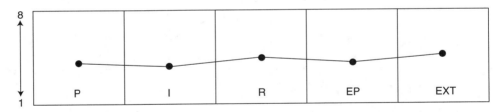

FIGURE 3.3   Pattern 1

Pattern 2. If your pattern is generally a slanting line across the grid, you show a strong structured (slanting down) or nonstructured (slanting up) orientation in your reported beliefs about schools. See Figure 3.4.

Pattern 3. If your pattern appears as a bimodal or trimodal distribution (two or three peaks), it indicates indecisiveness on crucial issues and suggests the need for further clarification. The closer the peaks (adjacent sets), the less contradiction in the responses. See Figure 3.5.

Pattern 4. If the pattern appears *U*-shaped, as in either of the graphs in Figure 3.6, a significant amount of value inconsistency is indicated. Such a response would suggest strong beliefs in very different and divergent systems.

Pattern 5. Finally, a pattern that is simply a flowing curve without sharp peaks and valleys may suggest either an eclectic philosophy or a person only beginning to study his or her own philosophy. See Figure 3.7.

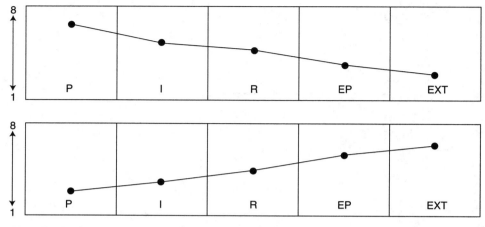

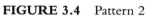

FIGURE 3.4 Pattern 2

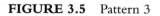

FIGURE 3.5 Pattern 3

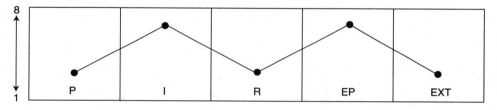

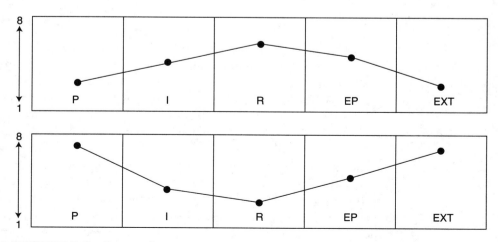

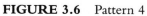

FIGURE 3.6 Pattern 4

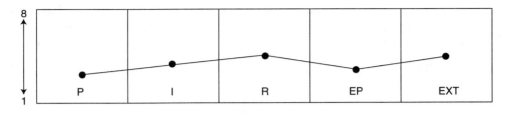

FIGURE 3.7   Pattern 5

PHILOSOPHIES AS FOUND IN SCHOOLS

During the twentieth century, U.S. schools evolved from highly standardized content-focused institutions to more flexible and diverse institutions. Our understandings of human development and the learning process and the pressures on our rapidly changing society account for these alterations of the schooling form.

All schools are designed to promote an education, but the designs of school curricula differ just as philosophies differ. Schools represent a blueprint, or plan, to promote learning; because the ends sought by planners differ, all schools are not alike. This section introduces the fifteen dimensions of school design, dimensions by which schools can be compared and contrasted. Each dimension has been prepared to illuminate the various philosophical continua within schools. Although these continua do not match our five philosophies precisely, you can begin to see a rough parallel between these philosophies and the various dimensions of the school setting. Questions for planners are highlighted for your consideration.

The intentions of schooling might be thought of as a continuum of choices. On one end of such a continuum is the belief that education is the process of shaping raw human talent into something definitive and useful to society. This classic view of education sees schools as shaping and refining human thought and behavior through an increasingly controlled program of study. Such control, in the legitimate sense of the word, is accomplished by structuring the learning environment to facilitate highly predictable ends.

On the other end of that same choice continuum is the belief that human talents are best managed by allowing the natural capacities of individuals to develop through the removal of growth barriers. This definition of education would have schools acting to release the student from behaviors and perceptions that limit personal development. Thus, the institution of the school would formally seek the expansion of human potential in the process of learning by promoting flexibility in the learning environment.

Strong arguments can be made for either of these positions, as well as for the many intermediate stances on such a continuum. The crucial concept to be understood is that schools are institutions created by society to accomplish certain ends. Because there are many possible goals for the institution of the school, there are many legitimate forms of schooling. To the degree that the organization of the school corresponds with the objectives of the school, the school can effectively educate students.

The range of possible intentions for a school program, bordered on one end by a school seeking maximum control and on the other by a school promoting maximum freedom, can be translated into the universal variables of structure versus flexibility. These two variables are used to facilitate the analysis of fifteen major dimensions of schooling. These dimensions can all be readily observed by a visit to any school:

1. Community involvement
2. School buildings and grounds
3. Classroom spaces
4. Organization of knowledge
5. Uses of learning materials
6. Philosophy of education
7. Teaching strategies
8. Staffing patterns
9. Organization of students
10. Rules and regulations
11. Disciplinary measures
12. Reporting of student progress
13. Administrative attitudes
14. Teacher roles
15. Student roles

Examining the school by such criteria, in a systematic manner, will help you see a school in its totality. The underlying beliefs about educating will become more obvious, and the program congruence or inconsistencies will be more visible. In short, you will be able to analyze the dimensions of a school setting in a selective and regular way and to understand the philosophical intent of the curriculum. The numbered rating scales in the following sections refer to this list.

The Learning Environment

Environments, both real and perceived, set a tone for learning. What people feel about the spaces that they occupy or in which they interact causes them to behave in certain ways. For instance, churches call for discreet behavior, while stadiums elicit a different behavior altogether.

Traditionally, schools have been solitary, sedate, and ordered environments. This atmosphere was the result of many forces: a narrow definition of formal education, a limited public access to knowledge, and a didactic (telling–listening) format for learning.

In contrast, many innovative schools seem to be the organizational opposite of the traditional, structured school. They are often open, noisy, and sometimes seemingly chaotic activity centers. Such schools are the result of both a changing definition of education and a new understanding of the environmental conditions that enhance learning.

Three measures of the learning environments of schools are the relationship of the school and the surrounding community, the construction and use of buildings and grounds, and the organization of learning spaces within buildings. Within each of these three areas, selected dimensions have been identified that may help you to understand the learning environment of the school.

Community Involvement.   Individual schools differ according to the degree and type of interaction that they enjoy with the immediate community. Schools that perceive their role as shaping the behavior and thoughts of students into acceptable patterns normally seek to limit community access and involvement in the school program. By limiting community access, the school also limits community influence on the school program and thus ensures more predictable student outcomes.

Conversely, schools intent on expanding student responses to the educational process generally encourage community access and involvement in school activities. By encouraging community access, the school encourages community influence, thus ensuring the divergent input characteristic of most communities.

Measures of community access to and involvement with a school are plentiful. A simple measure readily available to the observer is to note how many and what kinds of nonschool personnel are in a school building on a given day. Perhaps a more analytical approach to the assessment of involvement, however, is to observe the school operation in terms of physical, legal, participatory, and intellectual access.

The descriptive continua in Figure 3.8 suggest the potential range of alternatives present in schools.

Physical access.   In a physical sense, community involvement can be measured by the amount of quasi-school-related activity occurring in the school building. Activities such as school-sponsored visits to the building, community-sponsored functions in the building, parental participation in school-sponsored activities, and school programs being conducted in the community are indicative of interchange and involvement.

On the other hand, schools in which the public is never invited to visit; in which classes never leave the building; and in which the public is fenced out or locked out, held at the office when visiting, not welcome after school hours, or discouraged from mobility within the spaces of the school have limited access and involvement.

Legal access.   Legally, the community is allowed to become involved with the school at varying levels. In a tightly structured or closed school, legal access is normally restricted to setting limits and voting on school bonds. Increasing participation is measured by electing school officials and the chief administrative officer of the school district. Further access is indicated by school-building-level committees (such as a textbook selection committee) that allow community members to play an active role in policy formation. Not surprisingly, so-called community schools allow the ultimate access; parents and the community-at-large serve in governance roles over school operation and activity.

Physical Access

No contact	Community functions in the school buildings	Scheduled community visits to the school	Regular community participation in school building activities	School learning activities in the community

S ├─────────┼─────────┼─────────┼─────────┤ F
  1   2   3   4   5

Legal Access

Voting for bonds	Electing school officials	Serving on official committees	Policy boards at school building level	Operational control over school programs

S ├─────────┼─────────┼─────────┼─────────┤ F
  1   2   3   4   5

Participatory Access

Ignored	Informed	Advisory	Planning	Participatory

S ├─────────┼─────────┼─────────┼─────────┤ F
  1   2   3   4   5

Intellectual Access

Never consulted about content	Advisory in goal setting	Set goals and parameters of school programs	Involved in planning implementation	Actively involved in implementing at classroom level

S ├─────────┼─────────┼─────────┼─────────┤ F
  1   2   3   4   5

General Access

Media access (the news)	Legal access (voting bonds)	Physical access (visitations)	Participatory access (school programs)	Intellectual access (goal setting)

S ├─────────┼─────────┼─────────┼─────────┤ F
  1   2   3   4   5

FIGURE 3.8   Types of Community Access to Schools (S = structured; F = flexible)

Participatory access.   In terms of participation in the daily operation of the school program, the community can be ignored, informed, included at an advisory level, or asked to participate wholly. Whether a school chooses to include the community in the type of school program that is being experienced by the students depends on whether such participation is seen as contributing to or detracting from the mission of the school.

Intellectual access.　Finally, there is an intellectual dimension to community involvement with the school that is indicated by access to goal setting, resource allocation, and program development. To the degree that the community is excluded from thinking about the substance of what is taught and the method of instruction, the school is characterized by limited intellectual access or high structures (S). If the school encourages programmatic and instructional participation from parents and members of the community, access or high flexibility (F) is evidenced.

Questions.　What is the relationship of the school to the community? What rights does the tax-paying public have in school governance? How much autonomy should professionals have in operating public schools?

There are great differences in the degree of access and community involvement with individual school buildings. As such, community involvement represents one salient dimension of the learning environment.

School Buildings and Grounds.　The physical nature of school buildings and school grounds may be subtle indicators of the school's perceived mission and, therefore, useful measures for a visitor or interested observer. Features such as access points, building warmth, traffic control inside the building, and space priorities may reflect the intended program of the school.

Architects have observed that buildings are a physical expression of content. A dull, drab, unexciting building may reflect a dull, drab, unexciting educational process. An exciting, stimulating, dynamic building may reflect an active, creative learning center. A building not only expresses its interior activity but may also reflect, and even control, the success of these functions. If school corridors, for example, are colorful, well lit, and visually expansive, this excitement and stimulation direct the individual in such a space. This is why most new airports have extremely wide and brightly colored corridors. The environment "sets up" the participant dispositionally.

School buildings changed a great deal during the twentieth century, and those changes in architecture and construction reflect more subtle changes in the programs of schools. A stereotypical evolution of school buildings in the United States would show a progression from a cellular lecture hall (many one-room schoolhouses together) to an open and largely unstructured space, as illustrated in Figure 3.9.[*]

Although many of these changes might be explained by evolutions in architecture and cost-effectiveness demands, a primary force behind the diminishing structure in school buildings has been the dissemination of knowledge through other media. As the essential curriculum of the turn of the century gave way to a more broadly focused academic preparation, buildings were designed to incorporate diversity. Because spaces had multiple uses, the construction was necessarily flexible in design. With the advent of interactive computers and a universe of

---

[*]In the 1990s, districts were opting to use site-constructed additions (portable) to expand capacity at school sites rather than construct totally new buildings. This modular strategy reflected an awareness of the ups and downs of school populations caused by mobility and fluctuations in birth rates.

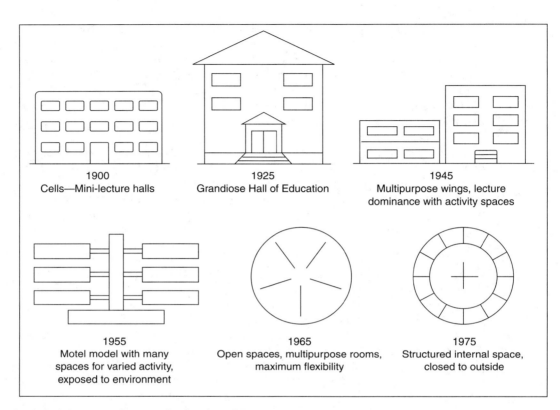

1900
Cells—Mini-lecture halls

1925
Grandiose Hall of Education

1945
Multipurpose wings, lecture
dominance with activity spaces

1955
Motel model with many
spaces for varied activity,
exposed to environment

1965
Open spaces, multipurpose rooms,
maximum flexibility

1975
Structured internal space,
closed to outside

FIGURE 3.9   Evolution of School Buildings

possible knowledge, the role of buildings is becoming less clear. Storefronts could serve learning as well as traditional schools, if home schooling and learning networks structure the curriculum.

The design of a school building, however, does not always reflect the current philosophy of the school. Many flexible programs are found in old "egg crate" buildings, and highly structured programs are sometimes found in modern open-space schools. Returning to our analytical tools—the degree of access, the warmth of the building, traffic control patterns inside the building, and space priorities—we can begin to guess the educational philosophy of the school.

The descriptive continua in Figure 3.10 suggest the potential range of alternatives present in schools.

Degree of access.   Many schools, because of genuine danger in the immediate neighborhood, limit the number of access points to the school building. Other schools deliberately limit public access as a means of controlling the environment and personnel in the building. Signs of extreme control in school buildings are a single entrance for all entering the building, constantly locked spaces such as

Degree of Access

Highly visible control of access exterior building	Access control visible interior only, high regimentation	Access control visible exterior only	Order visible but not excessive	Access not controlled exterior or interior

S ├─────────────┼─────────────┼─────────────┼─────────────┤ F
1   2   3   4   5

Building Warmth

Spaces drab, overwhelming, repulsive, cold	Spaces ordered and monotonous	Spaces neutral, neither pleasant nor unpleasant	Spaces pleasant, light, clean, attractive	Spaces inviting, cheery, colorful

S ├─────────────┼─────────────┼─────────────┼─────────────┤ F
1   2   3   4   5

Traffic Control Patterns

Movement in building highly controlled	Movement patterns structured by arrangement	Traffic patterns established	Traffic patterns not specified; options available to individuals	Movement patterns not discernible

S ├─────────────┼─────────────┼─────────────┼─────────────┤ F
1   2   3   4   5

Space Priorities

Space allocation grossly distorted	Space allocation highly disproportioned in building	Some priorities via space allocation obvious	Space equally allocated to various components, location key	No space priority observable by size or locale

S ├─────────────┼─────────────┼─────────────┼─────────────┤ F
1   2   3   4   5

Grounds

Grounds not in active use	Grounds used for informal activity	Grounds used for specific activity	Grounds use variable	Grounds used extensively for multiple activity

S ├─────────────┼─────────────┼─────────────┼─────────────┤ F
1   2   3   4   5

FIGURE 3.10 Alternative Uses of School Buildings and Grounds (S = structured; F = flexible)

bathrooms and auxiliary spaces, and purposeful physical barriers to movement, such as long unbroken counters in school offices.

Cues such as these tell visitors, students, and even teachers in the building that there are acceptable and unacceptable ways to enter the building and move in the building. Highly controlled access and mobility in school buildings indicate a belief that only certain types of movement in a building are conducive to successful education.

Building warmth.   Related to physical access is the concept of building warmth. The size of spaces, shape of spaces, scale of the environment (relationship between the size of the people and objects in the environment), coloration, and use of lighting all affect the warmth of a school building. Generally speaking, a combination of extreme space (large or small), extreme light (bright or dim), extreme coloration (too drab or too bright), repelling shapes (not geometrical or too geometrical), or disproportionate scale (too large or too small) can make occupants feel uncomfortable.

In the past, small classrooms with oversized furniture, drab coloration, and square walls were used purposefully to control environment stimulation and direct attention to the teacher. Such a discomforting setting presupposed that teacher behavior was the significant action in the learning environment.

More recently, schools have used bright colors, curved walls, large expansive spaces, and acoustical treatments to encourage student mobility and mental freedom. Such an environment presupposes that education is an act that is highly individual and conducted through exploration. Control under such environmental conditions can be difficult.

Although a few school buildings are constructed to promote an identifiable pattern of instruction, the effect of environmental warmth is great on instructional procedure. Failure to consider this factor has led to many unsuccessful and inefficient teaching episodes.

Traffic control patterns.   Traffic control within a school building, made famous by Bel Kaufman's book *Up the Down Staircase,*[15] is also a reflection of the school's belief about the nature of education. Many schools go to great lengths to communicate order to inhabitants of the building. Adhesive strips dividing hallways into acceptable paths, turnstiles, fences, and children marching single file along walls are indicative of such structure in a building.

Buildings in which flexibility is encouraged will have curved sidewalks, doorless entrances to learning spaces, seating spaces where occupants can stop and rest enroute to their destinations, and multiple patterns of individual progression from point to point in the building.

Space priorities.   Finally, space usage and priorities reflect the learning environment in school buildings. Priorities are indicated by both the size and location of spaces in the building. In some schools, old and new, a significant portion of total available space is dominated by single-event spaces such as auditoriums, gymnasiums, swimming pools, and central office suites. In terms of construction costs and use, these spaces speak subtly of the priorities of the resident educators.

The number, kind, and quality of spaces can be a measure of the definition of educational priority in a school building.

A second, and perhaps more accurate, measure of space priority in a school building is the location of various areas. Studies of school buildings have indicated that teachers who have more seniority in a building have better resource bases than do the other teachers. How much space, for instance, does the English department have? Where is the fine arts complex located? What new additions have been made to the building, and which program do they serve?

Grounds. Beyond the structural walls of the school building lie the school grounds. Sometimes, these spaces will reveal the attitude of the school toward learning. One interesting measure of the schoolyard is whether it is being used at all. Some schools located on ten-acre sites never plant a bush or add a piece of equipment to make the grounds useful to the school. Other schools, by contrast, use the grounds extensively and perceive them as an extension of the formal learning spaces.

Another question to be asked about the school grounds is whether they are generally used for student loitering, casual recreation, physical education, or comprehensive educational purposes. Equipment and student behavior will indicate which, if any, uses are made of this valuable resource.

Questions. In continuing to build traditional school buildings, do we force function to follow form? In this age of technology, could significant cost savings be realized by providing an alternative to school buildings?

There are great differences in how individual schools use their buildings and grounds. Thus, the use of these resources represents another relevant dimension of the school environment.

Classroom Spaces. Just as the school learning environment may be revealed in school dimensions such as community involvement and building use, the organization, movement, and ownership of physical space in the classroom are often indicative of the intentions of the school. In viewing these characteristics of the classroom, it is again obvious that not all schools are alike.

Classroom organization. One way of viewing the classroom spaces is in terms of the organization for instructional effectiveness. A traditional pattern would be to arrange the room so that all vision and attention are on the teacher. Figure 3.11 shows that there is little opportunity for lateral communication. Activity is fixed by the arrangement of furniture. The conditions are perfect for teacher lecture but little else.

Another possibility in organization of classroom spaces is to create multipurpose spaces with the focus of attention generally in the center of the classroom (as shown in Figure 3.12). This style permits increased student involvement, mobility,

FIGURE 3.11   Traditional Classroom Arrangement

FIGURE 3.12   Classroom with Multipurpose Spaces

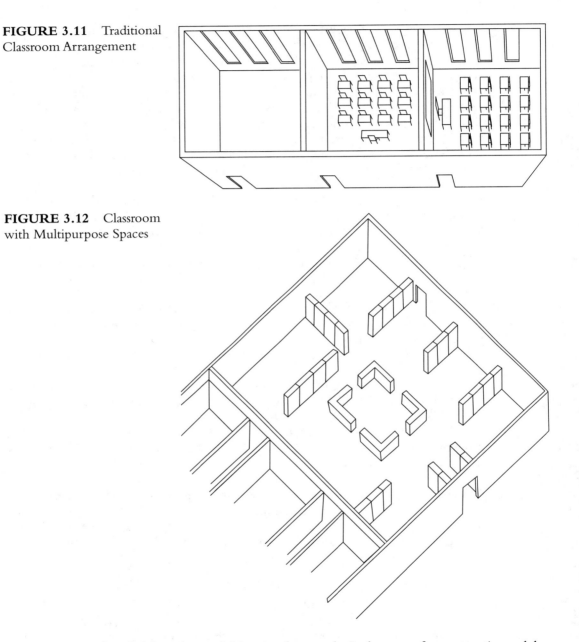

and varied learning activities simultaneously. It does not focus attention solely on the teacher and cannot easily be controlled in terms of noise or lateral communication among students.

The extreme degree of flexibility in organization of classroom spaces is, of course, to perceive the classroom as simply a place where learners meet to prepare for educational experiences both in the school building and in the community.

Classroom movement. Pupil movement within the classroom may be another subtle indicator of the structure or flexibility present in the learning environment (see Figure 3.13). Movement in some classrooms is totally dependent on the teacher. Students in such classrooms must request permission to talk, go to the washroom, or approach the teacher. Such structure usually minimizes noise and confusion but restricts activity to only verbal exchange. When movement occurs in such classrooms, it is generally to and from the teacher's desk.

In a less stationary classroom, movement is possible within controlled patterns monitored by the teacher. Movement is usually contextual, depending on the activity. During teacher talk, for instance, movement may not be allowed; at other times, students may be able to sharpen pencils, get supplies, or leave the room for water without complete dependence on teacher approval.

Pupil movement is sometimes left to the complete discretion of the student. Even during a lesson or a teacher explanation, a student may leave to use the washroom. In open-space buildings with high degrees of program flexibility, students are often seen moving unsupervised from one learning area to the next. Parents who have attended more structured, traditional programs often view such movement as questionable because they believe that the teacher must be in direct contact with students for learning to occur. Yet, self-directed, unsupervised movement is an integral part of any open, activity-centered curriculum.

Classroom ownership. A third consideration in viewing classroom spaces is what might be considered ownership, or territoriality, of the area. In most classrooms, this dimension can be seen by the spaces both the teacher and students occupy and by items that belong to those persons inhabiting the classroom.

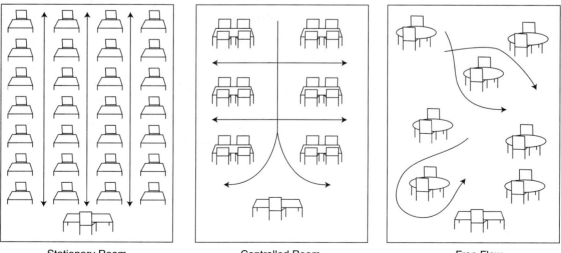

Stationary Room   Controlled Room   Free Flow

FIGURE 3.13 Patterns of Pupil Movement

FIGURE 3.14 Division of the Average Classroom

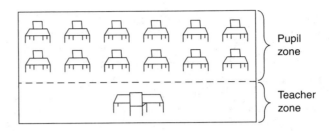

At the most structured end of an ownership continuum in a classroom, the teacher has total access to any area or space in the room, and the students "own" no space. In some classrooms, particularly in elementary schools, teacher ownership of space can extend even into the desks, pockets, and thoughts of students.

In somewhat less structured environments, students have zones where they can locate without being inspected or violating the teacher's territoriality. The average classroom is divided about two thirds for students and one third for the teacher (as illustrated in Figure 3.14).

The most flexible pattern of ownership is seen in the classroom with no overt symbols of territoriality. Either the teacher's desk is accessible for all purposes, or, in newer schools, the teacher has a private place somewhere else in the building. Furniture in such classrooms is uniform for students and teachers alike.

Another measure of ownership available to the observer is that of personal items on display in the room. In particular, the display of student work or student art is a useful indicator. When student work is displayed, for example, are samples drawn from the work of all students or simply a few? Are the samples on display uniform (everyone colors the same picture the same color) or diverse?

Ownership is also revealed by the kind of teaching visuals on display (standard or tailored), the presence or absence of living objects, and any signs of reward for creative or divergent thinking. A highly structured classroom will generally be bland and uniform; a highly flexible room will be nearly chaotic in appearance.

Questions.   How might teaching staffs use their limited spaces to better serve all learners? What does emerging research tell us about the organization of learning spaces?

There are great differences in school classrooms, and these differences reflect the intentions of the school in educating students. As such, classroom spaces represent another important dimension of the learning environment. The descriptive continua in Figure 3.15 suggest the potential range of alternatives present in schools.

Programs of Study

Schools differ to a great extent in how they organize and use knowledge and materials in their programs of study. The age of the Internet is also radically changing this conception. In highly structured schools, knowledge is, for all practical purposes, the curriculum, and ordering knowledge represents the major activity of

Classroom Organization

Uniform seating arrangement dominates room	Classroom furniture uniform but not symmetrical	Furniture arranged for each activity	Multipurpose spaces in room	Space outside classroom used for instruction

S ├────────┼────────┼────────┼────────┼─┤ F
1   2   3   4   5

Classroom Movement

Movement totally restricted by teacher	Total teacher control with noted exception	Pupil movement contextual	Pupil has freedom of movement within limit	Pupil movement at pupil discretion

S ├────────┼────────┼────────┼────────┼─┤ F
1   2   3   4   5

Classroom Ownership

Classroom space is dominated by teacher	Teacher dominates— some student zones	Classroom has areas of mutual free access	Territory only at symbolic level—open to all	All classroom spaces totally accessible to all persons

S ├────────┼────────┼────────┼────────┼─┤ F
1   2   3   4   5

FIGURE 3.15   Differences in Classroom Spaces. (S = structured; F = flexible.)

curriculum development. In highly flexible schools, by contrast, knowledge can be a simple medium through which processes are taught.

Organization of Knowledge.   The organization of knowledge can best be understood by viewing it in several dimensions: the pattern of its presentation, the way in which it is constructed or ordered, its cognitive focus, and the time orientation of the context.

Presentation of knowledge.   In most schools, knowledge is presented as an essential body or set of interrelated data, as shown in Figure 3.16(a). In some schools, however, this essential knowledge is supplemented by other useful learnings, which may appear as unequal satellites around the main body of information, as shown in Figure 3.16(b).

To the degree that student needs and interests are considered in planning the program of study, the satellites, or electives, are expanded and become a more important part of the program. In some schools, electives are equal in importance to essential knowledge areas and consume up to one half of school time (see Figure 3.16[c]). Once the school acknowledges the value of student-related content, it may find that it can teach the essential content in a form that accounts for student needs and interests (see Figure 3.16[d]).

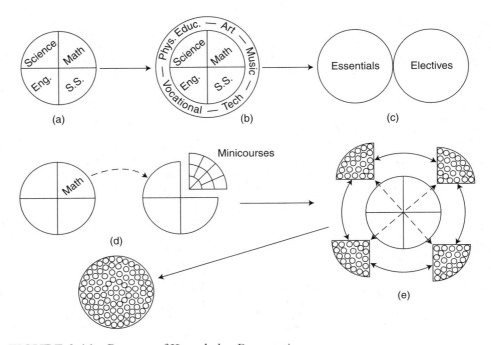

FIGURE 3.16   Patterns of Knowledge Presentation

As the interrelatedness of essential subcourses is verified, cross-referencing of course work may occur (interdisciplinary instruction). Finally, a maximum of flexibility in the ordering and use of knowledge may occur when a problem-oriented activity is the common denominator for organizing knowledge (see Figure 3.16[e]).

Construction or ordering of knowledge.   Another distinguishing dimension of the organization of knowledge is how it is constructed or ordered. Most programs of study employ one of three standard curriculum designs: (1) the building blocks design, (2) the branching design, or (3) the spiral design. It is also possible, however, to order knowledge in school programs in terms of (4) task accomplishment or (5) simple learning processes. These five patterns of knowledge construction are symbolized in Figure 3.17.

The building blocks design takes a clearly defined body of knowledge or skills and orders it into a pyramid-like arrangement. Students are taught foundational material that leads to more complex and specialized knowledge. Deviations from the prescribed order are not allowed because the end product of the learning design (mastery) is known in advance. Also, activities that do not contribute to this directed path are not allowed because of the efficiency of this model. Building blocks designs are the most structured of curriculum organizations.

Another common learning design found in schools is the branching design. Branching is a variation of the building blocks design but incorporates limited

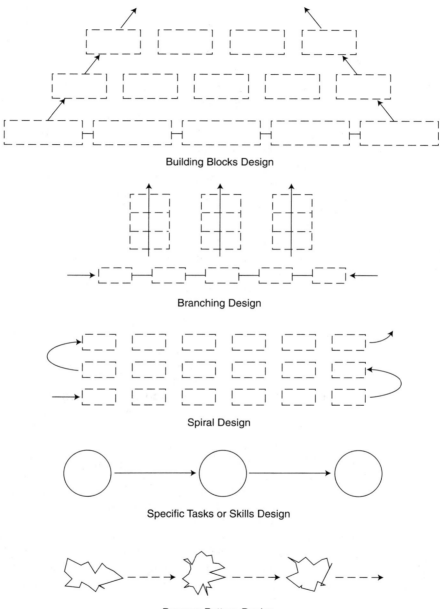

Building Blocks Design

Branching Design

Spiral Design

Specific Tasks or Skills Design

Process-Pattern Design
(interdisciplinary)

FIGURE 3.17 Patterns of Knowledge Construction

choice in the knowledge to be mastered. Branching designs recognize the value of foundational knowledge in learning but allow choice within prescribed areas beyond the common experience. Like the building blocks, branching prescribes the eventual outcomes of the learning program, although the prescription is multiple rather than uniform. The branching design allows for some variability in learning but only within tightly defined boundaries of acceptance.

A third organization of knowledge in programs of study is the spiral curriculum. In this design, knowledge areas are continually visited and revisited at higher levels of complexity. This design does have some flexibility, but it still controls what is taught and learned and even predetermines when it is to be received by the student.

A fourth possible organization of knowledge occurs when knowledge is organized to accomplish specified tasks. In specific tasks or skills designs, the purpose of the learning experience is predetermined, but the student interaction with data in terms of both content and order of content is flexible. Competency-based skill continua are an example of this design.

A final organization of knowledge in a school program of studies might use knowledge as simply a medium for teaching processes. Thus, reading could be taught regardless of the particular material used by the student. Such a process pattern features great flexibility in terms of the knowledge used, its order in learning experiences, and the expected outcomes for its selection and use.

Cognitive focus.   Still another dimension of the treatment of knowledge is the cognitive focus of instruction. In addition to a focus on factual material, such as learning important dates in history, knowledge can also be organized for teaching generalizations. Sometimes conceptual treatments of information are related to the lives of students. Maximum flexibility in the treatment of knowledge is gained by focusing on the personal world of the students, drawing concepts and facts from their experiences.

Time orientation.   A final area related to knowledge in school settings is the time orientation of the instructional material. In some classrooms, all information is drawn from past experiences of humankind. In other rooms, information from the past is mixed with that from the present. Some classrooms will be strictly contemporary and deal only with the here-and-now. Beyond the present-oriented instructional space are those that mix current knowledge with projected knowledge and some that deal only in probabilities. With each step from the known (past) to the speculative (future) content, flexibility increases.

The descriptive continua in Figure 3.18 suggest the potential range of alternatives found in schools.

Questions.   Why are schools unable to break away from the traditional content curriculum? Which format for organizing knowledge seems most applicable to life in the twenty-first century? How has new technology-assisted learning using the Internet altered our conception of "knowing"?

Presentation of Knowledge

Essential courses only	Essentials plus some satellite courses	Essentials and coequal elective courses	Cross-referenced courses	Integrated courses

S ├────────┼────────┼────────┼────────┼─ F
  1   2   3   4   5

Construction or Ordering of Knowledge

Building blocks	Branching	Spiral	Task focused	Process pattern

S ├────────┼────────┼────────┼────────┼─ F
  1   2   3   4   5

Cognitive Focus

Related facts	Series/set of facts	Conceptual organization	Concepts via world of the students	Concepts via personal life of individual

S ├────────┼────────┼────────┼────────┼─ F
  1   2   3   4   5

Time Orientation

Past only	Past and present	Present only	Present and future	Future only

S ├────────┼────────┼────────┼────────┼─ F
  1   2   3   4   5

FIGURE 3.18   Types of Knowledge Presentation (S = structured; F = flexible)

Uses of Learning Materials.   The ways in which learning materials are used or not used in classroom spaces vary tremendously from room to room. In some settings, no materials are visible to the observer except perhaps a single textbook. In other classroom spaces, the volume and variety of learning materials give the impression of clutter. Three measures of the use of learning materials are (1) the degree of sensory stimulation present, (2) the diversity of learning media found, and (3) the location of usable learning materials. The descriptive continua in Figure 3.19 suggest the potential range of alternatives found in schools.

Sensory stimulation.   On the most structured end of a continuum, the stimulation from learning materials can be fixed and absolute, as when all material is written or programmed. Sometimes stimulation from learning materials is prescribed or controlled, as during lectures. A slightly more flexible version of stimulation is available when the materials are interpreted, such as during an animated film or

Degree of Sensory Stimulation

Stimulation fixed	Stimulation prescribed	Stimulation interpreted	Stimulation experienced	Stimulation immersion

S ├———————┼———————┼———————┼———————┼———————┤ F
   1   2   3   4   5

Diversity of Learning Media

Single medium	Two media	More than two media	Multiple concerted media	Infinite learning media

S ├———————┼———————┼———————┼———————┼———————┤ F
   1   2   3   4   5

Location of Usable Learning Materials

Classroom-contained	Specia-purpose spaces	Clustered in special spaces	Found in school and out of school	All objects perceived as materials

S ├———————┼———————┼———————┼———————┼———————┤ F
   1   2   3   4   5

FIGURE 3.19   Types of Learning Materials (S = structured; F = flexible)

game playing. Still greater stimulation occurs when the learner is in physical proximity to the materials and has a tactile experience. Finally, stimulation that immerses the learner in multisense experiencing represents the greatest degree of stimulation to the learner.

Diversity.   Another measure of the effect of learning materials is found in the diversity of media present. Although some classrooms have only textbooks, others have printed matter, audiovisual aids, games, displays, and interactive materials. An important question is, How many types of learning media are interacting with the learner at any moment?

Location.   Finally, the location of usable learning materials is a variable in classroom settings. In some schools, all learning materials are contained in standard classrooms. Still others have special-purpose spaces in which students may interact with materials. A third, and more flexible, possibility is that the school possesses areas (instructional materials centers) where learning materials are clustered. An even more flexible pattern would be to identify and select learning materials both in the school and outside the school. Maximum flexibility, of course, would perceive all objects as being possible learning materials for instruction.

Questions.   How might teachers be provided with a greater variety of learning resources? How might technology be used to enhance learner–materials interface?

Instructional Format

Teacher drills	Didactic format with closure	Free exchange with summation	Experience learning with individual summation	Nonstructured learning with no summation

S ├────────┼────────┼────────┼────────┼ F
  1   2   3   4   5

Acceptance of Diversity Among Students

Teacher enforces conformity	Teacher communicates expectations for conformity	Teacher tolerates limited diversity	Teacher accepts student diversity	Teacher encourages student diversity

S ├────────┼────────┼────────┼────────┼ F
  1   2   3   4   5

FIGURE 3.20   Types of Educational Philosophies (S = structured; F = flexible)

How could these new media be directed to support the existing school curriculum? Should they be?

Instructional Orientation

Three measures of instructional orientation are (1) philosophy of education, (2) teaching strategies, and (3) staffing patterns.

Philosophy of Education.   The descriptive continua in Figure 3.20 suggest the potential range of alternatives found in schools.

Instructional format.   In some classes, learning is absolutely structured. The teacher controls the flow of data, communication, and assessment. Such a condition is characterized by drill. Slightly more flexible is a pattern of didactic teaching whereby the teacher delivers information, controls the exchange of ideas, and enforces the correct conclusions through a question–answer session. A balance between complete structure and flexibility in the learning process is for the teacher to allow the free exchange of ideas in the classroom but to enforce a standardized summation of the process. Even more flexible would be a pattern in which students are allowed to experience a learning process and then draw their own conclusions about meaning. Most flexible is an instructional process that is not uniformly structured for all students, allows an exchange of ideas, and leaves the process open ended.

Acceptance of diversity.   Yet another measure of philosophy in the classroom is the acceptance of diversity among students. Sometimes this is observable in norms relating to dress or speech enforced by the teacher. Sometimes such a measure can be assessed by the appearance of the learning space. The key to this variable is whether students are made to act in standardized ways or whether differences are allowed. On the most extreme end of structure would be a classroom in which no individuality is allowed. In a classroom with maximum flexibility, diversity among students in appearance and behavior would be significant.

Questions.   What evidence exists to show that learners are diverse or unique? What is the essential difference between education and training?

Teaching Strategies.   Like the actions that suggest educational philosophies, the teaching strategies found in classrooms often give clues regarding the degree of structure in the learning program. Such strategies can often be inferred from teacher behaviors and organizational patterns. For instance, some teachers behave in ways that allow only a single learning interface with students, as in the case of the didactic method. Other teachers provide multiple ways for students to interact and communicate during instruction.

Two behaviors that speak louder than words about the learning strategy employed in the classroom are the motivational techniques being used and the interactive distances between the teacher and student. By watching these phenomena, the observer can anticipate a pattern of structure or flexibility in other instructional areas.

The descriptive continua in Figure 3.21 suggest the potential range of alternatives found in schools.

Motivational techniques.   A range of motivational techniques is available to classroom teachers, and all are situationally legitimate. Some techniques, however, seek

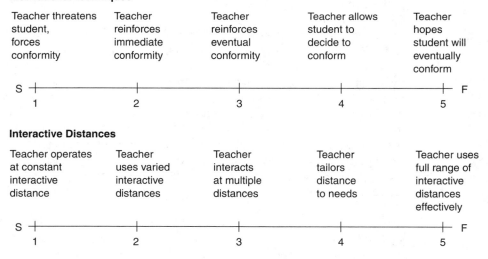

Motivational Techniques

Teacher threatens student, forces conformity	Teacher reinforces immediate conformity	Teacher reinforces eventual conformity	Teacher allows student to decide to conform	Teacher hopes student will eventually conform

S +————————+————————+————————+————————+ F
  1   2   3   4   5

Interactive Distances

Teacher operates at constant interactive distance	Teacher uses varied interactive distances	Teacher interacts at multiple distances	Teacher tailors distance to needs	Teacher uses full range of interactive distances effectively

S +————————+————————+————————+————————+ F
  1   2   3   4   5

FIGURE 3.21   Types of Teaching Strategies (S = structured; F = flexible)

to control and structure learning; others encourage flexibility. Teachers using threats or fear as a motivator generally seek maximum structure in the classroom. Coercion, as a rule, arrests behavior and encourages conformity to previous patterns of behavior. Extrinsic rewards, immediate or deferred, also encourage structure by linking desired behaviors with rewards. Intrinsic rewards, whether immediate or deferred, have an opposite effect. Intrinsic rewards encourage student participation in the reward system and thereby a wider range of acceptable behaviors. If the motivational technique is observable, the overall learning strategy (to constrict or expand student behavior) becomes evident.

Interactive distances.   Another dimension of the learning strategy in a classroom setting is the interactive distance between the teacher and students. To the degree that it is important to have two-way communication in the classroom, and to the degree that the instructional strategy values multiple learning styles among students, the teacher will make adjustments for differences.

In his book *The Silent Language,* Edward Hall made observations about the appropriateness of certain distances between persons for certain activities.[16] Some distances (fifteen feet and beyond) were appropriate for broadcasting; other distances (six inches or under) were reserved for intimate moments. In a classroom setting, it is possible to observe if the teacher makes adjustments in interactive distances during instruction or chooses to treat all situations alike.

Questions.   What are some combinations of teaching behavior that reflect motivational theory? What advantage can be gained by designing a classroom that allows for teacher mobility?

Staffing Patterns.   A final indicator of structure versus flexibility in schools, in terms of instruction, is found in the staffing patterns observed. Two staffing indicators are the role of teachers in staffing and the organization of teachers in the school building.

The descriptive continua in Figure 3.22 suggest the potential range of alternatives found in schools.

Role of the teacher.   In some school buildings, all teachers are hired and assigned on the basis of subject-matter preparation. Such teachers are perceived as solitary artisans with the highly structured task of teaching a subject to students. In other schools, a teacher might be hired as a subject specialist but assigned to an interdisciplinary team. A more flexible pattern would be to staff a school with teachers having two or more subject specialties. It might even be possible to have one teacher (as in the elementary grades) responsible for all subjects. Or, a teacher could be hired to teach students at a certain level, rather than specific subjects.

Organization of teachers.   Another staffing pattern is the organization of teachers in the building. Are all teachers isolated in self-contained classrooms? Do the isolated teachers have instructional aides? Do the classroom teachers meet to plan activi-

Role of the Teacher

Solitary subject specialist	Subject specialist on team	Subject specialist in multiple areas	Subject specialist in all areas	Specialist in teaching at a level

S +————————+————————+————————+————————+ F
1   2   3   4   5

Organization of Teachers

Teachers isolated in self-contained classrooms	Teacher and aide isolated	Teacher isolated except for planning	Two or more teachers work cooperatively	Teachers in active teams for instruction

S +————————+————————+————————+————————+ F
1   2   3   4   5

FIGURE 3.22   Types of Staffing Patterns (S = structured; F = flexible)

ties? Are teaching units ever combined? Do the teachers teach in teams or other cooperative arrangements?

Questions.   What is the critical difference between deploying a single teacher and organizing teachers into teams? At what level of schooling would teaming be most appropriate?

Administrative Conditions

Organization of Students.   The way in which a school organizes students can give an observer some measure of the degree of structure in the school. Two different measures of student organization are the criteria for organization and the actual grouping patterns found in the school.

The descriptive continua in Figure 3.23 suggest the potential range of alternatives found in schools.

Criteria for organization.   Because most schools in the United States admit children according to age, students are grouped by age. Schools use a more flexible criterion when students are organized by subject taught. Still greater flexibility is evidenced in schools that group students within grades and subjects according to capacity. Even greater organizational flexibility is found in schools that group students by needs and by student interests.

Grouping patterns.   Besides criteria for grouping, the actual organization patterns of students can indicate the degree of structure or flexibility in the school. Perhaps the most structured situation exists when the size of the room determines the number of students present. A uniform number of students for all activities is also a

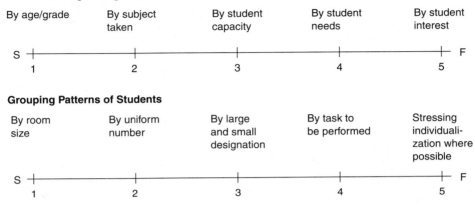

Criteria for Organizing Students

By age/grade	By subject taken	By student capacity	By student needs	By student interest

S +————————+————————+————————+————————+— F
1   2   3   4   5

Grouping Patterns of Students

By room size	By uniform number	By large and small designation	By task to be performed	Stressing individuali-zation where possible

S +————————+————————+————————+————————+— F
1   2   3   4   5

FIGURE 3.23   Ways of Organizing Students (S = structured; F = flexible)

highly structured condition. When a school begins to recognize that some activities should have large or small classes, a degree of flexibility is in evidence. The greatest flexibility in the organization of students is represented by the assignment of students on the basis of tasks to be accomplished and the individualization of instruction, whenever possible.

Questions.   What advantage is gained by organizing schools by age of students? Given what is known about human development patterns, what grouping criteria seem most promising?

Rules and Regulations.   Within schools and within individual classrooms, rules and regulations vary. Perhaps the most structured situations are those in which an excessive number of regulations exist based on historical precedent. Slightly less structured is the school with numerous and absolute regulations. A more flexible condition is when there are a few rules that are formal and enforced. When there are few rules and the rules are negotiable, or when no formal or informal regulations are stated, maximum flexibility is indicated. The descriptive continuum in Figure 3.24 suggests the potential range of alternatives in schools.

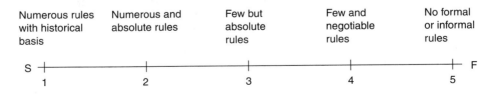

Numerous rules with historical basis	Numerous and absolute rules	Few but absolute rules	Few and negotiable rules	No formal or informal rules

S +————————+————————+————————+————————+— F
1   2   3   4   5

FIGURE 3.24   Types of Rules and Regulations (S = structured; F = flexible)

Disciplinary Measures.   Discipline techniques used in schools to influence student behavior cover a wide range of actions. In some schools, all infractions are given the same treatment regardless of severity. In more flexible schools, there is a hierarchy of discipline measures to deal with differing discipline problems. Sometimes the pattern found in schools will be to deal only with the severe or recurrent discipline problems. In schools where great flexibility is found, the pattern for discipline is sometimes unclear owing to the uneven application of discipline measures. In some schools, no discipline measures are observable.

The descriptive continuum in Figure 3.25 suggests the potential range of alternatives for discipline in schools.

Reporting of Student Progress.   The reporting of student progress in the most structured schools and classrooms is a mechanical process whereby students are assessed in mathematical symbols such as 83 or upper quartile. A generalization of such preciseness is a system whereby student progress in learning is summarized by a letter such as a B or U. Increased flexibility in reporting student progress is evidenced by narrative descriptions that actually describe student work and by supplemental reporting by other interested parties, such as the student or the parent. Maximum flexibility in reporting student progress is found when such reporting is informal, verbal, and continuous.

The descriptive continuum in Figure 3.26 suggests the potential range of alternatives for reporting student progress found in schools.

Questions.   What is the purpose of any student control system? What adult behaviors are learned in school settings?

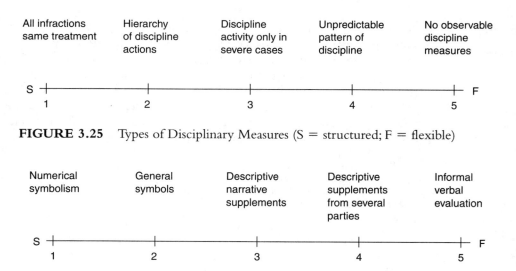

FIGURE 3.25   Types of Disciplinary Measures (S = structured; F = flexible)

FIGURE 3.26   Ways of Reporting Student Progress (S = structured; F = flexible)

Roles of Participants

Administrative Attitudes.   Administrative style, more than any other single factor, determines the atmosphere of a school building. How those in the school building perceive the administrator affects both teacher and student behavior. For this reason, clues about the structure or flexibility of a school or classroom can be gained by observing the administrator.

The descriptive continua in Figure 3.27 suggest the potential range of alternatives for administrative behavior found in schools.

Decision-making role.   Administrators often assume one of five attitudes that characterize their pattern of interaction with others. At the most structured end is a warden who rules by intimidation. Closely allied to this model is the benevolent dictator who maintains absolute control while giving the impression of involvement. A more flexible posture for the administrator is to act as the program manager, reserving key decisions for the only person with the comprehensive viewpoint. Still more flexible is the collegial leader who shares all decision making with the teaching faculty. Finally, there is a leadership style that is nondirective or laissez-faire.

Medium of communication.   A second interesting variable for studying administrative attitudes is the medium used to communicate with students. In some schools, the lead administrator is a phantom, known only by the presence of his or her portrait in the foyer. Such an administrator generally leaves communication with parents or students to an intermediary such as a vice principal. Another impersonal medium is the intercom, which is often used to communicate to students. Slightly more personal is a live address at assemblies. Finally, some administrators

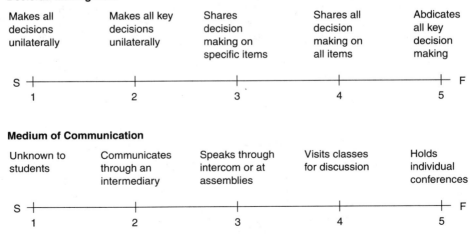

FIGURE 3.27   Types of Administrative Interaction (S = structured; F = flexible)

communicate with students by coming into the classrooms and even sometimes by individual conferences.

Teacher Roles.   The role of a classroom teacher in a school can vary from being an instructor who teaches a prescribed set of facts to being a multidimensional adult who interacts with students and others in the building. For the most part, such perceptions are self-imposed. A key observation can be made from teacher responses to the question, What do you teach?

The descriptive continuum in Figure 3.28 suggests the potential range of responses to that question.

Student Roles.   Like teachers, students in schools hold a role perception of what they are and what they can do in a classroom setting. Sometimes such perceptions are self-imposed, but more often they are an accurate reflection of expected behavior for students. A question that usually receives a telling response is, How do students learn in this classroom?

The descriptive continuum in Figure 3.29 suggests the potential range of responses to such a question.

Questions.   How might roles and relationships in school be altered to restructure education? What teacher and student roles seem appropriate for the twenty-first century?

School Assessment

The value of viewing school components on a continuum, such as the degree of structure versus flexibility, is that program congruence or inconsistencies can be

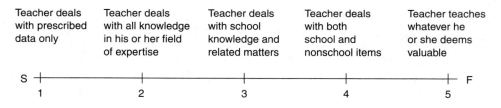

FIGURE 3.28   Teachers' Perceptions of Their Roles (S = structured; F = flexible)

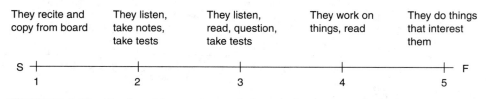

FIGURE 3.29   Students' Perceptions of Their Roles (S = structured; F = flexible)

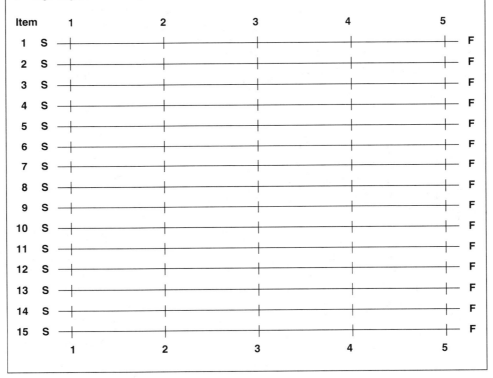

Directions: Using the descriptors found in this chapter, visit a school and mark an X on the description that most nearly describes what you see. Upon completion of the 15 items, connect the Xs vertically, thereby developing a profile of consistency. S = high degree of structure; F = high degree of flexibility.

FIGURE 3.30   School Assessment Worksheet

identified (see Figure 3.30). In schools in which the program intent (philosophy) is clear, the degree of structure or flexibility should be relatively constant. Said another way, if the fifteen dimensions were plotted across the five degrees of structure and flexibility, strong schools would have reasonably vertical columns. A zigzag pattern in such a school profile would indicate an inconsistency in the learning design.

SUMMARY

Educational philosophies are the heart of purposeful activity in curriculum development. Philosophies serve as value screens for decision making. Because educators today are confronted by multiple choices, it is vital that curriculum specialists understand their own values and beliefs about schooling.

Over the years, the American school has evolved from a highly structured and traditional institution to one with considerable flexibility. The degree of structure or flexibility found in the learning design of a school is a reflection of the undergirding philosophy of education being practiced. Whatever the philosophy, consistency in the design is the key to the effectiveness of the curriculum.

In this chapter, five major educational philosophies were presented, along with a philosophy assessment inventory to help you clarify your posture on key issues. To be decisive leaders, curriculum specialists must be aware of their own values and be able to assess accurately the value systems found in today's schools.

SUGGESTED LEARNING ACTIVITIES

1. Using the philosophy assessment inventory found in this chapter, analyze your beliefs about the roles of schools. If your profile does not correspond to what you think you believe, explain this discrepancy.
2. Using the scales found in this chapter, visit a school with which you are familiar and analyze its profile. What observations can you make about this type of analysis of a school?
3. Using Figure 3.9, describe the type of instructional program most likely to be implemented in the various structures. Where would you like to work? Why?
4. Describe how the following current concerns in public schools are philosophical in nature: school choice, cooperative learning, whole language reading, and middle schools.
5. Discuss how the Internet has changed any comprehensive description of schools.

NOTES

1. *Youth: Transition to Adulthood,* a report of the President's Advisory Commission on Science, 1973.
2. In Charley Reese, Associated Press, September 13, 2000, "Teacher of the Year Says Public Education Should Be Abolished."
3. Robert M. McClure, "The Reforms of the Fifties and Sixties: A Historical Look at the Near Past," *The Curriculum: Retrospect and Prospect,* National Society for the Study of Education, (Washington, DC: NSSE, 1971), p. 51.
4. Galen Saylor and William M. Alexander, *Planning Curriculum for Schools* (New York: Holt, Rinehart & Winston, 1974), pp. 144–145.
5. Robert Hutchins, *On Education* (Santa Barbara, CA: Center for the Study of Democratic Institutions, 1963), p. 18.
6. A. S. Neill, *Summerhill* (New York: Hart, 1960), p. 4.
7. Saylor and Alexander, *Planning Curriculum for Schools,* p. 146.
8. Daniel Tanner and Laurel N. Tanner, *Curriculum Development: Theory into Practice,* 3rd ed. (New York: Macmillan, 1995), p. 82.
9. Tanner and Tanner, *Curriculum Development: Theory into Practice,* p. 64.
10. John D. McNeil, *Designing Curriculum: Self-Instructional Modules* (Boston: Little, Brown, 1976), pp. 91–92.
11. Martin Mayer, *The Schools* (New York: Harper & Row, 1961).
12. James B. Conant, as reported in Charles Silberman, *Crisis in the Classroom* (New York: Random House, 1970).
13. Charles E. Silberman, *Crisis in the Classroom* (New York: Random House, 1970), p. 9.
14. Morris L. Bigge, *Learning Theories for Teachers* (New York: Harper & Row, 1971), p. viii.

15. Bel Kaufman, *Up the Down Staircase* (Englewood Cliffs, NJ: Prentice Hall, 1965).
16. Edward Hall, *The Silent Language* (New York: Doubleday, 1959).

ADDITIONAL READING

Benne, K. *The Task of Post-Contemporary Education.* New York: Teachers College Press, 1990.

Berube, M. *American School Reform: 1883–1993.* Westport, CT: Greenwood, 1994.

Callahan, R. *Education and the Cult of Efficiency.* Chicago: University of Chicago Press, 1962.

Coleman, J. *Equality and Achievement in Education.* Boulder, CO: Westview Press, 1990.

Foyle, Harvey. *Constructing Curriculum.* Dubuque, IA: Kendall/Hunt, 1999.

Goldstein, Arnold P. P. *The Prepare Curriculum: Teaching Prosocial Competencies.* Champaign, IL: Research Press, 1999.

Goodlad, J. *The Ecology of School Renewal.* Chicago: National Society for the Study of Education, 1987.

Knapp, L., and A. Glenn. *Restructuring Schools with Technology.* Needham Heights, MA: Allyn and Bacon, 1996.

Nolet, Victor, and Margaret J. McLaughlin. *Assessing the General Curriculum.* Thousand Oaks, CA: Corwin Press, 2000.

Oliva, Peter F. *Developing the Curriculum.* Dallas, TX: Pearson, 2000.

Slattery, P. *Curriculum Development in a Postmodern Era.* New York: Garland, 1995.

Wiles, Jon. *Curriculum Essentails: A Resource for Educators.* Needham Heights, MA: Allyn & Bacon, 1999.

chapter 4

BASIC TASKS OF CURRICULUM DEVELOPMENT

Curriculum development, at its best, is a comprehensive process that (1) facilitates an analysis of purpose, (2) designs a program or event, (3) implements a series of related activities, and (4) aids in the evaluation of this process. At its worst, curriculum development accomplishes none of these four activities. Clearly, there are basic tasks that distinguish quality curriculum work from accidental instructional change. It is also evident that modern curriculum development involves much more than the implementation of a new course of study or the updating of a guide to instruction. This is particularly true in the present technological era.

Curriculum development proceeds in a deductive manner using an if–then logic (see Figure 4.1). The initial step in curriculum work is to clarify purpose. This involves first identifying a philosophy and then deducing appropriate goals and objectives. Once this framework for program development is established, an assessment of need is conducted to sharpen the focus in terms of the target—the learner. Finally, the curriculum itself is analyzed through a mapping-out process, and the instructional activities are ordered and aligned for maximum effect. The curriculum worker strives to attain a near correspondence between the intention and the outcome of instruction.

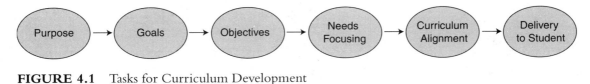

FIGURE 4.1 Tasks for Curriculum Development

ESTABLISHING THE PHILOSOPHY

A *philosophy*—the clarification of beliefs about the purpose, goals, and objectives of instruction—is the essential tapestry for all curriculum development efforts. School programs without this overarching backdrop either are disjointed, which makes them targets for social pressure, or operate in a state of programmatic contradiction. The development of a working philosophy of education is a prerequisite to all other leadership efforts in school improvement.

The task of goal setting is a national function in most countries (see Figure 4.2 for sample national goals). In the United States, by contrast, it is a continuous process led by curriculum workers at various operational levels (state, district, school, classroom). Such developmental work is generally done in three ways:

1. Other people can be asked to review existing statements of philosophy or related documents and restate them in terms of desired changes.
2. Others can be asked to transfer their own personal philosophy of living into a school context, setting goals for school from general life goals.
3. Others can be asked to look for patterns in current behavior in society that might suggest goals for schools.

Methods that can be used to help others achieve goal clarity and consistency include writing personal goal statements, assigning priorities to various items, surveying existing documents, and analyzing school programs. One widely practiced

Australia	1. Fulfilling lives and active citizenship 2. Joining the workforce 3. Overcoming disadvantage and achieving fairness in society
Taiwan (ROC)	The three principles: geography, history, and economy (the meaning of nation) Utilization of group life (operation of democracy) Productive labor (livelihood) Eight moral virtues: loyalty, kindness, love, faith, righteousness, harmony, peace, fidelity
People's Republic of China (Red China)	1. Develop good moral character 2. Develop love of motherland 3. Literacy and intellect 4. Healthy bodies 5. Interest in aesthetics

FIGURE 4.2   Sample Statements of Purpose for National Education Systems

Source: From national documents from respective state education departments. See also C. Postlethwaite, *Encyclopedia of Comparative Education and National Systems of Education,* Oxford, Pergamon Press, 1988.

method of clarifying philosophical positions is to have persons develop belief statements. These statements rest on a simple premise: each time a person acts, there is a rationale for action. Without a formalization of such rationales, it is impossible to coordinate or manage individual activities.

Belief statements can be organized in numerous ways, and the correct way for any individual district depends on the planning format. Figure 4.3 lists examples of belief statements organized around students, learning, teaching roles, grouping of students, and educational programs in general. The generic philosophy from which these are drawn is that the school exists to meet the needs and interests of students.

After identifying a philosophy and stating it in easy-to-understand belief statements, the school district or school is ready to develop goals that will serve to guide development. Such goals are drawn from the philosophical orientation of the district, the needs of the school population, and the unique characteristics of the community.

Students
1. WE BELIEVE that students are individuals with unique characteristics and interests.
2. WE BELIEVE that students should have an equal opportunity to learn, based on their needs, interests, and abilities.

Learning
1. WE BELIEVE that students learn best when content is relevant to their own lives.
2. WE BELIEVE that students learn best in an environment that is pleasant and one in which the democratic process is modeled.

Teaching
1. WE BELIEVE that the role of the teacher in the classroom is primarily that of a facilitator of learning.
2. WE BELIEVE that student learning may be affected more by what teachers do than by what they say.

Grouping
1. WE BELIEVE that a more effective program of instruction can be provided for students if they are grouped according to maturation level and similar interest.
2. WE BELIEVE that a high school should include those students who are mature enough to participate in a program that is more specialized than the middle school and those students beyond the age of 18 who have a need to complete the requirements for a high school diploma.

The Educational Program
1. WE BELIEVE that all special programs should incorporate specific educational objectives that complement the total school program.
2. WE BELIEVE that evaluating and changing programs to more effectively meet the needs and interests of students should be a continuous process.

FIGURE 4.3   Example of Belief Statements

As curriculum specialists clarify their own beliefs about the purpose of education and assist others in finding their value systems, the odds for meaningful curriculum development increase. Shared values can form the bond of commitment to change. The time spent in assessing group philosophies has significant payoff in areas such as continuity in school programs and articulation among school levels, the development of relationships and roles among school faculties, the selection of learning activities and materials, the evaluation of school programs, and the redesign of basic curriculum offerings.

Most important, however, is the connection of philosophy to leadership and decision making in education. To be decisive leaders and consistent decision makers, curriculum specialists must know their values and those of the persons around them.

FORMULATING GOALS

Educational goals are statements of the intended outcomes of education. The scope of the entire educational program can be found in the goals espoused by a school. Goals are also the basic building blocks of educational planning.

Goals may be stated at various levels of specificity. Many school goals are purposefully broad so that a majority of the public can support the intentions of the school. Sometimes there is an attempt to state the goals in terms of student behaviors that the school seeks to promote (see Figure 4.4). Over the years, commissions have attempted to define American education by developing formal goals.

Perhaps the most familiar goals were defined by the Commission on Reorganization of Secondary Education in 1918. Those goals were (1) health, (2) command of fundamental processes, (3) worthy home membership, (4) vocation, (5) citizenship, (6) worthy use of leisure time, and (7) ethical character. These became widely known as the Seven Cardinal Principles of Secondary Education.

A second attempt at defining the purposes of secondary education was expressed in 1938 by the Educational Policies Commission of the National Education Association and the American Association of School Administrators. The group developed a number of goals under the headings of (1) self-realization, (2) human relationships, (3) economic efficiency, and (4) civic responsibility.

The Association for Supervision and Curriculum Development, a national organization of curriculum specialists, identified a set of valued learning outcomes "that reflected the 'holistic' nature of individuals." Hundreds of organizations, including state departments of education and regional research and development centers, were requested to share their goals with the group. The group identified ten major goals for youth:[1]

1. Self-conceptualizing (self-esteem).
2. Understanding others.
3. Basic skills.
4. Interest and capability for continuous learning.
5. Responsible member of society.
6. Mental and physical health.
7. Creativity.

Academic Goals

Achievement
Maintain or improve test scores
Reduce failures and parental notices
Reduce retentions and dropouts
Produce better grade point averages
Increase honor roll (based on grades)
Institute new honor rolls in nonacademic areas
    (based on nonacademic achievement)
Meet needs of high achievers

Responsibility
Arrive on time
Decrease vandalism cases
Decrease discipline counts
Admit to wrongdoing
Take care of academic areas

Respect for Others
Decrease sarcasm and put-downs
Increase sensitivity to need of others
Increase their role in helping others (peer
    learning)

Behaviors

Exhibits Healthy Habits
Monitoring self
Exhibit smoking and drug awareness
Exhibit awareness of physical growth
Walk for health
Participation in intramural sports

Higher Self-Esteem
Increase openness to new experiences
Eliminate self-abusive behaviors
Increase ability to self-reveal
Exhibit school pride

Attendance and Participation
Increase daily attendance count
Increase club memberships
Decrease make-up work

Stress and Misbehavior
Decrease visits to counselor
Decrease outbursts in class
Decrease aggressive behaviors
(Teachers) distribute homework more evenly

Organized
Bring materials to class
Complete homework frequently
Maintain personal calendar
Bring gym clothes
Manage time wisely
Ask questions to clarify responsibilities

Problem-Solver
Possess analysis skills
Solve word problems
Apply subjects to "real world"
Possess creative thinking skills
Learn in hands-on manner

Love of Knowledge
Belong to an academic club
Read designated books
Meet with adult tutor/mentor
Develop a personal library
Exhibit awareness of state, national, and world
    events

Attitudinal Goals

Positive Attitude
Exhibit enthusiasm about learning
Participate in school activities
Volunteer/join school service clubs

Mannerly and Courteous
Exhibit ability to introduce self to adults
Dress neatly and appear well groomed
Know etiquette

FIGURE 4.4   Goals for Students in Terms of Behaviors

Source: Authors' work with Kellogg Foundation Model Middle School, Ishpeming, Michigan. Our thanks to Principal Ed Sansom for his contribution to this set of ideas.

8. Informed participation in the economic world of production and consumption.
9. Use of accumulated knowledge to understand the world.
10. Coping with change.

In the late 1980s and early 1990s, numerous prestigious commissions, such as America 2000, suggested additional goals and directions for public education. Many standards were developed. Among the most widely circulated and discussed recommendations were the following:

☐ *Time for Results, The Governors' 1991 Report on Education* (Chicago: National Governors' Association Center for Policy Research and Analysis, 1991)
☐ *A Nation Prepared: Teachers for the 21st Century* (New York: Carnegie Forum on Education and Economy, 1986)
☐ *Turning Points* (New York: The Carnegie Commission, 1990)
☐ *What Works: Research about Teaching and Learning* (Washington DC: U.S. Department of Education, 1986)

The findings of these commissions, however, should not be considered final. Educators and curriculum specialists continue to ponder both the ends and the means necessary to implement public education goals; this process will continue well into the twenty-first century.

In the following sections, we consider the steps and procedures involved in clarifying goals and objectives. The focus of this discussion is the school and classroom level.

Classifying Goals and Objectives

Educational goals inherently reflect the philosophical preferences of the writer of the goals. Objectives, too, have a philosophical underpinning and form the fabric of instructional development at the school and classroom levels.

Goals for educational planning generally occur at three levels (see Table 4.1). Level I goals are broad and philosophical in nature, for example, "The environment of the school must be conducive to teaching and learning—safety for all is a primary concern."

Level II goals are more specific than Level I goals and are often used to define or give form to such aspirations. For example, the following indicators might be used to define an orderly and safe environment:

Indicators
1. The school climate reflects an atmosphere of respect, trust, high morale, cohesiveness, and caring.
2. Expectations for student behavior are clearly stated in a student handbook.
3. A variety of classroom management skills are used to create a businesslike, orderly, and comfortable classroom environment, conducive to learning.
4. Discipline within the school is enforced in a fair and consistent manner.

TABLE 4.1   The Relationships Between Levels I, II, and III Learning Objectives

Level of Objectives	Type	Origin	Features
Level I	Broad goals or purposes	Formulated at district level by councils or school board	Seldom revised
Level II	General but more specific than Level I	Formulated at school or department level	Contains an outline of process to accomplish Level I objectives
Level III	Behaviorally stated	Formulated by teams of teachers or single teacher	Describe expected outcome, evidence for assessing outcome, and level of performance

5. Parents are informed of disciplinary action as it relates to their child.
6. Positive reinforcement of expected behavior is observable throughout the school.
7. Student work is attractively displayed throughout the school.
8. The physical plant is
   a. clean
   b. aesthetically pleasing
   c. safe
   d. well maintained
9. School improvement needs are assessed annually, the needs are prioritized, and the principal is resourceful in getting the tasks accomplished.
10. The principal is involved in prioritizing countywide maintenance requests.

Finally, Level III objectives are specific to the classroom level and are stated in terms of student behavioral outcomes. These objectives structure learning activities and tell the teacher if the intention of the curriculum has been met.

Behavioral objectives are statements describing what learners are doing when they are learning. Teachers need to describe the desired behaviors well enough to preclude misinterpretation.

An acceptable objective lets students know what is expected of them. It also enables teachers to measure the effectiveness of their own work.

Behaviorally stated objectives contain three essential elements:

1. The terminal behavior must be identified by name. An observable action must be named indicating that learning has taken place.
2. The important conditions under which the behavior is expected to occur should be described.
3. The criteria of acceptable performance should be specified.

A simple method of developing a complete behavioral objective is to apply the *A, B, C, D* rule. *A* stands for the audience, *B* for the behavior, *C* for the condition, and *D* for the degree of completion. A behavioral objective containing all of these elements will be a complete objective. For example:

A. The student will (the audience)
B. successfully complete the multiplication problems (behavior)
C. during the class period (condition)
D. getting 80 percent correct (degree)

The advocacy of behavioral objectives by those seeking to clarify educational purpose has met resistance from those who believe describing learner outcomes in this fashion is simplistic and reduces education to training.

In the rush to write clear, precise statements, teachers sometimes choose simple objectives that require little thinking on the part of their students. These teachers are actually writing objectives at the lowest levels of cognitive behavior. Through in-service training, teachers can master the skill of writing objectives requiring higher forms of thinking on the part of their students. In addition, teachers should write objectives leading to affective and psychomotor behaviors, which are discussed next.

Using Objectives to Order Learning

Anyone familiar with program development in schools knows that there is regularly a discrepancy between the intentions of the curriculum and what the teacher actually delivers to students. This "disorder" is a result of not refining goals and objectives, not specifying what the teacher is to do with the student, or not defining what the student is to do after having been taught. A wonderful tool for "ordering" the curriculum are the three taxonomies of learning: (1) the cognitive domain, (2) the affective domain, and (3) the psychomotor domain (see Figures 4.5, 4.6, and 4.7).

Each of these hierarchies of learning was developed to assist planners in "targeting" the level of learning desired and to direct the complexity of the teaching act and the materials encountered by the student. Cognition, the mental processing of information, is conceived by Bloom as a six-tier model from the simplest processing (knowledge) to the most complex (evaluation). Krathwohl's affective domain, a five-level model, addresses the degree of "feeling" experienced by the student about the material encountered. Harrow's psychomotor behaviors suggest an order of physical response to learning situations.

When planning learning, the curriculum worker should ask, What is specifically intended for the learner? and then write an appropriate objective to guide the teacher in the classroom. For instance, if we teach the student about the Civil War, what is our intention? Do we want them to know about it (Bloom's first tier) or be able to analyze the activities (Bloom's fourth tier)? A corresponding degree of feeling would accompany the learning experience. Seen in this way, planning a

	Knowledge (ability to recall; to bring to mind the appropriate material)	Comprehension (ability to comprehend what is being communicated and make use of the idea without relating it to other ideas or material or seeing fullest meaning)	Application (ability to use ideas, principles, theories in new particular and concentrated situations)	Analysis (ability to break down a communication into constituent parts in order to make organization of the whole clear)	Synthesis (ability to put together parts and elements into a unified organization or whole)	Evaluation (ability to judge the value of ideas, procedures, methods, using appropriate criteria)
Knowledge						
Comprehension	Requires knowledge					
Application	Requires knowledge	Requires comprehension				
Analysis	Requires knowledge	Requires comprehension	Requires application			
Synthesis	Requires knowledge	Requires comprehension	Requires application	Requires analysis		
Evaluation	Requires knowledge	Requires comprehension	Requires application	Requires analysis	Requires synthesis	

FIGURE 4.5   The Taxonomy of Educational Objectives: Cognitive Domain

Source: Adapted from *Taxonomy of Educational Objectives: The Classification of Educational Goals. Handbook I: Cognitive Domain* edited by Benjamin S. Bloom et al. Copyright © 1956 by Longman, Inc.

Receiving	Responding	Valuing	Organization	Characterization
(attending; becomes aware of an idea, process, or thing; is willing to notice a particular phenomenon)	(makes response at first with compliance, later willingly and with satisfaction)	(accepts worth of a thing, idea or a behavior; prefers it; consistent in responding; develops a commitment to it)	(organizes values; determines interrelationships; adapts behavior to value system)	(generalizes certain values into controlling tendencies; emphasis on internal consistency; later integrates these into a total philosophy of life or world view)
				Requires organization of values
			Requires development of values	Requires development of values
		Requires a response	Requires a response	Requires a response
	Begins with attending	Begins with attending	Begins with attending	Begins with attending

FIGURE 4.6 The Taxonomy of Educational Objectives: Affective Domain

Source: Adapted from *Taxonomy of Educational Objectives: The Classification of Educational Goals. Handbook II: Affective Domain* edited by David R. Krathwohl et al. Copyright © 1964 by Longman, Inc.

Reflex Movements	Fundamental Movements	Perceptual Abilities	Physical Abilities	Skilled Movements	Expressive Movements
(actions without conscious volition in response to stimuli)	(formed by combining reflex movement, e.g., walking)	(interpreting the environment and making adjustments, e.g., dodging ball)	(use of organic vigor, e.g., lifting weights)	(efficiency in performing complex movements, e.g., dancing)	(communication through body movement, e.g., facial expression)
	Begins with movement	Begins with movement	Begins with movement	Begins with movement	Begins with movement

FIGURE 4.7 Levels of Psychomotor Behavior

Source: Adapted from Table 5, pp. 104–106, in *A Taxonomy of the Psychomotor Domain: A Guide for Developing Behavior Objectives,* Anita J. Harrow (New York: Longman Publishing Group), Copyright © 1972 by Anita J. Harrow. Reprinted by permission of the author.

FIGURE 4.8   Curriculum
Planning Matrix

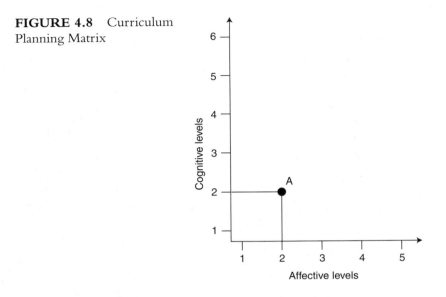

curriculum at the instructional level might be thought of as a matrix as shown in
Figure 4.8. At point *A,* the junction of cognitive level 2 and affective level 2, the
student should comprehend the material and respond to it.

SPECIFYING BEHAVIORAL OBJECTIVES

Following the development of goals and general descriptors of direction, long-
range planning requires the specification of objectives that will guide the creation
of school programs. *Objectives* are written operational statements that describe the
desired outcome of an educational program. Without such objectives, the translation of general goals into programs is likely to be haphazard.

The objectives developed by a school district should be derived from existing
goal statements. If objectives are developed that do not directly relate to a goal
area, they may suggest goals that need to be addressed by the district. The major
purpose of identifying objectives, from a planning perspective, is to manage and
evaluate the population to be served, the timing, and the expected outcomes.

Many school districts become bogged down in an attempt to translate goals
into objectives because of the behavioral aspect of stating objectives. In general,
objectives attempt to communicate to a specific group the expected outcomes of
some unit of instruction. They identify both the capability learned and the performance that the capability makes possible. The process can become mechanical and
sometimes threatens individualized programs when the objectives are stated in
behavioral terms. If the emphasis of the school program is on experiencing rather
than on being able to exhibit behaviors, such specificity may be altogether inappropriate for curriculum planning.

The following are advantages of using behavioral objectives in planning curricula:

- They help identify the specific behaviors to be changed.
- They increase interschool and intraschool communication.
- They direct instructional activities in the classroom.
- They provide a meaningful basis for evaluation.

The following are disadvantages that can occur when using behavioral objectives to plan curricula:

- They are sometimes simplistic; human behavior is more than the sum of the parts.
- They disregard the interrelatedness of human activity.
- They frequently limit choice by removing or prohibiting alternatives.
- They limit concomitant learning in the classroom.

While general or conceptual descriptors can serve as planning objectives, some school districts may wish to pursue instructional objectives that are behaviorally stated. Many guides are available to assist such a task. Examples of planning objectives in the area of science are shown below:

Develop Scientific Observation and Description Skills
a. Observe and identify phenomena, objects, and their properties
b. Observe and identify changes in physical and biological objects
c. Order a series of observations

Develop Scientific Hypothesis Formation Skills
a. Distinguish among hypothesis, prediction, inference, and opinion
b. Formulate a simple hypothesis and give explanations for various phenomena on the basis of known information and observations

Understand the Content and Concepts of Advanced Science
a. Understand concepts about the life of man
b. Understand the concepts relating to physical science
c. Understand the concepts relating to ecology

ASSESSING NEEDS: FOCUSING FOR RESULTS

Once the basic framework of the curriculum plan is in place, a substantial amount of focusing is necessary to increase efficiency and meet intentions. In many school districts, a failure to assess the true needs of the learners results in a dysfunctional curriculum. The needs assessment technique represents a comprehensive inquiry into the educational status of a district or school. The major intent of the process is to determine if the real intentions are being met through the existing instructional form. Such inquiry often leads to adjustments in goals, instructional technique, and expectations for students.

The actual data gathered in a needs assessment is determined locally. Figure 4.9 shows a typical outline of areas that may be reviewed. Needs assessments are characteristically conducted locally by school or district staffs, as opposed to accreditation visits and surveys that usually use outside experts to make observations about the condition of the program. The emphasis in the needs assessment is not so much a matter of what conditions exist, but rather how those conditions affect the program.

The first steps of a needs assessment are to decide what data are needed for decision making and to develop a strategy for data gathering. A typical needs assessment in a school district will use citizens' groups or study teams comprised of a mixture of persons from the school community. Sometimes natural resources that might affect local school operation should be included. Information should also be included about local commerce and industry, which may indicate the tax support for schools in the area as well as the relative wealth of the parents of schoolchildren.

Special social or economic conditions in an area should also be noted. For instance, if a nearby military base is served by the district, or if there is a seasonal migrant population, it is important to acknowledge these variables.

General data about the community, regardless of location, are available in public libraries in standard census reports. Current information dating from the last census data can generally be gained from the local chamber of commerce, or from various Internet sources.

General Information

It is important in any needs assessment that the meaning of educating in a public school be put in perspective. Each of the 12,500 school districts in the United States has unique variables that are reflected in schools. Failure to know and understand such variables often leads to school plans that are either inappropriate for community standards or impossible to implement, given community resources. Any needs assessment should begin with an accurate but brief description of the school setting. The size of the district, its population, the governance pattern (elected or appointed officials), and its resource capacity are information items critical to school planning.

General Population Characteristics

In gathering information about the people who live in the area served by the school district, an attempt should be made to understand the community's educational and cultural levels, general attitudes about schools, and expectations for education in the area.

Some of the most important information to be gathered about the people who are served by the school district is their cultural heritage and set of traditions.

I. General Information
   a. Location of school district
   b. Demographic characteristics of immediate area
   c. Natural resources of region
   d. Commercial–industrial data
   e. Income levels of area residents
   f. Special socio-economic considerations
II. General Population Characteristics
   a. Population growth patterns
   b. Age, race of population
   c. Educational levels of population
   d. Projected population
III. School Population Characteristics (Ages 3–19)
   a. School enrollment by grade level
   b. Birthrate trends in school district
   c. In-migration, out-migration patterns
   d. Race/sex/religious composition of school district
   e. Years of school completed by persons over 25 years of age
   f. Studies of school dropouts
IV. Programs and Course Offerings in District
   a. Organization of school programs
   b. Programs' concept and rationale
   c. Course offerings
   d. Special program needs
V. Professional Staff
   a. Training and experience
   b. Awareness of trends and developments
   c. Attitudes toward change
VI. Instructional Patterns and Strategies
   a. Philosophical focus of instructional program
   b. Observational and perceptual instructional data
   c. Assessment of instructional strategies in use
   d. Instructional materials in use
   e. Decision-making and planning processes
   f. Grouping for instruction
   g. Classroom management techniques
   h. Grading and placement of pupils
   i. Student independence
   j. Evaluation of instructional effectiveness
VII. Student Data
   a. Student experiences
   b. Student self-esteem
   c. Student achievement
VIII. Facilities
   a. Assessment of existing facilities and sites
   b. Special facilities
   c. Utilization of facilities
   d. Projected facility needs
IX. Summary of Data

FIGURE 4.9   Basic Needs Assessment Framework

In areas where populations are stable, both in terms of turnover and composition, there is usually minimal social or cultural change. Because schools tend to reflect the communities they serve, a comparable stability should be present in school data. In communities that have experienced considerable growth or turnover of population, however, school planning data tend to be more varied, and expectations for change in the schools is increased.

Along with information about population changes, data about economic development in the community often indicate anticipated population changes that will affect schools. The closing of key industries, declining farm populations, the closing of military bases, or seasonal industries can signal new patterns for school districts. Out-migration of urban population, regional economic prosperity, or the development of new industries based on natural resources can also affect school planning.

A number of population composition variables are important indicators for school planners. Birthrate projections, population stability patterns, racial and economic composition, and special social and cultural characteristics such as languages spoken or national origin of parents all have planning implications for school leaders.

Another influential variable to include in a formal needs assessment is the educational level of parents and persons in the community over twenty-five years of age. Data about the educational achievement in the community often indicate the amount of belief in, and support for, education.

School Population Characteristics

Among the most stable and useful data available to school planners are the birthrate trends in the district and the school enrollment patterns by grade level. Because of the rise in births in the late 1980s, school populations showed an increase at the elementary levels in the early 1990s, in the intermediate grades in the late 1990s, and in the high schools starting in 2002. Using such data, planners can determine how many classrooms and teachers will be needed, as well as how many programs will be needed for special students (one in nine students in 1990 was categorized as special). Birthrate information is available through county health department records.

The racial, ethnic, religious, and sexual composition of a school district is also important to school planners. The population in the United States is increasingly mobile due to changes in family structure and the economy. As a result, primary characteristics of communities can change rapidly, and the educational organization may need to make adjustments. When such change goes unnoticed, obsolescence is often a major problem.

Perhaps the most important data about school population come from our study of dropouts. Most school districts in the United States have an alarming number of students who terminate their formal education prematurely. The school and the communities should be particularly concerned about any student who walks out the door, never to return, by personal choice. Not only can such an exodus indicate a deficiency in school programming, but such dropouts have severe implications for the community, which must absorb them. In Florida, for example, 80 percent of all persons incarcerated are school dropouts, and the cost for each person in prison is five times the cost of each person attending a public school.

Students who quit school prior to graduation are usually faced with employment difficulties, limited job opportunities, low earning power, lessened opportunities for promotions, and emotional stress from related cultural and social pressures. To accept a high dropout rate as a normal event in the schooling process is a short-sighted position for an agency charged with the task of preparing the young to become citizens. Table 4.2 illustrates how one school monitored dropout numbers.

Programs and Course Offerings in the District

The general scope and depth of an educational program can be best identified by reviewing the number and types of courses and special activities offered by individual schools. Of importance in understanding the programs of a school district are the organization of school programs, the rationale for such organization, the breadth and scope of course offerings, and the degree to which special education needs are met.

Many school districts conceptualize schooling according to levels of attainment and reference programs such as primary school, elementary school, middle school, and high school. In such an organization, students advance through the program by grades rather than by age, maturation, achievement, readiness, or interest.

In such programs, content and skill development are dominant organizers; there is little consideration for individual differences, and curriculum planning focuses on the sequencing of experiences. Such programs are usually organized in quantitative units, with teachers, students, classrooms, and textbooks assigned by a predetermined formula. Supplemental activities, enrichment experiences, and student services are added to the core program as resources allow.

Regardless of the avowed purpose of schooling and the primary organization of the educational program, the heart of the assessment process should address the course offerings and experiences that the students have. Most school districts in the United States, because of history and state and local requirements, arrange school into subject areas. Nearly all schools provide a core of activities that

TABLE 4.2 Sample Dropout Grid

Year	Number of Dropouts	Total Number of Students	Dropout (percentage)
1997–98	34	258	13
1998–99	38	253	15
1999–2000	44	239	18
2000–01	30	234	13
2001–02	48	277	17
	Total 194	Total 1,261	Average 15

includes mathematics, science, English, and social studies. Most districts also provide supplemental programs in physical education, art, music, and vocational arts. Beyond such basic programs, courses and experiences are offered that reflect the capacity of the district to address individual differences. Often, the degree to which a school district tailors such offerings indicates how aware school leaders are of the needs of students.

In recent years, owing to research and legislation, school districts in the United States have become sensitive to the needs of special groups of students found in the school. A list of all such special students would be lengthy, but addressing programs to serve special education, career education, and adult education can illuminate course offerings outside the general curriculum.

Every community has children and youth with special educational needs that cannot be met within the operation of the general program of instruction. Many definitions of students with special needs exist; most include those children with emotional, physical, communicative, or intellectual deviations that interfere with school adjustment or prevent full attainment of academic achievement. Included in such a broad classification are children who are intellectually gifted, as well as those who have mental, physical, or speech disabilities; behavioral disorders; visual or hearing impairments; autism; or multiple disabilities, and those who are homebound or hospitalized. School districts vary in how they serve these special learners. Legislation at the national level (Public Law 94–142 and IDEA) has set strong guidelines for special education programs, which affect about one child in nine (see Table 4.3).

Career and vocational education is fast becoming a major curriculum component of many school districts in the nation. The impetus for this trend comes from many sources, but career and vocational education still represents the major alternative for secondary school students who choose a noncollege preparatory program.

Student interest in vocational programs is generally high among all types of students. The mandate for school districts to provide quality vocational experiences is heightened given that the majority of all students graduating from secondary schools do not go on as full-time students in postsecondary institutions.

A valuable resource for those assessing student vocational interests is the *Directory of Occupational Titles*,[2] produced by the U.S. Department of Labor. This directory identifies over 21,000 job titles that may be of interest to students. Using instruments such as the Ohio Vocational Interest Survey, students can identify areas in which vocational experiences might be developed. Questionnaires that seek to pinpoint students' plans following graduation can also provide school leaders with rough indicators of need.

A third type of special education program provided by some school districts is adult education. A program for adults will depend on their level of educational attainment, the skills and knowledge needed by adults in the community, and whether interests are for occupational or personal development. School districts can effectively use adult education programs to increase community involvement as well as to build bridges to parents of schoolchildren.

TABLE 4.3 Students with Special Education Needs

Year	Elementary School			Middle School			High School			Total		
	99–00	00–01	01–02	99–00	00–01	01–02	99–00	00–01	01–02	99–00	00–01	01–02
Educable mentally retarded	24	26	28	26	28	31	20	23	25	70	77	84
Trainable mentally retarded	4	5	7	2	3	4	1	2	3	7	10	14
Behavioral disorders	4	7	8	9	10	12	2	5	6	15	22	26
Visually impaired	0	4	5	0	1	2	0	2	3	0	7	10
Hearing impaired	2	4	5	0	1	2	0	0	1	2	5	8
Speech impaired	18	20	21	16	19	20	0	2	3	34	41	44
Multihandicapped	1	2	2	1	1	1	0	0	0	2	3	3
Hospital/homebound	5	6	6	3	4	4	2	2	2	10	12	12
Gifted	14	15	15	13	13	13	14	14	14	41	42	42
Learning disability	15	18	20	30	34	35	31	31	31	76	83	86
						Total				257	302	329

Adults in the community who have less than a high school education may be interested in programs geared to meeting basic education needs. Such programs often lead to completion of a high school equivalency test. Other adults may be interested in education for job opportunities. Still other adults in the community may participate in education for personal improvement. Popular courses include family-oriented courses, household mechanics, child development, computers, and record keeping.

Schools providing educational experiences for adults in the community can use questionnaires and other devices to assess needs and interests effectively. The following list is illustrative of the types of offerings regularly requested by adult learners:

Job-Oriented Courses	**Personal Development Courses**
a. Keyboarding	a. Reading improvement
b. Bookkeeping	b. Arts/crafts
c. Computers	c. Horticulture
d. Office machines	d. Aerobics
e. Income tax	e. Self-projection
f. Electrical wiring	f. Home improvement
g. Brick masonry	g. Photography
h. Cosmetology	h. Interior decorating
i. Sales clerking	i. Leisure activities
j. Carpentry	j. Basic sewing

Professional Staff

A thorough needs assessment also reviews the professional staff in the school district. Among primary concerns are the training and experience of teachers, supervisors, and administrators; the balance among the various teaching positions; and anticipated staff needs. Also subject to analysis is the staff's awareness of recent trends and developments in the field, as well as their attitudes toward change.

A review of staff often will indicate a dominance of age, race, or sex among school faculties. These patterns are important in terms of the goals of the district and the specific programs being promoted in the buildings. Such an assessment will sometimes reveal an excessive number of graduates from a single university or a pattern of regional dominance among teachers. The latter situation is sometimes unavoidable in remote regions; however, a diversity among teaching backgrounds is desirable in terms of the experiences that teachers bring to the classroom.

A districtwide assessment of allocated teaching positions will often reveal overstaffing in particular subject areas at the expense of other equally important areas. Such a districtwide review will also indicate trends in staffing that can assist planners in projecting future staffing needs.

An analysis of faculty familiarity with new trends and developments in subject areas and new innovative concepts is important if the district anticipates new programs. Such a review can often pinpoint staff development needs that can be addressed in in-service sessions.

Finally, school districts can find extremely useful the analysis of professional staff attitudes toward change in general and toward specific curriculum alterations in particular. Such attitudes are the result of many factors, and experience has shown that the age and experience of teachers are poor predictors of readiness to change.

Data for Instructional Planning: Instructional Patterns and Strategies

By far the most important segment of a needs assessment in schools is the part that focuses on instructional patterns and strategies. Such teacher behaviors should reflect uniformly the intentions of the district to deliver quality programs to students. The types of instruction found in classrooms should result from an understanding of the goals of the district; an assessment of strategies and techniques can occur only following a clarification of the district philosophy.

In some districts, the predominant goal of instruction is to have all students master the essential data that will distinguish them as educated persons. Other school districts place greatest emphasis on the needs, interests, and abilities of students. A key distinction in these two extreme positions is the role of the student in the learning process. Because needs assessments tend to use subjective perceptual data about schools, they are most useful in districts favoring a student-centered curriculum.

Two major techniques can be used to assess instructional patterns and strategies: (1) the observation technique and (2) the administration of projective instruments. The projective approach is by far the most common method of reviewing instruction in needs assessments.

The projective data technique, commonly referred to as the *opinionnaire,* requires the administration of instruments to teachers and, in some cases, students and parents. This perceptual survey is based on findings of phenomenological psychology, which holds that people behave in terms of personal meanings that exist for them at a given moment. In short, behavior is based on perception because we behave and react to what we believe to be real. A personal perception may or may not be supported by facts, but such perceptions serve as facts to each of us.

Projective instruments possess several distinct advantages. First, they are quick to administer and tally. Second, they are easily managed and are less time consuming than interviews or quantitative measures. Most important, however, is that such perceptual techniques allow all teachers in the district to participate in the data-gathering stage. Such involvement is critical if programmatic responses to such findings are to be credible and supported.

Data for Instructional Planning: Student Data

School districts that attempt to serve the individual needs of learners, as opposed to giving all students the same academic treatment, must gather student data. Data relating to student experiences are valuable for preplanning input, and information about student feelings and achievement can assist school planners in making adjustments to the existing curriculum.

In reviewing student experiences, a number of variables are useful indicators of both the breadth and depth of the student's world. A questionnaire that assesses student travel, recreational, aesthetic, and cultural backgrounds can provide teachers with invaluable points of reference for instruction. Examples of such questions at the elementary level might be the following:

- ☐ Have you ever seen an ocean?
- ☐ Have you ever flown on an airplane?
- ☐ Have you ever been to a band concert?
- ☐ Have you ever been in a public library?
- ☐ Have you ever visited a foreign country?

Questionnaires that deal with assessments of experiences, at the secondary as well as the elementary level, give teachers insights into students' backgrounds and levels of sophistication. When tallied as a percentage, the general level of experience for entire schools can be developed. Another equally valuable assessment device that may provide the same type of information is a projection technique that asks students how to spend extra money or to plan trips.

Information about student attitudes, particularly those relating to self-esteem, can assist school planners in personalizing the instructional program. Beyond learning of student interest, motivation, and attitudes toward learning itself, such assessments often give clear portraits of student confidence in the instructional setting. Research over the past twenty years has shown consistently that individuals who feel capable, significant, successful, and worthy tend to have positive school experiences. In contrast, students who have low self-esteem rarely experience success in school settings.[3]

Measures of self-esteem, an individual's personal judgment of his or her worthiness, are plentiful. Two measures used regularly in needs assessments are the *When Do I Smile?* instrument (grades K–3) and the *Coopersmith Self-Esteem Inventory* (grades 4–12). *When Do I Smile?* is a twenty-eight-item instrument that can be administered to nonreaders. Students respond by marking faces that are happy, blank, or sad. By this means, school planners can gain insight into attitudes about school, peers, and general self.

The *Coopersmith Self-Esteem Inventory,* a fifty-item instrument, assesses student attitudes about themselves, their lives at home, and school life. Students respond to statements such as "I can make up my mind without too much trouble" or "I'm pretty happy" and choose either a "like me" or "unlike me" response. Such instruments can tell school planners a great deal about student confidence, support from home, and attitudes toward the existing curriculum.

Assessments of student achievement can be either broad or narrow in focus. The measure of this essential category is really a reflection of the school district's definition of education. When an educational program is perceived as primarily the mastery of skills and cognitive data, standardized achievement tests can be used exclusively to determine progress. When education is defined more broadly, measures of achievement become personal and more affective in nature.

Standardized achievement testing is carried out in most school districts in the United States on a scheduled basis. Tests such as the California Achievement Test can provide computer-scored analyses in areas such as math, language arts, and reading. Such standardized tests give school districts an assessment of relative progress in terms of validated national norms. Achievement tests compare a student's progress with what is considered to be normal progress for students in the nation of approximately the same age or grade level, or both. These tests do not address a student's ability to perform.

It is useful for school planners to know if students in a district or particular school are achieving above or below grade level, for such information might suggest the retention or elimination of a specific curriculum program. More important, however, are general trends revealed by such tests. A continuing decline in reading scores, for instance, may indicate that a curriculum review is needed. In Figure 4.10, students in a district are displayed according to whether they are achieving above or below grade level in reading according to three commonly used standardized tests: (1) *Gates McGinitie* (lower elementary), (2) *Iowa Test of Basic Skills* (middle grades), and (3) *Test of Academic Progress* (secondary grades).

Indicates Below Grade Placement

Grade Level	Number of Students by Grade							Total
	2	3	4	5	6	8	11	
14.0–14.9								
13.0–13.9							6	6
12.0–12.9							6	6
11.0–11.9						1	8	9
10.0–10.9						5	16	21
9.0–9.9						6	21	27
8.0–8.9					1	14	16	31
7.0–7.9				1	7	9	9	26
6.0–6.9				2	16	29	7	54
5.0–5.9		3	7	9	29	27		75
4.0–4.9		5	27	25	43	13		113
3.0–3.9	3	14	28	55	26	2		128
2.0–2.9	16	40	30	21	9			116
1.0–1.9	75	41	3	11	0			130
0.0–0.9								
Total	94	103	95	124	131	106	89	742

FIGURE 4.10 Summary of Reading Achievement in One School District

In school districts in which education is defined in terms of comprehensive criteria, assessments of student achievement are generally multiple. Sometimes such assessments have multiple dimensions, such as achievement in knowledge use, skill acquisition, and personal development. Sometimes such assessments are criterion referenced, matching student achievement against goals rather than norms. Almost always the evidence of student achievement is multidimensional, supplementing standardized tests with samples of student work, teacher observations, and other such measures of growth.

Data for Instructional Planning: Facilities

A final area considered by most needs assessments is that of the educational facilities used by the district to accomplish its program goals. Ideally, such facilities should be designed on the basis of program concepts.

An in-depth study of facilities seeks to answer the following critical questions:

- What is the overall pattern of facilities in the district?
- How adequate is each plant and site for educational use?
- How are the facilities currently being used?
- What is the net operating capacity of each facility?

Assessments of facilities and sites attempt to analyze the adequacy and capacity ratings of all plants and grounds for maximum benefit to the educational program. A basic principle of most such studies is that flexible, multiuse facilities are more beneficial than those that limit programs to a single instructional pattern. A facility (school building) is considered adequate and modern if it provides the following:

- A variety of grouping patterns.
- The use of educational media, guidance.
- Health and food services.
- Special interest instruction (music, art, home economics, science, horticulture, and so on).
- Large-group assembly.
- Administrative functions.

One commonly used criterion for assessing school facilities is the *Linn-McCormick Rating Form for School Facilities,* developed by the Institute of Field Studies, Teachers College, Columbia University. The Linn–McCormick scale uses a point system that systematically evaluates school buildings from classroom through custodial facilities. Facilities are then rated on a scale from excellent to poor. Such a scale does not consider the financial capability of the district to provide such facilities.

For educational planning, the value of such a building-by-building analysis is that it allows school planners to see facilities in terms of the desired educational program. School plants can be compared and priorities for new building programs identified. If additional school sites are projected, lead time is available for survey and acquisition. Remodeling, where needed, can be scheduled.

In the assessment of facilities, an important phase is the identification and analysis of special facilities. In most school districts, special facilities are perceived as supplemental to regular instructional spaces and thus are considered a luxury. School districts must choose among a host of special rooms and spaces such as gymnasiums, art rooms, teacher offices, and so forth. Additionally, many schools have had to plan rooms specifically for students with physical handicaps or other special needs. The decision as to which kinds of special rooms and spaces to have should be based on school planning rather than convenience or familiarity.

When school facilities are assessed, considerable attention should be directed to the use of these facilities. Detailed studies can often lead to more efficient use of existing buildings and sites. Such studies also will often reveal multiuse potential in spaces with only a single use, for example, the "cafetorium."

The assessment of school facilities and sites, including special areas and use patterns, should assist school planners in developing long-range facilities planning. Such planning can eliminate an undesirable pattern of building schools and acquiring sites after needs are in a critical state. Under such conditions, educational facilities are rarely adequate or appropriate to the needs of the instructional program.

ALIGNING THE CURRICULUM: THE CURRICULUM MAP

Once the scope of the curriculum has been determined by an operational philosophy, complete with goals and carefully selected objectives for learning, the curriculum must be sequenced or aligned. Over the past decades, we have spent a great deal of time working with schools on curriculum mapping since it is a prerequisite to meaningful interdisciplinary teaching and is useful in gaining efficiency from the curriculum in the form of test results. A typical mapping format is found in Figure 4.11.

Curriculum mapping, whether carried out at the district or classroom level, is most effective when the materials and experiences encountered by the student are presented in a meaningful pattern. Not only does the teacher have to deal with the mundane task of pacing the coverage of the curriculum, but, even more important, the teacher must also give appropriate emphasis to the information being addressed. In curriculum mapping, the content, skills, and objectives are laid out and arranged in an optimal order. Where appropriate, these teaching acts are keyed to test items or other expectations. It is extremely important to identify the concepts or "big ideas" that guide all subsequent definition. Too often, teachers cover material without thinking about *why* they are teaching it to students.

This mapping process, which connects goals and objectives to programs, offers two major benefits. First, by viewing the intentions for students in totality, school planners can often identify redundancy in both the scope (breadth) and the sequence (order) of the general curriculum. Second, such an overview can help planners see commonality among parts of the curriculum. Understanding the

Grade Level _____			Subject _____	
Grading Period _____			Teacher _____	

Content	Concepts	General Skills	Specific Skills/Objectives	Texts/Materials

FIGURE 4.11   Curriculum Mapping Format

interrelatedness of the curriculum can have payoffs in both instructional coordination and a maximum use of district resources.

Once objectives have been generated for each desired goal and placed in a format that allows a review of the total blueprint for educating students in the district, it is necessary to identify program concepts that will give form to instruction. Program concepts are, in essence, sets of instructional and organizational strategies that are philosophically based.

The program concept phase of curriculum development is perhaps the most difficult step in building school programs. Although the need is to develop programs that are compatible with the district philosophy, there is always a tendency to return to the familiar. Hence, the conceptual objectives often end up being translated into school programs with standard characteristics such as a textbook-dominated, six-period day. At this stage, the educational philosophy adopted before specific objectives were developed can assist in answering the question of which is the best teaching method to achieve the desired ends.

Schools and school districts differ tremendously in how they interact with students to accomplish desired goals and objectives. Generally speaking, however, schools vary according to how much structure they demand in the instructional program. Structure, as opposed to flexibility in instructional organization, is a reflection of the anticipated conciseness of the desired outcomes. School districts

FIGURE 4.12 Concepts for Child-Focused Program

Philosophy Statement

We desire in each school, kindergarten through adult education, a program that will focus on the individual student to provide learning experiences in the affective, cognitive, and psychomotor areas.

Program Concepts

1. A program of individual instruction will be implemented.
2. A basic diagnostic-prescriptive approach to teaching will be used.
3. A variety of materials, both commercial and teacher-made, will be used.
4. A flexible schedule will be implemented.
5. Instructional assistance will perform teaching, planning, and clerical tasks.
6. Instructional leaders (teachers) will serve as facilitators of program planning and implementation
7. A facility that provides as much flexibility in programming as possible will be promoted.

that desire highly predictable outcomes for all students should not encourage instructional flexibility, for each variable encourages diversity of outcome.

In schools where there is a philosophy focusing on the student as an individual, there is a wider choice for instructional patterns. The program concept, when translated into instructional arrangements, indicates to school planners how desired outcomes should be approached. In the example in Figure 4.12 a school district identifies seven concepts that are felt to reinforce their goal to develop a program focused on the individual child.

Planning flows from philosophy to goals to objectives. Within this sequence of if–then logic, there should be consistency (if we believe this, then our objectives should be thus and so).

CURRICULUM PLANNING IN A TECHNOLOGICAL ERA

In Chapter 1 we reported on a Florida district trying to leave behind the textbook curriculum and have students learn using Internet resources. We suggested that this particular effort was not following a logical cycle of curriculum improvement.

The Internet age presents curriculum leaders with a host of new problems. With web-based learning, which is highly individualized and nonlinear, the traditional deductive logic of philosophy/goals/objectives/programs/activities/lessons may not be an appropriate procedure for curriculum construction. In Chapter 6, "Instruction in a Technological Era," we introduce eight learning designs common in schools that might serve to organize the varied resources of the Internet. It appears, however, that we must still first ask what we want for students and then select experiences (web sites) that will promote learning. To do otherwise would result in a learning experience without structure.

PROVIDING LEADERSHIP FOR CURRICULUM DEVELOPMENT

The term *curriculum worker* applies to most educator-teachers, central office administrators, or principals. *Curriculum leader* refers to anyone in a school district who is primarily responsible for planning, coordinating, or managing curriculum activity. Curriculum leaders may be teachers chairing departments or committees, supervisors, or school administrators.[4]

There is a growing emphasis on curriculum development at the school or district level. The identification of curriculum leaders who can facilitate curriculum development is essential to the success of any change process. Many competencies have been compiled for the curriculum leader. Because the success of a curriculum leader depends on good human relations, the following competencies have been identified that will help the curriculum leader coordinate the curriculum planning and development activities of an educational staff. The curriculum leader should be able to do the following:

- ☐ Produce and implement a year-long plan focused on curriculum planning and the development of problems involving staff, parents, students, and support personnel; indicate their specific assignments and responsibilities; and provide a schedule of steps toward completion.
- ☐ Coordinate programming for instructional development at a variety of levels and areas (locally as well as regionally).
- ☐ Define, with staff, common problems and help staff with the solution of these problems.
- ☐ Develop, with staff, behavioral objectives that will be measurable and compatible with the content area.
- ☐ Schedule periodic interdepartmental meetings within a school or a school system to define common curricular problems and seek solutions.
- ☐ Help and encourage teachers to be innovative and to accept different methods as long as they produce the desired outcomes.
- ☐ Develop a program for continuous curriculum development.
- ☐ Accept the individual differences of adults in conducting workshops for the development of curriculum.
- ☐ Be a primary resource person.
- ☐ Help integrate subject areas into the total overall curriculum.
- ☐ Evaluate the current educational trends and know the philosophical basis for these trends.
- ☐ Recognize the dangers to educational development inherent in each of these trends.
- ☐ Assist the group in pursuing various possible solutions to a problem.
- ☐ Summarize various solutions clearly and concisely.
- ☐ Assist the group in coming to decisions based on the alternative choices.
- ☐ Follow through on a course of action decided.

☐ Evaluate the effects that course of action may have on those affected by the program change.

☐ Disseminate information on current **innovations** to staff members directly involved in a specific area of innovation.

☐ Promote and encourage the direct involvement and participation of teachers in planning, implementing, and evaluating curricular innovations and adjustments.

☐ Describe the various points of view and the proper relationships of different subject areas to each other.

☐ Coordinate curriculum planning and development for the local district, K–12.

☐ Open channels of communication among professional staff members that will allow crossing grade levels, ability levels, and individual discipline structures.

☐ Develop an attitude of commitment to local, district, state, and national curriculum development and improvement programs.

☐ Determine the needs of the community and of individual pupils in planning and developing programs at all levels of instruction to fulfill these needs.

☐ Plan budgetary allocations to ensure that curriculum plans can be inaugurated.

☐ Improve personal ability to communicate positively and influentially with many different personalities.

☐ Offer, by example, personal philosophy of education.

☐ Provide vision for long-range planning.

☐ Seek help and cooperation from staff members in setting up programs of curriculum development or improvement, or both.

☐ Use research on child development and learning in selecting and sequencing concepts for curriculum development.

☐ Communicate progress, plans, and problems between staff members and curriculum-making bodies.

☐ Speak competently before faculty and critically appraise their efforts.

☐ Understand both elementary and secondary education (with a strong background in one of the levels).

☐ Establish a personal philosophy or a frame of reference from which to operate; act in a manner consistent with such a philosophy or frame of reference.

SUMMARY

Curriculum development is a process of development that creates educational experiences to meet the intentions of planners. The basic tasks of curriculum work have been clearly defined in recent decades. Using an if–then logic, curriculum development identifies purpose, sets goals and objectives, aligns curriculum content, focuses on the critical needs of learners, and delivers a program. This process is more difficult in the United States because of the decentralization of control. New interactive technologies have also challenged this linear and sequential procedure.

Much of the difficulty in schools today stems from the lack of definition at the school and classroom level. Seeing the teacher (instruction) as an extension of curriculum calls for curriculum planners to use taxonomies and behavioral objectives to focus instructional activities. The curriculum mapping process and a needs assessment can further adjust the curriculum to the specific target of the design.

Leading curriculum development efforts call for standards and clusters of skills to guide program development.

SUGGESTED LEARNING ACTIVITIES

1. Develop an outline of events that would lead a school or district from no clear philosophy to a state of logical internal consistency in program development.
2. Develop a list of "quality indicators" that a district might want to review in conducting a needs assessment.
3. Using the list of skills for a curriculum worker found at the conclusion of this chapter, rank the ten most important skills for a school-level curriculum specialist.
4. Develop a response to our observations that the Internet challenges a sequential and logical (deductive) process in curriculum development efforts.

NOTES

1. Report to the Executive Committee of the Association for Supervision and Curriculum Development, Research and Working Group, 1982.
2. *A Directory of Occupational Titles,* 3rd ed. (Washington, DC: U.S. Department of Labor, Bureau of Employment Security, 1965).
3. G. Brookover, *Self-Concept* (Alexandria, VA: Association for Supervision and Curriculum Development, 1981), pp. 13–14.
4. Working group on "The Role, Function, and Preparation of the Curriculum Worker," in *Curriculum Leaders: Improving Their Influence* (Alexandria, VA: Association for Supervision and Curriculum Development, 1976), p. 16.

ADDITIONAL READING

Bean, J. *Affect in the Curriculum.* New York: Teachers College Press, 1990.

Centron, M., and M. Gayle. *Educational Renaissance: Our Schools at the Turn of the Twenty-First Century.* New York: St. Martins Press, 1991.

Drake, Susan M. *Creating Integrated Curriculum: Proven Ways to Increase Student Learning.* Thousand Oaks, CA: Corwin Press, 2000.

English, F. *Deciding What to Teach and Test: Developing, Aligning, and Auditing the Curriculum.* Thousand Oaks, CA: Sage, 1999.

Heinich, R., M. Molenda, J. D. Russell, and S. E. Smaldino. *Instructional Media and Technologies in Learning,* 5th ed. Upper Saddle River, NJ: Prentice Hall, 1996.

Idol, Lorna et al. *Models of Curriculum-Based Assessment: A Blueprint for Learning.* Austin, TX: Pro-Ed, 1999.

Longstreet, W., and H. Shane. *Curriculum for the New Millennium.* Needham Heights, MA: Allyn and Bacon, 1993.

Mager, Robert. *Preparing Instructional Objectives.* Palo Alto, CA: Fearon Press, 1962.

Reavis, George H., and Joyce Orchard Garamella. *Animal School: The Administration of the School Curriculum with References to Individual Differences.* Peterborough, NH: Society for Developmental Education, 2000.

Seels, Barbara, and Zita Glasgow. *Making Instructional Design Decisions.* Englewood Cliffs, NJ: Prentice Hall, 1997.

Siskin, L. *Realms of Knowledge: Academic Departments in Secondary Schools.* Bristol, PA: Falmer Press, 1994.

Sowell, Evelyn J., and Debra A. Stollenwerk. *Curriculum: An Intergrative Introduction.* Upper Saddle River, NJ: Prentice Hall, 1999.

Steffy, Betty E. *Curriculum Alignment: A Facilitator's Guide to Deciding What to Teach and Test.* Thousand Oaks, CA: Corwin Press, 1999.

Wiles, Jon. *Curriculum Essentials: A Resource for Educators.* Needham Heights, MA: Allyn and Bacon, 1999.

chapter 5

CURRICULUM MANAGEMENT PLANNING

In previous chapters we observed that the curriculum development process is a cycle, whether at the macro (state, district, school) or micro (classroom) level. Curriculum development begins with an analysis of purpose, proceeds to a design or plan for learning, is implemented, and is then assessed for results. This cycle, with its recurring tasks, is adaptable to any philosophy or starting point. It is a prerequisite to orderly program development, even in a technological age. Although philosophies are value laden, the development process is essentially value free.

The impurity of the work environment (distortions) in schools often means that what is intended is not what is delivered to children in the classroom. The goal of the curriculum worker is to ensure that any distortions of the intent of a plan are minimized and that the intentions are carried out to the degree possible. Failure to acknowledge this probable theory–practice gap, and to use sound management techniques to overcome it, results in many of the failures in today's curriculum work in schools and using Internet-assisted resources.

Bridging theory and practice requires sound planning and the management of change in schools. In our consulting work in schools we use a technique known as *curriculum management planning*, which is covered later in this chapter. First, however, let's begin with how schools traditionally improve their programs.

HOW DISTRICTS IMPROVE PROGRAMS

The methodology of school district reviews depends on both an understanding of curriculum development and the sophistication of the district in carrying out a review procedure. Sometimes districts review themselves in terms of external criteria, such as when professional accreditation is sought. Sometimes districts rely on expert opinion by having consultants survey the district. Finally, some districts choose to conduct an internal needs assessment. This occurs, in many instances, after a change of leadership when new leaders wish to have a status report. These three approaches are compared and contrasted in Table 5.1.

School districts can be differentiated by the degree to which they succeed in assessing themselves and projecting improved programs. This behavior is rarer in schools than would be imagined. Some districts, of course, never enter into such a cycle; for them, school programs are simply a historical accident. Others seemingly go through the motions, year to year, but don't seem to gain direction or momentum for all of their efforts. These districts have beautiful documents, but programs rarely change. Still a third pattern is seen in districts that plan well but are interrupted time and again by external social forces such as law, finance, or pressure groups. They are characterized by numerous false starts and some serious frustration with the lost investment of curriculum development. Finally, and happily, we

TABLE 5.1   Three Methods of Assessing School Conditions: Characteristics and Data

	Characteristics	
(1) Accreditation	*(2) Survey*	*(3) Needs Assessment*
Organization orientation	Administrative orientation	Programmatic orientation
Concern with structure, organization	Concern with structure and management	Concern with clients and corresponding programs
Analysis of what actually exists (descriptive)	Analysis of what actually exists (descriptive)	Assessment of what should be in existence (prescriptive)
Scheduled	Self-contained	Ties to remediation
Comprehensive	Quasi-comprehensive	Focused on client needs
Validation emphasis	Judgmental	Objective with design
	Data	
(1) Accreditation	*(2) Survey*	*(3) Needs Assessment*
Pupil-teacher ratio	Community background	School-community history
Number of library books	Administration and organization	Achievement patterns
Statement of purpose	Instructional patterns	Attitudes toward school
Quality of buildings	Finance	Motivation, self-concepts
Financial patterns	Extracurricular	Student interests
Pupil-personnel services		Teacher perception
Standards	Standards	Problems
External	External	Internal
Postevaluation	Postevaluation	Preevaluation

can report that some school districts do it right and get the satisfying results of an ever-improving program. The next section focuses on what these more fortunate districts seem to do to ensure success.

COMPREHENSIVE PLANNING

As early as 1970, Kathryn Feyereisen[1] and others called for the application of a "systems" concept of curriculum work. These early systems analysts realized that despite a rigorous process of curriculum review, and honorable intentions by school leaders in assessing their programs, sometimes nothing happened. All of the regular methods of upgrading school programs could not guarantee results because they couldn't control or manage the many variables of curriculum change. These early advocates of a systems approach to curriculum development called for more comprehensive planning and an integration of the many functions involved in school improvement.

The nature of a comprehensive process is shown in Figure 5.1. Here, each of the deductive steps following the identification purpose is outlined for study. Note that actions to implement the desired change occur after the direction has been set, not vice versa.

In working with some of the better school districts in the United States, we have uncovered four premises that seem critical to successful and lasting curriculum improvement:

1. For lasting change to occur, the persons to be affected must be involved in planning the change.
2. In a bureaucratic environment (schools), change must be directed from the top level of leadership.
3. Good decisions are best made on the basis of data, and such data should be shared with all those involved in planning.
4. Evaluation and expectation can drive change efforts forward.

The traditional failure patterns in curriculum development disappear in schools or school districts that develop a management plan for curriculum development that ensures these conditions. A review of the traditional cycle of development reveals some of the most common problems.

In the analysis stage, many districts fail to engage fully in a dissection of the current program. Reasons for this vary but include the following:

☐ The existing program has no design and therefore cannot be analyzed.
☐ Leaders fear that analysis will reveal weakness or problems that will reflect on them in their leadership role.
☐ The analysis never gets beyond words (jargon), and true assessments are not made.
☐ Leaders enhance the assessment because they feel it is expected.

If any of these conditions occurs in the analysis stage, subsequent curriculum development will fail because a deductive logic rests on its original premise.

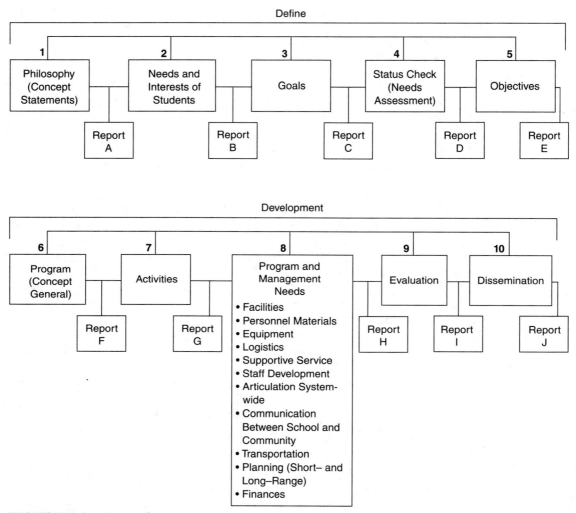

FIGURE 5.1 Comprehensive Management System
Source: Florida Department of Education, Tallahassee, FL.

In the design stage, numerous possible failures can sabotage the process, including the following:

☐ The design is "blue sky" (unreal) in nature or follows a bandwagon (everyone else has it).

☐ The design is unachievable because of existing conditions (financial, academic).

☐ The design challenges bedrock values of those who must implement it.

☐ The design is couched in terms that are vague or wordy.

In the implementation stage, regular conditions that undermine successful efforts include the following:

☐   The primary supporter of the design (such as the school board or superintendent) changes or leaves.
☐   The change is too complex, and the purpose is obscured.
☐   Time frames for changing are unrealistic, and the design is abandoned.
☐   Training to implement the design is not sufficient to carry the change.

Finally, in the traditional cycle, an evaluation step assesses the completion of the effort. This step can break down if any of the following occurs:

☐   No baseline data were secured for a comparison to the desired condition.
☐   Evaluation is not in a form that is useful in redirecting efforts.
☐   Those involved in the process do not trust those evaluating the process or believe the reported outcomes.

These common failure conditions are not meant to be all inclusive, but they do illustrate some of the things that can go wrong. If such errors are commonplace, curriculum development can be an unbelievable, frustrating, and even boring process. If

"So much for curriculum development this school year. I hear you asking yourself, 'What about 2000, 2001, and the year 2002?' "

Source: Phi Delta Kappan. September 1981. Used by permission of Ford Button.

these conditions are controlled through management actions, the cycle of curriculum development becomes the most important function of school leadership.

In the following section we introduce our own model of a curriculum management plan, developed over the past ten years in school districts such as Denver, St. Louis, Miami, and Jacksonville.

CURRICULUM MANAGEMENT PLAN

A curriculum management plan (CMP) increases the odds that the curriculum cycle will be completed successfully by providing structure for (1) how changes are made and (2) the order of those changes. Such a plan also seeks to provide continuity across a district or school effort. When implemented, the CMP will minimize political interference and single-issue crises. Most important, the CMP provides a way in which the philosophy of education desired by planners can intersect the development process over a long period.

A curriculum management plan begins with an acknowledgment of power; that is, an understanding that certain persons in each district or school have the power to make decisions, set or alter policy, allocate resources, and use procedures and regulations to emphasize activities. Curriculum leaders must realize that without such top-down support, instructional improvement efforts will not usually succeed.

In the Wiles-Bondi CMP model, curriculum leaders form a management team that initiates action, communicates upward and downward for logistical purposes, and helps define political reality in districts or schools. This group "allows" a process to be initiated, pursued, and completed. Figure 5.2 shows the relationship of this group to other groups in the CMP.

FIGURE 5.2 Committee Structure for Curriculum Management Plan (CMP)

Source: J. Wiles and J. Bondi, copyright © 1988. *Planning for Middle School Programs,* Wiles, Bondi & Associates (Tampa, FL: 1988), p. 12.

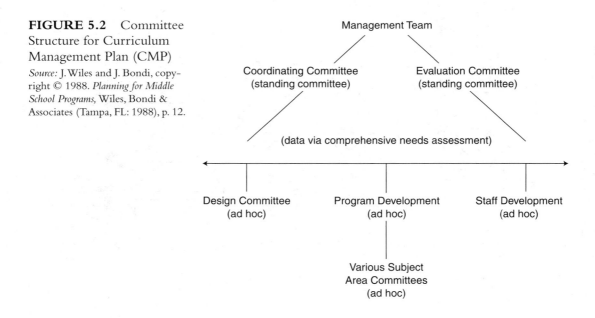

Analysis Stage

In the Wiles–Bondi curriculum management plan, the management team plays a crucial role in the analysis stage of development. Many of the proposed changes in American education during the past thirty years have come from external sources or have bypassed this influential group. In practice, as opposed to theory, this management team can facilitate or sabotage any change effort. Securing this team's endorsement, as a formal step in the development process, will eliminate problems of ownership down the road. Such an endorsement is best if it is in written form (see Figure 5.3). The management team's endorsement is also a necessity for conducting a true assessment

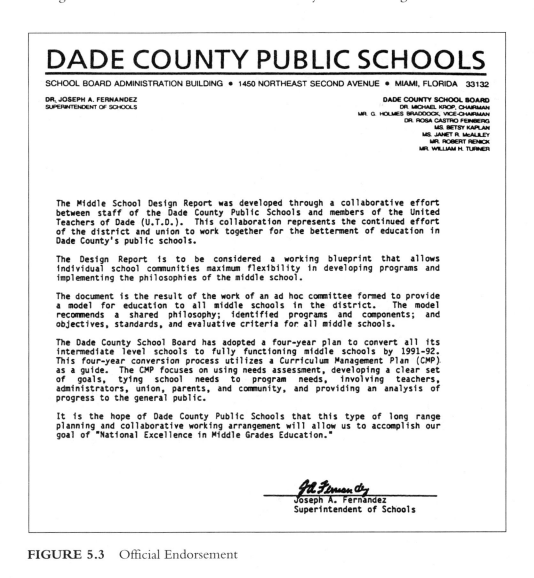

FIGURE 5.3   Official Endorsement

(see Figures 5.4, 5.5, and 5.6), coordinating efforts across the district, and gaining true and accurate evaluation data. Without this group, the effort to improve curriculum will be external, lack coordination, and be destined to failure from an absence of internal support.

There are, of course, other groups to be consulted if the change process is to succeed, such as the teachers union, parents, political action groups, and so on. These groups are combined in the Wiles-Bondi CMP model into something

A. *Pupil Performance*
1. Standardized tests—teacher-made tests
2. Pupil grades
3. Dropout data
4. Pupil attendance
5. Observation of pupil performance
6. Inventories—skill continua
7. Observations of teaching-learning situations in the classroom
8. Degree of student attention and involvement

B. *Questionnaires—Polls of Opinions of Pupils, Teachers, Parents*
1. Polls of parents regarding the success of certain school programs
2. Group interviews with students, parents, teachers about the success of curriculum innovations
3. Attitude surveys of students about certain programs
4. Comparison of attitudes of pupils and teachers toward contrasting programs
5. Systematic questionnaires, rating sheets, and interviews with small random samples of students

C. *Follow-up Studies of Learners*
1. Success at the next grade level
2. Continuation of schooling
3. College success
4. Success at work
5. Application of skills learned, interests generated in school, for example, participation in lifetime sports, the arts

D. *Examination of Learning Materials*
1. Examining learning materials to see if they are feasible and practical for use by teachers in the schools—accuracy and soundness of materials
2. Determining if costs of materials are too great
3. Checking materials to see if they are at the right level for students
4. Determining whether teachers get special retraining in order to understand and use new materials
5. Matching materials to students' interests, needs, and aspirations—relevancy of materials

FIGURE 5.4   Sources of Data about an Instructional Program

FIGURE 5.5 Outline of Baseline and Projective Data to Be Gathered in Needs Assessment

Source: From *Making Middle Schools Work,* Fig. 2, p. 16, by J. Wiles and J. Bondi. Copyright © 1986, by Association for Supervision and Curriculum Development, Alexandria, VA.

Baseline Data (Where are we now?)
1. Existing Conditions
   a. Average daily attendance
   b. Absences per teacher per month
   c. Number of low socio-economic students
   d. Student mobility
   e. Corporal punishment patterns
   f. Grade distribution patterns
   g. Achievement analyses
   h. Teacher, student, parent attitudes toward present program
   i. Follow-up survey of junior high graduates
   j. Teacher training and certification patterns

2. Existing Resources
   a. Condition of facilities
   b. Analysis of instructional materials
   c. Community resources for education

Projective Data (Where do we want to go?)
1. Attitude Scales
   a. Parent attitudes and opinions
   b. Teacher attitudes and opinions
   c. Administrator attitudes and opinions
   d. Student instructional preference patterns

2. Program Definition
   a. Student self-concept ratings
   b. Teacher skills checklist
   c. Values surveys

---

known as the *coordinating committee*—a group of all-powerful individuals and organizations outside of the management team. This standing committee (as opposed to a temporary or ad hoc committee) is a vehicle for involvement and dissemination. Involving the teachers union, for example, may help planners gain access to classrooms, which revealed the pattern of instruction found in Figure 5.7.

In this stage, the primary task is to clarify purpose and goals. The following criteria can be applied to any set of goals as a measure of their usefulness to the organization:

☐ *Are the goals realistic?* If goals are attainable, they possess a quality that allows members of the organization to relate to them in daily work.

☐ *Are the goals specific?* Specific goals imply behaviors that need to be changed.

☐ *Are the goals related to performance?* Goals that are developed in an organizational context suggest patterns of interaction.

	Low	High
Enrollment range	670	1389
Average daily attendance (May 1984)	83%	95%
Absences per teacher per month	.36	1.27
Number of low socio-economic students (percentage)	11%	56%
Ratio of gifted students to other exceptional education students	1/104	179/63
Number of students moving in or out during year	33%	70%
Number of students experiencing corporal punishment	44	619
Number of students experiencing suspension	37	240
Number of students dropping out in academic year	0	22
Average score of students on CTBS total battery	36	80

Findings: These data confirm that a wide range of conditions and performance exists in the junior high schools of Orange County. The single greatest variable reflected in these data is variance in student population.

Implications: These statistics suggest that the quality of intermediate programs experienced in Orange County may depend upon the individual school. Efforts should be made to equalize programs and performance of the individual schools during the transition to middle schools.

FIGURE 5.6   Sample Baseline Summary of Existing Conditions in the Junior High Schools in District

Source: From *Making Middle Schools Work,* Fig. 5, p. 18, by J. Wiles and J. Bondi. Copyright © 1986, by Association for Supervision and Curriculum Development, Alexandria, VA.

- ☐ *Are the goals suggestive of involvement?* To be effective, goals must be stated in a way that allows individuals in the organization to see themselves as being able to achieve the objective.
- ☐ *Are the goals observable?* Can people in the organization see the results of their efforts and monitor progress toward the desired condition?

After surfacing, stating, and reviewing goal statements, the next major step is to determine if these goals are realistic. A preliminary needs assessment, which views both hard data and perceptions of key groups, tells planners what actually exists and what aspirations are present.

Although many districts conduct this assessment informally using internal staff, we believe that such a step must be formal and open to the public. Failure to reveal true conditions at this point will deter setting attainable goals and will prevent a consensus of shared goals and beliefs. Using data (numbers) of decision making, as opposed to philosophical statements, will promote meaningful curriculum change. Use of the coordinating committee to monitor an assessment and interpret the reality will provide assurances to the public that there are no hidden agendas. We also recommend a standing evaluation committee, with at least some

	Grade Level			
	6 (%)	7 (%)	8 (%)	Total (%)

Teaching Is Personal

	6 (%)	7 (%)	8 (%)	Total (%)
1. Student work is displayed prominently in the classroom.	37	25	12	25
2. Teacher/student-made bulletin boards rather than purchased displays are in use; ideally, bulletin boards are activity-oriented.	56	43	37	45
3. There is a seating pattern other than straight rows.	12	25	0	12
4. Living objects (plants, animals) are found in classroom.	43	68	25	45
5. Teacher moves about room freely while instructing.	50	75	43	56
6. Teacher calls students by first name without difficulty.	56	56	50	54
7. Constructive student-to-student communication is allowed during class.	18	25	6	14
8. Teacher frequently uses specific praise and encouraging comments.	25	43	25	31

Teaching Is Individualized

	6 (%)	7 (%)	8 (%)	Total (%)
9. Multilevel texts or materials are in use for instruction.	50	25	6	27
10. Some students are doing independent research or study in the classroom.	0	18	12	10
11. Learning centers are present in the room.	12	6	6	8
12. Students are working together in small groups on assignments.	6	6	0	4
13. Supplemental learning materials are available in the classroom for student use.	75	81	62	72
14. Student work folders are used by teacher for work management.	18	37	18	25
15. Skill continuum cards are kept on individual students.	12	6	12	10
16. Instructional activity allows for creative or multiple outcomes over which the student has some choice.	18	6	0	8

Teaching Skills Are Utilized

	6 (%)	7 (%)	8 (%)	Total (%)
17. Conferences one-to-one with student in the classroom.	50	50	25	41
18. Diversifies instructional approach or method during observations.	12	31	6	16
19. Uses small groups to increase learning.	0	25	0	8
20. Groups and re-groups students for instructional purposes.	0	18	6	8
21. Teaches at varying level of difficulty around an idea or concept.	18	12	0	10
22. Uses stylized learning materials for the group.	0	6	6	4
23. Uses real-life illustrations or examples during instruction.	25	25	25	25
24. References student interests or needs during instruction.	0	12	12	8
25. Maintains student discipline through nonpunitive behavior.	37	37	31	35
26. Uses student–teacher contracts for learning.	6	6	0	4
27. Works with other teachers across subject-matter lines.	0	6	6	4
28. Teaches general study skills while instructing.	18	12	12	14
29. Uses teacher-made interdisciplinary units during instruction.	0	0	6	2
30. Uses questioning techniques that encourage participation.	43	25	25	31

FIGURE 5.7 Middle School Instructional Checklist: Summary of Forty-Eight Classroom Visits in Eight Middle Schools

lay citizens, to provide continuous access to information from the coordinating committee.

Since most schools and districts have access to computers, the process of assessing and testing data is easier than it was in the past. Whether we are working with 500 pupils in a school or 50,000 pupils in a school district, the task is to gather data and look for patterns. Figures 5.8 and 5.9 show a typical questionnaire

---

Please rate each of the following statements in terms of *their importance to you for the middle school.* Choose the answer that tells how you feel about each one and blacken the bubble below the letter of that choice on the separate computer answer sheet. *Use a Number 2 pencil only.* Use the following key to show your feelings.

A	B	C	D	E
Very Important	Important	Fairly Important	Not Very Important	Not Important at All

1. Specialized guidance and counseling services should be available.
2. Both teachers and counselors should be involved in guidance.
3. Emphasis should be on group guidance.
4. Emphasis should be on individual guidance.
5. Each student should have at least one teacher who knows him/her personally.
6. Each student should meet with that teacher individually.
7. Opportunities for social activities for students (dances, athletic games, boosters, etc.) should be provided.
8. Club activities should be scheduled during the day to provide opportunities for group work in areas of common interest.
9. School-wide opportunities should be provided to help students develop good attitudes and standards for themselves.
10. The middle school program should be more child-centered than subject-matter-centered.
11. The middle school program should be a unique program bridging the gap between the elementary schools and the secondary schools.
12. Provisions should be made for students to explore their individual interests through exploratory elective courses.
13. Provisions should be made fo short-term exploratory/enrichment activities in addition to the regularly scheduled electives.
14. Behavior problems of students should be handled, when possible, by teachers and parents without the involvement of the administrators.
15. An alternative program to suspension should be provided for students having behavior problems (In-school Suspension Program).

FIGURE 5.8 A Sample Opinionnaire with Likert Scale Response

Source: From *Making Middle Schools Work,* Fig. 6, p. 19, by J. Wiles and J. Bondi. Copyright © 1986, by Association for Supervision and Curriculum Development, Alexandria, VA.

EAST BATON ROUGE PARISH SCHOOL BOARD

SURVEY OF: MIDDLE SCHOOL TEACHERS
GROUPING: OVERALL TOTALS

1.		%		2.		%		3.		%		4.		%		5.		%		6.		%
A	497	71.10		A	309	44.20		A	77	11.00		A	292	41.80		A	374	53.50		A	189	27.00
B	152	21.70		B	280	40.00		B	235	33.60		B	267	38.30		B	178	25.50		B	239	34.20
C	42	6.00		C	87	12.40		C	283	40.50		C	119	17.00		C	106	15.10		C	184	26.30
D	7	1.00		D	19	2.70		D	91	13.00		D	16	2.50		D	26	3.70		D	72	10.30
E	1	.10		E	4	.50		E	12	1.70		E	1	.10		E	14	2.00		E	14	2.00
M	1.37			M	1.75			M	2.61			M	1.81			M	1.75			M	2.26	

7.		%		8.		%		9.		%		10.		%		11.		%		12.		%
A	264	37.80		A	243	34.80		A	341	48.90		A	136	19.50		A	403	57.60		A	290	41.50
B	264	37.80		B	272	38.90		B	245	35.10		B	216	30.90		B	201	28.70		B	254	36.30
C	113	16.10		C	146	20.90		C	98	14.00		C	240	34.40		C	85	12.10		C	112	16.00
D	42	6.00		D	26	3.70		D	9	1.20		D	71	10.10		D	7	1.00		D	27	3.80
E	15	2.10		E	11	1.50		E	4	.50		E	34	4.80		E	3	.40		E	15	2.10
M	1.97			M	1.98			M	1.69			M	2.50			M	1.58			M	1.89	

13.		%		14.		%		15.		%		16.		%		17.		%		18.		%
A	192	27.50		A	166	23.30		A	292	41.80		A	559	79.90		A	284	40.60		A	292	41.80
B	275	39.50		B	225	32.30		B	189	27.10		B	108	15.40		B	212	30.30		B	281	40.20
C	164	23.50		C	158	22.70		C	112	16.00		C	24	3.40		C	113	16.10		C	109	15.60
D	43	6.10		D	82	11.70		D	49	7.00		D	1	.10		D	60	8.50		D	9	1.20
E	22	3.10		E	65	9.30		E	55	7.80		E	7	1.00		E	30	4.20		E	7	1.00
M	2.18			M	2.50			M	2.12			M	1.27			M	2.06			M	1.79	

19.		%		20.		%		21.		%		22.		%		23.		%		24.		%
A	369	52.80		A	197	28.30		A	262	37.50		A	150	22.80		A	494	70.60		A	306	43.80
B	236	33.80		B	239	34.40		B	263	37.60		B	249	35.60		B	161	23.00		B	267	38.20
C	74	10.50		C	196	28.20		C	134	19.10		C	204	29.10		C	35	5.00		C	106	15.10
D	13	1.80		D	45	6.40		D	28	4.00		D	57	8.10		D	6	.80		D	15	2.10
E	6	.80		E	17	2.40		E	11	1.50		E	29	4.10		E	3	.40		E	4	.50
M	1.64			M	2.20			M	1.94			M	2.35			M	1.37			M	1.77	

25.		%		26.		%		27.		%		28.		%		29.		%		30.		%
A	267	38.10		A	288	41.20		A	353	50.50		A	486	69.60		A	474	68.30		A	303	43.40
B	263	37.60		B	296	42.30		B	189	27.00		B	163	23.30		B	171	24.60		B	195	27.90
C	133	19.00		C	101	14.40		C	101	14.40		C	37	5.30		C	43	6.20		C	123	17.60
D	29	4.10		D	12	1.70		D	34	4.80		D	9	1.20		D	2	.20		D	53	7.60
E	7	1.00		E	2	.20		E	22	3.10		E	3	.40		E	3	.40		E	23	3.20
M	1.92			M	1.78			M	1.83			M	1.40			M	1.40			M	1.99	

31.		%		32.		%		33.		%		34.		%		35.		%		36.		%
A	221	31.70		A	151	21.70		A	196	28.00		A	267	38.40		A	264	37.90		A	363	52.20
B	192	27.50		B	237	34.10		B	212	30.30		B	185	26.50		B	271	38.90		B	226	32.50
C	141	20.20		C	181	26.00		C	165	23.60		C	134	19.30		C	128	18.40		C	84	12.00
D	82	11.70		D	80	11.50		D	76	10.80		D	65	9.30		D	16	2.30		D	13	1.80
E	60	8.60		E	45	6.40		E	50	7.10		E	43	6.10		E	16	2.30		E	9	1.20
M	2.38			M	2.47			M	2.39			M	2.18			M	1.92			M	1.67	

FIGURE 5.9 Sample Printout of Teacher Response

Source: Reprinted courtesy of East Baton Rouge School District.

that asks teacher position and the summary response of those teachers. Here, 94 percent of the teachers felt that the school should have a child-centered focus—certainly a strong enough consensus for planners to proceed.

When a philosophy has been established (by consensus) and documented (by numbers), and when recommendations for change are presented to the board by a representative body of citizens and groups, and when the superintendent and his or her staff have been responsible for coordinating all such activities, then planners can advance to the design stage.

One of the key points of such a process is that it keeps political interference in schools to a minimum, thus overcoming one of the largest problems for school planners in the last twenty-five years. If someone stands up at a parent–teacher association or school board meeting and objects to a book, a program, or a practice, and if the planners have done their homework, the intrusion can be countered if compelling data and hard facts are on hand.

In the Wiles-Bondi CMP model, the school board receives information from the coordinating committee in small bites rather than as a grand plan. Using semester or quarterly reports, the board is walked into change, much like a novice swimmer walks into the water. First, a philosophy is determined, then general goals and objectives are set, then the plan is endorsed by the public (evidenced by numbers) and decisions are made. As time goes on, a track record of progress is established, making it increasingly difficult for a new player to change the game. This gradual unfolding process is crucial because school board composition can change each year and superintendents may last less than four years. Establishing this track record prevents a worst-case scenario in which massive planning is undone by a change of players.

The needs assessment, because it is internal and seeks instructional direction, provides both macro and micro vantage points. This is in contrast to accreditation, which seeks endorsement, or surveys, which are often for consumption. Figure 5.10 outlines some of the problem areas that may be revealed by a comprehensive needs assessment. Figure 5.11, by contrast, reveals a larger pattern for planners. This display shows that the district is doing quite well until students reach the intermediate years, when achievement drops off sharply.

In the Wiles-Bondi model for curriculum management, a series of temporary committees (ad hoc) are used to process this information into school programs. A design committee, a program development committee, and a staff development committee are used to involve people in the process of curriculum work and to eliminate distortion of the process.

Design Stage

The design stage of the Wiles-Bondi CMP model is carried out by a new, temporary committee whose job is to define the goals for the school or district in broad strokes that establish a framework for subsequent curriculum work. This critical committee needs to be visionary, but it must work within the parameters of both the endorsed philosophy of the board and the realities of data gathered. We provide examples of this process for both a district and a school.

1. **Improvement of Basic Academic Achievement**
   9 Pupils perform below real ability
   9 Students not prepared for grade level
   9 Students consider curriculum irrelevant
   9 Instructional materials are too difficult
   9 Advanced course offerings not available in some subjects
   9 Low standardized test scores
   9 Students do poorly on daily work
   9 Graduates seem unprepared for job market or higher education
   9 High rate of student failure
   9 Students cannot apply basic skills

2. **Continued Commitment to Reduction of Racial Isolation**
   9 Student polarization along racial lines
   9 Division among faculty along racial lines
   9 Student-teacher antagonism along racial lines
   9 Racially motivated hostility in the community
   9 Unequal status roles for minorities in curriculum materials
   9 Transported students feel unwelcome
   9 Racial groups establish certain areas of the school as their territory
   9 School lacks unified approach to reducing racial isolation
   9 Parents of transported students are not involved in the school
   9 Avoidance of problem situation by school personnel

3. **Improvement in Staff Attendance and Continued Upgrading of Staff Performance**
   A. Attendance
       9 Frequent staff absences
       9 Habitual staff tardiness
       9 Patterns of staff absences and tardiness

   B. Performance
       9 Low expectations for student achievement and behavior
       9 Apparent lack of productive teaching techniques and methods
       9 Instruction not geared to student needs
       9 Resistance to progressive change and professional growth
       9 Learning experiences seem passive
       9 Lack of positive learning environment
       9 Poor classroom management
       9 Lack of staff cooperative effort

FIGURE 5.10   Some Symptoms of School Problems

4. Improvement in School Morale and Community Relations

A. School Morale

    9   School administration viewed as cold and detached from student concerns

    9   Administrator and staff feel isolated; lack of mutual support

    9   Low status of some subject areas in teacher's view

    9   Extensive vandalism

    9   Negative student attitude toward learning

    9   Students are uninvolved, unmotivated

    9   Lack of harmonious staff relationships

B. Community Relations

    9   Inadequate efforts to involve students in community

    9   Lack of parent interest

    9   Lack of teacher involvement in the community served by the school

    9   Principals and teachers do not try to involve parents and community in the school program

    9   Lack of communication between school and community

5. Student Attendance, Behavior, and Discipline

A. Attendance

    9   Frequent truancy

    9   Frequent tardiness

    9   Frequent class cutting

    9   High absentee rate

    9   High dropout rate

    9   High rate of student mobility

B. Behavior and Discipline

    9   Vandalism

    9   Violence

    9   Disruptive classroom behavior

    9   Use of illegal drugs

    9   Disruptive behavior on campus or playground

    9   Frequent referrals to office for disciplinary action

    9   Disruption caused by outsiders

    9   Excessive noise level and confusion throughout the school

    9   Disrespect for authority

FIGURE 5.10 *Continued*

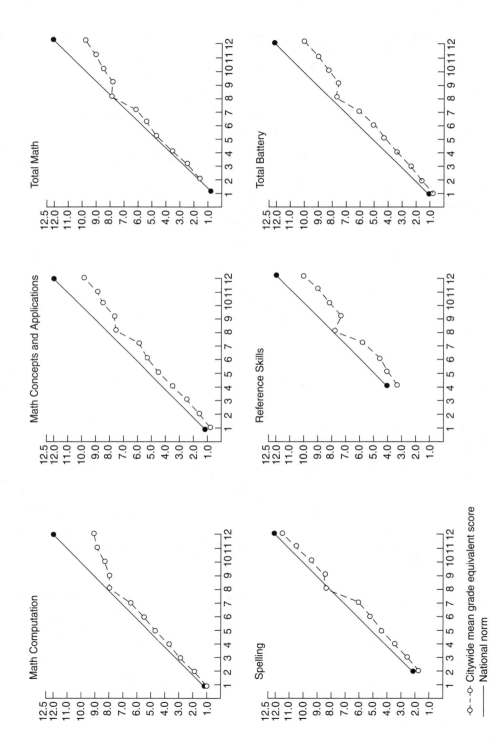

FIGURE 5.11 Graphs Showing the Relationship of Local District Achievement to National Norms by Grade Levels

Source: St. Louis School District One. Used by permission.

Curriculum Management Plan—District Example.   Our district example comes from Dade County in Miami, Florida, a district that undertook the largest curriculum change effort ever in American education. Under our direction, fifty-two schools housing nearly 60,000 pupils were converted to a middle school design over a five-year period (1987–1992). The effort began with a broad view of what students may need for life in the twenty-first century (see Figure 5.12) and the role of the middle grades in meeting those needs.

Once these broad strokes were passed to the design committee, their task was to provide more definition. Figure 5.13 provides an overview of the desired program, followed by a definitional statement concerning the critical elements of the desired program in Figure 5.14. In Figure 5.15, the organizational schema of the new program is outlined, and in Figure 5.16 one area—exploratory programs—is given further definition. Figure 5.17 illustrates the kind of thinking skills that will be taught to students across all subject areas.

As the program design is given form by the design committee, certain tasks begin to emerge, which will be handled by the new program development com-

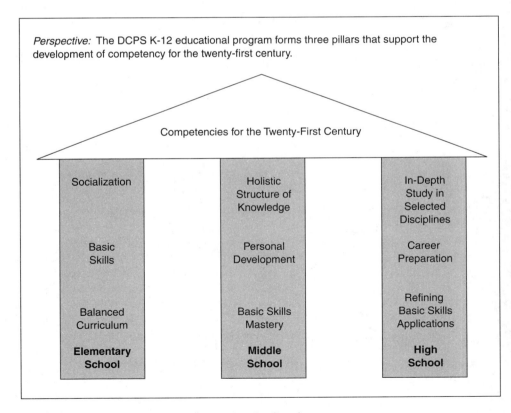

FIGURE 5.12   Generic Competencies Outlined

Source: Middle School Design Report, Dade County Public Schools, June 1989.

mittees or the staff development committee. A critical part of the Wiles–Bondi CMP model is that the function of the general program design (design committee) is separated from the specific development of programs (by the program development committees). This "fading away" of one committee, and the assumption of more detailed work by another committee, prevents "special pleading" by members of the design group for their subject area. The program development committees must stay within the design parameters, and their work is reviewed by the coordinating committee against the criteria of compliance that the board adopted.

Curriculum Management Plan—School Example. Our school example concerns a common move in the late 1980s—the establishment of state-mandated kindergarten programs. Such a program would come to the district from the state

FIGURE 5.13 Overview of Middle School Parameters

Source: Middle School Design Report, Dade County Public Schools, June 1989.

I. **Philosophy**
   A. Child-centered
   B. Holistic knowledge structure is developed
   C. Thinking skills are priority goals
   D. Safety is essential
   E. Students' developmental needs are important

II. **Curriculum**
   A. Academic excellence/social competence
      1. Academic core
      2. Exploration and developmental programs
   B. Personal development
   C. Mastery of continuous learning skills

III. **Organization**
   A. Interdisciplinary teams
   B. Advisement program
   C. Block scheduling and flexible scheduling within blocks
   D. Team planning and shared decision making
   E. Exploratory and developmental experiences
      1. Elective classes
      2. Wheels and exploration credits
      3. Mini-courses
      4. Clubs, activities, interest groups, intramurals
   F. Integrated curriculum
   G. In-service education and professional development

IV. **Implementing Strategies** (delivery systems)
   A. Cooperative learning
   B. Interdisciplinary teaching
   C. Learning styles
   D. Student services and career planning systems
   E. Home–school partnerships and communications

The Critical Elements Summarized

The middle grades education program has important functions different from the elementary and high school programs. Middle school students (transescents) have special needs that identify them as a unique group in the K–12 learning continuum. There are specific philosophical approaches, educational strategies, and school organizations that are effective during this period. Twelve critical elements are needed in the DCPS middle school.

1. The core of the middle school education program is based on the following beliefs:
   - Every child can learn
   - Middle school is a key time where students learn that the various disciplines and subjects are all related to humanity's search for understanding
   - Learners must feel physically and psychologically safe
   - Thinking skills instruction is a middle school responsibility
   - Every child's individual differences must be respected

2. To accomplish its mission, the middle school curriculum has three interwoven and connected threads. They are the pursuit of
   - Academic excellence as a way to achieve social competence in a complex, technological society
   - Self-understanding and personal development
   - Continuous-learning skills

3. The traditional academic core must be taught in a way that ensures that our students recognize
   - The relationships between such disciplines as math, language arts, science, and social studies and can transfer learning from one discipline to another
   - That their exploratory and developmental experiences are related to the academic core and are a way to broaden each individual's insights and potential for personal growth

4. The middle school curriculum contains a variety of exploratory experiences (into disciplines beyond the academic core), which will enable students to
   - Recognize, through exploratory experiences, that there are a multitude of routes to take to understanding and successful independence

FIGURE 5.14   Definitional Statement about Critical Elements of the Middle School Program

and be "fit" into an existing conception of early childhood programming. A sketch of one such program, its design, and some of the implications for management follows.

Plan for Establishing a Kindergarten

☐ *Population.* Approximately three hundred students, ages 3 to 5, and 6-year-olds who do not have the readiness for the first grade.

☐ *Program concept.* The kindergarten program will be divided into two distinct components. An A.M. program will be provided, with a basic instructional format that will match the individualized and continuous progress concepts. The major focus of the A.M. program will be readiness

- Sample fields they may wish to pursue in greater depth in high school or beyond
- Develop a realistic overview of talents, aptitudes, and interests
- Begin to develop talents and special interests in a manner that provides balance and perspective

5. Thinking skills expand in scope and nature during the middle grade years. While problem-solving strategies need to be part of the K–12 learning continuum, formal instruction in critical and creative thinking skills is essential in the middle grades program.

6. Middle school students need someone to whom they can relate as an advisor and guide during the transescent period. Middle schools provide such advisors and ensure that advisors and advisees have time to work on the developmental issues of early adolescence.

7. Middle schools integrate academic knowledge and skills through use of interdisciplinary teaching teams. The structure of such teams may vary widely, but the essential elements are common planning time and teaching the same group of students.

8. The teachers of the academic core and the exploratory/developmental programs work together to foster transfer of learning from one discipline to another, enhance application of basic skills, and to help students develop a "big picture" on the scope and nature of our efforts to understand ourselves and the environment.

9. The exploratory program is provided in a variety of ways in addition to formal classes. These may include mini-courses, clubs, special activities, and interest group meetings built into the school day at regular intervals.

10. In-service education and methods for teachers to share insights and information are an important part of the middle school conversion.

11. Instructional delivery strategies used at the middle grades allow for the developmental traits of the students. Cooperative learning strategies, accommodation of different learning styles, recognition of attention span limitations, and understanding the transescents' preoccupation with personal development issues are all needed in the middle grade program.

12. The middle school must develop a closer relationship with the parents and community and serve as a guide to the student's departure from childhood and embarkation on the route to adulthood and citizenship.

FIGURE 5.14   *Continued*

Source: Middle School Design Report, Dade County Public Schools, June 1989.

for the more formal education program to follow; the specific objectives will be to develop social skills, motor skills, self-direction, self-esteem, and communication. During the P.M. program, a child-care service will be provided for those students whose parents both work away from the home. The program will follow an action format that will have little structure. Focus will be primarily on socialization.

☐ *Areas of learning.* Socialization, school readiness, independence, motor skills, communication.

☐ *Program organization.* The student population will be divided into instructional units of thirty students each and will be comprised of students of

III. Organization of the Middle School

A middle school is organized so that students experience the integrated nature of our knowledge base and have opportunities to grow and expand.

The organization is flexible so that teachers have many options in meeting student needs and in implementing the mandated content and skills curriculum set forth by the school board and state board of education.

The following diagram illustrates the relationship between the parameters that are essential to middle school organization.

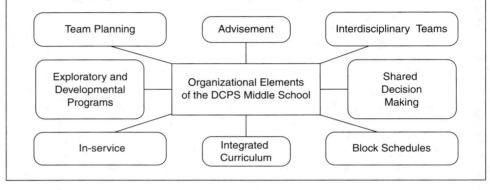

FIGURE 5.15   Organization of the Middle School Program
Source: Middle School Design Report, Dade County Public Schools, June 1989.

varying ages, but with similar maturation characteristics. The formal program will be scheduled from 8:00 A.M. to 12:00 noon, with a breakfast and lunch program provided. Students who are eligible for the child-care program will remain at school until 3:00 P.M. The kindergarten program will operate five days a week, twelve months of the year when year-round school is in session.

☐ *Staff organization.* The staff will be organized to complement the instructional unit approach. One teacher and three instructional aides will work as a team in each unit.

☐ *Staff requirement.* The kindergarten school staff will consist of one program coordinator, ten teachers, thirty instructional aides, one school nurse, and one secretary/bookkeeper.

☐ *Teaching strategies.* Some examples of teaching strategies to be used by the kindergarten staff are role playing; field trips; educational games; regular planned rest; rhythmical activities; positive reinforcement; creative expression; peer teaching; and exploration of self, school, and community.

☐ *Facilities.* The kindergarten school will use the cafetorium and the auditorium located at the current high school site. Both buildings need remodeling in order to be adequate for an early childhood program. Floors and restrooms of the auditorium need remodeling; lighting, controlled air, and carpeting should be updated.

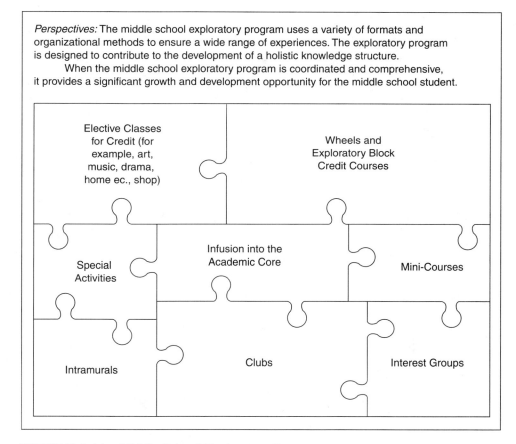

Perspectives: The middle school exploratory program uses a variety of formats and organizational methods to ensure a wide range of experiences. The exploratory program is designed to contribute to the development of a holistic knowledge structure.

When the middle school exploratory program is coordinated and comprehensive, it provides a significant growth and development opportunity for the middle school student.

Elective Classes for Credit (for example, art, music, drama, home ec., shop)

Wheels and Exploratory Block Credit Courses

Special Activities

Infusion into the Academic Core

Mini-Courses

Intramurals

Clubs

Interest Groups

FIGURE 5.16   Middle School Exploratory Program

Source: Middle School Design Report, Dade County Public Schools, June 1989.

Using such a sketch of the program to be organized, management planners can then begin to translate the needs into the resources needed to implement such a plan. In Figure 5.18, for example, the financial implication of such a program for three hundred students is calculated in rough form.

Implementation Stage

After clarifying the goals and objectives and setting the parameters of programs within an overarching structure, the next curriculum task is to coordinate the many efforts needed to implement such programs. In our opinion, this is where 90 percent of all curriculum work fails. In the future, curriculum specialists will need managerial skills to succeed in curriculum development. Under the Wiles–Bondi CMP model, efforts now shift to the implementation phase.

C. Teaching skills needed for continuous learning in school and in life are the joint responsibility of the entire educational staff.

The middle school seeks to instill mastery of the basic communication and mathematical skills taught in elementary school.

Due to the emergence of abstract thinking abilities during the transescence period, critical and creative thinking skills are infused through the curriculum and taught as specific skills.

Social cooperation skills and their application to problem solving are infused throughout the curriculum.

Perspective: Middle school students develop a unified set of skills that promote continuous learning, as the diagram illustrates.

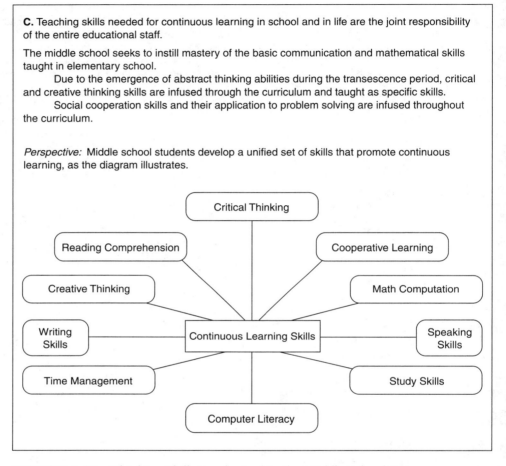

FIGURE 5.17   Thinking Skills Emphasized in the Middle School Program
Source: Middle School Design Report, Dade County Public Schools, June 1989.

One of the first tasks for the planner is get the "big picture" in order. This requires that a time frame be established and that a natural order of development be decided on. All work from here on will be a refinement of basic concepts and programs into instructional prescriptions; the project can be envisioned as a basic distance-rate-time problem with resources determining the rate. If resources are interrupted, for example, the project will simply take longer. Figure 5.19 shows the outline of steps in one such project.

The process of actually developing the curriculum under the Wiles-Bondi model falls to subject area subcommittees and special groups who are assigned to develop their areas. Math and science, for example, would define their areas anew in terms of the parameters of the design report to the board. Standards would be formed to give further definition to the subject area (see Figure 5.20). In areas that teach skills, the same process would occur (see Figure 5.21). These standards would

Item	Cost	
	Start-up	**Continuing**
1. Personnel		
a. 10 Regular teachers		$300,000
b. 30 Instructional aides		300,000
c. 1 Program coordinator		25,000
d. 1 Secretary/bookkeeper		12,000
2. Fixed Charges		
Social Security and teacher retirement @ 15% of $637,000		95,500
3. Materials		
Continuous cost—10 teachers @ $1,000/teacher	20,000	10,000
4. Equipment		
Cots, chairs, tables, learning center equipment, playground equipment	30,000	4,000
5. Facilities		
Renovation of the cafeteria and auditorium on the present high school site	150,000	
6. Maintenance and Operation of Plant		
10 teachers @ $4,000/teacher		40,000
7. Staff Development		
a. Consultant honorarium and travel	3,000	15,000
b. Materials		800
Subtotal	$203,000	$802,350
Total Cost of Kindergarten School Program		$1,005,350

FIGURE 5.18   Cost of Proposed Kindergarten

further establish purpose and guarantee that other areas could see the contribution of this part to the whole. Subsequent action plans in each area would help planners understand the logistical needs of the area to meet its goals. The collection of all action plans would form the bulk of the implementation plan.

General administrative standards would also be established to envelope the program areas and service them. Among concerns would be areas such as grouping and use of time (Figure 5.22), facilities (Figure 5.23), and staff development (Figure 5.24). When these concerns are wedded to the program standards and identified needs of specific areas, an overall calendar of activity and budget can be developed.

The calendar of events is a projection of what is going to occur, when it will occur, how much it will cost, and what is expected (in terms of the overall program intention) of this component. Calendars (Figure 5.25) and time lines (Figure 5.26) usually follow next, which lead to products of activity. These products are

Analysis Stage
1. Identify Denver Public Schools' philosophy
2. Identify board policy relative to middle schools
3. Superintendent (public) statement on middle schools
4. Outline time frame for implementation
5. Form centralized coordinating group
6. Delineate tasks and appoint subcommittees
7. Develop "definition" of Denver middle schools
8. Structure awareness/orientation campaign
   a. administrators
   b. teacher groups

Design Stage
9. Translate philosophy into goal statements
10. Project preliminary budget/resource base
11. Prioritize goal statements
12. Translate goal statements to objectives format
13. Block out 3–5 year plan for implementation
14. Establish management/information system to monitor progress of implementation (external audit)
15. Establish evaluation targets, time, responsibilities, resources; identify baseline data needed
16. Conduct needs assessment
17. Develop final management system (PERT)

Implementation or Management Stage
18. Provide advanced organizers (simple plan) to all interested persons
19. Provide each school with resource kits, glossaries, data bank from needs assessment (local planning/decision-making data)
20. Form teams in each school to serve as
    a. study group for mapping curriculum/skills
    b. planning group/house plan
    c. team/cooperative teaching unit
21. Provide preliminary staff development (demonstration teaching) in all schools on
    a. advisor/advisee program
    b. continuous progress curriculums
    c. team planning and teaching
22. Require school-by-school development plan including curriculum, staff development, evaluation, community involvement
23. Provide local budget supplement based on plan

Evaluation Stage
24. Conduct formative evaluation (external audit) every 6 weeks to monitor management outline
25. Conduct major review after 6 months—revise time line, goals, needs, and so on
26. Develop master evaluation plan (sum of all schools) for 3-year period

FIGURE 5.19   Comprehensive Plan of the Denver Public Schools

Source: Author's notes, Denver, Colorado.

Mathematics

The mathematics program provides for the sequential development of skills that enable students to comprehend our number system, to perform mathematical calculations, and to use mathematical thinking in solving problems.

_____ A skills profile card is maintained on each student.
_____ Diagnostic/prescriptive teaching techniques are used.
_____ Opportunities are provided to practice creative problem solving and computational skills in daily living situations.
_____ A variety of diagnostic test results are utilized to meet the needs of the students.
_____ Instruction is provided at different levels of achievement and understanding.
_____ Opportunities are provided to develop computer literacy.

Science

The science program reflects the character of science, encourages students to explore in order to increase scientific and technical knowledge, including computer literacy, and creates an awareness of the problems associated with science. The program ensures that each student can investigate and learn at his/her own level of understanding and guarantees that the scope of learning be broad enough to encompass contemporary issues of the scientific domain.

_____ The science program is exploratory in nature.
_____ The program is laboratory-centered.
_____ Scientific methods are utilized.
_____ Contemporary issues discussed in daily newspapers are emphasized.
_____ Scientific problems facing our community today, such as environmental problems, air pollution, and water pollution, are addressed.
_____ Instruction is provided at different levels of achievement and understanding.
_____ The range of topics studied by students includes the major areas of science.
_____ Computers and appropriate software are made available whenever possible.

FIGURE 5.20   Subject Area Standards

chronicled in regular public board reports that tell everyone where the school or district is in its pursuit of this educational program.

Evaluation Stage

The CMP emphasizes evaluation from the beginning to support the curriculum development cycle. Evaluation is used in at least five ways:

1. To make explicit the rationale of the instructional program as a basis for deciding which aspects of the program should be evaluated for effectiveness and what types of data should be gathered
2. To collect data upon which judgments about effectiveness can be formulated
3. To analyze data and draw conclusions

Curriculum Area: Computer Education

Purpose: The overall goal in the educational use of computers is to integrate computer literacy into all content areas of the middle school curriculum, thus providing an additional tool for interdisciplinary curriculum development. In addition, elective computer courses in application and programming provide for personal development and the reinforcement of essential skills.

Program Descriptors

Program Descriptors	Status		
	Yes	No	Action Plan to Achieve
1. Microcomputers, either permanently located in all classrooms or on mobile carts, are available for classroom use.			
2. Additional mobile computers will be available to move into classrooms when necessary or to develop a mini lab when desired.			
3. Each school will have at least two qualified full-time computer education teachers.			
4. Each school will have at least two complete computer labs containing a minimum of sixteen microcomputers and have a ratio of two students per computer. Each lab shall include necessary computer-system hardware, software, and peripheral equipment to meet current and future trends and developments. The complete computer lab will consist of necessary space, lighting, seating, air-cooling system, electrical system, and security, plus access to telecommunications.			
5. Daily lab schedules should include time set aside for independent student use.			
6. All students in grades 6 and 7 will be scheduled into one of the computer labs for a minimum of three hours a week in order to meet the state requirements for computer literacy.			
7. A minimum of two computers with needed peripherals will be located in the teachers' work area for teacher use (for grade recording, software review, word processing, and so on).			

Note: The Computer Literacy Program for the 6th and 7th grades should be interdisciplinary and taught through the team concept.

Both the media center and administrative offices need computerization. These noninstructional needs should be addressed by the appropriate middle school ad hoc committee.

Essential Skills: (Skills reinforced regardless of discipline or program spiral)

Reading	Writing	Problem solving	Thinking	Computation or calculation
Listening	Vocabulary	Decision making	Computer literacy	Motor

FIGURE 5.21   Mapping Worksheet with Standards in Skill Areas

The organization of the middle school is such that a smooth transition may be made from the self-contained classroom of the elementary school to the departmentalized high school. Provision is made to meet the unique social, academic, and personal needs of children as they emerge from childhood into adolescence. Flexibility in time utilization, and in the grouping of students and teachers, is provided to allow for balanced instruction.

1. Teacher grouping
   - Teachers are organized into interdisciplinary teams to provide instruction in the core subjects of reading, language arts, science, mathematics, and social studies.
   - The interdisciplinary team serves a common group of students.
   - The interdisciplinary team controls a block of time.
   - The members of the interdisciplinary team are assigned classrooms in close proximity to one another.
   - The members of the interdisciplinary team have a common planning period.
   - A member of the interdisciplinary team shall be designated as team leader.

2. Student grouping
   - The students are organized by grade levels.
   - Each grade level is divided into teams of approximately 90 to 135 students as is compatible with the interdisciplinary instructional team.
   - Provision is made for instruction at differing ability levels, at differing skills levels, and in different interest areas.

3. Time
   - Provision is made for a flexible daily time schedule.
   - A block of time equivalent to five 45-minute time segments (225 minutes) is assigned to the interdisciplinary team for academic instruction.
   - A 90-minute block of time is provided for exploration and physical education activities.

Proposed Middle School Student Schedule

25 min. A/A	225 min. Academic Block	25 min. Lunch	45 min. Enrich.	45 min. P.E.	25 min. Passing

The day schedule contains:
   7—45-minute periods
   1—25-minute A/A period (Advisory Activities)
   1—25-minute lunch period
   passing times (total of 25 minutes)

Total student day of 6 hours, 30 minutes

FIGURE 5.22 Proposed General Organization Standards

Source: From *Making Middle Schools Work,* Fig. 12, p. 26, by J. Wiles and J. Bondi. Copyright © 1986 by the Association for Supervision and Curriculum Development, Alexandria, VA.

Proposed Facilities Standards

The instructional program and the organizational pattern of the middle school dictate the facility requirements. The facilities should allow for varied instructional experiences, support the middle school concept, and meet the personnel and support-staff needs.

1. Essential considerations
    - ☐ Increased attractiveness by use of color schemes and graphics
    - ☐ Adequate instructional space and equipment for each curricular program
    - ☐ Clustered interdisciplinary team instruction rooms
    - ☐ Team planning/work/conference area
    - ☐ Flexible classroom space
    - ☐ Computer instruction area
    - ☐ Alternative education area
    - ☐ Clinic area
    - ☐ Closeable restroom stalls for boys and girls
    - ☐ Adequate area for physical education and recreational activities
    - ☐ Appropriate private shower and changing facilities for boys and girls
    - ☐ Appropriate exceptional education/student services

2. Desirable considerations
    - ☐ In-house television capability
    - ☐ Adequate acoustical treatment (ceiling tile, floor covering, and so on)

Note: Existing science facilities are clustered, which poses difficulties in the adjacent team room concept. It is suggested that the sixth-grade science program be taught in convenient classrooms, which are equipped with a water source, portable lab facility, storage, and student stations at tables. Seventh- and eighth-grade science classes should be taught in existing science rooms at the expense of being removed from the team area.

Any new facility or any major renovation of an existing facility should address the decentralization of science rooms.

FIGURE 5.23   Middle School Facility Needs

4. To make decisions based on the data
5. To implement the decisions to improve the instructional program

These questions need to be asked prior to setting up an evaluation design to monitor curriculum development:

- ☐ What are the criteria for evaluating the program?
- ☐ What type of evaluation do we want to conduct?
- ☐ What constitutes good research?

These questions are addressed in the following section.

Individual Professional Development Summary		Incentives	Source	Delivery
Sec. I Basic Certification Information	From Personnel Records	• Required for hiring and tenure		• Preservice college courses
Sec. II Basic Required In-Service Growth and Development of Preadolescents Middle School Philosophy and Curriculum Fundamental and Specialized Instructional Strategies for Preadolescents Counseling, Guidance, and Human Relations Teaching of Basic Skills Teaming and Team Teaching	• 6 required 4-hr. courses (over 3 yrs. on release time) • Introduction courses to each of the 6 basic competency categories • 25 Professional Development points each (150 for teachers, 225 for administrators) 3 additional for Administrations	• Professional Development points awarded • On paid contract time (release) • Provided free of charge • Required by district for Middle School Specialist designation	• Needs assessment • Staff development committee	Location: on-site (e.g., teaming); area offices (e.g., philosophy); T.O.R.C. (e.g., basic skills); other central locations Time: release time (partial day—sub provided) on rotating basis by content area, by grade release time (full in-service day—school closed) by school, by position
Sec. III Renewal In-Service _____ _____ _____	• Allows in-depth in any of the 6 basic Competency Categories • Specialist designation requires 6 basic (150 points) + 3 add'l (75 pts.) • Minimum of 150 points (6 courses) every 3 yrs. for Specialist renewal • Fills in specific skills needed by individual (self and principal assessment)	• P.O. points awarded • Required by district for Specialist designation and renewal • Provided free of charge • Release time • College credit • Guarantees better choice of openings • State certification?	• Needs assessment • Staff development committee • Individual skill assessment profile	Location: T.O.R.C.; other central locations Time: release time (see above) evenings (college credit)

FIGURE 5.24   Comprehensive Middle School Staff Development Design

Source: Pinellas County Schools, Clearwater, Florida.

Individual Professional Development Summary	Incentives	Source	Delivery
(Completion of Sections I–III provides District Middle School Specialist Designation)			
Sec. IV Supplemental In-Service • Additional courses as needed or desired • Recorded on I.S.P. check-list	• College credit (tuition paid if for state certification) or • Extra P.D.U. points or • Stipend w/minimum P.D. points	• Individual skill assessment profile • School improvement	Location: on-site (school based req., activity tailored to school; T.O.R.C.; area offices; colleges Time: evenings (w/stipend P.D.U. or college credit); staff meetings; team meetings
Professional Self-Development	• Self-growth • Available, convenient, and free of charge	• Requests for service • Identified needs	Location: central location; I.S.S. Time: evenings, Saturdays, summer
Sec. V Program Development/Training/Consulting Experience Program Development _____ Contracts _____ Internal Presentations _____ External Presentations _____	• Opportunity for release time to develop special programs/units • Release time for presentation • Preparation time • Presentation time (if after school) • Experience, pride, broadening of skills		

FIGURE 5.24 *Continued*

Source: Pinellas County Schools, Clearwater, Florida.

FIGURE 5.25 Middle School Staff Development and Meetings Schedule

Source: From *Making Middle Schools Work*, Fig. 21, p. 36, by J. Wiles and J. Bondi. Copyright © 1986 by the Association for Supervision and Curriculum Development, Alexandria, VA.

	August			September								October							November							December				
	22	26	27	5	6	12	13	19	20	26	27	10	11	17	18	24	25	31	1	7	8	14	15	21	22	5	6	10	12	13
Teachers																														
Leadership Group						1					1	4	2			3		3	4	8	5	9	6	10	7		8			
Principals										1							2						3							
Assistant Principals				1								2						3			4									
Management Team	1									2			2												3					
School Visits (as needed)						1					2															5	6	7	8	
School Board																												1		
Coordinating Committee																1			3							2				
Staff Development														1		1														
Grant																1					2		2				3			
Evaluation Committee										1																5				
Program Consultants				1								2						3				4								
Public Relations Committee							1																	2						

Task	Time Line	Responsible Person(s)
23. Coordinating Committee meeting three	March 31, 1998	Paul Bell

24. Progress Report I to board
  a. Results of needs assessment
  b. Tasks completed
  c. Tasks pending
  d. Evaluation or progress of year one implementation
	June, 1998	Joseph Fernandez
		Paul Bell
		J.L. DeChurch
		Wiles-Bondi

25. Summer training of staff. This will lead to middle school endorsement and internal certification.	June–August 1998	Kenneth Walker Karen Dreyfuss Margaret Petersen Wiles-Bondi
26. Clinical assistance-visitation to pilot schools	Ongoing 1997–2000	Wiles-Bondi District Staff Area Superintendents and Staff
27. Curriculum development, refinement of middle school subject areas	Spring, 1998–Ongoing	J.L. DeChurch
28. Development of middle school intramural program	Summer, 1998	District Staff
29. Piloting of intramural program	Fall, 1998	District Staff
30. Coordinating Committee meeting four	October, 1998	Paul Bell
31. Midpoint assessment/sharing of team implementation in second group of middle schools	November, 1998	Wiles-Bondi Team Leaders
32. Coordinating Committee meeting five	December, 1998	Paul Bell
34. Team Fair two	March 30, 1999	Wiles-Bondi Middle School Principals

FIGURE 5.26   Time Lines of Activity

Source: Dade County Public Schools, Miami, Florida.

Criteria for Evaluating Instructional Programs.   The first consideration in the evaluation of instructional programs must be the purposes for which the instructional program is being planned. Whether these are the objectives stated for a particular lesson in a classroom or the general educational goals for a school or district, planning occurs on the basis of the purposes defined. As stated earlier, we believe that a good instructional program must adequately reflect the aims of the school or agency from which they come. At the school level, the faculty, students, and parents need to define comprehensive educational goals, and all curriculum opportunities offered at the school should be planned with reference to one or more of those goals.

A good instructional program must provide for continuity of learning experiences. Students should progress through a particular program on the basis of their achievement, not on the basis of how much time they have spent in the program. Instructional programs in a school that are planned over several years lend themselves to better vertical progress. Continuity of learning experiences within a program dictates that a relationship between disciplines be established. Core, or interdisciplinary, programs allow students to see purpose and meaning in their total instructional program.

All principles of learning need to be drawn upon in selecting an instructional program. Programs that rely solely on operant conditioning as a psychological base for teaching neglect the important theories of Combs, Piaget, and others. All of those associated in education understand the difficulty of putting psychological principles into practice. A careful analysis of new programs can reveal the psychological bases of those programs.

Programs selected should make maximum provision for the development of each learner. Any program selected should include a wide range of opportunities for individuals of varying abilities, interests, and needs. Each child is characterized by his or her own pattern of development. Youngsters are curious, explorative, and interested in many things. An instructional program must promote individual development in students rather than make them conform to a hypothetical standard.

An instructional program must provide for clear focus. Whether a program is organized around separate subjects such as history or science, or around related subjects such as social studies, it is important that whoever selects the program knows which dimensions to pursue and which relationships of facts and ideas should stand out and which should be submerged. The problem for those who are reviewing programs is to decide which element of the program is the center of organization. Instructional programs may be organized around life problems, content topics, interests, or experiences. In selecting instructional programs, however, the organizing focus must also be examined to see which topics are emphasized, which details are relevant, and which relationships are significant.

A good instructional program should be well planned and must include a built-in process for evaluation. Steps need to be defined that would include a periodic assessment of the success of the program and a continuous process for reviewing and updating the program.

In the Wiles–Bondi CMP model, evaluation is built in from the beginning by establishing a standing committee to review and report on progress. As stated earlier, this committee includes several laypersons, which helps allay suspicions, and its purpose is to communicate all results. Assumed in the design of if–then logic is that if the program is built correctly, it will produce the results desired. If such results are not forthcoming, the program should be redesigned.

While many types of evaluation exist, we find the following outline of evaluations, by D. L. Stufflebeam, to be a useful paradigm:

A. Focusing the Evaluation
   1. Identify the major level(s) of decision making to be served, for example, local, state, or national.

    2. For each level of decision making, project the decision situations to be served and describe each one in terms of its locus, focus, timing, and composition of alternatives.

    3. Define criteria for each decision situation by specifying variables for measurement and standards for use in the judgment of alternatives.

    4. Define policies within which the evaluation must operate.

B. Collection of Information
    1. Specify the source of the information to be collected.
    2. Specify the instruments and methods for collecting the needed information.
    3. Specify the sampling procedure to be employed.
    4. Specify the conditions and schedule for information collection.

C. Organization of Information
    1. Specify a format for the information that is to be collected.
    2. Specify a means for coding, organizing, storing, and retrieving information.

D. Analysis of Information
    1. Specify the analytical procedures to be employed.
    2. Specify a means for performing the analysis.

E. Reporting of Information
    1. Define the audiences for the evaluation reports.
    2. Specify means for providing information to the audiences.
    3. Specify the format for evaluation reports and/or reporting sessions.
    4. Schedule the reporting information.

F. Administration of the Evaluation
    1. Summarize the evaluation schedule.
    2. Define staff and resource requirements and plans for meeting these requirements.
    3. Specify means for meeting policy requirements for conduct of the evaluation.
    4. Evaluate the potential of the evaluation design for providing information that is valid, reliable, credible, timely, and pervasive.
    5. Specify and schedule means for periodic updating of the evaluation design.
    6. Provide a budget for the total evaluation program.[2]

Another useful resource for curriculum leaders responsible for designing evaluation systems is a classification outline developed by the Phi Delta Kappa National Study Committee on Evaluation. This outline presents four types of evaluation commonly found in schools and breaks them down according to their objective, method, and relationship to the decision-making (DM) process:

    1. Context Evaluation

        Objective: To define the operation context, to identify and assess needs in the context, and to identify and delineate problems underlying the needs.

        Method: By describing individually and in relevant perspectives the major subsystems of the context; by comparing actual and intended inputs and outputs of the subsystems; and by analyzing possible causes of discrepancies between actualities and intentions.

        Relation to DM Process: For deciding upon the setting to be served, the goals associated with meeting needs and the objectives associated with solving problems, that is, for planning needed changes.

2. Input Evaluation

Objective: To identify and assess system capabilities, available input strategies, and designs for implementing strategies.

Method: By describing and analyzing available human and material resources, solution strategies, and procedural designs for relevance, feasibility, and economy in the course of action to be taken.

Relation to DM Process: For selecting sources of support, solution strategies, and procedural designs, that is, for programming change activities.

3. Process Evaluation

Objective: To identify or predict, in process, defects in procedural design or its implementation, and to maintain a record of procedural events and activities.

Method: By monitoring the activity's potential procedural barriers and remaining alert to unanticipated ones.

Relation to DM Process: For implementing and refining the program design and procedure, that is, for effecting process control.

4. Product Evaluation

Objective: To relate outcome information to objectives and to context, input, and process information.

Method: By defining operationally and measuring criteria associated with the objectives, by comparing these measurements with predetermined standards or comparative bases, and by interpreting the outcome in terms of recorded input and process information.

Relation to DM Process: For deciding to continue, terminate, modify, or refocus a change activity, and for linking the activity to other major phases of the change process, that is, for evolving change activities.[3]

When developing comprehensive programs, curriculum workers may wish to go beyond academic achievement as a goal for education. We see public education as no less than a program for future citizens; therefore, curriculum workers should recognize the need for the physical, social, intellectual, and emotional growth of students while under the auspices of the school. Areas that are regularly assessed, and the instruments that are used to assess them, are shown in Figure 5.27.

Informal measures of student development are sometimes created internally in a school or district to monitor changes in students as they respond to the new program. Over time, using a time series design, evidence of growth can be recorded and used to rationalize the program, make decisions, and reinforce the attitudes of teachers and parents. Figure 5.28 shows some of the categories that might be assessed in this way.

Assessing Educational Research. Another task for curriculum workers that is related to school evaluation activities is to assess educational research. In some cases, such research will be conducted externally to the school district; in other

Instrument	Use	Author
Myers-Briggs Type Indicator	Team formation	Myers-Briggs
Teacher Preference Inventory	Teaching style	Canfield
Teacher Styles Inventory	Teaching style	Canfield
Curriculum Inventory Guide	Curriculum	R.S. Fox
Case Study Interview	Relationships	R. Havelock
Climate Questionnaire	Climate type	Litwin & Stringer
Community Power Interview	Leaders	Kimbrough
Organizational Climate Descriptor	Climate	Halpin-Croft
Group Cohesiveness Scale	Groups	S. Seashore
Community Attitude Scale	Community	Bosworth
Powerlessness Scale	Anomie	Neal and Seeman
Change Readiness Measure-C	Change	Duncan

FIGURE 5.27   Sample Assessment Instruments

cases, it will be in-house. The curriculum specialist should be able to identify good research and be able to assess research reports.

Good research possesses a number of characteristics that distinguish it from mediocre research. The following guidelines will assist the review of research efforts:

- ☐ The problem should be clearly stated, be limited, and have contemporary significance. In the proposal, the purpose, objectives, hypotheses, and specific questions should be presented concisely. Important terms should be defined.

- ☐ Previous and related studies should be reported, indicating their relationship to the present study.

- ☐ The variables, those that are controlled and those to be manipulated, should be identified.

- ☐ A description of procedures to be used should be clear enough to be replicated. Details such as the duration of the study and the treatments used should be spelled out in depth.

- ☐ The groups being studied should be defined in terms of significant characteristics.

- ☐ The report should note the school setting, describing things such as organization, scale of operations, and any special influences.

- ☐ The evaluation instruments should be applicable to the purpose of the study. Growth in self-concept, for instance, is not measured by standardized achievement tests in reading. Evidence of validity (Is this test the correct one?) and reliability (Does this test measure what it should?) should be given for all evaluation instruments used.

- ☐ Scoring of measures should be done by the most appropriate method whether it be means, medians, percentages, quartiles, rank, or whatever.

Growth Areas for Consideration	Measures of Development
Aspects of Thinking	Achievement Tests in Subjects
Work Habits and Skills	Academic Aptitude Tests
Reading	Reading Tests
Content Mastery Measures	Social/Emotional Adjustment
Development of Social Interests	Health Assessments
Appreciations of New Areas	Home Conditions
Development of Social Sensitivity	Pupil Questionnaires
Social Adjustment	Behavior Ratings
Creativeness	Interest Indexes
Development of a Personal Philosophy	Writing Sample Inventories
Physical Health	Work Habit Measures
Mental Health	Teach-Behavior Assessments

FIGURE 5.28   Growth and Measures of Development

☐ Results or findings should be clearly stated in the report in a prominent location.

☐ Limitations on findings (and there usually are limitations) should be clearly stated.

In addition to understanding what goes into good research, the curriculum specialists may sometimes be asked to assess specific research reports that have application to the schools in which they work. The following questions will help in such an assessment:

☐ *Problem presentation.* Is the question an important one? Will the question add to further understanding? Will the question aid in decision making? Is the problem explained well in light of limitations in the research area? Are the concepts reasonable and testable?

☐ *Methodology.* Are the hypotheses stated in a manner that will reveal expected differences? Can this research be replicated? Is the sampling adequate and representative? Is the study designed to show evidence of causation or correlation? Will the results be generalizable to other groups with similar characteristics?

☐ *Results.* Are the observational categories used relevant to the purpose of the study? Are the statistical treatments appropriate to the data presented? Are the reported differences statistically significant? (Significant at the 0.01 level of confidence, for instance, means that there is only one chance in one hundred that differences as observed occurred by chance.) Are the results presented in a manner that makes them understandable?

☐ *Conclusions.* Are logical inferences drawn from the findings? Are inferences of any use to decision making? Are the limitations of the research identified?

Using such organizers as targeted data, evidence data, standards of excellence, and relevant data, evaluation decisions can help schools and districts measure the kinds of items that help them to assess real progress. What curriculum workers really need to know is if they are on task and accomplishing what they intended.

If the evaluation stage in a CMP can tell the school board and other planners of their status, give general direction to planning, and answer the question, Did we do what we wanted to do? evaluation is a functional part of the curriculum cycle.

SUMMARY

Comprehensive school planning means seeing all areas of school operations as a system. All planning in a system must begin with a clear conception of purpose. The formalization of that purpose is important for the sake of continuity in program development. Assessing present conditions, usually through a needs assessment, provides planning data to support philosophical goals.

A curriculum management system (CMP) can be used to tie together the many activities needed to accomplish the planned change. Activation of this system depends on identifying responsible agents to carry out tasks and setting a time frame for the planned change. Various technical aids can assist the curriculum leader in managing the many variables.

The design phase of curriculum development proceeds deductively from goals previously identified and endorsed. Broad conceptualizations of the programs desired are projected, and plans for specific components of the program are developed. Placing these plans into one holistic understanding of the desired change leads to the management or implementation stage of the cycle.

Evaluation, a fourth step of the curriculum development cycle, is the critical stage. Accountability by school leaders for their performance should encourage them to be both effective and efficient in developing quality school programs. Historic criteria for curriculum quality, plus sound educational research, will guide curriculum leaders in their evaluation of school programming.

SUGGESTED LEARNING ACTIVITIES

1. Develop a checklist for selecting new instructional programs in your school.
2. What sources of data would you use for a follow-up study of students leaving an elementary school? Middle school? High school?
3. You are chairing a committee to suggest an evaluation design for a new science program at your school. What things would you consider in the design?
4. What is the role of an accrediting agency? Which association of colleges and secondary schools represents your area?
5. You have been asked by your PTA to explain the accountability movement. Outline in detail what you would say.

6. Develop a program for the continuing evaluation of your school.
7. Describe the relationship between educational research and educational evaluation. Can you reduce this relationship to a model or outline?

NOTES

1. Kathryn Feyereisen, *Supervision and Curriculum Renewal* (New York: Appleton Century Croft, 1970), p. 138.
2. D. L. Stufflebeam, "Toward a Science of Educational Evaluation," *Education Technology* (July 30, 1968).
3. *Defining Evaluation Systems* (Bloomington, IN: Phi Delta Kappa, 1978).

ADDITIONAL READING

Elmore, R., and S. Fuhrman. *The Governance of Curriculum*. Alexandria, VA: ASCD, 1994.

Geisert, P., and M. Futrell. *Teachers, Computers, and Curriculum*. Needham Heights, MA: Allyn and Bacon, 1995.

Glasser, W. *Quality School*. Port Chester, NY: National Professional Resources, 1990.

Hersey, P., et al. *Management and Organizational Behavior*, 7th ed. Upper Saddle River, NJ: Prentice Hall, 1996.

Joyce, B., et al. *The Self-Renewing School*. Alexandria, VA: ASCD, 1993.

Rossman, G. *Change and Effectiveness in Schools: A Cultural Perspective*. Albany, NY: SUNY Press, 1988.

PART III

INSTRUCTIONAL CONCERNS

chapter **6**

INSTRUCTION IN A TECHNOLOGICAL ERA

Teaching and learning, as we all have always understood them, are in a period of transition. The 3,500-year-old dependency relationship of the learner and the teacher is lifting as the Internet provides a tool for direct-to-learner information flows. Much like 200 years ago, when teachers were tutors, the computer is becoming the critical information source for both formal and informal learning. New teacher–pupil relationships are emerging, and the century-old goal of being able to individualize instruction for each student is becoming a near possibility. This chapter will attempt to describe this transition, as it is now occurring, from teacher-centered instruction to student-centered instruction.

THE TRADITIONAL RELATIONSHIP

The traditional role of instruction in schools is as a subset of curriculum planning. As seen in previous chapters, curriculum planning evolves through a cycle in which a situation is analyzed, a program is designed, steps are taken to implement the program, and then an assessment is made to ascertain the degree to which the program achieved its goals. Classroom instruction traditionally has followed a similar cycle; it is a cycle within a cycle.

In the instructional cycle, a teacher enters the classroom with the planned curriculum and analyzes that plan in terms of the students being taught. The plan is then adjusted to fit the students in terms of such variables as ability, interest, motivation, or relevance. The teacher then proceeds to implement the plan (teach the lesson). Normally, this teaching is followed by some sort of student assessment. This teaching act can only be understood or rationalized by the purpose or objectives of the curriculum. In this traditional model, the teacher is like an interior decorator, rather than an architect—that is, the teacher is not in charge of the purpose or design of instruction, only the delivery.

Various controls assist the teacher in assuring that what is intended (the curriculum) is taught. Students are contained in a space and there is a scheduled duration for the learning. The teacher is the primary source of access to learning by the student. Curricula have boundaries (scope) and order (sequence). The format or media (textbook, software program, video) is generally linear and predetermined. The teacher directs the student in "learning."

Dysfunctions can occur in this process if the teacher is unaware of or lacks allegiance to the curriculum intent. In selecting content, media, grouping, pacing, and evaluation options, for example, the teacher "colors" the curriculum. This emphasis at the classroom level either will reinforce or detract from the "plan." Since values are at the heart of all curricula, it is very important for the teacher to understand and "buy into" the purpose of the curriculum and its intended outcomes.

This adoption of the curriculum at the classroom level can be seen as a six-step cycle (Tyler model) of instructional delivery.

1. Determine teaching tasks and student outcomes.
2. Match objectives to student abilities.
3. Design the instructional process.
4. Deliver the planned curriculum.
5. Use feedback to analyze curriculum and instruction.
6. Adjust instructional delivery.

In the first step, the teacher must arrive at an understanding of the teaching tasks, including any mandated student outcomes. Having extracted these critical measures of purpose, the teacher views the planning process as a distance-rate-time problem: Can I get students to master these objectives by the end of the semester?

The tools a teacher will use at this stage include textbooks, teacher guides, curriculum maps or outlines, and testing standards. In some schools, it is assumed that the teacher will conduct such an assessment. In better schools, this "talking through" the curriculum is a planned process resulting in all teachers understanding their part and the role of others in meeting the student objectives.

A second step at the classroom level is to attempt to match these expectations with the actual capacity of the students being taught. A rough rule of thumb is that for each year in school there will be a year of range. This means that a fourth grade teacher must accommodate a four-year range of achievement, maturation, and native ability in planning. This rule continues until high school (a nine-year range in the ninth grade) and trails off as students drop out of school.

By questioning student ability, background, and motivation, the teacher may begin to adjust the planned curriculum in significant ways. At this point, understanding the intent of the curriculum (orientation, mastery, application) is very important. What is the meaning of the Treaty of Ghent, periodic tables, or Pi?

In the third stage, the teacher becomes an actual designer of the instructional process. Here, experience and professional knowledge are essential to decision making. Most teachers learn by trial and error, and experience gives insight as to what actually works under certain circumstances. Teachers become "professionals" when they discover that research can provide guidance in this process beyond their own experience. Education has a rich literature and an extensive research base that can be used by teachers who understand this "designing" function.

Of course, any experienced teacher knows that different students require different strategies. Individual strategies for individual students is a noble goal, but as long as the teacher is assigned thirty-five students, these strategies must be global (workbooks, reading groups) rather than individual. For fifty years teachers in American schools have labored to meet the needs of individual students without having the physical ability to do so.

A fourth step in this planning process finds the teacher actually delivering the planned curriculum at the classroom level. In making minute-to-minute adjustments, and confronting some 3,500 classroom variables, there are numerous possibilities for distortion of the intended curriculum. The elements of time, space, materials, and media are woven together according to the perceptions of the teacher. The key to success in this stage is organization. The exemplary teacher has a plan, a contingency plan, materials, equipment, and an understanding of the purpose of the lesson when she or he enters the classroom. Corrections or improvisations as conditions warrant, during the school day, are the elements of the "art" of teaching. Figure 6.1 identifies some of the options open to the teacher who understands this "art".

A fifth phase of the traditional teaching act is a feedback phase in which the teacher weighs the appropriateness of both the planned curriculum and the delivered instruction and makes adjustments for future teaching episodes.

In most states, students are given standardized mastery tests that reflect how well they have learned predetermined skills and objectives. Content mastery from prescribed textbooks would be another measure of student learning. It is important for the teacher to view teaching as a purposeful act; teaching is about students learning rather than teachers talking. The successful teacher will have a way of documenting such progress including the grade book, portfolios, test scores on standardized tests, and other student applications. In the best districts, these "proofs" of student learning are passed on from year to year as the student progresses.

A final phase in instructional design is the act of "redesigning" the way a curriculum is delivered. A teacher's ability to be reflective and make mature adjustments in teaching behaviors depends on that teacher's intrinsic motivation. Professionalism and pride will drive even the twenty-year veteran teacher to seek new skills (staff development) and materials in order to be more effective. This professional assessment, of course, begins the cycle once again.

In addition to this cycle, teachers must possess a "way of thinking" about learning to be effective in the classroom. Teachers who have not conceptualized an

1. *Comparative Analysis.* A thought process, structured by the teacher, that employs the description, classification, and analysis of more than one system, group, or the like in order to ascertain and evaluate similarities and differences.

2. *Conference.* A one-to-one interaction between teacher and learner in which the learner's needs and problems can be dealt with. Diagnosis, evaluation, and prescription may all be involved.

3. *Demonstration.* An activity in which the teacher or another person uses examples, experiments, or other actual performance, or a combination of these, to illustrate a principle or show others how to do something.

4. *Diagnosis.* The continuous determination of the nature of learning difficulties and deficiencies, used in teaching as a basis for the selection, day by day or moment by moment, of appropriate content and methods of instruction.

5. *Direct Observation.* Guided observation provided for the purpose of improving the study, understanding, and evaluation of that which is observed.

6. *Discussion.* An activity in which pupils, under teacher or pupil direction, or both, exchange points of view concerning a topic, question, or problem to arrive at a decision or conclusion.

7. *Drill.* An orderly, repetitive learning activity intended to help develop or fix a specific skill or aspect of knowledge.

8. *Experimentation.* An activity involving a planned procedure accompanied by either the control of conditions or a controlled variation of conditions, or both, together with observation of results for the purpose of discovering relationships and evaluating the reasonableness of a specific hypothesis.

9. *Field Experience.* Educational work experience, sometimes fully paid, acquired by pupils in a practical service situation.

10. *Field Trip.* An educational trip to places where pupils can study the content of instruction directly in its functional setting, for example, factory, newspaper office, or fire department.

FIGURE 6.1   Eighteen Common Methods Used by Teachers

approach to the teaching–learning act often present an unclear instructional pattern to their students, thereby causing students to fail in the achievement of intended outcomes. Teachers in the preparatory phase may want to ask themselves the following questions: (see also Figure 6.2).

1. *What am I expected to teach?* Upon arrival in any classroom the teacher will be confronted with materials and equipment thought to be generically valuable for any occasion: texts, soft-sided instructional supplements, perhaps projection devices (overhead projectors), and hopefully, computers and software. Better school districts will offer detailed curriculum maps or frameworks and guides to instructional resources indicating a degree of specificity for the instructional process. Since teaching is perceived in the traditional model as the delivery of the curriculum, the absence of these items is certainly cause for alarm.

11. *Group Work.* A process in which members of the class work cooperatively rather than individually to formulate and work toward common objectives under the guidance of one or more leaders.

12. *Laboratory Experience.* Learning activities carried on by pupils in a laboratory designed for individual or group study of a particular subject-matter area, involving the practical application of theory through observation, experimentation, and research, or, in the case of foreign language instruction, involving learning through demonstration, drill, and practice. This applies also to the study of art and music, although such activity in this instance may be referred to as a studio experience.

13. *Lecture.* An activity in which the teacher gives an oral presentation of facts or principles, the class frequently being responsible for notetaking. This activity usually involves little or no pupil participation by questioning or discussion.

14. *Manipulative and Tactile Activity.* Activity by which pupils use the movement of various muscles and the sense of touch to develop manipulative or perceptual skills, or both.

15. *Modeling and Imitation.* An activity frequently used for instruction in speech, in which the pupils listen to and observe a model as a basis upon which to practice and improve their performance.

16. *Problem Solving.* A thought process structured by the teacher and employed by the pupils for clearly defining a problem, forming hypothetical solutions, and possibly testing the hypothesis.

17. *Programmed Instruction.* Instruction using a workbook together with either a mechanical or electronic device, or both, which has been programmed by (a) providing instruction in small steps and (b) asking one or more questions about each step in the instruction and providing instant feedback if the answer is right or wrong.

18. *Computer-Assisted Instruction.* Software programs provide students with practice in key skill areas or are used to search for further information about selected topics.

FIGURE 6.1   *Continued*

2. *To whom am I teaching this curriculum?* Since nearly all school learning is associative (learned in terms of what you already know), it is important for the teacher to learn about the students. What are the backgrounds of these students? What previous experience of theirs can be used as a reference point? What are their reading levels and other related skill mastery levels?

3. *What is the expected outcome or product of my teaching?* Understanding the exact expectation of these teaching episodes is vital to being successful. Any variable in the classroom can be manipulated by the teacher (seating arrangements, use of time) and each such adjustment will change the "meaning" of the curriculum being delivered. The taxonomies (cognitive, affective, psychomotor) are helpful in targeting the desired outcome and the appropriate teaching behavior to gain such a result.

4. *How can my classroom be best organized to reach these student outcomes?* Teachers can make their classrooms into an infinite number of learning

1. Is the room prepared? Is furniture arranged to promote desired learning? Is the environment conductive to what I intend to teach?
2. Do I have a plan for getting students into the room and settled in their seats?
3. Have I thought of a "motivational opener" to make the transition from the last class they attended to this one?
4. Can I give the students a preview (advanced organizers) of what we'll be doing during the period so they'll know what to expect?
5. Have I estimated the time required for each activity this period?
6. Are the major concepts for this lesson covered by my planned activities?
7. Are the essential facts I want taught in the materials to be used?
8. Have I planned for the appropriate level of affect desired?
9. Have I planned to allow each student to participate at an appropriate level of learning?
10. Are the necessary and appropriate materials present in the room?
11. Do I have a plan for discussion? Have I clarified what kind of discussion will contribute to the lesson objectives?
12. Have I planned for relevance? Do I have some real-life examples?
13. Have I considered handout procedures and steps for collecting homework?
14. How will I involve special students in this lesson?
15. What is my plan for grouping? What directions will I give?
16. Do I have a plan for possible deviant behavior today?
17. Do I want to emphasize a certain format/standards for today's homework or assignment?
18. What kind of test questions would I ask about today's material? Do I want to share these expectations with students?
19. What kind of a technique will I use for closure of today's class?
20. What is my procedure for dismissal of the class?

FIGURE 6.2   Twenty Questions before Teaching

environments by making instructional decisions prior to teaching. Generally speaking, if the planned curriculum is global (comprehension, familiarity, understanding), then a great deal of flexibility is called for so that the greatest number of students can achieve "access" to learning. If, on the other hand, the curriculum is specific (mastery, skill acquisition), then high degrees of structure are called for. These "adoption" decisions by the teacher are critical to student success. An understanding of how the curriculum and instruction interface is an essential element in curriculum work.

5. *What can I do to get my students to learn in the intended manner?* This may at first seem an odd question unless you recognize that curriculum planners "predetermine" the outcome and its form. This condition has been rein-

forced by the testing movement, which operates under the assumption that students have only "learned" if they can demonstrate mastery under specific testing conditions.

If this is the case under the traditional teaching–learning model, then the classroom teacher must "design" learning for that specified outcome. As the classroom is perceived as a "system," refining itself more and more to do less and less, test scores will rise. Unfortunately, such a definition of schooling is more like training than education.

Having addressed these questions, the teacher proceeds to develop a 'lesson plan' that includes such elements as objectives, rationale, primary content, instructional procedures, material needs, and evaluation criteria. Along the way, the teacher may develop some instructional strategies and some delivery modifications. But, in reality, the very fact that instruction is always planned for a space housing thirty to thirty-five students, a time period of about one hour, and the use of predetermined and standardized materials and evaluative criteria means that not much variety will exist from room to room, school to school, or district to district. This traditional curriculum planning procedure has seen very little change in nearly a century!

CURRICULUM PLANNING AND TECHNOLOGY

In sharp contrast to this traditional era of curriculum development and instruction is a new technological age in which all the rules are changed. No longer is the curriculum absolute in its prescription, nor are teachers dependent in their instructional delivery. In addition, the traditional relationship between the teacher and student is altered. Teachers are no longer the access point for knowledge acquisition. In contrast to the "old way," students now have unrestricted access (seven days and twenty-four hours) to a universal source of information. This source is not contained by time or space, is not dependent on a teacher for access, and is largely unordered. By the old definition, this information is not a curriculum because it lacks definition and structure (boundary, scope, sequence).

The new information is rarely assessed for relevance or accuracy and is not dedicated to student mastery. Learning in this new era is student centered because the student "controls" the learning medium and the ordering of any intended "curriculum." Learning is nonlinear or nonsequential. Obviously, what is defined as "curriculum," "teaching," and "learning" is radically different in the new technological era, an era that began with the establishment of the Internet in May 1995.

The Internet in a Nutshell

Computers first appeared in American schools in the 1980s. These simple early machines, with very limited memory and very little software, were initially perceived as processing tools and entertainment devices. After considering a rash of brand names, including Texas Instruments, Commodore, and Apple, schools finally adopted the Apple IIe as a kind of standard because it was "teacher friendly." By the early 1990s schools had entire labs of these machines, and advanced districts even created in-school and interschool local area networks (LANs) and wide area networks (WANs). At this time these machines were still perceived to be supplements to the classroom teacher, and most of the software was of a drill and practice variety.

Outside of school, however, a lot more was going on with computers. As early as 1969, the U.S. military linked sites in the South Pacific and the Caribbean basin through something called ARPAnet (Advanced Research Project Agency net). In 1986, the National Science Foundation network (NSFnet) was created as a noncommercial network to service the space program. This net linked six "super computer sites" for tracking and analyzing space launches. Finally, on April 30, 1995, most of the functions of NSFnet were made available to commercial services, and the modern Internet was born. This network of networks, or information 'superhighway,' connects most computers in the world into one gigantic communication system.

Before the Internet was created, it took a special computer language called UNIX to navigate the network channels. Soon, however, search engines or "browsers" such as Yahoo and Magellan emerged to help "nontechies" get around on the net. These search engines use hypertext (http, or hypertext transport protocol) to provide a multimedia environment that can combine print, video, and sound enhancements. Together, all of this good stuff is known as ISDN (Integrated Services Digital Network).

The essential point here is that search engines have made the Internet a magnificent tool for learning. At "warp speed" learners can access almost any information source in the world. When tandem searches (Boolean) are used, highly specific answers can be gained to complex questions. As an example of how many sites there are on any topic, the term 'quadratic equations,' brings up 10,000 sites.

Schools have been very slow to understand that this new information resource will change everything we have known about curriculum and schooling. This medium is a superior source of information and an unparalleled learning tool for any individual wishing to know more about anything. It will break the monopoly of the school as the learning place, and it will change the concept of what constitutes a curriculum forever. This transition is occurring as this book is being written.

The roles of teachers and students no longer constitute a dependency relationship as we have known it for nearly 3,500 years. Teachers in the immediate future will have different roles and may operate in very different institutions. As the transition occurs, teachers will begin to use the Internet to alter their instructional delivery. Eight such uses are listed here:

1. Teachers, students, and parents will communicate by e-mail. Seventy-five per cent of all classroom teachers now own computers with an Internet provider. Slightly more than half of all public school students are so equipped.

2. Regular stand-up teaching in the classroom can now be supplemented by identifying Internet sites for enlargement and enrichment at school or at home.
3. Teachers can individualize learning for students by identifying Internet sites or creating curriculum journeys for special purposes. Such Internet-assisted lessons have an infinite number of possible formats.
4. The Internet can serve as a source of rewards for students. Pleasure learning at sites such as Disney or Legoland, or under topics such as dinosaurs and volcanoes can be built into regular lessons.
5. Teachers can make interdisciplinary connections for students using various subjects and tying them to problems, issues, or interest areas.
6. Students can take electronic field trips to places such as Yosemite National Park, the Smithsonian Institute, or the Louvre. Student backgrounds for future learning can be enlarged by such exploration.
7. The Internet can be used for skill-building and mastery practice in skill areas such as reading, spelling, and mathematics. Advanced thinking skills (critical and creative) can be enhanced.
8. The Internet is a great tool for advanced learning or independent study.

The arrival of the Internet in 1995, with its simple-to-use search engines, provided teachers with an opportunity to become leaders in curriculum development in schools. While schools have been slow to recognize this "systems break," this dramatic change will alter education as we have known it all of our lives. As more and more teachers "get on board," new paradigms will be needed in the field of curriculum development to define the novel teaching and learning process.

Defining the New Technological Classroom

Author Jon Wiles has been instrumental in forming a new nonprofit Florida corporation dedicated to helping teachers enter this new age of technological learning. The corporation, Learning Webs, Inc. (www.learnweb.org), is dedicated to teacher leadership in curriculum work and has focused its first year on helping teachers develop Internet-assisted lessons.

Internet-assisted lessons, which use Internet resources to supplement regular classroom lessons, are a first step toward a textbook-free curriculum for the twenty-first century. Using a bank of useful Internet sites (see Figure 6.3), teachers develop classroom lessons and insert "hot links" (links to Internet sites) to supplemental resources. This allows teachers to create individualized and personalized lessons for any group of students or individual students in the classroom.

For example, imagine a fourth grade teacher who is about to begin a unit on space exploration. The content of this unit will include such topics as planets, astronomy, satellites, space travel, and the landing of men on the moon. While most adults are still in awe of such events, students who have known reality all of their lives are sometimes 'bored' by such a unit. The question of motivation is a concern.

Bluweb'n	http://www.kn.pacbell.com/wired/blueweb'n
ERIC	http://ask.eric.org/virtual lessons/other.html
Gateway to Educational	
Materials	http://www.thegateway.org
Help Web	http://www.imaginarylandscape.com/helpweb/
Internet 101	http://www.www2.famvid.com/internet101.html
Kathy Schrock's Guide	
for Educators	http://school.discover.com/schrockguide/
LearningWebs, Inc.	http://www.learnweb.org
Natonal Educational	
Technology Standards Group	http://cnets.iste.org/condition.htm
PBS Teachersource	http://www.pbs.org/teachersource
Tappedin	http://www.tappedin.org
Teacher Pathfinder	http://teacherpathfinder.org
TeacherVision	http://teachervision.com.
Web Quest	http://www.edweb.sdsu.edu/webquest.htm
Web Teacher	http://www.webteacher.org/macnet/indextc.htm
21st Century Teachers	
Network	http://www.21ct.org

FIGURE 6.3   Useful Sites for Classroom Teachers

The teacher decides to take the students on a preview "virtual trip" and create a little story line about how a student "just like you" will be the first student in outer space. The goal of this lesson is to explore and inquire, to motivate, not to master subject content.

The teacher takes control of this broad topic by creating a path of Internet sites that will lead the student through topic areas such as space camp, the space center, the Discovery missions, the Hubble Telescope, and planets in outer space. The lesson will be called "First Kid in Space" (see Figure 6.4), and the student who interacts with this lesson will be the star of the show. Nothing is quite as motivational as studying ourselves!

Our teacher goes to a bank of preselected and 'safe' sites (Figure 6.3) and pulls Internet sites in topics such as the Cape Kennedy Welcome Station, the Discovery Program, and the Hubble Telescope. Numerous resources exist that identify safe sites, including *Learning Webs: Curriculum Journeys on the Internet* (Keating, Wiles, Piazza, Prentice-Hall, 2001), a source of 1,200 sites in 240 topic areas. Armed with these lesson "enhancers," the teacher puts together a script about the first student to be selected to travel in space and enters the URLs in the script. Depending on the software being used, these sites become active in a number of ways. Sending them to the student by e-mail (over the Internet) automatically activates the sites. When the student reads the lesson and 'clicks' on the highlighted URL, the lesson will go straight to the enhanced resource site. A basic lesson in black and white print becomes bigger, more visual, and site specific.

Grade Level	**Fourth grade**
Type Activity	**Inquiry/exploration**
Journey References	**Kennedy Space Center, planets, Hubble telescope**
Outcomes	**Awareness and conceptualization**

Just imagine yourself (insert student name) the first kid ever to go into outer space. Out of all of the schoolchildren in America you have been selected to go to the Kennedy Space Center and ride with the astronauts to the Hubble telescope station. Once on site, you will conduct some experiments and be a working member of the crew. Are you up to this challenge? Lets go!

First stop for you will be the space camp in Florida (http://spacecamp.com/main.htm), where kids learn about some of the activities in our space program. You will then proceed to the spaceport at Cape Kennedy (http://www.kennedyspacecenter.com/index.html) where you'll be given a virtual tour of the place. This will take a while since so much is going on there.

Before things get too serious, they will send you to two places to learn more about your task. The first is http://www.kidsinspace.org, and the second is the Starchild Learning Center (http://starchild.gsfc.nasa.gov.docs/StarChild/). During these visits you will select some of the experiments you will carry out while in outer space and learn more about the Hubble space telescope.

The pictures you have just seen were taken by a massive telescope that has broadened our understanding of outer space considerably. Take a look at how big this telescope really is (http://starchild.gsfc.nasa.gov/docs/StarChild/space_level2/hubble_kennedy.html).

Before leaving earth, you can study in great detail the first pictures ever taken by Hubble. Visit http://oposite.stsci.edu/pubinfo/pictures.html and the NASA photojournal (http://wwwas.wvu.edu/~planet/lnk_solr.htm). NASA will give you copies of these pictures when you get back to earth, but you'll be the only student to really have seen what space looks like from the Hubble.

We will, of course, be riding the space shuttle today on our way to outer space.

If you are unfamiliar with the take-off procedure, check out this site: http://www.j-2.com/space/landing.htm.

As you might imagine, we can't pay a kid for being a part of our crew on this mission, but the mission commander says you can have anything you want from the space shop when you return (http://www.thespaceshop.com/). Why don't you browse around and select something for your family and school friends?

OK (insert student name), time to suit up! All of the kids in America will be cheering for you today. Good luck.

FIGURE 6.4 First Kid in Space

The teacher could send this curriculum journey to any student by e-mail, or could list it on a web page so any student could access it from school or home. The lesson could be differentiated from easy to hard allowing the student to self-select the amount of knowledge acquired. This lesson is not intended for mastery, but rather as an "inquiry lesson" to bring the subject to life in the classroom. If teachers developed and exchanged such lessons, they could revolutionize the standard school curriculum in a matter of months. Now, let's see how Internet-assisted lessons fit into the process of curriculum development.

Title of Activity: _____ Time Required: _____

Grade Level(s): _____ Lesson Designer(s):

_____

Curriculum Design (check off below):

☐ Content Based
☐ Skill Based
☐ Inquiry and Exploration
☐ Conceptual
☐ Interdisciplinary
☐ Cooperative
☐ Problem Solving
☐ Critical and Creative Thinking

Online Resources/References:

State Standards (Outcomes):

Materials Needed:

FIGURE 6.5 Internet Lesson Planning Template Part 1

1. Introduction
General description in narrative form. It could contain an overview of the process/tasks, expected outcomes, evaluation criteria, and roles of participants—for example, "You are an astronaut exploring our solar system."

_____
_____
_____
_____
_____
_____
_____

2. Questioning and Planning (Could be eliminated for more linear curriculum design models)
Students should create their own questions to help guide their inquiry.
☐ What do we know?
☐ What do we need to know?
☐ Who is going to do what?
☐ What resources/materials do we need to complete the tasks?

3. Process/Tasks: (Depends on curriculum design, but uses online references/resources on first page)

_____
_____
_____
_____
_____
_____
_____
_____
_____
_____
_____

Outcome and Evaluation
☐ Outcome could simply be heightened interest, acquired skills, or a tangible product such as a
  project, presentation, or paper.
☐ Evaluation method—Explain how students will be graded. Will a rubric be developed?

_____
_____
_____
_____
_____
_____

FIGURE 6.5 _Continued_

Technological Lessons

The primary problem for classroom teachers who want to use the Internet is that it is unorganized. A wealth of knowledge is available, an overwhelming amount really, but its randomness renders it almost useless for school as we know it. Accessing topic sites isn't the problem, the search engines can do that. The problem with the Internet, by the old definition of curriculum, is that it is nonlinear.

Sticking to the old definition of curriculum, and ignoring whether a linear curriculum is desirable at all, we can best understand the use of new technologies in classrooms by seeing how lessons might be constructed using eight common instructional designs: content-based designs, skill based-designs, inquiry and exploration models, conceptual models, interdisciplinary designs, cooperative designs, problem-solving models, and critical and creative thinking designs (Table 6.1). On the cognitive taxonomy (Bloom 1956), these designs go from simple to complex, involving the student to a greater degree in each instance. See Appendix 6.1 for the eight curriculum journey lessons created using the common instructional designs. We will follow the same format as we did in the curriculum journey "First Kid in Space" so you can compare and contrast these lessons.

Even within the old "linear learning" model of a knowledge-based curriculum, the Internet can enhance almost any design. We believe that this is how the transition to a twenty-first-century curriculum will begin. However, as we look closer, the Internet and its resources offer much more than simply a linear enrichment with branching. The National Educational Technology Standards Group (1999) identified ten significant changes that result from the use of technology in education:

FROM	TO
Teacher-directed instruction	Student-directed instruction
Single sense stimulation	Multisensory stimulation
Single path progression	Multipath progression
Single medium	Multimedia
Isolated work	Collaborative work
Information delivery	Information exchange
Passive learning	Interactive participative learning
Factual, literal learning	Exploratory, inquiry learning
Reactive student response	Proactive student initiation
Isolated and artificial context	Authentic, real-world context

A simple glance at this list reveals that the Internet is much more than a supplement to the historical linear content curriculum that has dominated American schools for two hundred years. The Internet revolutionizes teaching and learning by eliminating teacher control of the access to learning. It is a learning tool that puts the user (the student) in the driver's seat and allows that user to access and construct knowledge without assistance. The role of a teacher will be completely redefined by this instrument.

Type	Purpose	Activity
Content-Based Instruction	Knowledge acquisition	Facts, representative form
Skill-Based Instruction	Manipulation, patterns	Rules, practice, ordering
	Awareness, interest	Stories, unknowns
Inquiry Approach	Understanding	Big ideas, familiarity
	Connecting information	Organizing, ordering
Conceptual Learning	Social Skill development	Cooperative activity
Interdisciplinary	Shared decision making	Group work
Cooperative Learning	Issues analysis	Current events
Problem Solving	Skills application	Futurism
Critical/Creative Thinking	Construction of new knowledge and forms	Model building Free imagination

TABLE 6.1   Eight Common Curriculum Designs

For nearly a decade, the educational literature has spoken of "constructivist classrooms" (called "connectionism" one hundred years ago). This literature speaks of active and involved learners, social learners dialoguing with others, and creative learners experiencing personal knowing. Following are the five premises of the constructivist classroom:

1. The learner controls learning.
2. The search for understanding is the source of motivation.
3. Students will determine the relevance of information.
4. Lessons will necessarily be structured around big ideas.
5. Evaluation of learning will be contextual.

Constructivist literature may give us a way of thinking about technological learning and the role of a formal teacher in some kind of learning space. Following are three basic constructivist premises about student learning:

1. Lessons must be connected to the prior knowledge and experience students bring to the classroom (associative learning).
2. The teacher's role is to focus on student thinking, not provide information.
3. Teachers can help students to transform (organize or give meaning to) knowledge.

We endorse these three premises, but observe that these things have always been true in school settings. Many of the failures of organized schooling have stemmed from the attempt to control and standardize learning outcomes by ignoring student background, by providing information, and by telling students what such information means. If the twentieth century in education demonstrated anything, it was that students are not alike and that standardizing unlikes is difficult if not impossible. If twenty-first-century schools acknowledge student diversity and interest, guide students in study, and help students to understand what they are learning, they can be a part of the transformation to the new technological age. Failure to do these things will result in the erosion of support for schools by a public already living in the new technological age.

Some Instructional Assumptions

Curriculum development and instructional designs will have to work from the same page to be effective in the twenty-first-century. We believe the following to be true of instruction in a technological age:

1. Students and teachers will both be learners.
2. The formatting of knowledge will give meaning to what the student learns.
3. The primary role of a teacher will be that of a guide, a mentor, and a tutor.
4. A set of essential learning skills will be required for learning.
5. Learning environments will be totally redesigned to encourage individual learning experiences.
6. Most learning experiences will be in the present or future, not directed to the past.
7. Student evaluation will no longer, and should no longer, be standardized.

ADVANTAGES OF THE NEW TECHNOLOGIES

There are some promising benefits for teachers, students, and parents as we transition to a high-tech future in schools. For teachers, there will be a greatly reduced burden of storing information and record keeping. At the same time, student progress information will be plentiful and detailed. Teachers will also see improved communication with parents, other teachers, and support personnel. Student learning time (on-task) will increase, and the time lost to student absences will be eliminated to a great degree. Of course, there will be greater access to instructional resources from the Internet.

Students will also gain from the new technologies. They will have a greater knowledge of what is going on at school and in their classrooms. They will have full-time access to assignments and resources. There will be better parent–teacher communication about student progress. The student will have more individual contact with the teacher and more immediate feedback on learning efforts. The student will be able to learn at his or her own pace and will have more control over the way learning occurs.

For the parent, there will be "real-time" information about a student's academic and social progress. The teacher and school will be directly accessed by e-mail. Homework will be forwarded home to the parent, and students who are sick or absent can access their assignments anywhere, worldwide. Parents will have access to training and continuing education.

An important side benefit of the new technologies will be to reduce inequities in learning by providing all students with access to the best resources. Language support for non-English speakers is now available, as is assistance for those students with learning disabilities (e.g., sign language instruction).

SCHOOLS MAKING THE TRANSITION

Thousands of schools in the United States are currently making the transition to a new technological age. Unfortunately, thousands of schools are still unaware of the change occurring in our educational institutions. Writing in *Business Week* magazine, William Symonds described one school that has succeeded:

> Union City, New Jersey—A failing district near New York City, Union City secured help from Bell Atlantic Corporation to provide computers to students at school and at home. This networking forced a change in the curriculum from rote learning to project method. Last year, Union City topped all New Jersey cities on the state tests.

While Union City is certainly a success story, it is hardly typical. In reality, most districts have focused on obtaining hardware rather than on the purpose of these machines. From nearly zero schools with computers in 1984, today nearly 95 percent of all public schools are wired to the Internet. This does not mean, of course, that all students in such schools have Internet access. At the time of this writing, the computer-to-student ratio in the United States was 1 to 5, and schools were spending about $133 per pupil on technology. This represents less than 2 percent of the total education budget. Only 8 percent of this amount is allocated to training teachers to use this technology. Today, approximately 30 percent of all teachers use the Internet in their classroom lessons.

To be successful in making the transition from nineteenth-century format to a twenty-first century format, schools will have to spend much more on both equipment and training. In the 1990s many U.S. corporations "downsized" their personnel significantly to finance the purchasing of technical equipment. So far, schools have been unable to conceptualize a realignment of their budgets to encourage a new form of learning.

Without the intersection of some major force, the clientele served by public schools (53 million in 2000) will likely "slip away" to various competing media. Virtual schools, for example, are proving popular with high school students wanting to graduate early or gain specialty courses for college entrance. Home-schoolers, to name another group, are no longer handicapped by a lack of learning materials since the Internet allows access to the finest libraries in the world without charge. Once school leaders realize they can pare down building costs, teacher salaries, and textbook purchases by more creative uses of time, space, and media, the technological age will find the financial base it needs to bloom fully. In the interim, the technological future of public schools in the United States is certainly a broken front, and the so-called digital divide gets wider each day.

SUMMARY

Certainly, we have no crystal ball to predict how the new technologies will affect the schools that house and transmit the planned curriculum to future generations. Traditionally, change in schools has been very slow, suggesting that not much will change in the next decade. However, given the impact of the Internet on our society during the period 1995–2000, only a fool would take a "wait and see" attitude toward this social force. We believe it isn't a matter of *if* the Internet will change the teaching–learning process, but *how* it will change our historic conception of schooling. The *when* is right now!

We see many signs of a schism in public education, with the standards-based movement digging in its heels and doing 'more and more' to achieve less and less. We believe this is symptomatic of an archaic institution defending its turf in the face of overwhelming evidence that education can no longer be contained in time and space; it is somehow reminiscent of the fall of the Soviet Union after the Berlin Wall came down. On the other hand, there is every indication that the clients of our schools are voting with their feet, leaving public schools for other viable options: charter schools, magnet schools, home schools, virtual schools, or any other option that challenges the nineteenth-century model under which we now educate our children.

What becomes of curriculum workers in this era of transition depends heavily on which camp they choose to follow. There may be a role for some in what has been called the "mechanistic wing" of curriculum development. But, as textbooks, tests, and other forms of standardization are challenged or fall away, this camp will be increasingly challenged to ignore all that is going on about them. They will likely become isolated and dysfunctional.

On the other hand, if the curriculum field acknowledges the excitement of an instrument that frees learners from the rigor of lockstep learning and allows the teacher to return to the historic role of a knowing guide to learning, the future is bright. The technologies of the past ten years have revolutionized our society and can do the same for our largest institution. Leadership will be needed, and new learning will be required. But, after all, curriculum work has always been about making choices and organizing learning experiences. Whether this is done in the old format of schools with teachers or in some new and interesting format in the new century, there is a role for this important function in educating our youth.

SUGGESTED LEARNING ACTIVITIES

1. Identify those forces currently pushing schools toward greater use of technology in the classroom.
2. How can schools deal with the "digital divide," where some children have technology and some children don't?
3. Develop a job description for the teacher in a school fully utilizing the new interactive technologies.

NOTE

1. LearningWebs is a new Florida-based nonprofit corporation run by teachers to assist in the transition to a technological future.

ADDITIONAL READING

Adams, Jacob E. *Taking Charge of Curriculum: Teacher Networks and Curriculum Implementation.* New York: Teachers College Press, 2000.

Davis, Stan. *Blur: The Speed of Change in the Connected Economy.* Reading, MA: Addison-Wesley, 1998.

Henderson, James George et al. *Transformative Curriculum Leadership.* Upper Saddle River, NJ: Prentice Hall, 1999.

Henderson, James George et al. *Understanding Democratic Curriculum Leadership.* New York: Teachers College Press, 1999.

Tapscott, Dan. *The Digital Economy: Promise and Peril in the Age of Networked Intelligence.* New York: McGraw-Hill, 1996.

APPENDIX 6.1
WEB-BASED LESSONS USING INSTRUCTIONAL DESIGNS
Content-Based Curriculum

This type of curriculum design identifies in advance things to be mastered by the student and is usually organized as a discipline of study. Lessons in such a curriculum consist of facts, critical data, and knowledge representative of a greater knowledge base in that area.

All the World's a Stage:	**Internet Scavenger Hunt**
Grade Level	10–12
Type Activity	Data gathering in specific content area
Journey References	British literature, drama, museums, world literature
Outcomes	Students will acquire knowledge about British literature and arts.

Today we are going to England. Specifically, we will tour some sites in London's most historic borough—Southwark. While in Southwark, we will stop at the newly constructed Globe Theater and other locations. Then we will venture to other sites about the Globe, William Shakespeare, and Shakespeare's plays. This journey will take an hour and a half.

First Stop: *http://www.southwark.gov.uk/discovering/index.html*
Read "Dicovering Southwark," then click on the "History of Southwark" link on the right. Click on the "Shakespeare's Southwark" link and read it to answer the following questions:

1. Find the name of the area of Southwark where the playhouse boom was centered.
2. In addition to the Globe, list in order of their construction the other three theaters in Southwark.
3. In 1850, where specifically in South London was the first playhouse built?
4. In what year did the Globe burn down?
5. What other entertainment was popular besides theater-going? (Hint: Especially on Thursdays)
6. Find three additional interesting facts about the Globe, Shakespeare, and/or Elizabethan theater-going from this site.
7. At the same site, choose a different London link to follow from the following: "The Mayflower," "London Bridge," "Southwark Prisons," and "John Harvard." List the link you followed and three facts about your choice.

Second Stop: *http://www.rdg.ac.uk/Globe/*
Click on the "Shakespeare's Globe" link.

8. What year did the Puritans finally close the Globe?

Now, on the left scroll bar, click on and explore interesting links such as the time line. Then, scroll down and click on "Virtual Reality Views of the Rebuilt Globe." Then click on "Virtual Tour of the Globe Theater," NOT "Virtual Reality Views of the Unfinished Globe."

Navigate around following the links, viewing pictures, reading the informative text, and gathering the following data:

9. In Elizabethan times, how much was admission to view the play from the following three sections of the theater:
    a. Groundlings (in the yard)
    b. Lower gallery
    c. Gentlemen's rooms
10. Based on the information, name two advantages of sitting in the Gentlemen's section.
11. What was the favored sitting area of the aristocracy? (Hint: It's not one of the three above.)
12. Why do you think they favored this area?
13. What is pictured on the "Frons Scenaie" (stage wall/backdrop)?
14. Visit the yard section and list two facts you found interesting.

Third Stop: *http://www.calvin.edu/academic/engl/346/proj/nathan/globe.htm*

Fourth Stop: *http://www.cybervillage.com/ocs/globe.htm*

15. From the above sites, find five additional facts about the Globe Theater or Elizabethan drama (NOT already covered in your other answers).

Fifth Stop: Using the search engine of your choice, search for informative sites about William Shakespeare.

16. Find a good site and list its address and five facts about Shakespeare.

Sixth Stop: *http://www.pathguy.com/hamlet.htm*

17. What college was Hamlet attending?
18. Who did Old Hamlet kill the day Hamlet was born? (Act I)
19. What country is Hamlet set in?
20. What is the name of the castle in Hamlet?
21. Name two themes in Hamlet.

Seventh Stop: Search for informative sites on Hamlet.

22. List the web address of a particularly good Hamlet site.
23. From the site you identified, list five facts about Hamlet NOT covered in previous questions or in class.

For the truly adventurous web explorers:

☐ **Bonus #1** What is the name of the real castle in Denmark that Hamlet's castle is representing? Provide the address of the site where you find the name.
☐ **Bonus #2** Who built this castle between 1574 and 1585? Provide the address of the site where you find the name.

Skill-Based Designs

Teachers encounter two common types of skill-based curricula. On the one hand, various standards in schools today require students to exhibit what are referred to as "basic skills," such as reading, writing, and computing. Most often, work in these areas consists of manipulation of an operation in a repetitive pattern (practice effect). A second kind of skills-based curriculum addresses sequencing or understanding and applying a process. Both of these types of skills-based instruction can be aided by Internet resources.

Quadratic Equations

Grade Level	7–12
Type Activity	Understanding and applying a process
Journey References	Algebra, math history, quadratic equations, satellites, sputnik
Outcomes	a. Students will understand the use of quadratic equations.
	b. Students will practice problem solving using quadratic equation problems.
	c. Students will master practice test on quadratic equations.
	d. Students will draw relationship of the quadratic equation formula to satellite programs.

Students learn in the primary grades that numerals represent real objects. They also learn that these objects/numerals can be manipulated through basic operations (addition, subtraction, multiplication, and division), and that this can be done with incomplete or partial objects as well (fractions and decimals).

When students enter a second level of mathematical abstraction (algebra, geometry, trigonometry, and calculus), they are no longer manipulating real objects, but instead are using formulas to solve problems. The proof that this is indeed a mathematical world, and that fixed relationships that can be reduced to mathematics exist on earth and in space, is proved by these course processes. Algebra is the first instance in which formulas are shown to be reliable in solving problems involving unknowns.

http://www.ms.uky.edu/~carl/ma330/project2/al-khwa21.html

http://www.museums.reading.ac.uk/vmoc/algebra/

Quadratic equations are formulas for nonlinear or irregular mathematical relationships. They are used to solve puzzles. Visit the site: http://www.unican.es/sosmath/algebra/quadraticeq/bdef/bdef.html. Answer the question, What is meant by the statement that quadratic equations are puzzles that are glued together?

Solving problems using quadratic equations is a process of finding relationships among knowns. Visit the following sites: http://members.tripod.com/~kselva/quad.html and http://www.webmath.com/quad.html. Using the thirteen-step process provided at http://quickmath.com/www02/pages/modules/equations/ solve a quadratic equation. When finished, take the practice test. If you need further assistance, visit these sites: http://math.holycross.edu/~little/A2AS/node2.html and http://cne.gmu.edu/modules/dau/algebra/quadratic_eqns/exercises.html.

Finally, what problems relating to orbits in space are faced in launching satellites such as the first satellite, Sputnik (http://sputnik.infospace.ru/)? Can you identify a quadratic equation that would serve as a useful tool in our space program?

Inquiry And Exploration Designs

Children are naturally inquisitive, and so are adults. It is the nature of human beings to learn, and life is a never-ending learning process. Such natural exploration is an immediate source of motivation in students. Teachers can identify areas for exploration, such as countries of the world, and allow the natural curiosity of students to drive learning forward. The choice of country studied isn't nearly as important as seeking information about several countries as a reference point for future learning.

The Adventures of Miss Shell

Grade Level	4–9
Type Activity	Acquisition of background information, writing practice
Journey References	Paris, Africa, South Africa, Kruger Park, Italy, Sri Lanka
Outcomes	a. Students will gain knowledge of at least three countries of their choosing.
	b. Students will develop an interest in knowing about other countries.
	c. Students will apply learning skills in planning their trip.
	d. Students will practice writing skills in developing their stories.

Note: Although Miss Shell would love to travel, she is a full-time teacher. However, during her lunch hour she often slips back to the room to get on her computer and take an imaginary trip. Follow Miss Shell as she goes on her adventures:

Day 1: Paris
Day 2: Germany, Austria, and Italy
Day 3: Safari
Day 4: Sri Lanka
Day 5: India

Conceptual Designs

Curriculum designs that are organized around concepts seek to promote student understanding of "big ideas" or provide organization for large amounts of detailed information. Global in their focus, these lessons introduce students to formal bodies of knowledge.

Flight Exploration

Grade Level	5–7
Type Activity	Study of detailed information followed by application; leads to general understanding of how man has achieved flight
Journey References	Inventions, experiments, machines science museums
Outcomes	a. Students will master specific factual information about flying.
	b. Students will apply skills of inquiry to information.
	c. Students will develop an understanding of the theory of flight.

Work with a partner to become an expert aerospace engineer and airplane pilot. These activities will take from three to five hours to complete. The basics:

1. Draw a simple Venn diagram to compare aeronautical engineering and aerospace engineering.
   http://wings.ucdavis.edu/Book/Flight/intermediate/aeronautics-01.html
2. Describe the difference between aerodynamics and gas dynamics.
   http://wings.ucdavis.edu/Book/Flight/intermediate/gas-01.html
3. What five units of measurement are useful in the study of flight? Give an example of each.
   http://wings.ucdavis.edu/Book/Flight/intermediate/measure-01.html
4. What is Mach 1, and how fast is it?
   http://wings.ucdavis.edu/Book/Flight/intermediate/move-01.html
5. Now it's time for a little flight training. Go to:
   http://www.planemath.com/activities/pmenterprises/index.html

Enter the training department and choose "Forces of Flight" to complete the following:

1. Describe the four forces that allow a plane to fly.
2. Explain in words or pictures Bernoulli's Principle.
3. Sketch an aeordynamic plane.
4. Why does a crumpled piece of paper fall to the floor more quickly than a flat sheet of paper?
5. Which of the following will increase a plane's speed? thrust $<$ drag; thrust $=$ drag; thrust $>$ drag.

Now choose "Tour of the Basics" and complete the following:

1. How does a propeller provide thrust?
2. What part of the plane's wing allows it to bank?
3. Explain why a pilot would lower the wing flaps during landing.
4. What allows the plane to yaw?
5. What controls the pitch of the plane?
6. Use your hand to demonstrate yaw and pitch to your partner.

They said it couldn't be done! Visit the Virtual Flight Museum at http://hawaii.psychology.msstate.edu/invent and complete the following:

1. Read an article from the 1905 *Scientific American* and
   a. Explain how the author feels about the Wright's first flight.
   b. Determine how much farther and how much longer (time) the September 29th Wright Brother's flight was than the September 26th flight. (Hint: Choose "Just Off the Runway.")
2. Describe Clement Ader's role in the development of the airplane. (Hint: Choose "Inventors' Gallery.")
3. Fly the 1903 Wright Flyer Simulator.

And now for some PlaneMath!
Visit PlaneMath at http://www.planemath.com/activities/pmactivitiesall.html and choose "Applying Flying." Then complete the following activities with your partner:

1. Flight Path
2. Plane Capacity
3. Filler Up
4. Lift-Off

Flying on your own. Design, build, and fly your own plane with your partner. Be sure to try modifications to improve your plane's flight speed and distance. Record data and graph your flight data or create a spreadsheet! You've earned your wings!

1. http://www.phxskyharbor.com/skyharbr/kids/planesub.html
2. http://www.sprocketworks.com/
3. http://www.al.com/children/flyact.htm

For more high-flying fun!

1. http://www.nasa.gov/kids.html
2. http://www.af.mil/aflinkjr/
3. http://wings.ucdavis.edu/index.html
4. http://www.planemath.com/

Interdisciplinary Designs

Curriculum designs that are featured in schools seek to pull information together for students so they may see the various connections and relationships. Since the "real world" is an interdisciplinary place by its very nature, this approach often features "hands-on" and applied learning. The Internet is very useful for this instructional approach because it is easy to find examples of any comparative item. The skills of organizing data, ordering information, comparing data, and contrasting data are natural planning avenues using the interdisciplinary approach.

Cultures of the World

Grade Level	5–8
Type Activity	Compare and contrast
Journey References	Cultures, religions, languages, flags, wedding customs, India, Madagasgar, Ireland, New Zealand
Outcomes	a. To familiarize students with at least three different cultures
	b. To compare and contrast these cultures by symbols, languages, history, religions, and customs
	c. To define culture in everyday operational terms

Culture is a difficult thing to understand. When confronted with a different language or religion or custom, we often wonder why other people aren't like us. In this unit you will be asked to learn about several cultures that are quite different and try to determine just what a culture is. You may select from the countries identified or pick out another culture, perhaps one where your ancestors came from.

First, let's find out what the dictionary says about culture. Copy down the official definition of culture from this site: http://work.ucsd.edu:5141/cgi-bin/http_webster.

Next, let's pick out some exotic cultures that are NOT alike and find out about them. One great source is the *CIA World Fact Book* at http://www.odci.gov/cia/publications/factbook/index/html. Another good general resource is the Web Virtual Library at http://www.vlib.org/. We will use India, New Zealand, Madagasgar, and Ireland for starters. If you don't know where these countries are, check out http://www.mapsofindia.com/ or http://www.maps.co.nz/ or any of the great maps from National Geographic at http://www.nationalgeographic.com/maps.

Just guessing, do you think the locations (latitude) and weather of these countries affect their culture? Do any of these countries have similar weather due to their latitudes?

What languages do you think are spoken in these places? Would you like to learn a few words of a foreign language? Check these out: phrases in 66 languages at http://www.travlang.com/languages or translate a phrase at http://www.logos.it. How about French at http://www.ambafrance.org/ALF or German at http://web.uvic.ca/german/149/ or Spanish at http://www.studyspanish.com, or even romantic Italian at http://www.cyberitalian.com. Of course, they teach more of this in high schools.

Flags of countries are interesting because they are symbolic of things important to any culture. Many Muslim countries, for instance, have swords on their flags. The United States' flag has thirteen red and white stripes representing our first colonies. Check out the flags of India, Egypt, Japan, and Brazil and see what they are saying with their flags. Can you draw any conclusions about flags and cultures?

Religions are very important in cultures. From the CIA factbook cited earlier, can you say what religions you might find if you visited Ireland? New Zealand? Madagsgar? What about India? What are three primary religions found in India?

Holidays often defines a culture. In the United States we celebrate the Fourth of July; the French celebrate a similar holiday on July 14th (Bastille Day). What do you suppose is a holiday in India (http://www.welcometoindia.com/culture/festival.html.) or Madagascar (http://www.madagascar-guide.com/top/HP_Fr1Eng.html) or New Zealand (http://www.nzway.co.nz/)

History also plays a part in defining the particular culture of any country. Read about the long history of India at http://www.itihaas.com or of Madagascar at http://iias.leidenuniv.nl/iiasn/iiasn7/iswa/ellis.html or of New Zealand at http://discovernz.co.nz/. What events in the history of India, Madagascar, and New Zealand do you think would influence the way they live and what they believe and value?

It's also interesting to note how some cultures value the same things even though their histories, religions, and languages are different. Both New Zealand (http://parks.yahoo.com/parks/international/new_zealand_s_parks/) and Madagascar (http://www.inforamp.net/~ornstn/madagascar.html) value their wildlife and are trying to protect rare birds, fish, and animals.

Finally, we can look at one custom, weddings, to see the diversity in the world in which we live. Check out the customs in these places: Africa (http://melanet.com/awg/), Scotland (http://weddingcircle.com/ethnic/scot/), Japan (http://www.japan-guide.com/e/e2061.htm), and Israel (http://weddingcircle.com/ethnic/jewish/).

So, now you've looked at history, holidays, languages, religions, climates, and other things that make up a culture. State in your own words a definition of culture.

Before leaving this activity, let's apply what we know to our own culture here in the United States. We've learned that our flag represents (the states, the colonies, independence, other).

List some of the events in our short history that have become important.

List some of our most celebrated holidays.

What is the national language, and some other languages, spoken in the United States?

Do we have a national religion? Do we celebrate religious holidays? What are some religious holidays?

Are there other questions you'd like answered about the topic of cultures?

Cooperative Learning Designs

Over the past decade, many schools have tried to implement cooperative learning as an instructional strategy. Cooperative learning is also a curriculum design because it purposefully uses mixed-ability groups and focuses on the quality of interaction among students in the learning process. By-products of Cooperative Learning strategies, beyond solid achievement, include work skills, sharing, and accepting others.

Cooperative Learning at the classroom level can take six or seven configurations such as the share-pair, jigsaw, teams-games-tournaments, and so forth. Each of these "subdesigns" or instructional designs affects how students act and react to learning opportunities in the classroom setting.

What Is Pollution?

Grade Level	5–9
Type Activity	Cooperative share pair / jigsaw models
Journey References	Acid rain, air pollution, wetlands, environment, global warming, rain forests, water pollution, waste management
Outcomes	Using cooperative learning techniques (jigsaw), students will:

a. Conduct a primary study of one kind of pollution
b. Present findings to other group members (share-pairs)
c. Collectively define what pollution is and is not
d. Identify common examples of pollution in the community

A primary study group of six students will be formed using mixed-ability grouping. The group will be asked to conduct a study of pollution and apply the findings to an analysis sheet on their computers. Three types of pollution will be assessed by the students: air pollution, water pollution and noise pollution. Two students (a share-pair) will be assigned to each kind of pollution. Within each group, individual students will have an assigned specialty (individual accountability) such as the greenhouse effect, wetlands, global warming, rain forests, or waste management.

Listed here are the sites the students will visit while completing the analysis sheets:

Topic 1: Air Pollution

Student 1: Acid rain
Student 2: Global warming

Air Pollution

Glossary of terms: http://www.shsu.edu/~chemistry/Glossary/glos.html
Update from the EPA: http://www.epa.gov/airnow/
Polluting industries: http://www.pirg.org/enviro/cleanair/fact.htm
World with no cars: http://radawana.cg.tuwien.ac.at/~martinpi/nocar.html

Acid Rain (Student 1—Topic 1)
ABC's of acid rain: http://qlink.queensu.ca/~4lrm4/
Frequent questions: http://www.ns.ec.gc.ca/aeb/ssd/acid/acidfaq.html
Laws and regulations: http://www.epa.gov/docs/acidrain/lawsregs/lraindex.html

Global Warming (Student 2—Topic 1)
Warming update: http://law.pace.edu/env/energy/globalwarming.html
Greenhouse network: http://www.greenhousenet.org
The future: http://www.enviroweb.org/edf/

Topic 2: Water Pollution
Student 1: Rain forests
Student 2: Wetlands

Water Pollution
About water pollution: http://www.nce.unr.edu/swp/
Clean water action plan: http://www.cleanwater.gov/action/overview.html
MBTEs in drinking water: http://www.epa.gov/safewater/mtbe.html

Rain Forests (Student 1—Topic 2)
Rainforest workshop: http://passporttoknowledge.com/rainforest/intro.html
Statistics and photos: http://www.rainforests.net
Ecology sites: http://www.world-science.com/biology/ecology.htm

Wetlands (Student 2—Topic 2)
Wetlands—EPA site: http://www.epa.gov/OWOW/wetlands/vital/toc.html
The estuary: http://www.estuarylive.org
Contaminants: http://www.time.com/time/reports/environment/heroes/contaminants/

Topic 3: Noise Pollution
Student 1: Sounds
Student 2: Controls

Noise Pollution
Effects of noise: http://www.nonoise.org/library/handbook/handbook.htm
Antinoise information: http://www.lhh.org/noise/index.htm

Sounds (Student 1—Topic 3)
Music and noise: http://www.lhh.org/noise/facts/music.htm
Sounds of a Rain forest: http://www.naturenet.com.br

Controls (Student 2—Topic 3)
Laws to control noise: http://www4.law.cornell.edu/uscode/42/ch65.text.html
All six students in the cooperative learning group will respond to the following questions while reading in their subareas:

1. What is meant by pollution?
2. Give an example from your sites of a kind of pollution.
3. Is this kind of pollution present where you live?

After each of the six students has read his or her sections, taken notes, and answered these questions, the students will meet to 'teach' one another about what they have found. Each student will take notes on the two-minute talk by the other five students.

After listening to what has been learned about the three kinds of pollution (air, water, noise), students will redefine pollution. What is pollution? What isn't pollution? A formal statement will be constructed for review by the teacher when completed.

Finally, the students will compile a collective list of examples of air, water, and noise pollution in their community. If the teacher wishes so, the students will identify these kinds of pollution at the school. A memo to the student council identifying these problems may be drafted by the cooperative learning group.

Problem-Solving Designs

Since the ultimate goal of any program of education is to produce useful citizens who can benefit from what they have learned and experienced, some curriculum designs focus squarely on real events and problems in our society. In such designs, students are asked to analyze and synthesize large amounts of information and then apply that knowledge skillfully to the problems addressed.

In the following activity, students learn about various kinds of disasters that disrupt our lives and then attempt to generalize how such events might be avoided or minimized.

Disasters

Grade Level	7–12
Type Activity	Analysis of information provided and application to issues or problems
Journey References	Plagues, fires, earthquakes, floods, tornadoes
Outcomes	a. Students will be able to generalize across large bodies of information.
	b. Students will be able to distinguish similarities and differences in the data sources.
	c. Students will be able to locate and apply useful information to address an issue or problem.

In this journey, students will visit various Internet sites to familiarize themselves with the scale of human disasters regularly occurring on earth. Despite our extensive knowledge and capacity to invent solutions to problems, disasters occur at regular intervals to "mock" our knowledge and powers.

In reading in each of the four areas (plagues, floods, fires, tornadoes), the student will seek to answer the following organizing questions that will form the basis of a position paper to be written:

1. What constitutes a disaster?
2. What do most disasters have in common?
3. How are the four types of disaster alike and not alike?
4. What have we learned about controlling disasters that would be generally useful in responding to any natural catastrophe?

To gain background information fc the position paper, the student will visit the following preselected Internet sites:

Plagues

Plagues in Renaissance Europe: http://jefferson.village.virginia.edu/osheim/intro.html
The Black Death: http://www.discovery.com/stories/history/blackdeath/blackdeath.html
The Centers for Disease Control on plagues:
http://www.cdc.gov/ncidod/dvbid/plagindex.htm
Prevention of plagues: http://www.cdc.gov/ncidod/dvbid/plagprevent.htm

Floods
FEMA fact sheet: http://www.fema.gov/library/flood.htm
The Oregon floods of 1997: http://www.teleport.com/~samc/flood1.html
Warning technology: http://www.alertsystems.org/
Prevention of floods: http://www.pbs.org/wgbh/nova/flood/

Fires
Great fires in the United States: http://www.acusd.edu/~dpuffer/greatfires.html
Forest fires in the United States: http://www.scd.ucar.edu/vg/FIRE/ClarkFire.html
Fire causation: http://www.facts-1.com/

Tornadoes
Facts about twisters: http://www.usca.sc.edu/AEDC442/442984001/tkng.html
National Weather Service: http://www.nssl.noaa.gov/NWSTornado
Tornado tracker: http://www.gopbi.com/FEATURES/tornadotracker
Stormchase Central: http://www.Stormchase.com

To write the policy paper, the student assesses the information about these four forms of disaster, focusing on the organizing questions, and writes an essay about the prevention of human catastrophes. The paper is limited to ten pages, double-spaced, and should be submitted to the teacher in one week by e-mail.

Critical and Creative Thinking Designs

Curriculum designs that feature critical and creative thinking seek to promote skills in data analysis, create new forms of knowledge, or further develop student imagination. Most such activities would be futuristic or treat conventional wisdom in unique or novel ways.

Methane Hydrates

Grade Level	7–12
Type Activity	Creative thinking
Journey References	Underseas, global warming, methane hydrates, antarctica, and earthquakes
Outcomes	To have students practice the following skills of creative thinking:*

a. Ask self-directing questions
b. Generalize beyond immediate data
c. Understand associations
d. Practice perceptual scanning
e. Practice model building.

Source: Jon Wiles, Skill Clusters for Creative Thinking. Taipei, Taiwan: ROC Press, 1980.

"New Energy Source Interests Congress" read the Associated Press story in newspapers across the United States in early April 2000. This story featured preliminary public awareness knowledge about a hot and controversial scientific topic, the discovery of a new and vast energy source called methane hydrates (MH). Essentially a crystalline solid consisting of a methane molecule surrounded by frozen water molecules, this controversial substance is found in abundance on the floor of the oceans and under permafrost on land. Visit http://www.hydrates.org/.

For energy companies, MH is an exciting new source of fuel that might solve the problem of depleted oil reserves. Scientist believe that hydrates contain twice as much energy as the world's coal, oil, and natural gas combined. This powderlike substance is produced through a combining of methane gas and water under high pressure and low temperature. Test drilling has begun in Canada and off the coast of Japan, and major deposits have been mapped in Antarctica (http://coolspace.gsfc.nasa.gov/nasamike/essays/vip/vip.htm), the Gulf of Mexico, and off the coasts of Oregon and South Carolina.

On the other side of this story is the very justifiable fear that methane hydrates are dangerous to humans and may be the real culprit in global warming (http://www.global change.org/center.htm). Methane hydrates contain three thousand times the methane found in our atmosphere! What would result if these gases were suddenly released? One government paper hypothesized that the warming of the earth during the late Permian period might have released methane gases at high levels and caused the extinction of plants and animals (http://marine.usgs.gov/fact-sheets/gas-hydrates/).

Environmentalists are particularly worried about drilling now being initiated and the hurried exploration of this energy source. The composition of the earth near MH deposits is unstable due to the icy nature of the soil composite, much like areas that experience landslides during earthquakes. Most drilling to date has caused landslides under the sea, thus releasing hydrates into the air (http://www.epm.ornl.gov/NEW/m/hydrates.html). A secondary concern from such excavation is the release of unknown bacteria trapped in ice for long periods of time.

Scientists from the energy companies are working hard to determine how methane hydrates can be mined safely. Models are being constructed (heat and mass transfer) to develop ways to maintain the cold conditions found three hundred feet below the surface of the oceans, while at the same time surface drilling occurs unchecked in the Arctic (http://www.gasandoil.com/goc/features/fex81086.htm).

Student Response

1. What five questions would you want to ask about methane hydrates?
2. Of these five questions, which two would most probably lead you to new understandings?
3. What is the connection between methane hydrates and other energy sources?
4. What is the connection between methane hydrates and the earth's atmosphere?
5. Are there underlying assumptions in the information that should be challenged?
6. As we think about a model of how to extract this resource, are there existing precedents or operations that we should study such as nuclear energy, gas pipelines, or blimps?
7. What seemingly unrelated items come to mind as you think about this problem (ice cubes, the formation of a diamond)?
8. Make a sketch of a machine or a model of how we might safely mine this precious resource without catastrophe.
9. Were there things you don't know that kept your drawing from being as good as possible (such as theories of heat and mass transfer)?
10. State any nonconventional or wild ideas (hunches or intuition) that you have about this situation.

Source: Michele Keating, Jon Wiles, Mary Piazza, *Learning Webs: Curriculum Journeys on the Internet* (unpublished manuscript).

APPENDIX 6.2
WEBSITES FOR PRACTICE

Listed here are web sites used in creating the curriculum journeys in appendix 6.1, and some that could have been used. These sites can be arranged in many other ways to make new journeys.

First Kid in Space

Kennedy Space Center

Welcome Station Info	*http://www.ksc.nasa.gov/*
Virtual Tour	*http://www.kennedyspacecenter.com/index.html*
Discovery Program	*http://www.ksc.nasa.gov/shuttle/resources/orbiters/discovery.html*
Night Launch	*http://www.ksc.nasa.gov/shuttle/missions/sts-103/images/medium/KSC-99PP-1476.jpg*
Shop the KSC Store	*http://www.thespaceshop.com*

All the World's a Stage

Shakespeare's Southwark	*http://www.southwark.gov.uk/discovering/shakes.htm*
Hamlet	*http://www.pathguy.com/hamlet.htm*

Math Review

Practice	*http://www.worksheetfactory.com/*
Applications	*http://www.pbs.org/teachersource/math/elementary_analysis.shtm*
Baseball Math	*http://www.funbrain.com*

Quadratic Equations

Practice	*http://www.quickmath.com/www02/pages/modules/equations/*
Problem Solving	*http://www.unican.es/sosmath/algebra/quadraticeq/bdef/bdef.html*
Sputnik	*http://sputnik.infospace.ru/*

Miss Shell Visits Paris

Eiffel Tower	*http://www.tour-eiffel.fr*
Tourist Spots	*http://paris-tourism.com/places/notredame/index.html*
More Information	*http://www.francetourism.com*

Flight

Aerodynamics	*http://wings.ucdavis.edu/Book/Flight/intermediate/measure-01.html*
Flight Training	*http://www.planemath.com/activities/pmenterprises/index.html*
Go Fly	*http://www.al.com/children/flyact.htm*

World Cultures

Definitions	*http://work.ucsd.edu:5141/cgi-bin/http_webster*
CIA Facts	*http://www.odci.gov/cia/publications/factbook/index.html*
Maps	*http://www.nationalgeographic.com/maps*
Languages	*http://www.travlang.com/languages/*
Flags	*http://www.theodora.com/flags.html*

What Is Pollution?

Air	*http://www.epa.gov/airnow/*
Water	*http://www.nce.unr.edu/swp/*
Noise	*http://www.nonoise.org/library/handbook/handbook.htm*

Disasters

Plagues	*http://jefferson.village.virginia.edu/osheim/intro.html*
Floods	*http://www.fema.gov/library/flood.htm*
Fires	*http://www.acusd.edu/~dpuffer/greatfires.html*
Tornadoes	*http://www.stormchase.com*

Methane Hydrates

Definitions	*http://www.hydrates.org/*
Global Warming	*http://www.globalchange.org/center.htm*
Drilling	*http://www.gasandoil.com/goc/features/fex81086.htm*

APPENDIX 6.3

PROFILES FOR TECHNOLOGY-LITERATE STUDENTS

Grades Pre-K–2

Prior to completion of grade 2, students will

1. Use input devices (mouse, keyboard, remote control) and output devices (monitor, printer) to operate computers, VCRs, audiotapes, telephones, and other technologies.
2. Use a variety of media and technology resources for directed and independent learning activities.
3. Communicate about technology using developmentally appropriate and accurate terminology.
4. Use multimedia resources (interactive books, educational software, elementary multimedia encyclopedias) to support learning.
5. Work cooperatively and collaboratively with peers, family members, and others when using technology in the classroom.
6. Demonstrate positive social and ethical behaviors when using technology.
7. Practice responsible use of technology systems and software.
8. Create multimedia products with support from teachers, family members, or student partners.
9. Use technology resources (puzzles, logical thinking programs, writing tools, digital cameras, drawing tools) for problem solving, communication, and illustration of thoughts, ideas, and stories.
10. Gather information and communicate with others using telecommunications, with support from teachers, family members, or student partners.

Grades 3–5

Prior to completion of grade 5, students will

1. Use keyboards and other common input and output devices (including adaptive devices) efficiently and effectively.
2. Discuss common uses of technology in daily life and advantages and disadvantages those uses provide.
3. Discuss responsible uses of technology and information and describe personal consequences of inappropriate use.
4. Use tools and peripherals to support personal productivity, to remediate skill deficits, and to facilitate learning throughout the curriculum.
5. Use technology tools (multimedia authoring, presentation, Web tools, digital cameras, scanners) for individual and collaborative writing, communication, and publishing activities to create knowledge products for audiences inside and outside the classroom.
6. Use telecommunications to access remote information, to communicate with others, and to pursue personal interests.

7. Use telecommunications and online resources (e-mail, online discussions. Web environments) to participate in collaborative problem-solving activities.
8. Use technology resources (calculators, probes, videos, educational software) for problem solving, self-directed learning, and extended learning activities.
9. Determine when technology is useful and select the appropriate tools and technology resources to address tasks and problems.
10. Evaluate the accuracy, relevance, appropriateness, comprehensiveness, and bias of electronic information sources.

Grades 6–8

Prior to completion of grade 8, students will

1. Apply strategies for identifying and solving routine hardware and software problems.
2. Demonstrate knowledge of current changes in information technologies and the effect those changes have on the workplace and on society.
3. Exhibit legal and ethical behaviors when using information and technology and discuss consequences of misuse.
4. Use content-specific tools, software, and simulations (environmental probes, graphing calculators, exploratory environments, Web tools) to support learning and research.
5. Apply multimedia tools and peripherals to support personal productivity, group collaboration, and learning throughout the curriculum.
6. Design, develop, publish, and present products (Web pages, videotapes) using technology resources that communicate curriculum concepts to audiences inside and outside the classroom.
7. Collaborate with peers, experts, and others using telecommunications and collaborative tools to investigate curriculum-related problems, issues, and information and to develop solutions or products for audiences inside and outside the classroom.
8. Select and use appropriate tools and technology resources to accomplish tasks and to solve problems.
9. Demonstrate an understanding of concepts underlying hardware, software, and connectivity and of practical applications to learning and problem solving.
10. Research and evaluate the accuracy, relevance, appropriateness, comprehensiveness, and bias of electronic information sources concerning real-world problems.

Grades 9–12

Prior to completion of grade 12, students will

1. Identify capabilities and limitations of contemporary and emerging technology resources and assess the potential of these systems and services to address personal, lifelong learning, and workplace needs.
2. Make informed choices among technology systems, resources, and services.
3. Analyze advantages and disadvantages of widespread use and reliance on technology in the workplace and in society as a whole.

4. Demonstrate and advocate legal and ethical behaviors regarding the use of technology and information.
5. Use technology tools and resources for managing and communicating personal or professional information.
6. Evaluate technology-based options, including distance and distributed education, for lifelong learning.
7. Routinely and efficiently use online information resources for collaboration, research, publications, communications, and productivity.
8. Select and apply technology tools for research, information analysis, problem solving, and decision making in content learning.
9. Investigate and apply expert systems, intelligent agents, and simulations in real-world situations.
10. Collaborate with peers, experts, and others to contribute to a content-related knowledge base by using technology to compile, synthesize, produce, and disseminate.

Source: Engage: A Framework for Effective Technology Work in Schools. Presented at the Worth Central Regional Educational Laboratory Regional Conference, Atlanta, Georgia, June 2000.

chapter 7

ELEMENTARY SCHOOL PROGRAMS AND ISSUES

> The period we're living through has been marked by extraordinary challenges that test our determination, our creativity, and our resources. It is a time of transition not only for education, but for all our society. As we move from the Industrial Age of the 20th Century to the Information Age of the 21st, we keep tripping over remnants of the past, old ideas that we have failed to change.[1]

The elementary school of the first decade of the twenty-first century will represent a dramatic change from the conservatism of the previous three decades. Following the 1960s experimentation with open space, nongrading, team teaching, and extended enrichment, the decades of the 1970s, 1980s, and 1990s followed with, "Let's get back to the basics."

Fueled by legislation, national concerns about comparisons of U.S. students with those of other countries, and new demands of U.S. workers in a global economy, "basics" were redefined from minimum skills to higher standards, benchmarks, and a more rigorous curriculum. Although the attention was focused on exit skills for high school students to make sure they were not deficient in basic literacy and mathematic competency, major changes occurred at the elementary level. By the late 1990s, the elementary curriculum in many school districts included the following:

- ☐ Implementation of national standards in reading, writing, and mathematics
- ☐ The use of performance-based assessments with rubrics

- ☐ Competency-based instruction
- ☐ Academic skills placement tests
- ☐ State standards and frameworks along with assessment items and benchmark tests
- ☐ Portfolio assessment systems
- ☐ Aligning the curriculum through a deliberate approach designed to teach essential learning skills in a systematic and sequential manner

In addition, some elementary schools have implemented inclusion programs and "full-service" schools to cope with large numbers of children from single-parent and poverty households, and continue to deal with increasing cultural diversity and mobility of parents. Elementary teachers continue to be "all things to all children." Characterizing those teachers is the statement shown in Figure 7.1, which was posted in an elementary teachers' area.

The struggle between those who would narrow the elementary curriculum to testable areas and those who desire a broader school program continues in many school districts. With many children attending daycare centers years before they enter elementary school, the socialization function of the early grades (children

---

Plans, writes daily notes, prepares weekly progress reports, distributes fluoride, collects supermarket receipts for free computers, bundles newspapers, collects soup labels, writes clinic passes, takes a lunch count, collects money for book orders, collects money for ticket sales, collects money for after-school movies, collects money for pictures, writes a monies collected form, handles cumulative folders, handles science cards, handles reading and math folders, keeps insert cards current, computes grades and writes report cards by hand, comes up with a positive comment for each child, creates a science fair project, keeps track of "book it" and writes pizza slips, escorts children wherever they go, takes attendance, ties shoes, fastens clothes, wipes noses, evaluates the kids in all areas, files papers, directs programs, cleans, refers kids for programs (Chapter One, MWA, small group, ESE), delivers textbooks and keeps track of them, conducts head lice checks, teaches social skills (burping, nose picking . . .), breaks up fights, takes place of mom or dad for eight hours a day, watches for signs of abuse, lends lunch money, creates bulletin-board masterpieces, survives class parties and room mothers, remembers birthdays and other special events, has tremendous bladder control, eats lunch in 27 minutes or less, gives up much free time, counsels parents, works school fairs, sells candy bars, sings the school song, orders materials, buys hundreds of girl scout cookies, organizes field trips, teaches many levels in one subject, deals with the same kiddos for eight hours, prepares honor roll list, locates appropriate clothing, has bus duty, interns, calls parents, prepares perfect attendance lists, quarterly rewards, finds lost articles, attends PTA meetings, laminates materials, remediates standardized tests, . . . and, of course, teaches.

FIGURE 7.1   Roles of the Elementary School Teacher

getting to know adults other than parents and children other than siblings) needs updating. Programs need to be designed to help children cope with disruptions of home routines and limited parent contact. According to the last census, over one half of mothers of children under the age of two are in the workforce, so this trend will continue. The "Ozzie and Harriet" family of the 1950s no longer exists in the United States.

Millions of new immigrants have dramatically increased the number of non-English-speaking students in public schools. The elementary school is now serving as the great melting pot of the nation as new languages, customs, and cultures are brought to the school. With the great diversity of student populations in our schools, some favor ability grouping and tracking for the gifted. However, such programs most often exclude the minority child, the poor child, and the non-English-speaking child.

Additionally, school districts and state legislatures have begun to explore the concept of school choice, in which parents have an opportunity to select public school affiliation. By 1997 most states had considered or enacted choice initiatives.

The idea of choice has an appeal because it seems to be more consistent with our democratic commitment and lends itself to the revitalization of schools. However, there are a number of risks involved in the idea and many questions to be answered. For example, will school choice

- ☐ Prove culturally divisive?
- ☐ Provide sufficient common learnings?
- ☐ Increase racial isolation?
- ☐ Increase social class isolation?
- ☐ Result in "skimming" and "dumping"?
- ☐ Yield ability grouping or tracking?
- ☐ Harm nonchoice schools?
- ☐ Harm nonchoosers?
- ☐ Harm poor choosers?
- ☐ Undermine the forging of a public?
- ☐ Give way to an undesirable stress on marketing?
- ☐ Yield indifference and inequity as the best programs become overenrolled?
- ☐ Deny parents an operating base?
- ☐ Compromise professional integrity?

Balancing academics and exploration in early childhood programs is another issue confronting the elementary school. Many teachers of young children are faced with pressures to stress academics at the same time that early childhood specialists urge early childhood programs to be more developmentally appropriate. The goal of developmentally appropriate teaching is to provide instruction suited to the age and cognitive readiness of each child.

Although the concept of developmentally appropriate instruction is not new, schools during the 1970s, 1980s, and 1990s surrendered this principle under pressure to give children a more rigorous academic preparation—pressure fueled in part by the back-to-basics movement and overreliance on testing.

Other issues in elementary education will be discussed later in this chapter. In this new century, it is useful to examine the history and purposes of the elementary school and to study the major components of the elementary curriculum.

BASIS OF THE ELEMENTARY SCHOOL CURRICULUM

The modern elementary curriculum has evolved over the past two hundred years from a narrow curriculum devoted to the teaching of reading, writing, and arithmetic to a broad program encompassing not only basic skills, but also a variety of learning experiences. Because schools in the United States, as in other countries, are mechanisms for social change, schools often become battlegrounds for diverse groups with conflicting interests. The history of the elementary school during the past several years has been one of continuous change. Schools in the United States, like the nation itself, are in transition. By examining the history of the elementary school, we can see that elementary schools have been responsive to the needs of our expanding and increasingly diverse society.

Elementary School History

The establishment of free elementary schools for all children by state legislation was a grand and unique experiment in this country. Free elementary schools became associated with the highest ideals of our citizens.

Unlike most other countries, the United States has no national system of education. Under our Constitution, control of schools has been delegated to the states. Precedents were established early in the history of our country for the exercise of state legislative authority in educational matters. As early as 1642, the colonies were enacting legislation concerning educational matters. The Colonial Assembly of Massachusetts enacted compulsory education laws in 1642 and 1647. The 1647 legislation compelled communities over a certain size to set up grammar schools. That legislation, known as the Old Deluder Satan Act, passed by the General Court of the Massachusetts Bay Colony, required towns to establish common schools and grammar schools so men could read the Scriptures and escape the clutches of Satan. The act was not only the first law in America requiring that schools be established, but was also the first example in history of legislation requiring that children be provided an education at the expense of the community.

By 1693 legislation was passed allowing selectmen authority to levy school taxes with the consent of the majority of the townspeople. Previously, each town could determine how buildings, salaries, and other matters were handled.

For more than one hundred years, elementary teachers relied heavily on the *New England Primer,* a book that used Bible verses and books to teach reading and number skills. Disciplinary practices also followed religious lines, with flogging and other measures designed to "drive the devil out of children."

In addition to religious purposes, early elementary schools served another purpose—rallying support for the new American political system. James Madison and Thomas Jefferson both spoke out against ignorance and in favor of an educated populace. Elementary schools were established for the maintenance of society by inculcating not only religious but also political doctrine.

As the nation expanded westward with new states admitted to the Union, the elementary school experienced reforms. Many of the reforms were influenced by European examples. Perhaps the person most responsible for building the base for the modern elementary school was the Swiss educational reformer Johann Heinrich Pestalozzi (1746–1827). Pestalozzi viewed child growth and development as organismic (natural) rather than mechanistic. He recognized that the narrow curriculum, consisting mainly of mechanical exercises in reading, was inadequate to prepare children for intelligent citizenship. Through teacher training programs, he helped prepare elementary teachers to provide a variety of learning experiences for children. His ideas were best expressed in his book, *How Gertrude Teaches Her Children.*[2]

In the early 1800s, Prussian educators borrowed many of Pestalozzi's methods to build a national system of education. Horace Mann and other educators of the day visited Prussia and returned to the United States with glowing reports of the Prussian-Pestalozzian system. That system, imitated in this country, included grading students on the basis of ability, better methods of instruction and discipline, setting up a state agency for education, and developing special teacher-training institutions.

Public education became increasingly popular in the first half of the 1800s. The first state board of education was established in Massachusetts in 1837 with Horace Mann as its first secretary. By 1876 the principle of public elementary education had been accepted in all states. The period from 1826 to 1876, known as the *public school revival,* led to a new American conscience regarding educating children. Legislators were pressured to provide more money for elementary schools, and the curriculum was enriched.

Expansion and Continued Reforms of Elementary Schools

From 1876 to the mid-1930s, the United States became a great industrial nation. As the country moved from a simple agricultural society to an industrial power, schools as instruments of society became instruments of change. Elementary enrollments doubled, many new subjects were added to the curricula, and the school day was lengthened. World War I had resulted in demands for new skills on the part of youth, and curriculum change included a back-to-basics movement in 1918 to ensure that all children could read and write. Teacher education is often an influence in curriculum change, and because new courses in psychology and methods were introduced in teacher-training institutions, the elementary curriculum began to change. By the 1930s, standardized tests were used to determine achievement in school subjects, and individual and group intelligence tests were administered. Efforts were made to differentiate instruction for slow, average, and above-average elementary children.

During the 1920s and 1930s, educational philosophers such as John Dewey had a great influence on the elementary curriculum. Dewey and other "progressive" educators saw schools as agencies of society designed to improve our democratic way of life. Dewey believed that schools should be a reflection of community life, with students studying about the home, neighborhood, and community. By studying what is familiar to them, students become more curious about the disciplines of science, geography, and mathematics. "Learning by doing" is a principle of learning that was central to Dewey's ideas about schools. Because Dewey believed that active children learn more, he argued that learning in the elementary school should not include simply rote, mechanistic learning activities, but a variety of creative activities in which students are active participants in the learning process. Dewey maintained that the curricula of the elementary school should build on the interests of students and should represent real life by discussing and continuing the activities with which the child is already familiar at home.

The progressive education movement, led by John Dewey, George Counts, Harold Rugg, and others, heavily influenced the elementary curricula until 1957, when *Sputnik* forced a reexamination of the purpose of the elementary school. Critics such as Admiral Rickover and Arthur Bestor censured progressive education as failing to provide students with the necessary skills and knowledge to compete in a scientific world. Congressional acts establishing the National Science Foundation (NSF) and the National Defense Education Act (NDEA) pumped millions of dollars into the development of science and mathematics programs and materials. The elementary curriculum began to reflect a growing emphasis on science and mathematics in student courses such as "Science: A Process Approach" and in-service programs designed to improve teachers' skills in teaching science and mathematics.

The 1960s began an era of innovation in the elementary curriculum. Many of the innovations dealt with organizational changes such as nongrading, open classrooms, and team teaching. Elementary school buildings were designed to facilitate those organizational changes. As with other innovations involving organizational changes, teachers were not necessarily prepared to cope with such new ideas. Lack of in-services and continued turnover of elementary staffs resulted in growing resistance to nongrading, open space, and teaming. Moreover, elementary leaders who jumped on bandwagons sometimes confused organizational *means* with *ends*. Although their schools were advertised as "open and nongraded," little change occurred in teaching methods or in curriculum substance. Process had been confused with product, and the results of the innovations were disappointing.

Educators in the 1970s and 1980s, for the first time in the history of American education, saw a decline in elementary enrollment. Retrenchment, funding problems, and dissatisfaction with the experimentation of the 1960s led to legislated accountability measures and increased testing programs in the elementary school. Another back-to-basics movement began, with demands for an elementary curriculum emphasizing reading, writing, and arithmetic. By the late 1980s, with enrollment growing for the first time in two decades, the elementary curriculum had expanded to include a variety of learning experiences, but it had narrowed its focus to the basic skills of written and oral communication and mathematics. The shape of the elementary curriculum of the new century has been determined by radical changes in parenting, new job opportunities for adults, and other societal changes leading to the need for schools to provide a myriad of services that used to be offered by other agencies and institutions, and by the family.

ORGANIZING THE CURRICULUM

The curriculum of the elementary school is organized around the bases of knowledge, the needs of society, and human learning and development. As discussed in the previous section, early elementary schools were concerned simply with the transmission of knowledge. Later, schools were seen as an instrument of society to foster religious views and the political doctrine of early America. In the first half of the 1900s, elementary schools were seen as serving an emerging industrial society and as an instrument for the improvement of democratic institutions. Human learning and development did not influence the curriculum until the late 1920s and 1930s when psychologists began to introduce educators to research on student learning and child growth and development. Not until the 1960s did major changes in curriculum and in training curriculum leaders result from research studies of learning and development.

From the 1960s through the 1990s, many new programs were introduced into the elementary program to accommodate young learners and those learners with special needs. Free public kindergarten programs were implemented for five-year-olds in all states, along with a variety of other programs such as Head Start for disadvantaged young children. Special education programs for elementary students with physical and mental disabilities were greatly expanded, and programs for gifted learners were made available to more elementary students. Nursery school programs for three- and four-year-olds, extended-day centers for children before and after school, daycare centers, and even prenatal centers are now found in many elementary schools.

Individualizing Instruction in the Elementary Grades

A consistent theme of elementary school learning for years has been that of individualizing instruction to accommodate differences among students. Owing to the complexity of the concept, the term *individualization* is often misunderstood. Individualization has other dimensions besides the rate of progress. Among the variables that may be manipulated in individualized instruction are

- □ *Materials for study.* Prescribed or individually chosen; various levels of difficulty and with varying purposes.
- □ *Method of study.* Prescribed or chosen methods of learning.
- □ *Pace of study.* Timed or untimed, structured or fluid.
- □ *Sequence of study.* Ordered or providing the option for personal coverage of material.

- □ *Learning focus.* Factual, skill-based, process, or values.
- □ *Place of learning.* Classroom, school, environment, or optional.
- □ *Evaluation of learning.* Exam-based, product-based, open-ended, or student-evaluated.
- □ *Purpose of learning.* Mastery, understanding, application, or experiential.

In most elementary programs, students work with similar materials at about the same pace in the same spaces, and they usually have similar, if not identical, learning criteria for evaluating their progress. Some widespread techniques are used to accommodate differences, however, including grouping, use of materials with differing levels of reading difficulty, and special programs for students at the greatest range from group norms.

Grouping.   Flexibility is the key in any grouping arrangement. The major reason for employing grouping as an instructional technique is to provide more effectively for students' individual differences. Some common groups found in the elementary school are the following:

- □ A *class as a whole* can function as a group. Teachers sometimes have guilt feelings about whole-class activities, but there are occasions when the teacher can address the whole class as a single group. New topic or unit introductions; unit summaries; and activities such as reports, dramatizations, and choral reading may be effectively conducted with the total class.
- □ *Reading level groups* formed according to reading achievement levels are commonly found in classrooms. These groups are not static and must accommodate shifts of pupils from group to group as changes in individual achievement occur.
- □ *Reading need groups* are formed to assist students in mastering a particular reading skill such as pronouncing a phonic element or finding the main idea in a paragraph.
- □ *Interest groups* help students apply reading skills to other language arts and other content areas. Storytelling, recreational reading, writing stories and poems, and dramatization are activities that can be carried out in interest groupings.
- □ *Practice or tutorial groups* are often used to allow students to practice oral reading skills, play skill games, and organize peer teaching situations.
- □ *Research groups* allow for committee work, group projects, and other research activities. Learning centers in the classroom and research areas in the media center are often developed for research groups.
- □ *Individualization* allows a student to work as an individual in selecting books and references for learning projects. Developmental programs provide for individual progress through a series of lessons.

Two common terms used in grouping in the elementary school are heterogeneous (mixed) and homogeneous (like) groups. Usually, these two types of groups are used interchangeably during a school day. Teachers who organize skill groups in the classroom are using homogeneous grouping. The key is flexibility. Students are moved from group to group as they achieve required skills. Also, the skill groups are organized only for a portion of the school day. The rest of the day, students are organized into heterogeneous groups where they can interact with students of varying abilities.

Reading Levels. Another common means of providing for student differences is in providing books of varying degrees of difficulty. Textbook publishers regularly provide grade-specific texts (fourth grade math, for example) with several "leveled" versions. Teachers use the readability of the text as a means of tailoring instruction to the student.

Programs such as Accelerated Reader, STAR Reading, and others provide statistical data collected on students, which allow teachers to assess their students better. Those data can be put into reports for parents. *Readability* is the objective measure of the difficulty of a book or article and usually involves the use of a specific formula, with results reported in terms of grade level. Seven such formulas are listed here.

1. *Flesch Reading Ease Score.* Involves checking word length and sentence length (grades 5–12).
2. *Wheeler and Smith—Index Number.* Involves determining sentence length and number of polysyllabic words (grades primary–4).
3. *Cloze Technique.* Can be used to compare the readability of two pieces of material. Measures redundancy (the extent to which words are predictable), whereas standard readability formulas measure the factors of vocabulary and sentence structure. It can be used to determine relative readability of material but cannot predict readability of a new sample. It does not give grade-level designations.
4. *Lorge Grade Placement Score.* Uses average sentence length in words, number of difficult words per 100 words not on the Dale 769-word list, and number of prepositional phrases per 100 words (grades 3–12).
5. *Fry Graph.* Method is based on two factors: average number of syllables per 100 words and average number of sentences per 100 words. Three randomly selected 100-word samples are used.
6. *SMOG Grading Plan.* Involves counting repetition of polysyllabic words (grades 4–12).
7. *Spache Grade Level Score.* Looks at average sentence length and number of words outside of the Dale list of 769 words to give readability level (grades 1–3).

Armed with such assessments, the teacher can provide students with reading materials tailored to their needs and abilities.

Approaches to teaching reading vary according to how the teacher thinks children learn. Table 7.1 outlines seven approaches now found in public schools and cites their advantages and disadvantages.

Advantages	Disadvantages
I. Basals	
1. Is comprehensive and systematic	1. Is stereotyped and uncreative
2. Presents reading skills in order	2. Limits students to one reading book
3. Is flexible	3. Has an overabundance of material
4. Has a well-established basic vocabulary	4. Is geared to middle-class whites
5. Is equipped with diagnostic tools	5. Tends to be very expensive
6. Builds themes around familiar situations	6. Depends heavily on visual or sight word methods
7. Gives a well-rounded reading choice	7. Leaves little time for creativity
	8. Facilitates little transfer from skill to functional reading
II. Language Experience	
1. Integrates all listening and speaking skills	1. Has limited materials
2. Utilizes student's own language	2. Does not sequence skills
3. Develops sensitivity to the child's environment	3. Has no concrete evaluation process
4. Can be used with the culturally different	4. Limits word-attack skills
5. Encourages sharing of ideas	
6. Develops confidence in language usage	
7. Develops self-expression	
III. Individualized Approach	
1. Enables the child to select appropriate books	1. Allows for insufficient skill development
2. Gives greater opportunity for children to interact with one another	2. Requires a large amount of record keeping
3. Fosters self-confidence with the child progressing at his or her own rate	3. Requires vast amounts of books and supplementary materials
4. Establishes one-to-one relationships through conferences with the teacher	4. Tends to allow children to limit their own selection
5. Diminishes competition and comparison	5. Makes little provision for readiness
6. Is flexible	6. Allows for no advance preparation for words or concepts
	7. Requires teachers with a wide knowledge of books
IV. Linguistic Approach	
1. Begins with familiar words that are phonetically regular	1. Has many different linguistic approaches

TABLE 7.1   Seven Basic Approaches to Teaching Reading

Whole Language vs. Phonics: A Continuing Debate

During the last decade, debate continued on whether phonics or whole language was the better approach to teach beginning readers. *Phonics,* explicit decoding instruction, is known as basic-skills instruction. Phonics builds on a series of basic steps that introduces emergent readers to such fundamental skills as linking sounds and letters, combining sounds, and recognizing words with similar letter–sound patterns.

Whole language, as a teaching approach, embraces the theory that children-learn to read the way they learn to talk—naturally. The whole-language teaching

Advantages	Disadvantages
2. Presents words as wholes	2. Lacks extensive field testing
3. Shows letters as a function by arrangement in the words	3. Has too controlled a vocabulary
4. Develops sentence order early	4. Encourages word-by-word reading
	5. Lacks emphasis on reading for meaning

V. Phonics

Advantages	Disadvantages
1. Develops efficiency in word recognition	1. Tends to isolate speech sounds in an unnatural manner
2. Helps develop independence in word recognition	2. Involves too much repetition; is boring
3. Creates interest because of immediate success for the child	3. Uses the slow process of sounding out words
4. Shows association between print and sounds	4. Has too many exceptions to the rule

VI. Alphabetic Approach

Advantages	Disadvantages
1. Is simpler	1. Lacks clarification regarding techniques and materials
2. Gives opportunity for free expression	2. Makes transition from Initial Teaching Alphabet (ITA) difficult
3. Engenders enthusiasm to read due to quick success	3. Is very expensive
4. Encourages the learning of words more rapidly	4. Confuses children because they see ITA only at school
	5. Has not been around long enough to know its validity

VII. Programmed Instruction

Advantages	Disadvantages
1. Allows child to proceed at his or her own pace	1. Uses limited research
2. Reinforces student after each step	2. Does not consider limited attention span of student
3. Records student progress	3. Becomes repetitious
4. Is self-instructional	4. Bypasses comprehension because it is difficult to program
5. Helps teacher to understand sequencing	5. Gives little room for child to develop his or her own interests or tastes in reading
	6. Is expensive

TABLE 7.1 *Continued*

philosophy builds on a variety of reading and writing activities in which children choose their own books, construct meaning from their own experiences, sound out words in context, and decipher words from syntactical clues.

Many researchers today feel that it is not an either/or choice in selecting reading approaches. Studies suggest that a balanced approach, combining basic skills and whole language, works best for teaching beginning readers.

Studies by the National Institute of Child Health and Human Development in the mid-1990s suggested that most reading disabilities stem from a deficit in the most basic level of the language system—the phoneme.

About 75 to 80 percent of the population will respond to almost any type of teaching method, but others need explicit instruction. Thus, a balanced instructional approach that combines the best elements of whole-language and phonics instruction seems to be the best way to reach the majority of emergent readers.[3]

SELECTION OF CONTENT

Subject content in the elementary school is selected from the basic disciplines of language arts, mathematics, social studies, science, the arts, and health.

Curriculum developers at the national, state, and local levels help to select content. Because the United States does not have a national system of education, the work of curriculum developers and researchers must fit a variety of learning needs and expectations of students in the 13,000 school districts of this country. Although textbook series and curriculum projects may be designed to accomplish that task, the classroom teacher has the final choice on content selection. So, although geography may be taught in grade 7 and American history in grade 8 in most school districts, how these courses are taught and which materials and texts are used are decided by the teachers in local school districts. Indeed, the sequence of courses may be altered in some districts to allow the teaching of American history before geography.

Determining Appropriate Elementary School Curriculum Content

Determining what content is appropriate for elementary schoolchildren is not always easy. Testing programs today often dictate the selection of content. "Teaching for the test" has become a common practice in many classrooms.

Another problem facing elementary educators is the changing nature of our society. Divorce, mobility of families, and pressures brought on by the economy have influenced the achievement of elementary students. Testing programs and accountability legislation in many states have resulted in demands to teach more reading, writing, and mathematics.

Language Arts

Language arts includes the communication skills: reading, writing, listening, and speaking. These four modes of learning are interrelated in a developmental sequence. From listening to speaking to reading to writing, children begin to comprehend and use language skills. The reciprocal relationship among all four of the communication areas implies a need for those areas to be taught in a holistic approach.

The reading component of a total language arts program must include the development of skills in decoding and comprehension in order to use functional and literary written material. Although reading educators differ on their approaches to teaching reading, students who fail to master these skills will likely face a lifetime of underachievement.

Reading.   Reading, perhaps the most controversial area of the elementary program, is not only an emotional issue, but also a political one in many districts. Reading becomes the concern of parents long before their children enter school. Reading has also become the center of national rage and the focus of numerous research studies and a federal crusade in the past quarter century. In recent decades, millions of dollars have been poured into the development of reading programs. There are scores of reading programs that all work, yet we still have millions of nonreaders in our schools. It is debatable whether we are any closer to solving the mysteries of reading. We do know that reading has engaged the time of more teachers and received a larger share of the school dollar than any other subject in the curriculum.

What makes some students find success in reading whereas others find only failure? Some students fail because they deem certain classroom stimuli less important and tend to ignore them; others succeed because they are in tune with the teacher and react positively to instructional stimuli.

Grouping students into high and low groups usually ensures students will be treated differently by teachers. Students in high groups usually

- Read first, when they are more alert and eager.
- Meet for a longer time frame.
- Face a warmer, more receptive teacher, one that smiles, leans toward them, and makes eye contact more frequently.
- Are criticized in a softer, more respectful manner.
- Are disciplined with warnings instead of actions.
- Read approximately three times as much as other reading groups (of which 70 percent will be silent reading) and make more progress.
- Are expected to self-correct reading errors. If teacher-corrected, it is at the end of the section, which doesn't disrupt the reader's fluency.
- Are asked questions that are comprehension checks and require higher-level thinking skills.

However, a totally different atmosphere usually exists for students in low groups, who

- Meet for less time and later in the day, when they have already begun to tire.
- Read more orally, which is slow, halting, and labored; they are therefore reading less and getting further behind.
- Have each error pointed out as it's made. Errors are made three to five times as often and as often as once every ten words. Less time is allowed for self-correction.
- Are asked questions that tend to be literal—checking only to see whether they are listening.
- Face a teacher whose body language is negative—frowns, pursed lips, glares, leaning away, and fidgeting.

- ☐ Read silently only 30 percent of the time.
- ☐ Are aware that as "lows" they "can't read" and avoid it as much as possible.
- ☐ In large groups, are seated farthest from the teacher. These "slow" learners are given less time to respond to questions and have to think faster, thus increasing their chance of failure.[4]

Until teachers see all students as having potential and provide the same stimuli to all students, low and high, reading will continue to be a problem in the elementary school.

Spelling.   Two methods of teaching spelling are found in most elementary schools today. One method, *invented spelling*, involves students writing how they think a word is spelled and checking it later. This method allows students to concentrate on what they are trying to communicate. It also increases the writer's freedom.

The second method, the traditional way, has students memorizing ten to twenty words a week. Students are tested on their spelling rather than on their ability to apply rules to new words. Exercises focus on dictionary use, handwriting, and writing words several times.

New models of spelling in the elementary school suggest that spelling should not be treated as a separate subject, but instead should be seen as a total language system involving writing and reading. Learning to spell should be pleasant, natural, and as easy flowing and unconscious an act as learning to speak.

Writing.   Writing has again become a center of focus in today's elementary schools. Responding to demands of colleges that students know how to write better, elementary and secondary schools have devoted more time in the day to the teaching of writing skills.

Research on children's writing implies that focus on skill instruction in grammar and spelling may come at the expense of composition. Daily writing, conferences, and the focus of skills in the context of writing appear to be more effective.[5]

Elementary schools are striving to integrate composition and literature into their language arts program and to make remedial and regular language arts programs congruent. The goals of an integrated approach are to

1. Place genuine reading and composing at the center of the language arts curriculum.
2. Place skills instruction within rather than before genuine reading and writing.
3. Integrate the various components of language arts through content rather than skills.
4. Insist that all readers and writers—not just the most able learners—gain equal access to genuine reading and writing.[6]

Mathematics

Mathematics is more effective if it is carefully adapted to the developmental characteristics of elementary children. Early in the history of our schools, objectives of mathematics instruction centered on the development of computational skills. By the 1920s and 1930s, objectives shifted to a more practical application of mathematics. Today, mathematics educators are concerned with providing a balanced program in mathematics in which students not only attain computational skills, but also have an understanding of mathematics concepts and reasoning. The rapid increase in the number of microcomputers in elementary schools has resulted in the need for elementary students to perceive and understand structure in mathematics, including concepts, relationships, principles, and modes of mathematical reasoning.

Much of mathematics instruction in the elementary school involves the use of textbooks. A study in 1989 provided an analysis of the overlap between textbook content and content taught.[7] The results challenged the popular notion that elementary school teachers' content decisions are dictated by the mathematics textbooks that they use. In each classroom studied, researchers found important differences between the curriculum of the text and the teacher's topic selection, content emphasis, and sequence of instruction.

The use of computers, whole curricular approaches, and interdisciplinary units are giving elementary teachers new instructional options for delivery of content and skills. Practice sheets and end-of-chapter problems are giving way to these new approaches for teaching elementary mathematics.

The 1990s saw a host of efforts to reform curriculum and instruction in mathematics. *Professional Standards for Teaching Mathematics,* published by The National Council of Teachers of Mathematics (NCTM),[8] led the way in redefining elementary mathematics. The standards developed by the NCTM offer detailed images of the mathematics teaching promoted by many reformers in mathematics education.

Approaches in teaching mathematics include cooperative learning, the use of themes and real-life problems, and the use of group grading on cooperative assignments.[9]

Science

Science in the elementary school has also been influenced by the rapid advancements in technology in this country. During the 1960s, a reform movement urged a shift in science education away from an emphasis on the learning of facts and toward an understanding of the processes of science.[10] Recently, the emphasis has shifted toward the technological applications of science.

Learning scientific concepts, principles, and generalizations allows elementary children to understand better the universe in which they live by enabling them to see orderly arrangement in the natural world and to explain the continual change in the world. A functional competency with the tools of science must also be developed to help students live in a highly technological society.

The *whole approach* to teaching science in the elementary school is the teaching of science with an interdisciplinary scope. In contrast to traditional science instruction, the whole-science approach reinforces the required science curriculum with content from all subject areas in a thematic approach. The integrated approach to teaching science moves science teaching away from lectures and textbooks to a variety of materials and activities. Activities incorporate reading, writing, and mathematics while science concepts are developed. Cooperative learning and a team approach to teaching and learning science are also integral features of the whole-science approach.

In 1990, President Bush stated his goal to "make American students first in the world in mathematics and science achievement by the year 2000." Although no plan of action was presented, elementary schools began to build science programs that nurtured conceptional understandings and targeted scientific attitudes and skills that lead to those understandings.

Figure 7.2 illustrates methods of integrating science with other subject areas.

Reading and Social Studies
Reviewing scientific literature in children's science books, magazines, and reference
    books. A surprising amount of scientific information is also found in social studies
    and state studies books.
Map reading

Mathematics
Learning to gather data and record observations
Graphing data such as measurements and recorded data

Language Skills
Note taking
Summarizing
Report writing

Writing
Storytelling
Process writing: Developing poems and stories to communicate how weather has
    affected students' lives; writing "rap songs" to reinforce learning about proper body
    care

Artistic Expression
Poster designs
Murals
Models

Critical Thinking Skills
Redesign of the human body
Summarizing information from literature review, experiments, and other observa-
    tions for report writing

FIGURE 7.2   Integration of Science with Other Subject Areas

Social Studies

Social studies instruction in the elementary school focuses on the interaction of people with each other and with their natural and human environments. Although there has been less reform in the social studies area than in the other major areas of the elementary curriculum, educators have recently begun to develop a more relevant program for elementary school students.

Of prime importance today is using social studies in the elementary school to teach critical thinking, develop civic responsibility, build self-concept, and improve human relationships. Children are more open to diversity in the early elementary years than they are in the later years. Positive self-concepts, important in positively perceiving and judging social interactions, form in the critical early years of schooling. Social studies education that moves beyond the mere acquisition of facts is being developed in many school districts. Citizenship education, in which young children are active participants in examining political feelings—social issues as well as historical and geographical understanding—is forming the basis for social studies education in the elementary school. This approach fits with the instructional practices of cooperative learning and interdisciplinary instruction.[11]

Geography

Efforts have been made in recent years to revitalize the teaching of *geography* in elementary schools. The National Geographic Society contributed $40 million in 1996 to a geography education foundation. The purpose of the foundation was to provide additional training for teachers and to develop classroom materials to increase geography literacy among students.

Health and Physical Education

Health and developmental physical education are core components of a complete elementary school curriculum. *Health education* includes learning all aspects of healthful and safe living. Physical education includes adaptive and developmental activities that lead to better coordination and psychomotor skills.

Because the physical being cannot be separated from the mental or social being, health and physical education programs must include activities designed to interrelate all three areas of the person—the physical, the mental, and the social.

The National Association for Sports and Physical Education (NASPE) defines a physically educated person as one who

- □ has the skills necessary to perform a variety of physical activities,
- □ participates regularly in physical activity,
- □ is physically fit,
- □ knows the implications of and the benefits from involvement in physical activities, and
- □ values physical activity and its contributions to a healthful lifestyle.[12]

AIDS Education.   Schools have been among key American institutions in which the meaning of AIDS has been debated and deciphered. Because AIDS is fatal and linked in people's minds with homosexuality and drug use, it evokes strong opinions and fears. How to protect children and also provide information to them is a growing concern. Schools must accept students who are HIV positive or who have been diagnosed with AIDS, so the need for educating students and parents about this disease is crucial. The elementary school represents the first contact of students who have AIDS with others in the classroom and is also the first forum to provide students with an understanding of the disease. Programs are continuing to be developed to assist elementary staffs in implementing AIDS education programs.

Comprehensive School Health Education Program.   In September 2000, the Centers for Disease Control and Prevention published the CDC's definition of the key elements of comprehensive health education. They include the following:

1. A documented, planned, and sequential program of health instruction for students in grades kindergarten through twelve.
2. A curriculum that addresses and integrates education about a range of categorical health problems and issues at developmentally appropriate ages.
3. Activities that help young people develop the skills they need to avoid: tobacco use; dietary patterns that contribute to disease; sedentary lifestyle; sexual behaviors that result in HIV infection, other STDs and unintended pregnancy; alcohol and other drug use; and behaviors that result in unintentional and intentional injuries.
4. Instruction provided for a prescribed amount of time at each grade level.
5. Management and coordination by an education professional trained to implement the program.
6. Instruction from teachers who are trained to teach the subject.
7. Involvement of parents, health professionals, and other concerned community members.
8. Periodic evaluation, updating, and improvement.

The Arts

The *arts* in the elementary school include the visual and performing arts. Aesthetic education brings together cognitive, affective, and psychomotor areas of learning and includes experiences in music, fine arts, dance, theater, and other artistic modes of expression.

Until recently, mathematics and language were assumed to be cognitive in nature; the arts, on the other hand, dealt with feelings and emotions and were in the affective domain. Reading, writing, and arithmetic, moreover, were assumed to be essential skills that made information processing possible; the ability to read or to produce in the arts was an end in itself, leading to nothing more than inner satisfaction. Recent research indicates that the basic distinction between intellect and emotion can no longer be rationalized. It is now more clearly understood that our mental activities always involve both intellect and feelings, that we communicate in a rich variety of modes of symbolization, and that each art medium contributes a "language" and experience that adds cognitive data to the functioning brain.[13]

In the push for basic skills in the elementary school, the arts must not be left out of the curriculum. The arts are a necessary part of human experience. Nothing could be more basic.

HOLISTIC APPROACHES TO CURRICULUM

School curricula have become fragmented because of budgeting, bureaucratic turf-doms associated with textbook selection, media resources, and accountability aimed at attempting to prove year-to-year performance. Covering the information in a textbook may not relate to objectives in a curriculum or to a school's standardized achievement tests.

Those utilizing holistic approaches to curriculum development are asking the five questions that Tyler posed:

1. What educational purposes are being sought?
2. Is there a range of learning experiences that will facilitate the attainment of the educational purposes?
3. Are the experiences effectively organized and readily available to learners?
4. How well are we determining that the school's purposes are being attained?
5. Are we striving to get wholeness among curricular activities?[14]

DIVERSE NEEDS OF CHILDREN

Children with Attention Deficit Disorder

Attention Deficit Disorder (ADD) is characterized by these symptoms: difficulty remaining seated, calling out without request, interrupting others, and talking excessively. Biochemical abnormalities in the brain are thought to be the cause of ADD. Children with this disorder are easily distracted, disorganized, lacking in motor skills, and have a limited attention span. The majority of children with ADD are found in regular classrooms rather than in special programs.

ADD affects 3 to 5 percent of school-age children and occurs six to nine times more frequently in boys than in girls. ADD behaviors continue to be a concern throughout a person's life.

Teachers can aid the child with ADD by getting the child organized, giving effective instructions, having consistent discipline, using nonverbal cues, developing the child's self-esteem, and communicating regularly with parents.

Attention Deficit with Hyperactivity Disorder (ADHD), as defined by the American Psychiatric Association, is exhibited in a child with eight or more of fourteen symptoms that reflect difficulties in attention, impulsivity, or motor hyperactivity with the onset before age 17. Self-control strategies are very important in dealing with children with ADHD, but it is important to first determine whether a child has other behavioral or even cognitive deficits that need to be remediated before self-control strategies are implemented.[15]

Children from Impoverished Families

Poverty remains a problem in the United States even though President Johnson declared the official War on Poverty in the mid-1960s. Figures in 2001 indicated that the younger the family, the poorer the children. Fifty percent of all U.S. children living in a household headed by a person twenty-five years of age or younger are poor. If a child lives in a family headed by a woman, chances are better than 50 percent that the child is poor. The U.S. Census Bureau stated that 50 percent of children born in 2000 live with a single parent. Contrary to popular belief, the majority of poor people live in semi-isolation in towns across the country rather than in the inner cities. Two thirds of Americans that are poor are white.[16]

Children living on the edge of homelessness are usually prevented from finding the stability that makes successful schooling possible. It was estimated in 2000 that 200,000 children were homeless each night.[17]

Foster children and other displaced children often come from poor families. Drug and alcohol abuse by parents has contributed to large numbers of children in juvenile detention centers.[18]

One fourth of mothers receive no prenatal care.[19] Teachers are seeing more learning disabilities as a result of poor health care and drug abuse by mothers. Children who were cocaine babies continue to enter school in large numbers, and their care is adding huge costs to already overburdened school budgets.

Children from Different Cultures

America's newest students speak many languages, practice many religions, come from many different backgrounds, and carry both hopes and frustrations into their new life.[20] The 1990 census figures showed large increases in students who speak Spanish as a first language. In Florida, for example, Hispanics were the largest minority group in 1996. The number of Asian students continues to grow in American schools as well. Providing the melting pot, schools are helping non-English-speaking students by creating a safe and warm learning environment for them. English as a Second Language (ESL) programs have been revised to allow students to learn English while retaining their cultures. Students are encouraged to express themselves and relate their experiences. Working with parents by giving them make-and-take materials and showing them techniques for playing with their children are also important elements of bilingual education programs.

Finding teachers and aides who speak the language of students remains a challenge. Finding qualified instructors who speak Cambodian or Creole (for Haitian students) often frustrates district educators who have large concentrations of those non-English-speaking students.

Several school districts are experimenting with peer tutoring programs in which older students tutor younger students who speak the same language. "Buddy systems" are also used to pair non-English-speaking students with English-speaking students.

Changes in the world continue to bring fresh young faces into our classrooms. They come from ancient empires, modern cities, remote villages, or refugee camps with one quest—freedom. Figure 7.3 provides information on who these ESL students are.

Children with Disabilities

The period from 1975 to 2000 represented an era of significant progress for students with special needs or disabilities. Public concern resulted in laws guaranteeing access to the curriculum and public dollars to ensure implementation of special programs for these children.

Although some 195 federal laws specific to those with disabilities were enacted between 1927 and 1975, the National Advisory Committee on the Handicapped reported in 1975 that only 55 percent of children and youths with disabilities were being served appropriately. Of the 195 acts passed, 61 were passed between March 1970 and November 1975. Public Law 93-380, the Education

---

An ESL* student is an individual

□ who was not born in the United States and whose native language is not English;

□ **or** who comes from a home environment where a language other than English is spoken;

□ **or** who is an American Indian or an Alaskan native and who comes from an environment where a language other than English has a significant impact on his or her level of English language proficiency;

□ **and** who, for the above reasons, has difficulty listening, speaking, reading, or writing in English, to the extent that he or she is unable to learn successfully in classrooms where English is the language of instruction.

ESL students have learned another language before English and need time to make the transition to a curriculum that uses only English. As students learn more English, the use of the native language is deemphasized.

ESL students need to develop both communicative skills and cognitive academic skills in English.

Children are not handicapped cognitively by bilingualism; some types of intelligence, such as creativity, may be enhanced by the child's being bilingual.

* English as a Second Language. May also be referred to as LEP (Limited English Proficiency) or ESOL (English for Speakers of Other Languages).

FIGURE 7.3 Who Is an ESL Student?

Consolidation Improvement Act (ECIA) passed in 1974, was the most important of the laws passed; it extended and amended the Elementary and Secondary Education Act (ESEA) of 1965 and established a national policy on equal educational opportunity. Figure 7.4 notes changes in this original law.

The most far-reaching and significant federal act passed affecting those with disabilities was Public Law 94-142, the Education for All Handicapped Children Act of 1975, which was an amendment to Public Law 93-380. PL 94-142 has been described by many educators as a Bill of Rights for those with disabilities. This law sets forth specific procedures that school districts must carry out to establish due process for students with disabilities. The most important feature of the

This Part of ECIA	Replaces These Programs

Chapter 1—Financial Assistance to Meet Special Educational Needs of Disadvantaged Children	ESEA Title I
	  Basic Grants to Local Districts
	  Special Grants
	State-Administered Programs for Migratory Children, Handicapped Children, and Neglected and Delinquent Children
	State Administration

Chapter 2—Consolidation of Federal Programs for Elementary and Secondary Education	
Subchapter A—Basic Skills Development	ESEA Title II—Basic Skills Development (except Part C, Sec. 231), Inexpensive Book Distribution Program
Subchapter B—Educational Improvement and Support Services	ESEA Title IV Part B—Instructional Materials and School Library Resources Part C—Improvement in Local Educational Practices Part D—Guidance, Counseling, and Testing ESEA Title V—State Leadership ESEA Title VI—Emergency School Aid Precollege Science Teacher Training* (Sec. 3(a)(1), NSF Act of 1950) Teacher Corps (Part A, HEA) Teacher Centers (Sec. 532, HEA)

FIGURE 7.4   The Education Consolidation Improvement Act: How Merged Programs Fit into ECIA

*Separate FY 1982; consolidated FY 1983.

law is that all disabled students between ages 3 and 21 must have available to them a free and appropriate public education. That includes an emphasis on the regular class as the preferred instructional base for all children.

It is the feature of reversing the historical method of referring children with disabilities *out* of regular classes that makes PL 94-142 unique. It also has major implications for classroom teachers and supervisory personnel who implement the act.

The right to education means that children with disabilities are eligible for all programs and activities sponsored by the school. This includes cheerleading, athletics, and other extracurricular activities. Children with disabilities can no longer be excluded from course offerings, most notably, vocational courses.

PL 94-142 also prohibits discriminatory evaluation. Testing and evaluation materials must be selected and administered so as not to be culturally discriminatory. No single test or procedure can be used as the sole criterion for determining educational placement in a program.

Working with children with disabilities requires an individualized instructional plan similar to the plan used for all children in a regular classroom. It requires a substantial amount of diagnostic information about present and past academic and social performance. Finally, it requires teachers and supervisory personnel to project the specific needs of each child with a disability and prescribes special programs to meet those needs.

The individualized education program (IEP) provision of PL 94-142, which became practice on October 1, 1977, was really a model for instruction that all good teachers should follow for all students. Collecting diagnostic data, setting goals and objectives, selecting instructional materials, and evaluating student performance are all steps in the instructional process. There are important activities in the instructional process that teachers must consider for students with disabilities.

Mainstreaming has been defined in many ways, most of which center on moving children with disabilities from segregated special education classes into normal classrooms. Since the implementation of special education classes in the United States, segregated classroom environments have been the most popular method of educating these children. Because children were labeled according to the severity of their disabilities and grouped into uniform categories in special classes, they were removed from what educators titled the "mainstream."

PL 94-142 mandates that the most appropriate education for children with disabilities should be the least restrictive environment. This means that such students should be integrated into, not segregated from, the normal program of the school. It does *not* mean the wholesale return of all exceptional children in special classes to regular classes.

Mainstreaming means looking at educational needs and creative programs that will help general educators serve children with disabilities in a regular setting. It does not imply that specialists will no longer be needed, but rather that the specialists and the classroom teachers must be willing to combine efforts and work cooperatively to provide the most appropriate program for all children.

Legal decisions and legislation have made it clear that the rights of all children must be respected in our schools. Unfortunately, legal decisions and legislation won't ensure the development of adequate or appropriate programs. In-service education will be necessary to provide teachers with more specialized skills to deal with specific behavioral and academic problems. Mainstreaming can succeed only with a strong partnership of curriculum specialists, teachers, and supervisory personnel working cooperatively to provide the most appropriate education for all children.

Educating Children with Disabilities in the Regular Classroom. Although the Education for All Handicapped Children Act requires school districts to identify and label children with special needs, it has never mandated separate programs. Both federal and state laws have been amended since 1975 to insist on placing special needs students in the "least restrictive environment"—usually in the regular classroom unless their disabilities are severe.

The four most common labels—learning disabled, speech/language impaired, mentally handicapped, and emotionally disturbed—cover 95 percent of all students labeled as disabled. Labels are often confusing because some districts may classify 10 to 15 percent of students as disabled whereas other districts classify from 1 to 75 percent of their disabled children as learning disabled.

Labeling also lowers student self-esteem, and moving students out of the regular classroom often limits students' expectation of success.

Mainstreaming students with disabilities, even those with severe disabilities, seems to be a better approach. *Inclusion* is a term used to include teachers of students with disabilities who accompany their students into regular classrooms. The team approach with regular classroom teachers allows the special needs teacher to work in a more integrated instructional environment.

Two new areas in the education of students with disabilities are (1) the emphasis on preschool identification and services and (2) the transition from school to the world of work. At the preschool level, federal and state mandates require services for very young children. At present, the mandate is age 3, but very shortly it will begin at birth. The idea is that early intervention is best when dealing with disabling conditions.

As these students exit school, much more assistance is being given to them in seeking employment. For many students, vocational goals are identified as early as ninth grade. Many students with disabilities work with job coaches who assist them in functioning at jobs appropriate to their levels of performance. Businesses are encouraged to employ individuals with disabilities while they are still in school and then keep these students employed after graduation. Before this emphasis on transition services, only 25 percent of these students were employed at the end of their schooling. Students ranging from age 3 to 21 are included in these programs. Many students with disabilities have gained employment as a result of recent state and national efforts.

Inclusion.   What Does It Mean? *Inclusion* is a term for which few authors can agree on a definition. Some lump inclusion with mainstreaming. Others believe it means keeping all special needs children in the regular classroom while retraining the special staff. Still others believe inclusion means some children and full inclusion means *all* children. The most common definition of inclusion states that inclusion involves keeping special education students in regular education classrooms and taking support services to the child rather than bringing the child to support services.[21]

A major issue in inclusion has been whether placing severely dysfunctional children in a regular classroom without providing adequate training or support for the teacher puts the other students at risk. Without the training and support, teachers take up much instructional time dealing with distractions, disruptions, and sometimes violence.

Much progress has been made in the 1990s in building successful inclusion programs. When elementary schools have a clear philosophy of inclusion, mission statements that include goals for *all* students, and a curriculum that balances the needs of general and special education students, inclusion can be successful.[22]

Gifted Students

It has been estimated that over 2.5 million, or about 6 percent, of all young Americans are endowed with academic, artistic, or social talents far beyond the talents of their peers. These "gifted" children come from all levels of society, all races, and both sexes.

All fifty states have programs for gifted children, but there are still problems of identifying and providing for talented youngsters. For instance, many gifted children cannot be identified by I.Q. tests alone. New yardsticks for identifying gifted children have to be used, including measures of creativity, advanced social skills, and even exceptional physical aptitude such as the kind that marks fine surgeons, watch repairers, or engineers.

As a group, talented and gifted children tend to learn faster and retain more than their peers. A gifted child is also a divergent thinker. All of these characteristics can be unsettling in a class, and sometimes gifted and talented children have been seen as troublemakers. Other gifted children are turned off by boring classes and become alienated from school.

The Federal Office for the Gifted and Talented has adopted a national definition for giftedness, which is as follows:

> Gifted and talented children are those identified by professionally qualified persons who, by virtue of outstanding abilities, are capable of high performance. These are children who require differentiated educational programs in order to realize their contribution to self and society.

Additionally, the Office for the Gifted and Talented identified the following six specific ability areas included in giftedness:

1. General intellectual ability.
2. Specific academic aptitude.
3. Creative or productive thinking.

4. Leadership ability.
5. Ability in the visual or performing arts.
6. Psychomotor ability.

The debate over how to educate gifted children often centers on the equity versus excellence issue. Some question whether it is fair to give special treatment to some children and not to others. Some educators have also seen cooperative learning as a threat to gifted children because it holds such students back. Others say cooperative learning works just as well in a homogeneously grouped gifted class because its real strength is bringing out the potential of each child in class.

Tracking, often associated with gifted programs, has come under fire by many educators who see it as discriminating against poor children who are most often found in low groups.

The gifted and talented remain a group of students who need special attention whether it be in separate programs or differentiated instruction in a heterogeneous grouping. The models and research on gifted and talented children have helped provide a sound basis for differentiating instruction and evaluating programs for them.

Differentiating instruction, fostering creativity, allowing for independent study, and encouraging peer learning are all important tasks of teaching. They are especially important for nurturing the diverse aptitudes and abilities of gifted and talented children. Organizational procedures such as cluster grouping, mainstreaming, and part-day grouping have all been used with gifted and talented children.

Other Students with Needs

Between the special education student, who is categorically identified, and the gifted student, who is provided for by a special program, are all other students. Most of these "normal" students have needs, too, particularly during the elementary years. Figure 7.5 provides a checklist of needs for students who are not served by special programs but who may need assistance.

Early Intervention

Prekindergarten programs are designed to smooth the transition from home to school and also from kindergarten to the upper grades. Prekindergarten programs stress cooperative or shared learning experiences. The focus of the curriculum for preschool programs is on developmentally appropriate activities, which include equal emphasis on physical, cognitive, social, emotional, and creative development. Often, prekindergarten programs use other students as models. Retired teachers, grandparents, and other senior citizens also become involved in such programs.

In many districts, kindergarten is no longer a part-time, play-oriented introduction to school. It is "real" school where children go for the whole day and spend a great deal of their time in academic pursuits.[23] For that reason, many children are failing kindergarten, and educators are concerned about a skill-based academic program being inappropriate for those students. Kindergarten teachers and

1. Gross motor and motor flexibility
   _____ Incoordination and poor balance
   _____ Difficulty with jumping/skipping/hopping (below age 9)
   _____ Confusion in games requiring imitation of movements
   _____ Poor sense of directionality
   _____ Inept at drawing and writing at chalkboard
   _____ Inaccurate when copying at chalkboard
   _____ Eyes do not work together
   _____ Eyes lose or overshoot target

2. Physical fitness
   _____ Tires easily
   _____ Lacks strength

3. Auditory acuity, perception, memory/speech
   _____ Confuses similar phonetic and phonic elements
   _____ Inconsistent pronunciation of words usually pronounced correctly by peers
   _____ Repeats, but does not comprehend
   _____ Forgets oral directions, if more than one or two

4. Visual acuity, perception, memory
   _____ Complains that he or she cannot see blackboard
   _____ Says that words move or jump
   _____ Facial expression strained
   _____ Holds head to one side while reading

5. Hand–eye coordination
   _____ Difficulty in tracing/copying/cutting/folding/pasting/coloring at desk
   _____ Lack of success with puzzles/yo-yo's/toys involving targets, etc.

6. Language
   _____ Difficulty understanding others

FIGURE 7.5   Checklist for Identifying Students Who May Need Educational Therapy

elementary principals who are holding firm to a developmental approach are under increasing pressure to step up formal instruction.

With a focus on early childhood, one cannot forget the term *developmentally appropriate*. The National Association for the Education of Young Children (NAEYC), the nation's largest professional organization of early childhood educators, believes one index of the quality of primary education is the extent to which

_____ Difficulty associating and remembering

_____ Difficulty expressing him or herself

7. Intellectual functioning

_____ Unevenness of intellectual development

_____ Learns markedly better through one combination of sensory avenues than another

8. Personality

_____ Overreacts to school failures

_____ Does not seem to know he or she has a problem

_____ Will not admit he or she has a problem

9. Academic problems

_____ Can't tolerate having routine disturbed

_____ Knows it one time and doesn't the next

_____ Writing neat, but slow

_____ Writing fast, but sloppy

_____ Passes the spelling test, but can't spell functionally

_____ Math accurate, but slow

_____ Math fast, but inaccurate

_____ Reads well orally, but has poor comprehension

_____ Does poor oral reading, but comprehends better than would be expected

_____ Lacks word-attack skills

_____ Has conceptual/study skill/organizational problems in content areas

10. Parents

_____ Seemingly uninformed about nature of learning problem

_____ Seemingly unrealistic about student's problems

FIGURE 7.5 *Continued*

the curriculum and instructional methods are developmentally appropriate for children five through eight years of age.[24]

Other writers point out that cognitive psychology has generally reaffirmed the beliefs of Dewey, Piaget, and Elkind about the construction of meaning and the *constructivist* view of learning. In the constructivist view, students are more active agents in their own education. The constructivist approach would also work well with the use of information technology, according to other writers.[25]

Child-Care Programs

Child care, largely the domain of private enterprise in the 1980s and 1990s, is now being addressed by school districts. Both before- and after-school programs are being implemented across the country for school-age children and, increasingly, preschool-age children. The importance of high-quality, affordable child care is being recognized by policy makers. Legislation requiring higher qualifications for child-care workers, district matching programs with local businesses, tax credits, and minimum salaries for child-care workers are all helping shape child-care programs and services.[26]

Integrated Instructional Systems

Integrated instructional systems (IIS), also commonly known as *integrated learning systems,* are instructional systems that are replacing older computer-assisted instruction (CAI) systems. CAI became associated with dull drill-and-practice activities. Linking computer lessons to accepted standard curricula provides an integration often missing in CAI programs.

IIS are actually complex integrated hardware/software management systems that give districts the best return on an investment in instructional technology. As with any new program, staff training is a critical factor in the success of IIS. Costs vary for such systems, but hidden costs such as software licensing, updates, and staff salaries (for project managers) can often stretch existing school budgets.

LEARNING STYLES AND SYSTEMS

Learning styles of children have been under study in recent years. Researchers have been studying whether individual differences can result in different concept formation, problem-solving techniques, and shared meanings.

Studies have indicated that some children enjoy understanding the big picture before focusing on specifics. Other children enjoy a classroom atmosphere in which personal relationships are important. Still others do best when they verbalize what they learn. For other students, a structured and systematic approach is better suited to their learning.

Elementary teachers who have their own learning and teaching styles can be assured that their students also have individual styles. Effective elementary teachers can assess learning styles and address them by adding variety to their teaching activities.

Cooperative Learning

In cooperative learning, a technique that gained great favor in the late 1980s and 1990s, children are trained to use one another as resources for learning. Each child plays a specific role in a group such as facilitator, checker, or reporter. Teachers learn to delegate authority to a group of students and to encourage students to engage in a process of discovery learning. Cooperative learning requires assignments and curriculum materials that are different from those used in traditional classroom instruction. Tasks and materials that encourage student interaction are most needed in cooperative learning situations. Teachers who are not skilled in the organization and monitoring of small groups need in-service training in cooperative learning.

Grade-Level Retention

Two position papers in 1990—*Grade Level Retention: A Failed Procedure,* California State Department, and *Grade Level Retention,* Florida Department of Education— summarized studies on grade-level retention (the practice of requiring an under-performing student to repeat an entire grade in school). Research studies showed that grade-level retention is not an effective remedy for students who are not achieving their potential.

When students are held back, they fall behind the students entering the grade in which they are retained. Also, retained students are more likely to drop out of school. Finally, their self-concept is lowered so much that most such students are turned off to school.

Unfortunately, most teachers and the general public still believe that grade-level retention works. Alternatives to grade-level retention, such as using a continuous-progress model, intensifying efforts to involve parents in school, and earlier intervention efforts, have been proposed in place of the practice of failing students.

ORGANIZATION AND GROUPING IN THE ELEMENTARY SCHOOL

Vertical and Horizontal Organizational Patterns of Students and School Staff

Organizational patterns in elementary schools may include self-contained class-rooms, grade-level teams, cross-grade teams, a total ungraded structure, or a com-bination of these patterns. For instance, the primary grades may be nongraded while the upper elementary grades are graded. Also, teams may operate at certain grade levels while other grade levels may be self-contained. Classes may also be self-contained or departmentalized.

The two basic types of organization groups for instruction are *vertical* and *horizontal*. Vertical organization refers to the movement of students from grade to grade or level to level. Horizontal organization refers to the grouping of students within a grade or level and the assignment of teachers to a grade or level. Self-contained classes and departmentalized classes, with a separate teacher for each dis-cipline, fall within a horizontal organization. Vertical organization may include both graded and nongraded plans.

Two or more teachers may engage in team teaching, in which each teacher contributes his or her special competencies while the team is jointly responsible for providing instruction for a group of students. Interdisciplinary teams may teach all of the disciplines, or they may have lead teachers in each discipline who take the major responsibility for the teaching of a subject area. Teams may be organized within a grade level or across grade levels. Teams may employ self-contained departmentalized and interdisciplinary instruction during a school year.

Organization and grouping, however, should be flexible; schools should be counseled against using a single pattern of organization or grouping arrangement. A sound approach is to organize and group according to the needs of students, the abilities of teachers, and the availability of facilities and resources. No single pattern can fit all situations.

Figure 7.6 illustrates an elementary scheduling pattern that includes both a graded and nongraded grouping arrangement. The school is organized into two schools within a school. School A includes grades K through 3; School B, grades 4 through 6. In a block schedule, a unit of time is allowed for both graded and nongraded courses, thus allowing for time frames for instruction in the discipline to be used. Enrichment classes are taught by all faculty members and are nongraded within School A and School B.

School A (K–3)	School B (4–6)	Time
Homeroom *(Nongraded/Reading Level)*	*Homeroom* *(Nongraded/Reading Level)*	
		9:15–9:30
		9:30–9:45
Language Arts	Language Arts	9:45–10:00
(nongraded)	(nongraded)	10:00–10:15
		10:15–10:30
Mathematics		10:30–10:45
(nongraded)	Mathematics	10:45–11:00
	(nongraded)	11:00–11:15
Lunch		11:15–11:30
(nongraded)	Physical Ed.	11:30–11:45
	(nongraded)	11:45–12:00
		12:00–12:15
	Social Studies	12:15–12:30
	(graded)	12:30–12:45
		12:45–1:00
Social Studies	Lunch	1:00–1:15
(graded)	(graded)	1:15–1:30
Science		1:30–1:45
(graded)	Science	1:45–2:00
Physical Ed.	(graded)	2:00–2:15
(graded)		2:15–2:30
Enrichment	Enrichment	2:30–2:45
Program	Program	2:45–3:00
		3:00–3:15

FIGURE 7.6 Schedule with Graded and Nongraded Grouping

The governance of the school illustrated in Figure 7.7 includes the principal; the curriculum assistant, who also chairs the curriculum committee; and the chairperson of the steering committee. The steering committee consists of the chairperson of School A, the chairperson of School B, a representative from the specialists' group (physical education, art, special education, media, music), and one other teacher from School A and from School B (a total of five members). The chairperson of each school is selected yearly by staff members of that school. The chairperson of the steering committee is also selected by that group on a yearly basis.

Elementary Grouping Strategies

Three grouping strategies have influenced elementary schools in the first decade of the twenty-first century. They include continuous progress, multiage (mixed age), and looping (see Figure 7.8).

INFLUENCE OF THE MIDDLE SCHOOL ON ELEMENTARY CURRICULA

The middle school movement in the 1970s, 1980s, and 1990s resulted in curricular and organizational changes in the elementary school. Early in the middle school movement, grades 5 and 6 were taken from the elementary curriculum and combined with grades 7 and 8 of the junior high school or high school. The ninth grade went to the high school. Later, fifth grades were returned to the elementary school in most districts, resulting in a grades K–5, 6–8, 9–12 structure in many districts. By losing the sixth grade, the elementary school was left with two

```
                         Principal
                   Curriculum Assistant

                    Steering Committee
                   2 members of School A
                   2 members of School B
                        1 Specialist

                   Curriculum Committee
                 Language Arts Chairperson
                     Math Chairperson
                    Science Chairperson
                 Social Studies Chairperson
School A         Special Education Chairperson         School B
13 Teachers            Specialists                    11 Teachers
1 Chairman           Special Education                 1 Chairman
                     Physical Education
                           etc.
```

FIGURE 7.7   Governing Structure of Oakleaf Elementary School

Continuous Progress (cp)

What is it?

CP generally implies that children remain with their classroom peers in an age cohort regardless of whether they have met or surpassed specified grade-level achievement expectations.

- Learner-centered
- Holistic view of the child
- Flexible organization
- Integrated curriculum
- Family-like environment
- Removal of traditional grade levels

What it looks like:

- Flexible physical arrangement
- Student-centered activities
- Student choice
- Team of teachers spend 2–3 years caring for and teaching a group of students
- Active classroom
- Trade books, manipulatives
- Time divided equally among whole-group, small-group, and independent work

Intended outcome:

- High self-esteem
- Cooperative, independent thinkers
- Ability to set goals and manage own learning
- Confidence in own unique abilities
- Leaders

Concerns:

- Students at top may not get the encouragement they need to advance and perform to their abilities.
- Students who need more structure may not do well in this environment.

Multiage (Mixed Age)

What is it?

Grouping children so the age span of the class is more than one year. Multiage grouping attempts to maximize the benefits of interaction and cooperation among children of different experiences and stages of development in all classroom activities.

- Teacher plans for a wide range of abilities
- Teacher provides for varying rates of progress
- Teacher adjusts to different social/emotional needs
- Takes into account that all learners are different
- Larger span, developmental level
- Increased options for placement

What it looks like:

- Vertical grouping
- Two or more ages
- Same teacher/team for more than one year
- Learner-centered

FIGURE 7.8   Elementary Grouping Strategies

☐ Many opportunities for cooperative work;
   room arranged accordingly
☐ Flexible groupings

Intended outcome:

☐ Opportunities to interact with a wide variety of abilities
☐ Supportive of children who are performing below expectation
☐ Less competition, more cooperation

Concerns:

☐ Small class size may make it difficult for same-age or same-sex friendships
☐ Fewer challenges for older students
☐ Frustrated younger children
☐ More teacher planning

Looping

What is it?

Student remains with a single grade class with the same teacher for two or more years.

☐ No beginning-of-the-year transition time
☐ Less need for assessment of skills
☐ Family feel
☐ Benefits shy, quiet children
☐ Long-term student-teacher-family relationship

What it looks like:

☐ Could take any structure, teacher-centered or student-centered

Intended outcome:

☐ More on-task time
☐ Stronger teacher-student-family relationship
☐ Enhanced learning

Concerns:

☐ Possibility of more than one year with an ineffective teacher
☐ Poor teacher–student chemistry

FIGURE 7.8   *Continued*

developmental groups: early childhood youth in grades K–3 and late childhood youth in grades 4 and 5. Not having to cope with emerging adolescents in grade six allowed elementary schools to match their curricula better with the developmental levels of the youths they served. Figure 7.9 illustrates the developmental levels and curricular implications for students in elementary, middle, and high schools.

The elementary curriculum in the 1980s and 1990s was affected dramatically by demands brought about by testing and evaluation. Legislators and political

Program		
Elementary School	*Middle School*	*High School*
Introduction to school	Personal development	Comprehensive
Socialization	Refinement of skills	Vocational training
Beginning skills		College preparatory
Beginning learnings	Continued learnings	In-depth learnings
Introduction to disciplines	Education for social competence	Chemistry
Social studies		Algebra
Science		World history
		American literature
	Interdisciplinary Learnings	Career Planning
Organization Developmental Skills		
Elementary School	*Middle School*	*High School*
K–5	6, 7–8	9–12
K–3 4–5	6–8	
Early Late		
childhood childhood	Transescence	Adolescence

FIGURE 7.9 Developmental Levels of Students in the Elementary, Middle, and High School

groups led the change by insisting that the basic skills of reading, writing, and arithmetic be the focus of teaching in the elementary school. Single-series texts in reading, mandated instructional time for reading and mathematics, and minimum competency testing at various grade levels resulted.

The elementary school of the new century has been changing to a full-service school with a great variety of programs needed to meet the increasing diversity of the student population.

In looking at the history of the elementary school, we can see how various reform movements have affected the elementary curriculum. Examining lessons from the past, we can see that the elementary curriculum must include many different learning experiences for a variety of learners. A balanced program must be available for all elementary children if the elementary school is to meet the needs of students in the first decade of the new century and beyond. Figure 7.10 lists some organizations that focus on early childhood programs.

TRENDS IN ELEMENTARY EDUCATION: DETERMINING WHAT WORKS

Year-round schools were seen by proponents as a cost-effective and better learning environment for elementary students during the period of 1986 to 1996. In 1985 fewer than one-half million students were in year-round schools. By 1996 the total

Association for Childhood Education
  International (ACEI)
11141 Georgia Avenue, Suite 200
Wheaton, MD
(301) 942-2443

Association for Supervision and Curriculum
  Development (ASCD)
1250 North Pitt Street
Alexandria, VA
(703) 549-9110

Bank Street College of Education
610 West 112th Street
New York, NY
(212) 663-7200

Children's Defense Fund
122 C Street, N.W.
Washington, DC
(202) 628-8787

ERIC Clearinghouse of Elementary and Early
  Childhood Education
University of Illinois at Urbana-Champaign
805 West Pennsylvania Avenue
Urbana, IL
(217) 333-1386

High/Scope Education Research Foundation
600 North River Street
Ypsilanti, MI
(313) 485-2000

National Association of Elementary School
  Principals (NAESP)
1615 Duke Street
Alexandria, VA
(703) 684-3345

National Association for the Education of
  Young Children (NAEYC)
1834 Connecticut Avenue, N.W.
Washington, DC
(800) 424-2460 or (202) 232-8777

National Association of State Boards of
  Education (NASBE)
701 North Fairfax Street, Suite 340
Alexandria, VA
(703) 684-4000

National State Child Development Institute
1463 Rhode Island Avenue, N.W.
Washington, DC
(202) 387-1281

Southern Association for Children Under Six
  (SACUS)
Box 5403
Brady Station
Little Rock, AR
(501) 666-0353

FIGURE 7.10   Organizations Concerned with Early Childhood Programs

had reached 1.8 million students. The number of year-round schools increased 600 percent (from 408 to 2,308) from 1986 to 1996. The majority of students in these year-round schools were elementary students. Year-round schools had been established in thirty-nine states by 1996 with most located in California.

By 1997 the trend had begun to reverse, with over one hundred schools moving back to a traditional calendar. Orange County, Florida (Orlando), phased out all sixty-four of its year-round elementary students in 1987. By 2000, though, school districts had begun to rethink their opposition to this model.

Many year-round schools found little improvement in their scores, and parents complained that they could not coordinate their children's vacation time. Community support has to be present if year-round schools are to succeed, and there is still a debate over how much cost savings such schools actually realize.

"Back-to-the-basics" is a plea often heard from education critics, yet others plead for schools to move beyond teaching low-level, simplistic objectives. Reformers stress that children need more than the basics to perform today's jobs. It seems the public wants tougher academic standards, yet they feel children can't acquire higher skills unless they have mastered the basics.[27]

Multiage programs, particularly in the primary grades, became popular in the 1960s and reappeared in the 1990s. Many traditional age/grade level schools moved to a multiage, nongraded structure.

Although proponents point out studies that indicate less student retention, better student achievement, fewer discipline referrals, and better student achievement in nongraded schools, opponents quickly point out other studies showing just the opposite. Parental support, as in year-round schools, seems to be a critical element in determining whether nongraded programs last in schools.

Trends such as continuous progress programs, team teaching, and multiyear teaching of the same group of students all approach the teaching of elementary students in a climate in which uneven development is not viewed as a deficit, but as a normal part of human growth. The teacher or teacher team strives to create a caring learning community.[28]

Quality assessment is a topic that has remained both complicated and controversial. In a country whose culturally diverse population is becoming even more diverse, how do we assess student progress? Rather than recommending one type of assessment over another, many educators are focusing attention on a *set* of assessment practices,[29] including portfolios, "authentic" assessment, and others, rather than relying simply on standardized test results.

Multicultural education faced strong setbacks in the 1980s and 1990s with conservative voices regularly denouncing the topic. Yet as the nation becomes more diverse and we prepare children to live in the global interdependent society of the new century, we keep revisiting the concept of multiculturalism. In the politically changed arena of today's schools, this topic will remain a controversial one.

Technology and its use in the educating of young children remains on the front burner of educational change. In the fall of 1995, the U.S. Department of Education released a national action plan for the use of technology in education. Because technology is such a powerful tool for learning, any kind of comprehensive education reform will be difficult to achieve without using technology to its fullest potential. Quality software, teacher training, and schools equipped with the latest information retrieval systems are necessary to meet the challenge. In 2000 the U.S. Office of Education estimated that only about 10 percent of teachers were proficient users of technology. In an information age, we must understand that the use of technology means much more than simply using computers.

In concluding this chapter on elementary education, we pose the following common and recurrent curriculum questions:

1. With 25 percent of all American families moving each year, how can elementary programs deal with in-migration and out-migration?
2. Elementary children watch up to six hours of television each day. How can teachers compete with the influence of this medium?

3. School consolidations and busing have ended the century-old pattern of the neighborhood school in many communities. How can school identity and school spirit be maintained?
4. With only one family in twelve having a two-parent family in which the mother is home during the day, how can the school gain family support for achievement at school?
5. With fewer new teachers being hired and many staffs "aging in place," how can the school maintain a spirit of growth and an openness to new ideas?
6. Elementary children are coming to school with many new ideas. How can we meet children's many social needs and still carry out the academic function of the elementary school?
7. How can curriculum leaders promote a balanced school experience for learners in the face of accountability laws and policies that focus solely on student achievement of basic skills?

Must we do more for our young children? During the 1990 United Nations World Summit Conference for Children, President George Bush joined 34 other presidents, 27 prime ministers, a king, a grand duke, and a cardinal, among others, to discuss the plight of 150 million children under the age of five suffering from malnutrition, 30 million living in the streets, and 7 million driven from their homes by war and famine. A bold ten-year plan was adopted to improve access to immunizations and education.

In the United States, every eight seconds of the school day, a child drops out of school. Every twenty-six seconds, a child runs away from home. Every forty-seven seconds, a child is abused or neglected. Every seven minutes, a child is arrested for a drug offense. Every thirty-six minutes, a child is killed or injured by a gun. Every day, 135,000 children bring guns to school.[30] Yes, we must do more.

SUMMARY

The new century presents the elementary school with its greatest challenge ever. Social conditions and new understandings of human growth and development require change in both programs and the means of delivery.

In looking at the history of the elementary school, we can see how various forces have caused change and reform throughout our history. Examining those lessons from the past, we can see that the elementary curriculum must include a variety of learning experiences for a diverse population of learners. A balanced program must be available for all elementary students if the elementary school is to serve all learners in the years to come.

Elementary educators are hard-pressed to keep up with the changing conditions that affect the ability of pupils to succeed in school. The goals of this nation, and those of world leaders, are ambitious and present school planners with their greatest challenge ever at this level.

SUGGESTED LEARNING ACTIVITIES

1. Identify the major events in the evolution of the elementary school in the United States.
2. Analyze the curriculum of your elementary school to determine if a balanced curriculum exists.
3. A group in your community has called for the abolishment of all art and music programs in the elementary school. Prepare a paper defending the inclusion of art and music in elementary curriculum.
4. Develop a schedule for an elementary school that includes provisions for both graded and nongraded classes.
5. Prepare evaluative criteria for a committee charged with developing guidelines for the selection of content in the major areas of language arts, mathematics, science, and social studies.
6. Develop a plan to incorporate full-service school services in your school.

NOTES

1. Claudia Cohl, "The Future of Education," *Principal* (January 1996): 22–38.
2. Johann Pestalozzi, *How Gertrude Teaches Her Children,* ed. Daniel Robinson (Frederick, MD: University Publications of America, 1977).
3. Karen Diegmueller, "The Best of Two Worlds," *Education Week* (March 20, 1996): 32–33.
4. Marjorie A. Wuhrick, "Blue Jays Win! Crows Go Down in Defeat!" *Kappan* (March 1990): 553–556.
5. Bobbi Fisher, "Moving Beyond Letter of the Week," *Teaching K–8* (January 1996): 74–76.
6. Jim Henry, "What Is Excellent Writing?" *Instructor* (September 1995): 39–40.
7. Deborah Ball, "Teacher Learning and the Mathematics Reforms," *Kappan* (March 1996): 500–508.
8. National Council of Teachers of Mathematics, *Professional Standards for Teaching Mathematics* (Reston, VA: NCTM, 1991).
9. Maureen Stuart, "Effects of Group Grading on Cooperation and Achievement of Two Fourth-Grade Classes," *The Elementary School Journal* 95, 1 (1994): 11–21.
10. Kathleen Metz, "Reassessment of Developmental Constraints on Children's Science Instruction," *Review of Educational Research* 65, 2 (Summer 1995): 91–127.
11. Linda Leonard Lamme, "The Literature Based Approach for a Social Studies Curriculum," *Trends and Issues* 8, 1 (Spring 1996): 7–11.
12. National Association for Sports and Physical Education (NASPE) (Washington, DC, 2000).
13. http://www.edu.gov/nccdphp/dash/cshede.htm
14. Ralph Tyler, *Basic Principles of Curriculum and Instruction* (Chicago: University of Chicago Press, 1949), p. 5.
15. Maag and Reid, "Attention Deficit Hyperactivity Disorder."
16. Report of U.S. Bureau of the Census (Washington, DC, 2000).
17. Report of U.S. Bureau of the Census (Washington, DC, 2000).
18. Report of U.S. Bureau of the Census (Washington, DC, 2000).
19. Report of U.S. Bureau of the Census (Washington, DC, 2000).
20. Carol Ascher, "The Changing Face of Racial Isolation and Desegregation in Urban Schools," *New Schools, New Communities* II, 2 (Winter 1995): 42–45.
21. R. Smelter and G. Yudeewitz, "Thinking of Inclusion for All Students? Better Think Again," *Kappan* 76, 1 (April 1996): 35–38.
22. Richard Riley, Full Service School-Community Collaboration Conference. Demands as prepared for delivery by U.S. Secretary of Education. Richard W. Riley, Washington, D.C., March 26, 1999.
23. Gerald W. Bracey, "The Impact of Early Intervention," *Kappan* 7, 4 (March 1996): 510–11.
24. National Association for the Education of Young Children, *Appropriate Education in the Primary Grades—A Position Statement* (Washington, DC: NAEYC, 1997).
25. Gerald W. Bracey, "Change and Continuity in Elementary Education," *Principal* 75 (January 1996): 46–50.

26. "Reality Check: Six Untruths about Health and School Health Education That Undermine the Well-Being of Our Children," http://www.concern.oug/cshe/cshereal.html, August 30, 2000.

27. "At the Crossroads," *American Teacher,* American Federation of Teachers, 80, 5 (February 1996): 6–7.

28. Don Jeanroy, "The Results of Multiage Grouping," *The School Administrator* (January 1996): 18–19.

29. Brian Leving, "Quality Assessment Practices in a Diverse Society," *Teaching Exceptional Children* 28, 3 (Spring 1996): 42–45.

30. Children's Defense Fund, Annual Report, 1997.

ADDITIONAL READING

Bauer, Ann, and Thomas Shea. *Inclusion 101: How to Teach All Learners.* Baltimore, MD: Paul H. Brookes, 1999.

Bireley, Marlene, Judy L. Genshaft, and Constance L. Hollinger, eds. *Serving Gifted and Talented Students: A Resource for School Personnel.* Austin, TX: Pro-Ed, 1995.

Block, Cathy Collins. *Creating a Culturally Enriched Curriculum for Grades K–6.* Boston: Allyn and Bacon, 1995.

Bracey, Gerald W. *A Short Guide to Standardized Testing.* Bloomington, IN: Phi Delta Kappa Educational Foundation, 2000.

Charbonneau, Manon P. *The Integrated Elementary Classroom: A Developmental Model of Education for the 21st Century.* Boston: Allyn and Bacon, 1995.

Conroy, Mary Ann. *101 Ways to Integrate Personal Development into Core Curriculum: Lessons in Character Education for Grades K–12.* Lanham, MD: University Press of America, 2000.

Lockett, Jean B. *The Least Restrictive Environment: Its Origins and Interpretations in Special Education.* Mahwah, NJ: Erlbaum Associates, 1999.

Cuffaro, Harriet K. *Experimenting with the World: John Dewey and the Early Childhood Classroom.* New York: Teachers College Press, 1995.

Davidson, David M. *Integrating Science and Mathematics in the Elementary Curriculum.* Bloomington, IN: Phi Delta Kappa Educational Foundation, 1999.

Easton, Charles. *Coordinating the Curriculum in the Smaller Primary School.* London: Falmer Press, 1999.

Ford, Donna. *Multicultural Gifted Education.* New York: Teachers College Press, 1999.

French, Michael P. *Attention Deficit and Reading Instruction.* Bloomington, IN: Phi Delta Kappa Educational Foundation, 1995.

Joyce, Bruce R. *Models of Teaching,* 5th ed. Boston: Allyn and Bacon, 1996.

Lewis, Rean, and Donald Ddoorlag. *Teaching Special Students in General Education Classrooms.* Upper Saddle River, NJ: Prentice Hall, 1999.

Marshall, J. A., J. Serris, and W. Schubert. *Turning Points in Curriculum.* Columbus, OH: Prentice Hall, 2000.

Ornseln, A., and L. Beher-Horensteing. *Contemporary Issues in Curriculum,* 2nd ed. Boston: Allyn and Bacon, 1999.

Passe, Jeff. *Elementary School Curriculum.* Boston: McGraw-Hill College, 1999.

Readman, G. *Teachers in Today's Classrooms—Cases from Elementary School.* Columbus, OH: Prentice Hall, 1999.

Sewell, E. *Curriculum: An Integrated Instruction,* 2nd ed. Columbus, OH: Prentice Hall, 2000.

Smith, Tom E., ed. *Teaching Students with Special Needs in Inclusive Settings.* Boston: Allyn and Bacon, 1995.

Walling, Donovan, ed. *At the Threshold of the Millennium.* Bloomington, IN: Phi Delta Kappa Educational Foundation, 1995.

WEB SITES

Blue Web'n:
http://www.kn.pacbell.com/wired/bluewebn
Busy Teachers:
http://www.ceism@galech.edu/busyt
Education World:
http://www.education-world.com
Teachers Helping Teachers:
http://www.pacificnet/
LearningWebs, Inc.:
http://www.learnweb.org

chapter 8

MIDDLE SCHOOL PROGRAMS AND ISSUES

After over forty years, the middle school is still America's longest-running innovation. Like its predecessor, the junior high school, the middle school serves as a transition between the elementary school and the high school. In this chapter, the middle school will be explored as a preferred model for intermediate education in the new century.

The junior high school, originated in 1910, was intended to move the secondary program into the elementary grades. The familiar bulletin *Cardinal Principles of Secondary Education* recommended that a school system be organized into a six-year elementary school and a six-year high school designed to serve pupils twelve to eighteen years of age.[1] The bulletin also suggested that secondary education be divided into two periods, the junior period and the senior period. Thus, junior high schools were thought to be a part of the high school, and for fifty years the curriculum of the junior high school tended to parallel that of the high school. Activities such as varsity athletics, marching bands, and even cap-and-gown graduation exercises tended to exert considerable pressures on junior high students. Teacher-training institutions also prepared "secondary" teachers for positions in the junior high schools. Most junior high schools were organized with grades 7 through 9.

By 1960 a number of factors led to the emergence of a new school known as the middle school. Critics of the junior high school were beginning to try to reform the junior high school in the 1940s and 1950s but could not break the junior high from the high school mold.[2]

Four factors led to the emergence of the middle school. First, the late 1950s and early 1960s were filled with criticisms of American schools, classroom and teacher shortages, double and triple sessions, and soaring tax rates. Books such as *Why Johnny Can't Read*[3] triggered new concerns about the quality of schooling in the United States. The successful launching of *Sputnik* in 1957 led to a new wave of criticism about the curricula of elementary and secondary schools. *Sputnik* created an obsession with academic achievement, especially in the areas of science, foreign languages, and mathematics. A renewed interest in college preparation led to a call for a four-year high school in which specialized courses could remain under the direction of the college preparatory school—the high school. Likewise, the inclusion of grades 5 and 6 in an intermediate school could strengthen instruction by allowing subject area specialists to work with younger students. Many of the first middle schools were organized with grades 5 through 8.

A second factor leading to the emergence of the middle school was the elimination of racial segregation. *The Schoolhouse in the City* stated that the real force behind the middle school movement in the larger cities (New York City, for example) was the desire to eliminate de facto segregation.[4]

A third factor leading to the emergence of the middle school was the increased enrollments of school-age children in the 1950s and 1960s. The shortage of buildings resulted in double and even triple school sessions in some districts. Because older children in high schools were able to cope with overcrowding better than younger students, the ninth grade was moved to the high school to relieve the overcrowded junior high school. The same rationale was used to relieve the elementary school by moving the fifth or sixth grade to the junior high school.

A fourth factor resulting in middle schools was the *bandwagon effect*. Because one middle school received favorable exposure in books and periodicals, some administrators determined that the middle school was "the thing to do."

All of these factors may not have provided a valid reason for middle school organization, but they did provide the right opportunity for reform of the American intermediate school.

Throughout the 1970s and 1980s, junior high schools were converted to a middle school design in record numbers, with the same four factors at play. In the 1990s a new increase in school-age population caused more conversions to middle schools. By the end of the 1990s, 90 percent of intermediate schools were classified as middle schools.

We believe that the following reasons, related to providing a more relevant and appropriate program and learning environment for transescent (the period between childhood and adolescence) learners, are easier to justify:

- ☐ To provide a program especially designed for the ten- to fourteen-year-old child going through the unique transescent period of growth and development. Students age 10 to 14 constitute a distinct grouping—physically, socially, and intellectually.
- ☐ To build on the changed elementary school. Historically, the post-*Sputnik* clamor to upgrade schools prepared the way for elementary

school personnel to accept the middle school concept. The introduction of the "new" science, the "new" social studies, the "new" mathematics, and the "new" linguistics in elementary schools eroded the sanctity of the self-contained classroom. As part of the reorganization of curriculum that followed *Sputnik,* elementary teachers tended to cultivate a specific content area in the curriculum. This led to a departure from the self-contained classroom toward more sharing of students among teachers.

□ To counter dissatisfaction with the existing junior high school. The junior high school, in most cases, did not become a transitional school between the elementary and senior high school. Unfortunately, it became a miniature high school with all of the sophisticated activities of the high school. Instruction was often formal and discipline centered, with insufficient attention given to the student as a person.

□ To provide much-needed innovations in curriculum and instruction. By creating a new school—the middle school—rather than remodeling the outmoded junior high school, educators provided an atmosphere for implementing those practices long talked about but seldom effected.

FUNCTIONS OF THE MIDDLE SCHOOL

Both in recognition and in numbers, middle schools have become a separate, intermediate institution in the United States. Cumulative experience and research, and the fact that the middle school "works," have resulted in widespread acceptance of the middle school by children, teachers, administrators, and parents. We define the middle school as a transitional school concerned with the most appropriate program to cope with the personal and educational needs of emerging adolescent learners. The middle school should be an institution that has

1. A unique program adapted to the needs of the pre- and early adolescent (transescent) student.
2. The widest possible range of intellectual, social, and physical experiences.
3. Opportunities for exploration and the development of the fundamental skills needed by all, with allowances for individual learning patterns. An atmosphere of basic respect for individual differences should be maintained.
4. A climate that enables students to develop abilities, find facts, weigh evidence, draw conclusions, determine values, and that keeps their minds open to new facts.
5. Staff members who recognize and understand the students' needs, interests, backgrounds, motivations, and goals, as well as stresses, strains, frustrations, and fears.
6. A smooth educational transition between the elementary school and the high school that allows for the physical and emotional changes of transescence.
7. An environment in which the child, not the program, is most important and in which the opportunity to succeed is ensured for all students.

8. Guidance in the development of the mental processes and attitudes needed for constructive citizenship and the development of lifelong competencies and an appreciation for the effective use of leisure.
9. Competent instructional personnel who will strive to understand the students they serve and who will develop professional competencies that are both unique and applicable to the transescent student.
10. Facilities and time to allow students and teachers an opportunity to achieve the goals of the program to their fullest capabilities.

Table 8.1 illustrates the unique and transitory nature of the middle school.

The middle school, then, presents a renewed effort to design and implement a program of education that can accommodate the needs of the preadolescent population. It is a broadly focused program of education, drawing its philosophy and rationale from the evolving body of knowledge concerned with human growth and development. The middle school represents a systematic effort to organize the schooling experience in a way that will facilitate the maximum growth and development of all learners.

The middle school program consists of arrangements and activities that attempt to tie formal learning directly to the developmental needs of the students. To date, identified developmental tasks represent the most promising criteria for curriculum development that will intersect school activity with learner growth and development.

ESTABLISHING AN IDENTITY FOR THE MIDDLE SCHOOL

Education for emerging adolescents has received an intensive reexamination over the past decade. One result has been the verification of a need for a school with a differentiated function for early adolescents—those aged 10 to 14. The need for a

TABLE 8.1   Schools in the Middle

	Elementary	Middle	High
Teacher–Student Relationship	Parental	Advisor	Random
Teacher Organization	Self-contained	Interdisciplinary team	Department
Curriculum	Skills	Exploration	Depth
Schedule	Self-contained	Block	Periods
Instruction	Teacher-directed	Balance	Student-directed
Student Grouping	Chronological	Multi-age development	Subject
Building Plan	Classroom areas	Team areas	Department areas
Physical Education	Skills and games	Skills and intramurals	Skills and interscholastics
Media Center	Classroom groups	Balance	Individual study
Guidance	Diagnostic/ development	Teacher helper	Career-vocational
Teacher Preparation	Child-oriented generalist	Flexible resource	Disciplines specialist

distinct school, unlike the elementary, high, or even the junior high school, is more defensible than ever in light of recent information about the growth and development of emerging adolescents. Changing social conditions have also helped to establish the need for a school in the middle with an identity of its own. As middle schools have grown in number and quality, some of the following common elements have contributed to their special identity:

- ☐ The absence of the "little high school" approach
- ☐ The absence of the "star" system, in which a few special students dominate everything, in favor of an attempt to provide success experience for greater numbers of students
- ☐ An attempt to use instructional methods more appropriate to this age group: individualized instruction, variable group sizes, multimedia approaches, beginning independent study programs, and inquiry-oriented instruction
- ☐ Increased opportunities for teacher–student guidance; may include a home base or advisory group program
- ☐ Increased flexibility in scheduling and student grouping
- ☐ Some cooperative planning and team teaching
- ☐ Some interdisciplinary studies, in which teachers from a variety of academic areas provide opportunities for students to see how the areas of knowledge fit together
- ☐ A wide range of exploratory opportunities, academic and otherwise
- ☐ Increased opportunity for physical activity and movement and more frequent physical education
- ☐ Earlier introduction to the areas of organized academic knowledge
- ☐ Attention to the skills of continued learning, those skills that will permit students to learn better on their own or at higher levels
- ☐ An emphasis on increasing the student's ability to be independent, responsible, and self-disciplined
- ☐ Flexible physical plant facilities
- ☐ Attention to the personal development of the student: values clarification, group process skills, health and family life education when appropriate, and career education
- ☐ Teachers trained especially for, and committed to, the education of emerging adolescents

THE MIDDLE SCHOOL STUDENT

The middle school espouses the same goals as did the junior high: to provide a transition between the elementary and the high school and to help students bridge the gap in their development between childhood and adolescence.

Emerging adolescent learners in the middle school represent the most diverse group of students at any organizational level of schooling. As ninth-graders moved to the high school and sixth-graders came into the middle school, the middle school became a real transitional school with students found at all levels of physical, social, and intellectual maturity. Unlike junior high schools, which tended to treat all students as adolescents, middle schools have attempted to develop programs to help students bridge the gap in development between childhood and adolescence.

Pre- and early adolescents experience dramatic physical, social, emotional, and intellectual changes resulting from maturational changes. More biological changes occur in the bodies and minds of youngsters between the ages of 10 and 14 than at any other period in their lives except the first nine months of their development.

Because the transitional years between childhood and adolescence are marked by distinct changes in the bodies and minds of boys and girls, the success of the middle school depends on teachers and administrators who understand each learner and his or her unique developmental pattern.

Table 8.2 describes in detail the characteristics of emerging adolescents and the implications of those characteristics for the middle school.

THE MIDDLE SCHOOL TEACHER

The middle school teacher, more than any other factor, holds the key to realization of the type of effective middle school required for emerging adolescents.

The middle school teacher must have all of those characteristics that research indicates are good for teachers of all age groups. However, because of the ages embraced in the middle school, the middle school teacher is responsible for children who are striking in their diversity. What confronts a teacher in the middle school is a rapidly changing group of children in different stages of development.

A number of key competencies have been identified for teachers in the middle school (see Figure 8.1).

MANAGING MIDDLE SCHOOL PROGRAMS

A well-designed middle school features a balanced program focusing on personal development, basic skills for continuous learners, and use of knowledge to foster competence. The curriculum of a middle school thus follows closely the developmental stages represented in the students that it serves.

There has been much progress in recent years in developing new and exciting programs for emerging adolescent learners, yet much still needs to be done. New pressures brought on by the call for a return to basics has narrowed the curriculum of the middle school to the teaching of rote skills and the transmission of knowledge. Exploratory programs, guidance services, and health and physical education programs have been cut back in many schools. Thus, the curriculum area of personal development has been changed in many middle schools. This development forced an imbalance in the middle school program and a return to the more content-centered junior high or imitation high school model in many middle schools. With sixth-graders being housed in many middle schools, the result was the thrusting down of a

TABLE 8.2 Development of Emerging Adolescents and Implications for the Middle School

Characteristics of Emerging Adolescents	Implications for the Middle School
Physical Development	
Accelerated physical development begins in transescence, marked by increase in weight, height, heart size, lung capacity, and muscular strength. Boys and girls are growing at varying rates. Girls tend to be taller for the first two years and tend to be more physically advanced. Bone growth is faster than muscle development, and the uneven muscle/bone development results in lack of coordination and awkwardness. Bones may lack protection of covering muscles and supporting tendons.	Provide a health and science curriculum that emphasizes self-understanding about body changes. Guidance counselors and community resource persons (e.g., pediatricians) can help students understand what is happening to their bodies.
	Schedule adaptive physical education classes to build physical coordination. Equipment design should help students develop small and large muscles.
In pubescent girls, secondary sex characteristics continue to develop, with breasts enlarging and menstruation beginning.	Intense sports competition; avoid contact sports.
	Schedule sex education classes; health and hygiene seminars.
A wide range of individual differences among students begins to appear. Although the sequential order of development is relatively consistent in each sex, boys tend to lag a year or two behind girls. There are marked individual differences in physical development for boys and girls. The age of greatest variability in physiological development and physical size is about age 13.	Provide opportunities for interaction among students of different ages, but avoid situations where physical development can be compared (e.g., communal showers).
	Emphasize intramural programs rather than interscholastic athletics so that each student may participate regardless of physical development. Where interscholastic sports programs exist, number of games should be limited, with games played in afternoon rather than evening.
Glandular imbalances occur, resulting in acne, allergies, dental and eye defects—some health disturbances are real, and some are imaginary.	Provide regular physical examinations for all middle school students.
Boys and girls display changes in body contour—large nose, protruding ears, long arms—have posture problems, and are self-conscious about their bodies.	Health classes should emphasize exercises for good posture. Students should understand through self-analysis that growth is an individual process and occurs unevenly.
A girdle of fat often appears around the hips and thighs of boys in early puberty. Slight development of tissue under the skin around the nipples occurs briefly, causing anxiety in boys who fear they are developing "the wrong way."	Films and talks by doctors and counselors can help students understand the changes the body goes through during this period. A carefully planned program of sex education developed in collaboration with parents, medical doctors, and community agencies should be developed.

(Continues)

Source: From Jon Wiles and Joseph Bondi, *The Essential Middle School,* 2nd ed., pp. 29–34. Copyright © 1993 by Macmillan Publishing Company. Reprinted by permission.

TABLE 8.2 *Continued*

Physical Development *(continued)*	
Students are likely to be disturbed by body changes. Girls especially are likely to be disturbed by the physical changes that accompany sexual maturation.	
Receding chins, cowlicks, dimples, and changes in voice result in possible embarrassment to boys.	Teacher and parental reassurance and understanding are necessary to help students understand that many body changes are temporary in nature.
Boys and girls tend to tire easily but won't admit it.	Advise parents to insist that students get proper rest; overexertion should be discouraged.
Fluctuations in basal metabolism may cause students to be extremely restless at times and listless at others.	Provide an opportunity for daily exercise and a place where students can be children by playing and being noisy for short periods.
	Encourage activities such as special-interest classes and "hands on" exercises. Students should be allowed to move around physically in classes and avoid long periods of passive work.
Boys and girls show ravenous appetites and peculiar tastes; may overtax digestive system with large quantities of improper foods.	Provide snacks to satisfy between-meal hunger as well as nutritional guidance specific to this age group.

Social Development	
Affiliation base broadens from family to peer group. Conflict sometimes results due to splitting of allegiance between peer group and family.	Teachers should work closely with the family to help adults realize that peer pressure is a normal part of the maturation process. Parents should be encouraged to continue to provide love and comfort even though they may feel rejected.
	Teachers should be counselors. Homebase, teacher-adviser house plan arrangements should be encouraged.
Peers become sources for standards and models of behavior. Child's occasional rebellion does not diminish importance of parents for development of values. Emerging adolescents want to make their own choices, but authority still remains primarily with family.	Sponsor school activities that permit students to interact socially with many school personnel. Family studies can help ease parental conflicts. Parental involvement at school should be encouraged, but parents should not be too conspicuous by their presence.

TABLE 8.2 *Continued*

Social Development *(continued)*	
	Encourage co-curriculum activities. For example, an active student government will help students develop guidelines for interpersonal relations and standards of behavior.
Society's mobility has broken ties to peer groups and created anxieties in emerging adolescents.	Promote "family" grouping of students and teachers to provide stability for new students. Interdisciplinary units can be structured to provide interaction among various groups of students. Clubs and special-interest classes should be an integral part of the school day.
Students are confused and frightened by new school settings.	Orientation programs and "buddy systems" can reduce the trauma of moving from an elementary school to a middle school. Family teams can encourage a sense of belonging.
Students show unusual or drastic behavior at times—aggressive, daring, boisterous, argumentative.	Schedule debates, plays, playdays, and other activities to allow students to "show off" in a productive way.
"Puppy love" years emerge, with a show of extreme devotion to a particular boy or girl. However, allegiance may be transferred to a new friend overnight.	Role-playing and guidance exercises can provide the opportunity to act out feelings. Provide opportunities for social interaction between the sexes—parties and games, but not dances in the early grades of the middle school.
Youths feel that the will of the group must prevail and sometimes can be almost cruel to those not in their group. They copy and display fads of extremes in clothes, speech, mannerisms, and handwriting; very susceptible to media advertising.	Set up an active student government so students can develop their own guidelines for dress and behavior. Adults should be encouraged not to react with outrage when extreme dress or mannerisms are displayed.
Boys and girls show strong concern for what is "right" and for social justice; also show concern for those less fortunate.	Foster plans that allow students to engage in service activities, for example, peer teaching, which allow students to help other students. Community projects (e.g., assisting in a senior citizens club or helping in a childcare center) can be planned by students and teachers.
They are influenced by adults—attempt to identify with adults other than their parents.	Flexible teaching patterns should prevail so students can interact with a variety of adults with whom they can identify.

(Continues)

TABLE 8.2 *Continued*

Social Development *(continued)*

Despite a trend toward heterosexual interests, same-sex affiliation tends to dominate.	Plan large group activities rather than boy-girl events. Intramurals can be scheduled so students can interact with friends of the same or opposite sex.
Students desire direction and regulation but reserve the right to question or reject suggestions of adults.	Provide opportunities for students to accept more responsibility in setting standards for behavior. Students should be helped to establish realistic goals and be assisted in helping realize those goals.

Emotional Development

Erratic and inconsistent behavior is prevalent. Anxiety and fear contrast with reassuring bravado. Feelings tend to shift between superiority and inferiority. Coping with physical changes, striving for independence from family, becoming a person in his/her own right, and learning a new mode of intellectual functioning are all emotion-laden problems for emerging adolescents. Students have many fears, real and imagined. At no other time in development is he or she likely to encounter such a diverse number of problems simultaneously.	Encourage self-evaluation among students. Design activities that help students play out their emotions. Activity programs should provide opportunities for shy students to be drawn out and loud students to engage in calming activities. Counseling must operate as a part of, rather than an adjunct to, the learning program. Students should be helped to interpret superiority and inferiority feelings. Mature value systems should be encouraged by allowing students to examine options of behavior and to study consequences of various actions.
	Encourage students to assume leadership in group discussions and experience frequent success and recognition for personal efforts and achievements. A general atmosphere of friendliness, relaxation, concern, and group cohesiveness should guide the program.
Chemical and hormone imbalances often trigger emotions that are little understood by the transescent. Students sometimes regress to childlike behavior.	Adults in the middle school should not pressure students to explain their emotions (e.g., crying for no apparent reason). Occasional childlike behavior should not be ridiculed.
	Provide numerous possibilities for releasing emotional stress.
Too-rapid or too-slow physical development is often a source of irritation and concern. Development of secondary sex characteristics may create additional tensions about rate of development.	Provide appropriate sex education and encourage participation of parents and community agencies. Pediatricians, psychologists, and counselors should be called on to assist students in understanding developmental changes.

TABLE 8.2 *Continued*

Emotional Development *(continued)*	
This age group is easily offended and sensitive to criticism of personal shortcomings.	Sarcasm by adults should be avoided. Students should be helped to develop values when solving their problems.
Students tend to exaggerate simple occurrences and believe their problems are unique.	Use sociodrama to enable students to see themselves as others see them. Readings dealing with problems similar to their own can help them see that many problems are not unique.

Intellectual Development	
Students display a wide range of skills and abilities unique to their developmental patterns.	Use a variety of approaches and materials in the teaching-learning process.
Students will range in development from the concrete-manipulatory stage to the ability to deal with abstract concepts. The transescent is intensely curious and growing in mental ability.	Treat students at their own intellectual levels, providing immediate rather than remote goals. All subjects should be individualized. Skill grouping should be flexible.
Middle school learners prefer active over passive learning activities and prefer interaction with peers during learning activities.	Encourage physical movement, with small group discussions, learning centers, and creative dramatics suggested as good activity projects. Provide a program of learning that is exciting and meaningful.
Students are usually very curious and exhibit a strong willingness to learn things they consider useful. They enjoy using skills to solve "real-life" problems.	Organize curricula around real-life concepts (e.g., conflict, competition, peer group influence). Provide activities in formal and informal situations to improve reasoning powers. Studies of the community and the environment are particularly relevant to the age group.
Students often display heightened egocentrism and will argue to convince others or to clarify their own thinking. Independent, critical thinking emerges.	Organized discussions of ideas and feelings in peer groups can facilitate self-understanding. Provide experiences for individuals to express themselves by writing and participating in dramatic productions.
Studies show that brain growth in transescents slows between the ages of 12 and 14.	Learners' cognitive skills should be refined; continued cognitive growth during ages 12 to 14 may not be expected.
	Provide opportunities for enjoyable studies in the arts. Encourage self-expression in all subjects.

(Continues)

1. Possesses knowledge of the pre- and early adolescent physical development, which includes knowledge of physical activity needs and the diversity and variety of physical growth rates.

2. Commands knowledge of the pre- and early adolescent intellectual development, with emphasis on the transition from concrete to formal levels of mental development.

3. Has a knowledge of a recognized developmental theory and personality theory which can be used in identifying appropriate learning strategies for the pre- and early adolescent.

4. Understands the socio-emotional development, including the need to adjust to a changing body.

5. Possesses the necessary skills to allow interaction between individual students as well as the opportunity to work in groups of varying sizes.

6. Understands the cultural forces and community relationships, which affect the total school curriculum.

7. Has the ability to organize the curriculum to facilitate the developmental tasks of preadolescence and early adolescence.

8. Understands the transitional nature of grades 3 through 6 as they bridge the gap between the children of the lower elementary grades and late adolescents and early adults of the upper grades.

9. Possesses the skills needed to work with other teachers and school professionals in team teaching situations.

10. Has the ability to plan multidisciplinary lessons or units and teach them personally or with other professionals.

11. Commands a broad academic background, with specialization in at least two allied areas of the curriculum.

12. Possesses the skill to integrate appropriate media and concrete demonstrations into presentations.

13. Is able to develop and conduct learning situations that will promote independent learning and to maximize student choice and responsibility for follow-through.

14. Possesses the knowledge and skills that will allow students to sort information, set priorities, and budget time and energy.

15. Is able to teach problem-solving skills and develop lessons that are inquiry oriented.

16. Has the ability to teach students how to discover knowledge and use both inductive and deductive methods in the discovery of knowledge.

17. Possesses the knowledge and skills necessary to use role-playing simulation, instructional games, and creative dramatics in teaching the content as well as the affective domain in a middle-grade classroom.

18. Commands the knowledge and skill needed to organize and manage a class that allows individuals to learn at a rate commensurate with their ability.

19. Possesses verbal behaviors that will promote student input in a variety of group settings.

20. Is able to write behavioral objectives and design lessons to effectively conclude the objectives.

21. Has the knowledge and skills needed to diagnose strengths and weaknesses, to determine learning levels of individuals, to prescribe courses of action, and to evaluate the outcomes.

22. Has experiences in innovation and possesses the skill to experiment with teaching techniques to find those that are most effective in given situations.

23. Is able to teach the communication skills of reading, writing, and speaking in all subject areas.

24. Commands knowledge of reading techniques that will enable students to progress and improve their reading in the subject areas.

25. Possesses the skills needed to diagnose reading problems and provide a remedial program in regular classroom.

26. Has a knowledge of the techniques necessary to promote positive self-concepts and self-reliance.

FIGURE 8.1   Selected Teacher Competencies for Middle School Teachers

27. Is able to help students clarify values, consider alternative values, and develop a personal and workable valuing system.

28. Possesses a knowledge of group dynamics and the ability to organize groups that will make decisions and provide their own leadership.

29. Has a knowledge of careers and the ability to help students explore careers.

30. Commands knowledge of several major learning theories and the learning strategies that emanate from the theories.

31. Has a knowledge of how to deal with unusual classroom problems.

32. Possesses skills necessary to effectively manage groups of students in activity settings.

33. Possesses the ability to recognize difficulties that may be emotionally or physically based.

34. Possesses the knowledge and skills needed to effectively manage abusive and deviant behavior.

35. Works with extracurricular activities in the school.

36. Gathers appropriate personal information about students by using questionnaires, interviews, and observation.

37. Provides frequent feedback to students on learning progress.

38. Functions calmly in a high-activity environment.

39. Handles disruptive behavior in a positive and consistent manner.

40. Builds learning experiences for students based on learning skills (reading, math) obtained in elementary grades.

41. Works cooperatively with peers, consultants, resource persons, and paraprofessionals.

42. Exhibits concern for students by listening or empathizing with them.

43. Selects evaluation techniques appropriate to curricular objective in the affective domain.

44. Uses value clarification and other affective teaching techniques to help students develop personal value systems.

45. Provides an informal, flexible classroom environment.

46. Cooperates in curricular planning and revision.

47. Evaluates the teaching situation and selects the grouping techniques most appropriate for the situation: large-group instruction (100+ students), small-group instruction (15–25 students) or independent study.

48. Uses questioning techniques skillfully to achieve higher-order thinking processes in students.

49. Can move from one type of grouping situation to another smoothly.

50. Functions effectively in various organizational and staffing situations, such as team teaching, differentiated staffing, and multi-age groups.

51. Selects evaluation techniques appropriate to curricular objectives in the psychomotor domain.

52. Establishes positive relationships with the parents and families of students.

53. Works at understanding, accepting, and being accepted by members of the subcultures in the school and the community.

54. Understands the middle school concept and attempts to apply it in the classroom and in the school as a whole.

55. Manages the classroom with a minimum of negative or aversive controls.

56. Uses himself/herself as a tool in promoting the personal growth of students and colleagues.

57. Maintains harmonious and productive relationships with colleagues, administrators, and supervisors.

58. Is aware of the needs, forces, and perceptions that determine his/her personal behavior.

59. Maintains a balance between teacher-directed learning and student-directed learning.

60. Proceeds from a problem-solving framework involving the students in relevant inquiry.

61. Possesses skill in asking questions that encourage student thinking beyond the level of recall

FIGURE 8.1 *Continued*

Source: From J. Wiles and J. Bondi, *The Essential Middle School,* 2nd ed., pp. 55–58. Copyright © 1993 by Macmillan Publishing Company. Reprinted by permission.

high school program to an even younger group of students. Combined with a six- or seven-period departmentalized organizational model, the lack of emphasis on personal development signals a return to a secondary emphasis in the middle grades. The gains in program development won in the 1960s, 1970s, and 1980s by middle school educators were being washed away in the 1990s in many places by a return to the high school or secondary model, which was easier to schedule and administer. The lessons learned by the failure of the junior high school were lost in the face of doing what was easier and less costly.

The 1980s was a period of great activity in the middle school movement. Organizations such as the Association for Supervision and Curriculum Development (ASCD), local and state leagues of middle schools, the National Middle School Association, the National Education Association, the National Association of Secondary School Principals, the National Association of Elementary School Principals, and the National School Boards Association all began presenting conferences, publications, and position papers advocating the original purposes of the middle school as proposed in the national position document, *The Middle School We Need*.[5] Legislation encouraging middle school development and teacher training was passed in Florida, California, and other states that were active in the early middle school movement. The Carnegie Report, *Turning Points,* was the culmination of an active decade of middle school support.[6]

A milestone in the middle school movement occurred in 1986 with the publication of the best-selling ASCD publication, *Making Middle Schools Work*.[7] That publication addressed the major difficulty in getting middle schools to remain middle schools in program and organization as initially developed. The "shining light" syndrome with middle schools reflected the often-repeated situation in which a new middle school would be developed that would draw hundreds of visitors. That school would be a model for a year or two until the principal left or the staff changed. It would then revert to a junior high school type of program while a new shining light popped up somewhere else.

Seeing the frustration, and recognizing that there was an Achilles heel in the middle school success story throughout the United States, we introduced the Curriculum Management Plan (CMP)[8] model for development of middle schools. The CMP model recognized the fact that at the very heart of implementing true middle schools is solid, traditional curriculum development. The Wiles-Bondi CMP model draws from the previous work of Ralph Tyler and Hilda Taba and superimposes management techniques on a widely used accreditation format. Put simply, the CMP introduces regularity into the change process (manages it). Without such logic, the pitfalls for a complex design such as the middle school are multiple. The key to successful implementation of middle school programs remains successful planning.

Middle School Program: Overview

Successful middle schools using the Curriculum Management Plan model develop a design document that outlines program objectives and standards in detail.[9] Each design, or blueprint, is based on an extensive needs assessment outlining the academic, social, and physical needs of middle grade students.

Curriculum leaders must not lose sight of the purpose of the middle school. The middle school is a transitional school and must not be a replica of the high school or elementary school. The need for balance in the program and organizational flexibility has never been greater. In addition to the normal developmental changes that middle school students are experiencing, social changes have a major impact on the lives of emerging adolescents. Consider the following:

- The American family is breaking down. For every marriage today, there is a divorce. In the year 2000, 60 percent of children in the middle grades spent some time in a single-parent home.
- More adults moonlight now than at any other time in the history of our country.
- Only 8 percent of American homes today have the family pattern of a mother at home and father working.
- Alcoholism increased 800 percent among teenagers over the last twenty years. By the end of the ninth grade, 20 percent of adolescents will suffer a serious drinking problem.
- Forty-three percent of all persons arrested for serious crimes in the United States (rape, murder, robbery) are juveniles, yet juveniles make up only 20 percent of the population.
- One in two Americans moved during the past five years.
- One million girls between the ages of 10 and 18 gave birth to illegitimate babies in the United States in 2000. One of ten girls will be pregnant before age 18. An estimated 18 million teenage boys and girls are sexually active. AIDS is increasing at a very rapid rate among teenagers.
- The second leading cause of death among teenagers, after accidents, is suicide. The suicide rate among teenagers doubled in the decade between 1980 and 1990 and continued to increase in the 1990s.
- It is estimated that pre- and early adolescents spend one third of their waking hours watching television.
- Seventy-five percent of all advertising is aimed at ten- to eighteen-year-olds.
- Psychologists regard the lack of a stable home as the biggest contributor to delinquency.
- The most impressionable age group is that of youngsters twelve to fourteen years of age. It is no accident that the Hitler Youth, Red Guard, and even our Boy Scouts have age 12 as the starting point.

Dealing with emerging adolescents has become a national priority. In funding the National Institute of Education (NIE) during the 1990s, Congress mandated that the number one priority of NIE be research on emerging adolescent learners. The *Carnegie Report* on adolescent development in 1989 pointed out the serious deterioration of health care and the myriad social problems facing preadolescents and emerging adolescents. Consider the following:

- [ ] The middle grade years represent the last chance for students to master basic skills.
- [ ] The middle grades represent the last time for formal schooling for many of our youth. Low achievers drop out after the middle grades.
- [ ] The final attitude toward self and others, as well as a lasting attitude toward learning, is established in the middle grades.
- [ ] Future school success—indeed, future life success—can be predicted for most students in the middle grades.

Curriculum leaders must take a strong stance to prevent the middle school from becoming an imitation high school again. There are still many good models of middle schools and reformed junior high schools that offer promise for curriculum developers desiring to improve middle grade education. (See, for instance, the description for the significant results of the middle school program in St. Louis, "Miracle on Main Street—The St. Louis Story."[10]) In addition, the number of articles, texts, and research studies in the middle school area has grown both in quantity and quality in the last decade. Organizations such as the National Middle School Association and the Association for Supervision and Curriculum Development have organized numerous conferences and workshops for educators interested in middle school improvement.

Figure 8.2 illustrates the three major program elements needed in the middle school.

Balance in the Middle School Program

A balanced program needed to serve the diverse group of youngsters found in the middle grades should include the following:

- [ ] Learning experiences for transescents at their own intellectual levels, relating to immediate rather then remote academic goals.
- [ ] A wide variety of cognitive learning experiences to account for the full range of students who are at many different levels of concrete and formal operations. Learning objectives should be sequenced to allow for the transition from concrete to formal operations.
- [ ] A diversified curriculum of either exploratory or fundamental activities (or both) resulting in daily successful experiences that will stimulate and nurture intellectual development.
- [ ] Opportunities for the development of problem-solving skills, reflective-thinking processes, and awareness of the order of the student's environment.
- [ ] Cognitive learning experiences so structured that students can progress in an individualized manner. However, within the structure of an

I. Personal Development

Guidance—Physical Education—Intramurals—Lifetime Sports—Sex Education—Health Studies—Law Education—Social Services—Drug Education—Special Interest—Clubs—Student Government—Development Groupings—Programs for Students with Special Needs—Mainstreaming—Alternative Programs—Advisory Programs—Intramurals.

II. Education for Social Competence	III. Skills for Continuous Learning
Basic Studies	Communication
Science	Reading
Social Studies	Writing
Mathematics	Listening
Language Arts	Speaking
Exploratory Studies	Mathematics
Practical Arts	Computation
Home Economics	Comprehension
Industrial Arts	Usage
Business-Distributive	
Education	Observing and Comparing
Fine Arts	
Music	Analyzing
Art	
Foreign Language	Generalizing
Humanities	
Environmental Studies	Organizing
Outdoor Education	
Career Exploration	Evaluating
Consumer Education	
Media Study	

FIGURE 8.2 Program Design for the Essential Middle School

Source: From J. Wiles and J. Bondi, *The Essential Middle School,* p. 84. Copyright © 1986 by Bondi and Associates, Tampa, FL. Reprinted by permission.

individualized learning program, students can interact with one another. Social interaction is not an enemy of individual learning.

☐ A curriculum in which all areas are taught to reveal opportunities for further study, to help students learn how to study, and to help them appraise their own interests and talents. In addition, the middle school should continue the developmental program of basic skills instruction started in the elementary school, with emphasis on both developmental and remedial reading.

☐ A planned sequence of concepts in the general education areas, major emphasis on the interests and skills for continued learning, a balanced program of exploratory experiences and other activities and services for personal development, and appropriate attention to the development of values.

- [] A common program in which areas of learning are combined and integrated to break down artificial and irrelevant divisions of curriculum content. Some previously departmentalized areas of the curriculum should be combined and taught around integrative themes, topics, and experiences. Other areas of the curriculum, particularly those concerned with basic skills that are logical, sequential, and analytical, might best be taught in ungraded or continuous progress programs. Inflexible student scheduling, with its emphasis on departmentalization, should be restructured in the direction of greater flexibility.
- [] Encouragement of personal curiosity, with one learning experience inspiring subsequent activities.
- [] Methods of instruction involving open and individually directed learning experiences. The role of the teacher should be more that of a personal guide and facilitator of learning than that of a purveyor of knowledge. Traditional lecture–recitation methods should be minimized.
- [] Grouping criteria that involve not only cognitive, but also physical, social, and emotional criteria.
- [] As much consideration for who the student is and becomes, his or her self-concept, self-responsibility, and attitudes toward school and personal happiness, as for how much and what he or she knows.
- [] Experiences in the arts for all transescents to foster aesthetic appreciations and to stimulate creative expression.
- [] Curriculum and teaching methods that reflect cultural, ethnic, and socioeconomic subgroups within the middle school student population.

Advisory Programs

The advisory program helps to bridge the gap between the close, one-to-one relationship of the self-contained elementary school to the less directed, more independent world of the high school. It offers middle school students the best of both worlds. It provides every student with an advisor, a teacher who has a special concern for the student as an individual. Additionally, the program provides instruction that encourages the independence and personal growth needed at the high school level.

Finally, an advisor–advisee (A/A) program is designed to help students feel good about themselves and the contributions that they can make to their school, community, and society. An A/A program can serve as a prescriptive antidote for unmotivated, reluctant learners and at-risk students who face such societal influences as sexual promiscuity, suicide, substance abuse, unsupervised leisure time, and criminal activities.

Our country will be run someday by our middle school students of today. Such an awareness is certainly worthy of commitment, consistence, and effort on our part as middle-level educators to help young adolescents become happy, fully functioning citizens of our society. This is our role as advisors and the purpose of an advisory program.

The characteristics of an effective advisory program include the following:

- □ Advisory should be at a time and place where students feel comfortable and at home.
- □ Advisory should be in a place where students can foster peer relationships.
- □ Advisory student numbers should be as low as possible. An *optimum* number of students in one class is twenty.
- □ A student should ideally begin the day with his or her advisory teacher.
- □ All information concerning an advisee should be communicated to the advisory teacher.
- □ The advisory program should have a name decided on by the teachers, students, administration, and parents of a particular school, district, or county.
- □ A formal program consisting of a philosophy statement, operating guidelines, and activities should exist and should be formulated by the teachers, administration, parents, and students of a particular school, district, or county.

Physical Education Programs

The physical education program should address both the needs of the individual student and the diversity of the group. Each student should have the opportunity to grow physically, intellectually, socially, and emotionally. Through a broad range of experiences, students should have the opportunity to explore, to develop physical competence, and to view themselves in a positive light.

Traditionally, the grades 6–8 physical education curriculum has been activity centered. It has been organized around games/sports, gymnastics, and dance activities identified as the content of physical education. Units in basketball, volleyball, tumbling, and dance are examples of these activities. Specific skills are taught as they relate to a specific activity. They are means to developing the ability to perform in the activity. The activity has been viewed as the end.

A skill theme curriculum reverses the means–ends relationship. The curriculum is organized around specific skills or groups of skills, and the focus is on student outcomes. Activities become means through which the student can practice, refine, and develop competence in the skills. The end is the development of students who are able to use skills in a variety of contexts and situations.

Intramural Programs

Intramurals are activities that provide for the participation of students in an organized and supervised program. This participation takes place among all students within one school. The program is structured so that all students take part, regardless of their athletic ability or sex. Intramurals strive to offer success for everyone with a great deal of emphasis on fun.

The intramural program serves as an extension of the skills and activities previously learned in physical education. Middle school students are offered the opportunity to further develop these skills; intramural programs promote recreational activities, physical fitness, mental and emotional health, social contact, group loyalty, success, and a permanent interest in leisure-time activities.

The following are objectives found in most intramural programs:

☐ To offer a program within the school day to provide fun and enjoyment for all students.

☐ To provide skilled professional leadership through the physical education department for a varied number of activities.

☐ To offer activities that are adapted to the age and skill development of the students and to promote activities that afford wholesome use of leisure time.

☐ To provide opportunities for experience in human relationships, such as cooperation, development of friendships, and acceptance of group responsibility.

☐ To provide the opportunity for development of desirable personality traits, such as perseverance, self-confidence, self-discipline, self-direction, good sportsmanship, courage, and ethical conduct.

☐ To provide recognition to develop group pride, loyalty, and to serve as a means of motivation.

☐ To provide separation of grade levels on intramural days with the intramural program being the only activity at that time.

☐ To provide for the participation and cooperation of all teachers and instructional support staff.

☐ To provide an intramural advisory council, who will advise and counsel an intramural director.

☐ To provide funding for adequate staff, facilities, and equipment for a safe environment.

Exploratory Programs

The exploratory program offers students in the middle school a chance to explore many areas of interest. Courses taught by specialists include industrial technology, music, art, business, foreign language, agriculture, computer technology, and others. Special interest courses and clubs, taught by all staff members, allow further exploration for middle school students. Media persons and counselors also contribute to exploratory activities.

Special Programs

Special programs such as drug education, sex education, AIDS education, consumer education, and law education are found in many schools. A wide range of community resources, as well as in-house staff, are used for such programs.

Programs for Students with Special Needs

A full range of programs for special needs students, including those for students with physical and mental disabilities, non–English-speaking students, gifted students, and disruptive students are a part of middle school curricula. Through processes such as inclusion, mainstreaming, and teaming, students are included in team activities and other school programs.

Inclusion is a philosophy or belief that educational services to students with disabilities should be provided in general education settings, with the same peers, and in neighborhood schools to the extent appropriate for each school. There are many advantages of an inclusion component in the middle school, the most important of which is that labeling is deemphasized.

Guidance

Guidance is an integral part of the total middle school program. All instructional and special service personnel should be involved in guidance programs.

Guidance counselors serve as leaders of advisory programs and also provide instructional guidance to students while also dealing with the specific needs of individual students.

Despite much progress in the past ten years in developing new programs for emerging adolescent learners, much remains to be done. Whether programs for students in the middle grades are housed in organizational structures called middle schools or in upper elementary schools, junior high schools, or secondary schools, the focus of such programs should be the developmental characteristics of the emerging adolescent learner group itself. Figure 8.3 summarizes the middle school program in a sample philosophy/goal statement.

ORGANIZING FOR INSTRUCTION IN THE MIDDLE SCHOOL

Middle school educators, building on a philosophy and knowledge of the emerging adolescent learner, have structured a broad and relevant program for the varied needs of students found in the middle grades. To facilitate that program, the middle school must be organized to accommodate a flexible approach to instruction. Block schedules, teams of teachers with common planning periods teaching common groups of students, and special activity periods for advisory programs, intramurals, and other activities are essential elements of true middle schools. Inflexible, departmentalized high school organizational structures do not facilitate the broad program needed by middle grade students.

The interdisciplinary team approach to planning and implementing instruction has distinct advantages over a self-contained or departmentalized teaching pattern (see Figure 8.4). Some of these advantages follow:

    ☐   More than one teacher with the knowledge of scheduling, use of instructional materials, grouping, and instructional methods benefits individual student learning.

The middle school offers a balanced, comprehensive, and success-oriented curriculum. The middle school is a sensitive, caring, supportive learning environment that will provide those experiences that will assist in making the transition from late childhood to adolescence, thereby helping each individual to bridge the gap between the self-contained structure of the elementary school and the departmental structure of the high school.

Middle school curricula are more exploratory in nature than those of the elementary school and less specialized than those of the high school. Realizing that the uniqueness of individual subject disciplines must be recognized, an emphasis on interdisciplinary curriculum development will be stressed. Curriculum programs should emphasize the natural relationship among academic disciplines that facilitate cohesive learning experiences for middle school students through integrative themes, topics, and units. Interdisciplinary goals should overlap subject area goals and provide for interconnections such as reasoning, logical and critical thought, coping capacities, self-management, positive personal development, and career awareness.

The academic program of a middle school emphasizes skills development through science, social studies, reading, mathematics, and language arts courses. A well-defined skills continuum is used as the basic guide in all schools in each area including physical education, health, guidance, and other educational activities. Exploratory opportunities are provided through well-defined and structured club programs, activity programs, and special interest courses, thereby creating opportunities for students to interact socially, to experience democratic living, to explore areas not in the required curriculum, to do independent study and research, to develop and practice responsible behavior, and to experience working with varying age groups.

The middle school curriculum will be a program of planned learning experiences for our students. The three major components for our middle school curriculum are (1) subject content (2) personal development, and (3) essential skills.

FIGURE 8.3   A Sample Philosophy/Goal Statement

- ☐ Curricula among subject areas can be coordinated so that the students can relate one subject to another; this leads to greater breadth of understanding.
- ☐ Teachers can better understand individual differences in students when more than one person is making observations and evaluations. This enables teachers to cope with differences more effectively and handle discipline problems more easily. Guidance for students is discussed among the team.
- ☐ The team approach enables teachers to contrast a student's behavior and ability from class to class, thereby helping them develop a systematic and consistent approach to helping the child.
- ☐ Closer work with guidance and other specialists is possible.
- ☐ Block scheduling allows the teacher greater flexibility in grouping to accommodate large- and small–group instruction, remedial work, and independent study.
- ☐ Flexible time schedules are more conducive to children's developmental needs at this age level than are rigid departmentalized schedules.

Teams Should	**Teams Shouldn't**
Provide a constructive climate	Promote rivalry
Focus goals for students	Challenge school policy
Encourage self-esteem	Be fund raisers
Set discipline standards	Share negative feelings
Coordinate activities	Overburden one member
Help all students succeed	Isolate one member
Build school spirit	Take away one's teaching style
Be the parent contact	Handle severe student problems
Raise academic performance	
Share work burdens	
Set examples for students	
Make school fun	

Goals for the School Year

Get closer to elective teachers	Get team bulletin boards
Meet more often with administrators	Get more teacher input into team
Develop interdisciplinary instruction	formation
patterns	Make team leader councils really work
Involve counselors in team activities	

Indicators of a Successful Team

Attendance	Improved discipline
Academic achievement	School/team pride
Validating team goals	Funds allocated to team activities
Getting team bulletin boards	Family atmosphere
Establishing team-to-team communication	

FIGURE 8.4   Tasks of Teams in Middle Schools

Source: Dade County, Florida, workshop by authors, August 30, 1990. This list is the product of brainstorming by approximately 200 team leaders in Dade County schools, August 30, 1990.

- ☐ A number of instructors can lend their individual expertise to a given topic simultaneously.
- ☐ Large blocks of time are available for educational field trips, guest speakers, and so on; at the same time, scheduling is not disrupted. Less teaching time is lost to repetitious film showing.
- ☐ Teachers can be more aware of what their students are learning in other classes—what assignments, tests, projects are making demands on their time.
- ☐ Common planning time can lead to more creativity in teaching approaches and consistency in teaching strategies.
- ☐ Interdisciplinary teaching leads to economy of learning time and transfer among students.
- ☐ Student leadership is distributed among all of the teams because each team's students are typical of the total school community.

☐   Students are able to identify themselves with a smaller school within a school; with team representation on student council, they are more closely related to student government.

☐   Correlated planning of content and project work is more easily carried out.

☐   Parent conferences can be arranged by the guidance counselor for times when all of a student's academic teachers are available.

☐   Individual teams may rearrange time and period schedules without interference with the overall school program. For example, each team may individually manipulate their block of time to provide periods of various lengths. All students do not move in the hallways at the end of fifty-five minutes.

☐   Field trips can now be planned by teams, and built-in chaperoning is thus provided. Longer times for such trips are now available without disrupting a multiple number of classes.

☐   One of the greatest advantages of team teaching is the assistance provided to the beginning teacher.

☐   Building use is improved; large- and small-group space is used as well as regular classrooms.

☐   An interdisciplinary team scheduling arrangement promotes the professional growth of the teachers by encouraging the exchange of ideas among the members of the teaching team.

An example of block scheduling to facilitate interdisciplinary teaming is found in Figure 8.5.

Alternative Scheduling Models

Following the high school lead, some middle schools have implemented long blocks of time for classes—from seventy-five to ninety minutes. Longer periods provide teachers with fewer students to teach during the school day, cut down on the number of class changes for students (thus reducing potential discipline problems), and allow time for more depth of instruction.

The longer block schedule takes many forms. In the four-by-four block, students spend ninety minutes in four courses every other day, which creates eight subject loads in a school year. In the 75-75-3 plan, students follow a fairly typical middle school schedule for the first 150 days. Courses end after seventy-five-day terms, and students enroll in specialized courses during the last six weeks. The specialized courses can be academically enriching programs or remedial courses to help students master grade-level courses.

Two problems are created for middle school teachers with the longer teaching block—the need to carry out instructional activities and the difficulty in coordinating a common planning time for teachers teaching the same students, a major element of the middle school concept.

For additional information about scheduling in the middle school, see Resources for Information on Middle School Scheduling at the end of this chapter.

6th Grade	7th Grade	8th Grade	8:30
Advisory	Advisory	Advisory	← 1 8:50 ← 2

Basics
 	
90*
	Exploratory/
	Physical Education
	90
		Basics
		  English
		  Math
		  Reading
		  Science
		  Social Studies
		
		  210	

Exploratory/ Physical Education 90	Basics 60		
	Lunch 30		
Lunch 30	Basics 150		
Basics 120		Lunch 30	12:20 ← 3 12:50
		Exploratory/ Physical Education 90	← 4 2:20
Enrichment and Remediation 40	Enrichment and Remediation 40	Enrichment and Remediation 40	← 5 3:00

FIGURE 8.5   Parts of a Block Schedule

Source: From *The Essential Middle School,* p. 231, by J. Wiles and J. Bondi. Copyright © 1986 by Wiles, Bondi and Associates, Tampa, FL. Reprinted by permission.

In-Service Programs

Because in-service programs for middle school teachers have not been sustained in many schools, and preservice training has not changed from the old model of training secondary teachers, many teachers prefer the secondary program model and organizational pattern.

To counter that, a much more systematic approach has to be implemented to retool veteran teachers and prepare new teachers for the modern middle school (see Figure 8.6).

Certification Component   (Middle Level Education—Orange County Public Schools Component #20561)

This component will focus on the following topics of study:

1. The middle grades
2. Understanding the middle-grades student
3. Organizing interdisciplinary instruction
4. Curriculum development
5. Developing critical and creative thinking in students
6. Counseling functions of the teacher
7. Developing creative-learning materials
8. Planning and evaluating programs

To meet the requirements of the component, each participant will attend 10 two-hour workshops. The program will consist of 30 hours of instruction in a workshop setting and 30 hours of supervised in-school follow-up activities.

It is anticipated that successful completion of this component plus one year of successful teaching in a middle school will lead to middle school certification for the participants.

Leadership for Team Leaders and Grade Coordinators

This training will focus on group process and communication skills that will enhance the ability of team leaders and grade coordinators to carry out their assigned responsibilities. The participants will receive six hours of skills-based training. All participants will be expected to have successfully completed the Middle Level Education component prior to attending this training.

Overview of the Middle School

An audio-visual presentation giving an overview of middle level education in Orange County public schools. It addresses the planned structure and curriculum of the middle school.

This will be a one-hour activity.

Program of Instruction

An overview of the instructional program of the middle school. This would cover the subject content, areas of personal development, and essential skills. This activity will be one hour of information with opportunity for participants to ask questions.

Middle Level Education for School-Based Administration

The presentation will be modeled on the certification component (OCPS Component #20561—Middle Level Education) with emphasis in those areas of special interest to the school-level administrator. It will consist of 20 hours of instruction with specified activities to be carried out at the school site.

Selected Topics

The training will include topics from the certification that meet special needs of those personnel who deal with the middle school child in other than classroom settings. An example of this would be "Understanding the Middle Grades Student" for school secretaries, custodians, and other classified personnel. This would be a one-hour activity.

FIGURE 8.6   Middle School Training Components

Source: From *The Essential Middle School,* p. 35, by J. Wiles and J. Bondi. Copyright © 1986 by Wiles, Bondi and Associates, Tampa, FL. Reprinted by permission.

The National Education Association in 1985 adopted the *Wiles-Bondi Guide and Plan for Conducting Ten Workshops.* That plan has been modified and is now a part of the Wiles-Bondi Teachers Training Teachers (TTT) model,[11] which has been used by school districts implementing successful middle school programs. As part of the Curriculum Management Plan (CMP) model, the TTT program focuses on peers (teachers) teaching peers at school sites. Using the Wiles-Bondi training materials[12] (adapted to each school district), a systematic training program can be implemented that includes hands-on and practical materials and activities in workshops. This model eliminates the need for outside consultants who entertain teachers with stories and leave them wondering, What do I do on Monday? Since the in-service program is practical and delivered in school settings by teachers, it meets with the approval of middle school teachers. It also fits with the teacher empowerment model that dictates that teachers should be in control of their own improvement.

COMPREHENSIVE PLANNING FOR MIDDLE SCHOOLS: A REVIEW

The curriculum of the middle school, with its concern for the special needs of pre- and early adolescents, its comprehensive definition of education, and its promotion of continuity in learning and development, is more than a series of catch-phrases and education innovations. The middle school is, in fact, a highly complex plan for educating a special learner. Owing to the complexity of the educational design, successful implementation of the program calls for a significant degree of advanced planning.

The curriculum planning model suggested earlier is necessary if middle schools are to succeed. In assisting in the development of middle schools across the United States, we have noted that planning often determines the fine line between success and failure. Such planning is necessary at the district, school, and classroom levels. The following district-level planning steps, in sequence, are recommended for the establishment of middle schools.

Analysis

The middle school should arise from need. Ideally, school systems and communities will proceed through value-clarification processes that reveal the logic of the middle school design, and programs will be initiated on what is known about their students. Overcrowding, integration, or building availability are poor reasons for choosing the concept.

An important point in making such an analysis is not to allow the search to be focused only on problems. The analysis should also be projective—what kind of an educational experience do we want for students during this period of development?

Involvement

Preliminary investigations of the middle school concept should involve all parties with vested interests in intermediate education. A step often taken in planning the middle school is to explore the concept without involving those who will be most directly affected by its activation: students, teachers, parents, and the community. At a superficial level, the elimination of this stage will probably lead to future confrontations over both programs and policy (interscholastic athletics, social events, grading policies, community-based learning). More important from the planning standpoint, however, is the dedication and support that will be needed to put such a program in practice in the first place. The middle school cannot be implemented and maintained unless those involved believe in it.

Of the constituencies just mentioned, particular attention must be given to the community in which the middle school will reside. Unaccustomed to educational jargon and unfamiliar with national trends in educational programs, many citizens may resist the middle school idea because of misunderstandings about the academic nature of the program and the necessary organizational arrangements. Without a clear understanding of the rationale of the program and the reason for these arrangements, community resistance will be high.

By involving community members representing all segments of the population in the initial analysis of student needs, in the investigation of the middle school concept, in the drafting of documents, and in the planning of implementation stages, educators build in a means of communicating with the community at later times.

Commitment

Philosophical commitments to the middle school definition of education should be secured prior to activating the program. This text has repeatedly underscored the necessity of understanding and accepting the philosophical concept of the middle school as a prerequisite for successful implementation of such a program. A lack of understanding of the middle school concept represents the largest potential stumbling block to successful implementation. Without such understanding and a basic philosophical acceptance of the middle school concept, there can be no substantial rationale for practices and programs found in the middle school.

It is important to note that this understanding and acceptance must go beyond school board approval and superintendent acquiescence, although both are important. Such an understanding and commitment must be held by the building principal, the involved teachers, and the parents of involved students.

Funding

Appropriate monies must be earmarked for activation of the plan. An observable phenomenon in American education is that finance is the "fuel" of progress. Few major innovations of the past twenty years (middle schools being a notable exception) have really succeeded without substantial financial support.

Although it is not impossible for a building faculty to implement the middle school concept with sheer dedication, two simple facts about middle schools are worth noting: (1) middle schools are a much more complex form of education than traditional programs, and (2) due to this complexity, they require more energy and money to operate.

Every deviation from standardized patterns of education, such as uniform textbooks, the classroom-confined learning experience, and single-dimension instruction, requires effort and expense. School districts that commit to the middle school concept must also commit to financing building conversion, materials acquisition, staff development, and so forth.

Resources

Resources commensurate with the task must be allocated. One of the common pitfalls in establishing middle schools is to assume that they can operate on the same resource base as traditional intermediate schools. To rely on teacher-made materials exclusively, to overlook a consumable materials budget, to fail to allocate materials to build up the instructional resource center, to make no provision for off-campus experiences is to doom in advance the programs of the middle school. Middle schools, if properly operated, require substantial resources for instruction.

Personnel

Middle schools must be staffed with dedicated and enthusiastic teachers. The middle school will be only as effective as its personnel in succeeding at new roles. With only several colleges in the nation training teachers and staff members exclusively for middle school positions, most teachers and support personnel will enter the middle school from other more traditional educational designs. Such persons, regardless of their belief in and allegiance to the middle school philosophy of education, will need special assistance in adjusting to their new roles. Predictably, the middle school staff will need extensive assistance in assuming new roles.

A problem witnessed in many school districts is that middle school teachers are prone to return to traditional patterns if sufficient support is not maintained. Many middle schools open under the so-called Hawthorne effect (a term coming from the Hawthorne studies in which workers were found to be more productive, regardless of work conditions, if they first received sufficient attention as being special). Teacher enthusiasm and energy are understandably high in the beginning. However, as program development slows or resource bases erode with the gradual lessening of attention, it is not unusual for old patterns of teacher–pupil interaction and learning to creep in. Therefore, instead of offering only one short summer training session for the middle school staff, we suggest long-term, systematic training opportunities.

Detailed Planning

From an administrative/organizational perspective, it is crucial that schools conduct detailed planning to smoothly implement the middle school concept. The past experience of many middle schools suggests that a "broken front" approach to this concept does not work. Prior to the development of a middle school, the district must have an understanding of objectives, a commitment to this definition of educating, the involvement of those who support the school, money and resources to implement its components, and capable personnel willing to assume the required roles. The time frame for opening a middle school must allow for the magnitude of the process proposed.

Although the amount of preparation time required to open a fully functioning middle school depends on environmental conditions in the community, a minimum period appears to be eighteen to twenty-four months. This estimate is based on several definable steps of planning:

1. Awareness and study phases.
2. Educating the community and gaining commitments.
3. Budgeting for development.
4. Selection of staff, site.
5. Construction of a detailed implementation plan.
6. Intensive training of staff.
7. Development of curriculum.
8. Construction or conversion of site.
9. Opening of the middle school.

In some communities and school districts, it would be possible to accomplish these steps in six months or less because of central office organization and support from the community leaders. The experience of many middle schools, however, suggests that to hasten through steps 2, 6, and 7, or to proceed with step 8 prior to step 7 can lead to significant problems later on. Eroding community support, an ill-prepared staff, a superficially constructed curriculum, and a dysfunctional site are all causes of middle school failure.

Role of Technology

In the final years of the twentieth century, teachers and administrators in middle schools had to react to the avalanche of technology without a principle to guide selection. Each year something new and exciting supersedes the previous year's new and exciting item. Our continuous efforts to be high tech are distorting school budgets and skewing the schools' curricula. In this sense, technology has not been good for schools because it has distorted the existing system. However, technology has also piqued the curiosity of the better teachers who have recognized that the Internet might provide truly space age learning tools if the power of the instrument can be harnessed.

Evaluating the Middle School

Traditional Patterns.   Often missing in the development of middle schools is an evaluation plan that will measure the success of program and organization changes. The following middle school hypotheses, on which middle school evaluations in most school districts today are based, provide areas from which data can be compiled:

- ☐ The middle school will provide a rich program of exploratory courses.
- ☐ Social and psychological problems will be fewer and less intense.
- ☐ Students will develop more adequate self-concepts.
- ☐ Students will become more self-directed learners.
- ☐ Graduates will succeed better in high school.
- ☐ Teacher turnover will be lower.
- ☐ Teacher morale will be higher.
- ☐ The organization will facilitate better use of individual teacher competencies and skills.
- ☐ Attendance of students will increase.
- ☐ Teachers will use a greater variety of media to meet the diverse needs of preadolescent learners.
- ☐ Patrons (parents, students, teachers) will hold more positive attitudes toward the objectives and procedures.
- ☐ Student achievement on standardized tests will equal or exceed that of students in conventional schools.

Sample measures of evaluation appropriate for the middle school are offered in Figure 8.7.

The New Evaluation Pattern   While traditional criteria for existing middle schools suggest a comprehensive and flexible approach, the new technological middle schools of the twenty-first century will need highly individualized assessment designs. In these new middle schools, teachers will create instructional

Measures of Evaluation	Measures of Growth
Academic aptitude tests	Aspects of thinking
Reading tests (comprehension and vocabulary)	Work habits and skills
Achievement tests in subjects	Reading
Emotional and social adjustment measures	Development of social attitudes
Health assessments	Development of wider interests
Home conditions	Development of appreciations
Pupil questionnaires	Development of social sensitivity
Behavior ratings	Ability to make social adjustments
Interest indexes	Creativity
Writing sample inventories	Development of personal philosophy
Work habit measures	Physical health
Teacher classroom behavior assessments	Mental health

FIGURE 8.7   Measures of Evaluation

materials, and the degree of individualization for each student will be much greater. Districts will need to anticipate these changes to help teachers to prepare for this coming era.

As stated earlier, curriculum "frameworks" and "learning objectives" will guide teachers in their selection of learning experiences for students. All learning objectives should be specific to the following points:

1. Learning is defined in terms of global outcomes using measures such as the cognitive and affective taxonomies of Bloom and Krathwohl to target the desired results of instruction.
2. All learning should include thinking and problem-solving skills to emphasize that middle school learning is about life in the future and after school.
3. Affect (emotion) should be employed as a criterion for selecting learning opportunities for middle-schoolers. The higher the affect present, the more lasting or impressionable the learning episode.
4. Learning objectives should be sequential and within the scope of the curriculum. This is especially important when using the Internet due to the many enticing and interesting topics available.
5. Objectives should imply a level of attainment or a range of attainment, but not standardized growth. Underestimating, as well as overestimating, student capacity is a regular problem in many middle school classrooms.
6. All objectives should suggest evidences of participation or attainment, with the majority not being of the pencil-and-paper test variety.

As teachers begin to develop curricula (units, triptiks, exploratories) they should consider the following evaluative criteria:

1. Concepts should guide any content selection. Middle schools feature "big" learnings and detail is often forgotten.
2. Content is usually "sampling" rather than mastery oriented. We select a piece of literature as representative of a kind of literature rather than good in itself.
3. Information should be developmentally appropriate for middle-schoolers.
4. Information should be current and accurate. When using the Internet, the teacher must remember that there is no quality-control agent.
5. The scope of the learning is defined. With Internet learning, the information horizon is limitless. The student must have guidance in selection of experience.
6. Content on the Internet is always connected to more content, especially using search engines. Teachers should draw "information webs" or maps for the student with search guide words provided.

In terms of instructional design, teachers must understand that learning changes behavior. When we program a learning episode, we expect something to happen. The accidental curriculum is dangerous because it trivializes formal learning and suggests that all information is equally important. The following guidelines might aid in evaluating instructional plans:

1. All teaching strategies recognize and acknowledge that students have individual learning styles and preferences.
2. Lessons that are for self-directed learning should be defined by time and anticipated attention span.
3. All groups of lessons should be ordered and logical, and this order should reflect an overall curriculum plan for the subject or year.
4. Until individual student work habits are known, an instructional pace should be suggested for each student (expectations for learning materials).
5. Teachers should be able to build in optional learning activities and suggest peripheral learning paths for better students.
6. Middle school learning designs can be for groups of students (LANs) and should always show applications of the principles, concepts, or skills learned.

Selection of instructional materials is a very important part of any evaluation component. As we enter the age of Internet learning, we must be cognizant of the fact that materials of the Internet are extensive, dynamic, and easily accessible. The ultimate use of such "information superhighway" materials will be found in the meaning attached to the materials, not in the access to the materials. Use of computers allows the processing of information: deleting, adding, connecting, and constructing knowledge. Without guidance, students can easily become overwhelmed and lost. The teacher's role in the new middle school will be greatly enhanced.

Many teachers we speak with are anxious about students in their classrooms taking unguided learning trips on the Net. Providing the students with the appropriate addresses, "bookmarking" menu items on the browser, and even using existing "projection devices" to see what students are viewing will make early use of Internet materials less stressful for the teacher. The following guidelines are also suggested for evaluating criteria:

1. Select materials thought to be motivators for individual students.
2. Do not get trapped in using only the computer. Use books, films, and other media to engage students. Like television, computer viewing is hard on the eyes and has been shown by research to irritate some students.
3. Make sure the student understands the connection between suggested materials.
4. Use the Internet to supplement teacher lessons, not vice versa.
5. Try to ascertain the appropriate print size and reading difficulty for any assigned materials.
6. Take advantage of materials and plans recommended by state and national agencies. Most of these subject area plans are on the Internet.
7. Be on the lookout for inaccurate, false, or enticing information on the Internet. Remember, there is no filter beyond the classroom teacher for the new technological curriculum materials.

In addition to following these suggestions, the new middle school teacher needs to see himself or herself as in charge of learning. Over the past twenty years, publishing companies have taken away much of the control of learning in America's classrooms by producing "teacher-proof" learning systems. The advent of Internet technology changes all that—the teacher is once again in charge!

Teachers in the new middle school must become experts in philosophy and instructional criteria if they are to design learning once again. Middle school students are unique, and instruction in middle school is not like that at the elementary or secondary school.

Finally, teachers need to see evaluation of instruction as an assisting venture that makes learning more and more purposeful. The questions suggested in the preceding section are helpful, guiding questions designed to sharpen the instructional focus of the classroom teachers.

NEW STANDARDS FOR THE MIDDLE SCHOOL

We predict that a new and more responsive middle school will evolve in this century. Frankly, this must happen if the middle school is to survive! In a nutshell, everything has changed in terms of teaching and learning since the Internet became available to us in 1995. The curriculum, including what is offered, how it was developed, who developed it, how it's accessed or delivered, and the role of the teacher in delivering it, is in flux. What emerges from this change process will be completely new.

A century-old promise of intermediate educators to build an instructional program for a unique learner, the preadolescent, can now be fulfilled. The middle school can declare itself once and for all and be consistently progressive in its philosophy and its programs. The network of emerging technological middle schools is awesome and can only become more powerful through synergy.

Given these changes, new middle schools must clarify their mission and update their standards for evaluation. We offer the following list for the consideration of middle school leaders.

The Middle School Will
A. Use communicative technologies to redefine school learning.
  1. Provide each student with developmentally appropriate materials.
  2. Individualize learning for each student.
  3. Deliver learning experiences at the level of student readiness.
B. Develop a new and exciting exploratory curriculum.
  1. Expand on the natural growth of each student.
  2. Teach skills of access, assessment, and application.
  3. Stress an action learning format.
  4. Be future oriented, focusing on learning to solve problems.
  5. Be "high growth" in design, allowing for student expression.
C. Feature teachers who have transitioned to twenty-first-century learning.
  1. Teachers will be guides to and designers of learning.

2. Teachers will be the chief developers of curriculum.
3. Teachers will be at the center of a world learning community.
4. Teachers will train and be trained by other teachers.
5. Teachers will be lifelong learners.
    D. Possess evaluation measures that are relevant.
    1. Evaluation will be a joint venture among teachers, parents, and students.
    2. Evaluation will reflect the comprehensive nature of middle school education.
    3. Evaluation will assess students as individuals.

THE MIDDLE SCHOOL AS A PART OF THE TOTAL CURRICULUM

As is true of the elementary and high school, the middle school does not stand alone. It must build on the curriculum of the elementary school and, in turn, form a solid educational base for students entering the high school. Although early in the middle school movement, educational leaders fought for a separate identity for the middle school to prevent it from following the path of the junior high school, leaders are increasingly, emphasizing an articulated K–12 curriculum rather than building separate programs for elementary, middle, and high school students. The move toward developing a unified K–12 curriculum is a welcome one. Regardless of housing patterns or grade-level organization, students should be viewed as individuals progressing through definite stages of development. An articulated curriculum that accommodates the developmental needs of youngsters is more important than grade organizations of schools. The middle school, however, must be a strong bridge that holds together the total K–12 curriculum.

In concluding this chapter on middle grades education, here are some common and recurrent problems in middle schools:

1. Absentee rates for students in the intermediate grades are generally higher than those at the elementary and secondary levels. What may be some of the factors causing this condition? How can curriculum leaders address this problem?
2. Because many educators view the high school as a distinctive level of specialized academic preparation, many students are retained at the eighth-grade level. What price do we pay for such retention? What is a reasonable retention rate? What can curriculum personnel do about this problem?
3. Students in the intermediate grades have many interpersonal concerns related to growing up. Yet, the average student-to-counselor ratio for this age group is 1 to 450. What can be done in the curriculum to address this problem?
4. Declining achievement scores on national tests are a common phenomenon in the intermediate grades. What causes this to happen? What can curriculum teachers do about it?

GLOBALIZING THE CURRICULUM

Global systems identify our interdependence. As we work in a global economy, the world becomes a more closely knit community. Technology has shortened the distances around the world, and global issues and problems are shared and not isolated. They require cooperative and well-thought-out direction.

As we meet the challenges of the global economy in which work, workforces, products, and ideas are globally intertwined, students should be taught the values of human rights, dignity, self-reliance, and social justice and how they are and should be applied on a global scale. Human and universal values cover all attitudes and beliefs of the individual and humanity as a whole. We can help students stretch their identities beyond their own ethnic, national, and religious groups and understand the value of people who are different from themselves.

SUMMARY

By the year 2000, none of the goals listed in the Goals 2000 document (drafted in 1994) were realized. Although Americans still view those goals as very important, and we have made progress in reaching them, the resources, strategies, and will to meet them are still lacking. We must continue to work to reach those goals and not accept anything less than excellence in our schools.

Because of technology, for the first time in American history, education is seen as a direct gateway to the acquisition of power. Traditionally based on goods and property, power now to an astonishing degree stems from intellectual capabilities. In the twentieth century, it took an enormous labor force and kingdoms of land to build powerful enterprises such as railroads. In the new decade of the twenty-first century, power comes from the minds of people through the World Wide Web.

Public schools, as open-system organizations, are by their nature open to public policy demands and mandates. Those policies and demands are imposed by diverse coalition groups, court systems, and legislative bodies at the local, state, and national levels.

Schools today are standards-driven, and they are being measured by state assessment tests. State standards are usually based on national standards. With standards and tests have come alternative delivery systems for schools, both public and private.

The explosion of technology has brought new and exciting ways for students to learn, facilitated record keeping for schools, and forced the retooling of our teaching staffs. Challenges of how to use the technology and the information generated through technology remain with us.

Finally, the globalization of our economy and our shrinking world have brought on the need for globalizing the curriculum. Helping students to increase their understanding of ethnic and religious groups beyond our own borders and helping them to see our economic and social interdependence will be an important mission of the new American middle school.

The mission of the modern middle school has changed dramatically, and we must ensure that it succeeds.

SUGGESTED LEARNING ACTIVITIES

1. Prepare an outline of the standards and assessment tests your middle school will face in the coming school year.
2. Write a paper listing various types of assessment found in the modern middle school.
3. Develop an in-service plan to prepare teachers for using technology in the modern middle school.
4. Develop an outline of a global curriculum for your local middle school.
5. Organize a panel discussion on the topic "Challenges of Privatization."

NOTES

1. Commission on the Reorganization of Secondary Education, "Cardinal Principles of Secondary Education," *Bulletin 1918* (Washington, DC: U.S. Department of the Interior, Bureau of Education, 1918), pp. 12–13.
2. ASCD Commission on Secondary Education, *The Junior High We Need* (Alexandria, VA: Association for Supervision and Curriculum Development, 1961).
3. Rudolph Flesch, *Why Johnny Can't Read and What You Can Do About It* (New York: Harper-Collins, 1986).
4. Education Facilities Laboratories, *The Schoolhouse in the City* (New York: 1966), p. 10.
5. ASCD Working Group on the Emerging Adolescent, Joseph Bondi, ed., *The Middle School We Need* (Washington, DC: Association for Supervision and Curriculum Development, 1960), pp. 11–12.
6. Carnegie Council on Adolescent Development, *Turning Points: Preparing American Youth for the 21st Century* (New York: Carnegie Corporation, 1989).
7. Jon Wiles and Joseph Bondi, *Making Middle Schools Work* (Alexandria, VA: Association for Supervision and Curriculum Development, 1985).
8. The CMP model has been successfully used in the transition to true middle schools in such

districts as St. Louis, Denver, Dallas, Orange County (Orlando, FL), Dade County (Miami, FL), Duval County (Jacksonville, FL), Baton Rouge, Long Beach (CA), and hundreds of large and small school districts in the United States. It has also been used by the Kellogg Foundation in developing the model middle school program in Ishpeming. Michigan.
9. Design documents found in Dade County, FL; Duval County, FL; St. Louis, MO; San Bernardino, CA, and other school districts. See also Wiles and Bondi, *Making Middle Schools Work* for Orange County, FL, model.
10. Jon Wiles, Joseph Bondi, and Ron Stodghill, "Miracle on Main Street—The St. Louis Story," *Educational Leadership* (Alexandria, VA: Association for Supervision and Curriculum Development, November 1982), pp. 52–53.
11. Jon Wiles and Joseph Bondi, *A Guide and Plan for Conducting Ten Workshops with the NEA Middle School Training Program* (Washington, DC: National Education Association, 1985).
12. Wiles, Bondi and Associates, Inc., *Training Materials for Middle School Teachers* (numerous booklets and materials), P.O. Box 16545, Tampa, FL 33687.

ADDITIONAL READING

Allen, JoBeth. *Class Actions: Teaching for Social Justice in Elementary and Middle School.* New York: Teachers College Press, 1999.

Bondi, J., ed. *The Middle School We Need.* Alexandria, VA: Association for Supervision and Curriculum Development, 1975.

Carnegie Council on Adolescent Education. *Turning Points—Preparing American Youth for the 21st Century.* Washington, DC: Carnegie Council on Adolescent Education, 1989.

Elkind, D. *A Sympathetic Understanding of the Child: Birth to Sixteen.* Boston: Allyn and Bacon, 1974.

Jenkins, John M. *Banishing Anonymity: Middle and High School Advisement Programs.* Larchmont, NY: Eye on Education, 2000.

Koballa, Thomas R., Jr., and Deborah J. Tippins. *Cases in Middle and Secondary Science Education: The*

Promise and Dilemmas. Upper Saddle River, NJ: Merrill/Prentice Hall, 2000.

Lounsbury, J., and Donald Claus. *Inside Grade Eight: From Apathy to Excitement.* Reston, VA: National Association of Secondary School Principals, 1990.

Murphy. *Curriculum Guide for Middle School.* Thomson Learning, 2000.

Muth, K. Denise. *Teaching and Learning in the Middle Grades.* Boston: Allyn and Bacon, 1999.

Onstein, Allen. *Foundations of Education,* 7th ed. Boston: Houghton Mifflin, 2000.

Queen, J. Allen. *Curriculum Practice in the Elementary and Middle School.* Upper Saddle River, NJ: Merrill/Prentice Hall, 1999.

Rasool, Joan. *Multicultural Education in Middle and Secondary Classrooms: Meeting the Challenge of Diversity and Change.* Belmont, CA: Wadsworth, 2000.

Rettig, Michael D. *Scheduling Strategies for Middle Schools.* Larchmont, NY: Eye on Education, 2000.

Siskind, Theresa Gayle. *Cases of Middle School Educators.* Lanham, MD: Scarecrow Press/Technomic Books, 2000.

Snodgrass, Dawn M. *Collaborative Learning in Middle and Secondary Schools: Applications and Assessment.* Larchmont, NY: Eye on Education, 2000.

Ward, Phillip. "The Saber-Tooth Project: Curriculum and Workplace Reform in Middle School Physical Education." *Journal of Teaching in Physical Education* 18, 4. Champaign, IL: Human Kinetics, 1999.

Watson, Charles R. *Best Practices from America's Middle Schools.* Larchmont, NY: Eye on Education, 1999.

Wiles, J., and J. Bondi. *The Essential Middle School.* Tampa, FL: Wiles, Bondi and Associates, 1986.

Wiles, J., and J. Bondi. *Making Middle Schools Work.* Alexandria, VA: Association for Supervision and Curriculum Development, 1987.

Wiles, J., and J. Bondi. *The New American Middle School.* Prentice Hall, 2001.

WEB ARTICLES
General

"Technology and Teaching: A Turning Point," by Vivan H. Wright and George E. Marsh
http://computed.coe.wayne.edu/Vol5/Wright%26Marsh.html, March 25, 2000.

"Multimedia, Multilinearity, and Multivocality in the Hypermedia Classroom," by David Silver
http://info.ox.ac.uk/ctitext/publish/comtxt/ct14/silver.html, March 25, 2000.

"Computers and the Thinking Curriculum," by Christine De Matos
http://computed.coe.wayne.edu/Vol1/matos.html, March 25, 2000.

"Overcoming the Challenge of Internet Integration,"
http://computed.coe.wayne.edu/Vo12/media_designs.index.html, March 25, 2000.

"Thinking Styles and Assessing Information on the World Wide Web," by Jean Lumb
http://computed.coe.wayne.edu/Vo12/lumb.html, March 25, 2000.

Students with Special Needs

Individuals with Disabilities Act (IDEA 1997)
http://www.glef.org/edutopia/newsletters/6.1/ebooks.html, March 25, 2000.

"Digital Textbooks," by Mark Sargent
http://www.glef.org/edutopia/newsletters/8.1/ebooks.html, March 25, 2000.

"Assistive Technology Success Stories," by Yuri Wellington
http://www.glef.org/edutopia/newsletters/6.1/yuri.html, March 25, 2000.

"Leaping over Walls," by Mason Barney
http://www.glef.org/edutopia/newsletters/6.1/mason.html, March 25, 2000.

"Technology for the Constructivist Language Arts Classroom," by Rice, Stallworth, and Wilson
http://computed.coe.wayne.edu/Vo15/Rice(etal).html, March 25, 2000.

Math

"A Note on the Effective Implementation of Technology within the Mathematics Classroom"
http://computed.coe.wayne.edu/Vo15/lattimore.html, March 25, 2000.

Science

"Butterflies, Biology and Computers," by Robert Ceglie
http://computed.coe.wayne.edu/Vol4/ceglie.html, March 25, 2000.

"NASA Initiatives Transform Students into Star Scientists," by Marilyn Wall
http://www.glef.org/edutopia/newsletters/spring2000/wall.html, March 25, 2000.
"Connecting with Experts in the Real World," by Diane Demee-Benoit
http://www.glef.org/edutopia/newsletters/7.1/demme.html, March 25, 2000.
"Latinas en Ciencia: Making Science and Technology Real for Girls," by Roberta Furger
http://www.glef.org/edutopia/newsletters/spring2000/furger/article.html, March 25, 2000.

Students at Risk

"Street-Level Youth Soar," by Noel White
http://www.glef.org/edutopia/newsletters/spring2000/white.html, March 25, 2000.
"Student Creators," by Noel White
http://www.glef.org/edutopia/newsletters/spring2000/kidcreators/kidcreators.html, March 25, 2000.
Project-Based Learning
http://www.glef.org/edutopia/newsletters/spring2000/kidcreators/pbl.html, March 25, 2000.

WEB SITES

Busy Teachers—This award-winning site was created to help K–12 teachers find direct source materials, lesson plans, and classroom activities. Information is divided into nineteen categories, such as English, math, guidance/counseling, and even recess. To make things easier, each category includes background information:
http://www.ceismc.gatech.edu/BusyT
Discovery Channel School Online—Here's a monster site of information resources related to science, social studies, language arts, and the humanities for K–12 teachers. Search its database of lesson plans by grade level and/or subject area and explore links to other educational sites:
http://www.school.discovery.com
Education World—Offers lots of lesson-planning and curriculum resources. Information ranges from "outrageous women in history" to "Dr. Seuss celebrates reading." In addition to a huge education-oriented search engine, there's a message board and a searchable database of 50,000 web sites of interest to teachers: http://www.education-world.com
Educational Resources Information Center (ERIC)—Sponsored by the U.S. Department of Education, ERIC is the mother of all educational websites. It houses the largest database of educational materials in the world, including 850,000 abstracts of publications, lesson plans, a question-and-answer service, conference papers, and research: http://www.askeric.org
Learning Webs—A master site that focuses on curriculum resources at all levels. Includes examples of Internet-assisted curriculum journeys: http://www.learnweb.org

RESOURCES FOR INFORMATION ON MIDDLE SCHOOL SCHEDULING
The Copernican Plan

http://www.aasa.org/issues/Block/block1.htm.
Education consultant Joseph M. Carroll, developer of the Copernican Plan, says the approach is not about block scheduling but the relationship between time and learning. Read his explanation in the article at the American Association of School Administrators (AASA) website.

Intensive Scheduling

Corwin Press published *Intensive Scheduling: Restructuring America's Secondary Schools through Time Management* by David S. Hottenstein (1998). Order from Amazon.com.

Flexible Scheduling

The National Middle School Association's brief summary of research on flexible and block scheduling. http://www.nmsa.org

Looping

Links for teachers and schools interested in exploring "looping"—the practice of keeping kids and teachers together for more than one year. Also read the overview of looping in the Association for Supervision and Curriculum Development's *Education Update* (March 1998), *"Looping—Discovering the Benefits of Multiyear Teaching."*

Middle School Teaching That's "In the Loop"

Louisville math teacher Stacy Irvin relies on equal portions of standards-based instruction, backward lesson planning, and positive reinforcement to teach her "loopy" middle grades. A member of a team that "loops" through three grades with the same group of students, Irvin says the looping concept holds teachers and students accountable. From "Changing Schools in Louisville" (Spring 1999).

Multiyear Teaching in Middle and High School

While multiyear teaching or looping crops up regularly at the elementary level, it is unusual at the secondary level because of added complexities. For instance, teams of teachers must work together closely over the course of two to four years, and it requires teachers to instruct complex new curricula. But middle and high school teachers interviewed across the Expeditionary learning network said that the pros of staying with students for more than one year far outweigh the cons.

Multi-age Grouping in the Middle School

http://www.nmsa.org/ressum15.htm
What is the rationale for multi-age grouping? How is it defined and what are its characteristics? Are there academic benefits from such an organiza-

tional configuration? The National Middle School Association explores these and other questions in this research summary.

Sixth Grade Schools

Some school systems are creating sixth-grade-only schools—for space reasons, educational reasons, or both. Read "Where Does Sixth Grade Belong?" Also: a story about a sixth-grade "center" start-up in North Carolina and another in Wichita, Kansas.

Innovative Scheduling Is Powerful

Alternative schedules may not add hours to the school day, but they can vastly improve the quality of the time students spend at school, say authors Robert Lynn Canady and Michael D. Rettig in the article, "The Power of Innovative Scheduling," published in November 1995 in *Educational Leadership*. If you're interested in nontraditional school scheduling, you may also want to read Canady and Rettig's related article in the September 1996 issue of *School Administrator*, "All Around the Block: The Benefits and Challenges of a Non-Traditional School Schedule."

FAQs about Middle Level Education

http://www.nassp.org
This page from the web site of the National Association of Secondary School Principals answers questions about detracking, making the transition from junior high, characteristics of adolescents, the qualities of successful middle school teachers, and interdisciplinary teaming. Visit this page and find out how to join NASSP's National Alliance of Middle Level Services.

chapter 9

SECONDARY SCHOOL PROGRAMS AND ISSUES

The secondary school of today is receiving more attention than at any time since *Sputnik* in the late 1950s. As the exit school for a majority of American youth, the high school is viewed as the "finishing school" and as the means by which American society is renewed. Unfortunately, when the larger society experiences problems such as those plaguing the nation today, the secondary school is expected to find necessary solutions. When scientists, mathematicians, and technical workers are needed for a rapidly emerging high-tech/information society, for example, the schools draw criticism because the mathematics and science curricula are not rigorous enough.

Secondary schools in the United States are closely wedded to local communities and, therefore, to public opinion. Because schools reflect the weaknesses as well as the strengths of the larger society, they are caught up in the ebb and flow of continual revitalization.

The secondary school of today is not perfect, nor will it ever be in the eyes of society. We can learn from the past, however, and focus on those problems and issues that are important. We can also gain an increased knowledge of how the curriculum of the secondary school is developed and organized. Finally, we can attempt to chart a course for the future so that the secondary school can meet the great expectations our society has for it.

HISTORICAL DEVELOPMENT OF THE SECONDARY SCHOOL

Although elementary schools were developed for students at public expense from the mid–1600s, the public secondary school did not become a reality for a majority of American youth until late in the nineteenth century.

From the middle of the eighteenth century until the Civil War period, the principal instrument of secondary education in the United States was the academy. Benjamin Franklin is credited with the establishment of the first academy, the Philadelphia Academy and Charitable School, which opened in 1751. The academy achieved great popularity in New England and the Middle Atlantic states. Although the academy was neither wholly private nor wholly public (unlike the Latin grammar school, which was highly selective and private), it did not open the door to all youth in need of a secondary education.

In the mid–1800s, leaders in Massachusetts, such as Horace Mann, were successful in obtaining strong support for public schools. The first high school in the United States was founded in Boston in 1821. Known as the English Classical School, the school provided a three-year sequence of English, mathematics, history, and science.

The extension of secondary education in the United States was accomplished by state legislation and later by court cases. Again taking the lead, the Commonwealth of Massachusetts enacted laws that required towns with five hundred or more families to establish high schools with ten-month programs. Earlier, Massachusetts had required the establishment of elementary schools in towns of fifty families or more and had reorganized the state's responsibility for the preparation of teachers by establishing, under Horace Mann's leadership, the first state normal school. Massachusetts also passed the first compulsory attendance law in 1852. Today, all states compel students to attend school until a certain age, usually sixteen.

As secondary schools emerged in more and more states from the mid–1850s to the 1870s, there was great debate on whether high schools should be provided at public expense. The high school coexisted for a long time with the academy. With a frontier spirit of increased democracy, more youths were enrolling in high schools. Not until the famous Kalamazoo case in 1874 was the concept of a free high school education for all youths firmly established.

The Kalamazoo case resulted when a taxpayer in Kalamazoo, Michigan, challenged the right of the school board to establish a high school with public funds and to hire a superintendent. In 1874 the Supreme Court of Michigan ruled that a school district was not limited to the support of elementary schools but could establish whatever level of schools it wished as long as the voters were willing to pay the taxes. This historic decision affirmed the idea that secondary education was a legitimate part of the program of public schools.

After the Kalamazoo decision, public secondary schools grew in number. The most popular grade-level organization of schools was the eight-four pattern (eight years of elementary school and four of high school). Later, other patterns emerged, including the popular six-six pattern (six years of elementary school and six years of high school or secondary school). Not until 1910 was the junior high school established, and a three-level organizational system emerged. The popular organizational pattern then became the grades 1–6 elementary school, 7–9 junior high school, and 10–12 high school. For almost fifty years, the elementary/junior high/high school pattern dominated American schools. In the 1960s, a new school emerged—the middle school—which was to force a realignment of grade levels in American schools. Although grade patterns vary in the middle school in many school districts, the most common pattern is the grades 6–8 pattern. In the early 1980s, some large school districts (the St. Louis District, for example), which had ignored the junior high school and were still organized in a grades K–8 elementary and 9–12 high school pattern, organized separate middle schools for grades 6–8.

REFORM MOVEMENTS IN SECONDARY EDUCATION

Although many commissions and reports have called for high school reform in the last two decades, those working in American high schools have never lacked for advice on how to improve their school programs.

The tradition of secondary school reform began in the 1890s with a number of committees and commissions organized to examine the high school curriculum, especially its effectiveness in preparing students for college. The Committee of Ten on Secondary Schools, the Committee of Fifteen on Elementary Education, and the Committee on College Entrance Requirements organized in 1893–94, endorsed the idea of moving high school subjects down into the upper elementary grades (grades 7, 8, and 9).

In 1913 the National Education Association appointed the Commission on the Reorganization of Secondary Education, whose report was five years in the making. Their report in 1918 resulted in the famous seven Cardinal Principles of Education. The report recommended that every subject be reorganized to contribute to the goals expressed in the Cardinal Principles. Most important, the commission endorsed the division of secondary education into junior and senior periods. The commission recommended that vocational courses be introduced into the curriculum and that a comprehensive program be offered to both junior and senior high school students.

The moving down of the high school program into the upper elementary grades continued to be an issue even as district after district reorganized to include the junior high school. By the late 1970s, middle schools had all but replaced junior high schools as the dominant intermediate grade school in the United States.

The high school came under strong attack in the late 1950s and early 1960s following the launch of *Sputnik*. Although weaknesses in science and mathematics programs were attacked, other areas of the secondary school, such as foreign language instruction, also came under attack. The problem of "why Johnny can't read" was perceived primarily to be a problem of the elementary school.

James Conant and others led a movement in the 1950s to expand the high school curriculum to include both vocational and academic courses for students in a unitary, multipurpose school—the comprehensive high school. Conant and others were finally developing the kind of unitary high school recommended in the 1918 report of the NEA Commission on the Reorganization of Secondary Education. Such a comprehensive school would serve as a prototype of a democracy in which various groups could be federated into a larger whole through the recognition of common interests and ideals. The establishment of cooperative federal–state programs for vocational education in 1917 had resulted in separate specialized vocational schools, a pattern (modeled after the European system) that prevailed until the late 1950s.

The 1970s proved to be a decade in which serious reforms of the American high school were recommended and, in some cases, attempted. Throughout the land, prestigious commissions met to assess the needs of secondary education and to make suggestions for reform. Among those commissions were the following:

- The National Association of Secondary School Principals, whose report *American Youth in the Mid-Seventies* (1972) recommended increased "action learning" programs in the community.
- The President's Science Advisory Committee, whose report *Youth Transition to Adulthood* (1973) advocated the creation of alternative high schools and occupational high schools.
- The Institute for the Development of Education Activities (IDEA), whose report *The Greening of the High School* (1973) called for a new type of institution for modern students, with an emphasis on individual needs and student choice.
- The U.S. Department of Education, HEW, whose report *National Panel on High Schools and Adolescent Education* (1975) recommended decentralization of the comprehensive high school and reduction of the secondary school day by two to four hours.

These observations and recommendations were reflected in a number of innovative secondary schools that emerged and then receded when primary leadership was withdrawn, including the following:

- Nova High School (Ft. Lauderdale, Florida), an experiment with the application of technology to instructional processes.
- Parkway Schools (Philadelphia, Pennsylvania), an attempt to move learning out into the community—the school without walls.
- McGavok High School (Nashville, Tennessee), a truly comprehensive school with a broad range of occupational tracks under one roof and tied closely to business interests in the community.
- Melbourne High School (Cocoa Beach, Florida), an academic high school with five tracks, including Quest, an advanced placement program in which students could progress to their limits.
- Berkeley High Schools (Berkeley, California), employing the "public schools of choice" concept in which parents and students selected their high school by philosophy and purpose.

◻ Adams High School (Portland, Oregon), an experimental school in which students participated in the governance of the program, thereby learning basic democratic procedures for citizenship.

Typical of the broad goals for education at this period were those advocated by Harold Spears, a longtime advocate of the comprehensive high school (see Figure 9.1). In addition to many special programs, the actual course offerings of high schools grew extensively, as suggested by the English offerings of one high school shown in Figure 9.2.

Around 1974 the picture in secondary education began to change dramatically, and proposals for the expansion of the role of the American high school were no longer heard. Among the major factors causing this reversal were the following:

◻ *Declining enrollment.* Between 1970 and 1980, secondary enrollment declined by a full 25 percent. This decline, which was projected to last until 1992, meant falling teacher–pupil ratios and an increased cost per pupil in many districts.

1. Learn how to be a good citizen.
2. Learn how to respect and get along with people who think, dress, and act differently.
3. Learn about and try to understand the changes that take place in the world.
4. Develop skills in reading, writing, speaking, and listening.
5. Understand skills and practice democratic ideas and ideals.
6. Learn how to examine and use information.
7. Understand and practice the skills of family living.
8. Learn to respect and get along with people with whom we work and live.
9. Develop skills to enter a specific field of work.
10. Learn how to be a good manager of money, property, and resources.
11. Develop a desire for learning now and in the future.
12. Learn how to use leisure time.
13. Practice and understand the ideas of health and safety.
14. Appreciate culture and beauty in the world.
15. Gain information needed to make job selections.
16. Develop pride in work and a feeling of self-worth.
17. Develop good character and self-respect.
18. Gain a general education.

FIGURE 9.1 The Goals of Education

Source: From a lecture by Harold Spears given at George Peabody College, 1972.

English IX	Practical Communication	Films—Communications
English X	Science Fiction (Depth)	Creative Writing I
English X (AP)	Science Fiction (Survey)	Creative Writing II
English XI (AP)	Speech	Film Making
English XII (AP)	Sports Literature (Depth)	Folklore
Secretarial English I	Sports Literature (Survey)	American Literature
Secretarial English II	Techniques of Research	(Focus)
Humanities	Women in Literature	American Literature
American Dream	Themes: Modern Life	(Images)
Your America	Eng. as a Second Lang.	Contemporary Literature
American Novel	Reading—Grade 9	English Literature (Past)
Basic English Skills	Reading—Grade 9	English Literature
Directed Reading	Acting I	(Modern)
	Acting II	Journalism

FIGURE 9.2   The English Curriculum in One Comprehensive High School

☐ *Inflation.* By 1974 the inflationary effects of the Vietnam War were in full bloom, and taxpayers became painfully aware of the soaring cost of education in a time when the purchasing power of the dollar was shrinking.

☐ *Unionization of teaching staffs.* Between 1966 and 1977, the number of states recognizing the right of teachers to enter into collective bargaining rose from eleven to thirty. By 1977, 80 percent of all teachers were members of either the NEA (National Education Association) or the AFT (American Federation of Teachers). Because high school teachers tended to be more senior and, therefore, more expensive to the taxpayer, they were often identified with the union movement.

☐ *Declining achievement.* Throughout the 1970s and continuing in the 1990s, the media regularly reported declining achievement as measured by nationally normed standardized tests such as the Scholastic Aptitude Test (SAT). This was interpreted to mean, in the eyes of the public, that schools were failing.

Between 1975 and 1985 proposals for the expansion of the role of the high school were no longer heard. Two well-known projects were aimed largely at improving test scores and academic achievement rather than addressing larger social questions: the *Paideia Proposal* (1982), which proposed a twelve-year, single-track academic program with no electives,[1] and the Commission on Excellence, which produced the report *A Nation At Risk* in 1983. Other reform efforts after 1983 were aimed at specific problems such as the drop-out rate and mathematics and science achievement rather than overall school reform.

In the mid-1980s a book of significance, *A Place Called School,* was written by John Goodlad. In it, Goodlad shared the findings of a research project touching thousands of teachers and pupils, and his report was not glowing. Writing about the secondary school, Goodlad observed:

> Usually we saw desks or tables arranged in rows oriented toward the teacher at the front of the room. Instructional amenities, occasionally present in elementary classrooms, were rarely observed in the secondary classes.[2]

Regarding the organization of the standard secondary school, Goodlad observed:

> What begins to emerge is a picture not of two kinds of instructional activities in each class appealing to alternative modes of learning, but two curricular divisions in the secondary school. On one side are the more prestigious academic subjects, largely shunning manual activity as a mode of learning. On the other side are the nonacademics, generally characterized by the trappings of academic teaching but providing more opportunities to cultivate handedness and often featuring aesthetic qualities.[3]

The power of reputation and the reinforcement of observation by researchers made *A Place Called School* an important book of the 1980s and encouraged further inquiry into secondary school programs.

In *Horace's Compromise,* a 1984 study of public education, author Ted Sizer encouraged the push for a higher mission of secondary schools when he wrote:

> The best vocational education will be one in general education in the age of the mind.

Sizer led a partnership between Brown University and more than seven hundred schools called Coalition of Essential Schools to help students use their minds.[4] Sizer's nine principles committed restructured schools in the coalition not only to get students to use their minds well, but also to apply school goals to every student, allow students to have the opportunity to discover and construct meaning from their own experiences, and make teaching and learning personalized. Diplomas would be awarded on successful demonstration of mastery and exhibition.

The school reform movement that began in the 1980s continued in the 1990s. The secondary school reform movement was closely tied to the nation's quest for greater economic competitiveness fueled by a global economy and a revolution in the American workplace. The industrial age of the first half of the twentieth century was replaced by the technological age, then the high-tech age, and finally, at the end of the century, the information age. New jobs stressed brains over brawn. The lunch bucket was replaced by the briefcase and the personal computer. Rather than exit skills of basic reading, writing, and arithmetic, high school graduates were expected to exit with "thinking skills" and the ability to master new knowledge on the job.

In 1994, in a widely circulated report, the Secretary's Commission on Achieving Necessary Skills (SCANS) took a hard look at six goals in *America 2000;* they also identified five SCANS competencies. In particular, the SCANS report looked at National Goals 3 and 5, which stated:

> American students will leave grades four, eight and twelve having demonstrated competency in challenging subject matter including English, mathematics, science— and every school in America will ensure that all students use their minds so they will be prepared for responsible citizenship—and employment in our modern society. Goal 3 Every adult American will be literate and will possess the knowledge and skills necessary to compete in a global economy. Goal 5[5]

Although SCANS originated from the U.S. Department of Labor, educational implications were paramount. Two conditions were identified as changing what young people needed before entering the world of work: the globalization of commerce and industry and the explosive growth of technology on the job. Those developments meant that schools had to do a better job of preparing graduates.[6] The five competencies of SCANS are outlined in Figure 9.3.

The late 1990s brought many changes to secondary schools, including new national and state standards, more rigorous academic programs, large blocks of time for instruction, benchmark tests, academic skills placement tests, tech-prep programs that replaced traditional vocational programs, and an increasing number of students in advanced placement and international baccalaureate programs. Alternative schooling and alternative schools, including magnet schools, became commonplace in many school districts. Finally, the information superhighway ran right into many high schools, linking even the most remote and smallest schools with information sources, courses never before offered, and a rich variety of learning opportunities. For the first time in a hundred years, the high school had truly begun to change. Reform has not come easy to the high school, however; there are still problems and issues.

The push for school choice, charter schools, and tuition vouchers raises questions of whether the American public is still committed to a system of general and free public schools. Suggestions by some government and business leaders that secondary education can be offered better by private enterprise are strong evidence that public secondary education does not enjoy the same widespread support that it once did. Curriculum leaders must not let these changes be dictated entirely by those outside of our school system.

THE CHANGING CURRICULUM OF THE SECONDARY SCHOOL

For the first ninety years of the twentieth century, the high school curriculum remained the same. Basically, the high school consisted of a number of courses that a student must complete to graduate. Credits were given for successful completion of required courses. When a student earned a certain number of credits, he or she would graduate. To ensure that each student received a basic education during the

Resources: Identifies, organizes, plans, and allocates resources
  - A. *Time*—Selects goal-relevant activities, ranks them, allocates time, and prepares and follows schedules
  - B. *Money*—Uses or prepares budgets, makes forecasts, keeps records, and makes adjustments to meet objectives
  - C. *Material and facilities*—Acquires, stores, allocates, and uses materials or space efficiently
  - D. *Human resources*—Assesses skills and distributes work accordingly, evaluates performance and provides feedback

Interpersonal: Works with others
  - A. *Participates as member of a team*—Contributes to group effort
  - B. *Teaches others new skills*
  - C. *Serves clients/customers*—Works to satisfy customers' expectations
  - D. *Exercises leadership*—Communicates ideas to justify position, persuades and convinces others, responsibly challenges existing procedures and policies
  - E. *Negotiates*—Works toward agreements involving exchange of resources, resolves divergent interests
  - F. *Works with diversity*—Works well with men and women from diverse backgrounds

Information: Acquires and uses information
  - A. *Acquires and evaluates information*
  - B. *Organizes and maintains information*
  - C. *Interprets and communicates information*
  - D. *Uses computers to process information*

Systems: Understands complex interrelationships
  - A. *Understands systems*—Knows how social, organizational, and technological systems work and operates effectively with them
  - B. *Monitors and corrects performance*—Distinguishes trends, predicts impacts on system operations, diagnoses deviations in system's performance and corrects malfunctions
  - C. *Improves or designs systems*—Suggests modifications to existing systems and develops new or alternative systems to improve performance

Technology: Works with a variety of technologies
  - A. *Selects technology*—Chooses procedures, tools, or equipment including computers and related technologies
  - B. *Applies technology to task*—Understands overall intent and proper procedures for setup and operation of equipment
  - C. *Maintains and troubleshoots equipment*—Prevents, identifies, or solves problems with equipment, including computers and other technologies

FIGURE 9.3 Five Competencies of SCANS
Source: U.S. Department of Education, 1993.

Third International Mathematics and Science Study (TIMSS)

American business and educational leaders have been concerned about basic skill development in our students. In 1995, TIMSS was the largest and most ambitious study of comparative educational achievement ever undertaken. In total, TIMSS achievement testing in mathematics and science involved

- more than forty countries;
- five grade levels (third, fourth, seventh, eighth, and twelth);
- more than half a million students;
- millions of written responses to open-ended questions;
- performance assessment; and
- student, teacher, and school questionnaires about the contests for schooling.

TIMSS was conducted with attention to quality at every step of the way. Rigorous procedures were designed to translate the tests, and numerous regional training sessions were held in data collection and scoring procedures. Quality-control observers monitored testing sessions. The procedures for sampling the students tested in each country were scrutinized according to rigorous standards designed to maximize inclusion, prevent bias, and ensure comparability.

TIMSS is the most recent in a series of studies conducted by the International Association for the Evaluation of Educational Achievement (IEA). The IEA has been providing comparative information about educational achievement and learning contexts to policymakers, educators, researchers, and practitioners since 1959. The International Study Center for TIMSS is located at Boston College. International activities are funded by the National Center for Education Statistics (NCES) of the U.S. Department of Education and the U.S. National Science Foundation (NSF). Each country provides its own funding for the national implementation of TIMSS. In the United States, TIMSS was also funded by NCES and NSF.

For more information on TIMSS, or to download TIMSS reports, visit the World Wide Web site at http://www.ed.gov/NCES/timss, call the TIMSS customer service line at (202) 219-1333, or write to Lois Peak, TIMSS Project Officer, National Center for Education Statistics, U.S. Department of Education, 555 New Jersey Avenue, NW, Washington, DC 20208-5574.

---

high school years, certain courses and credit hours were required. The number of credit hours required by states varied, but most of the course titles and content were the same. Some states added a proficiency test that students needed to pass in order to graduate.

In the 1990s pressures brought on schools by the events discussed in previous sections, and accompanying state and national reports, resulted in a long-awaited curriculum reform movement. Rather than the solutions of more courses or credits and more tests, reforms reflected a concern about what was taught, how it was delivered, and how the curriculum could prepare students for the demands of a high-tech workplace and global economy. Leading the way were groups of educators building national standards in the major school disciplines of mathematics, English, science, and social studies. Other discipline groups followed with standards (see Figure 9.4).

The term *world class* began to be used to describe new standards. In other words, what would U. S. students need to know to compete with the best and brightest graduates from around the world?

In 1995 the American Federation of Teachers (AFT) published a 165-page book entitled, *What Secondary Students Abroad Are Expected To Know* (see Figure 9.4). This report offered a comprehensive look at what was expected of average achieving students in France, Germany, and Scotland and included a profile of each country's education system, including its school-to-work transition program, plus lengthy excerpts from the exams given to students at the ninth- or tenth-grade level. A comparative look at the U.S. GED was also included.

Although many countries have national examinations, the United States does not. Because our system of education is legislated at the state level, only if states agree to impose tests, or standards either for that matter, will any national standards or tests be implemented.

Not all educators agree on what "world class standards" are, which lends to even more confusion in the debate on how our students compare with those in other countries. The main comparisons of U.S. and foreign students occur in science and mathematics—the linchpins of a high-tech, global economy. However, surveys of business and industry leaders also point to problems in literacy, work ethic, and the ability to solve problems that crop up in any job on a daily basis.

SAT and ACT tests are general aptitude tests not intended to measure school performance. Since the United States has no national and few state-linked examinations (and states only began to spell out what every child should learn in the late 1990s), much still needs to be done to prepare to meet world standards.

With states jealously guarding their rights to determine what is taught, it appears that only a national crisis will precipitate any national approach to education. Americans are wary of the national government using schools as instruments of national policy. Who can forget the Hitler Youth and the Red Guards in the twentieth century?

Examining the content areas, a major shift in curriculum areas took place in the last five years of the twentieth century. New standards encouraged a move away from the mastery of low-level, isolated facts to a comprehensive curriculum emphasizing problem solving, integrated tasks, real-life problems, and higher-order thinking processes using portfolios and exhibitions. Assessments of students' work became more authentic. The NCTE Standards for Assessment of Reading and Writing reflect these approaches in their goals:

1. Students must constantly be encouraged about their work in terms of what they can do versus what they cannot do.
2. The primary purpose of assessment of writing is to improve teaching and learning.

World Class Standards

What Secondary Students Abroad Are Expected to Know, Defining World Class Standards. American Federation of Teachers (AFT), 1995.

Language Arts

Standards for the Assessment of Reading and Writing. Urbana, IL: National Council of Teachers of English, 1994.

NAEP Reading Standards. Washington, DC: National Assessment of Education Progress (NAEP), 1995.

NAEP Writing Standards. Washington, DC: National Assessment of Education Progress (NAEP), 1994.

Reading Standards. Newark, DE: International Reading Association, 1995.

Mathematics

Curriculum and Evaluation Standards for School Mathematics. Reston, VA: National Council of Teachers of Mathematics (NCTM), 1989.

Professional Standards for Teaching Mathematics. Reston, VA: National Council of Teachers of Mathematics (NCTM), 1991.

NAEP Mathematics Standards. Washington, DC: National Assessment of Education Progress (NAEP), 1994.

Social Science

NAEP Social Studies Standards. Washington, DC: National Assessment of Education Progress (NAEP), 1995.

National Content Standards for Civics. Calabasas, CA: Center for Civic Education, 1995.

National Content Standards for Economics. National Council of Economic Education (NCEE), 1995.

National Content Standards for Geography. National Geographic Society, 1994.

National Content Standards for History. National Center for History in the Schools, 1995.

National Content Standards for Social Studies. National Council on Social Studies (NCSS), 1995.

Science

Benchmarks for Science Literacy, Project 2061, American Association for the Advancement of Science (AAAS). New York: Oxford University Press, 1993.

National Science Education Standards, National Research Council. Washington, DC: National Academy Press, 1996.

NAEP Science Standards. Washington, DC: National Association of Education Progress (NAEP), 1995.

Science Performance Standards. New Standards Project, 1995.

FIGURE 9.4   Sources for Standards and Frameworks*

*You are encouraged to update this list of international, national, and state standards. The Association for Supervision and Curriculum Development (ASCD) in Alexandria, Virginia, is a prime source for such information: http://www.ascd.org.

3. Students need to realize that they have other audiences besides a teacher for which they can write.
4. Educators need to take into account the outside influences on a student's work when assessing it.
5. Assessment must be fair and equitable, taking into account the diverse ethnic and social groups in the country.
6. The consequences of assessment procedures are important, and each paper that a student writes should have a specific set of criteria to be used in grading it.[7]

Social studies instruction has undergone extensive changes as well, with students having less lecture, more collaborative learning activities, and interactive writing activities that are technology driven. Thematic teaching that integrates social studies with other disciplines has also made social studies instruction more relevant and more interesting.

Mathematics saw a host of inventive curriculum projects in the 1990s. Reformers invested much time and energy in the creation of new mathematics and state curriculum frameworks.[8] Mathematics context has moved from an almost exclusive focus on computation skills and measurement to a wide variety of activities requiring students to understand the processes and systems of mathematics and apply them to problem-solving situations. The Interactive Mathematics Program funded by the National Science Foundation resulted in programs that integrate traditional mathematics materials with additional topics recommended by the National Council of Teachers of Mathematics (NCTM), such as probability and statistics. It also uses graphing calculator technology to enhance student understanding.

Science, like mathematics, received much attention in the 1990s. New science programs using unifying concepts such as systems and change and the application of science concepts rather than the accumulation of unrelated facts replaced traditional programs. Themes demonstrating science's relation to other disciplines and contributions to solving world problems have also been an exciting focus of the new science curriculum of the secondary school.

Other content areas, including the arts, physical education, and the extracurricular curriculum, have been the focus of national groups, as the need for well-rounded youth has never been greater.

Vocational education and the practical arts faced demands for reassessment of their mission in the 1990s. The Carl D. Perkins Vocational Applied Technology Act of 1990 began an approach to use vocational courses to prepare all students for the world of work by integrating academic and vocational education. With the advent of technology in the workplace, "tech-prep" became the focus of most secondary schools, forcing production types of vocational courses out of the curriculum. Even in agriculture, new technology and the decline of the family farm forced a new approach.

By the late 1990s, the demands of a global economy forced even more drastic changes in vocational education. A high-tech workplace, the need for smarter workers, and the decline of traditional jobs blurred the traditional distinction between the academic and vocational curriculum.

The School to Work Opportunities Act of 1994 focused attention on how to help American schools help students make the connection between school and work. As students prepare for a new workplace, that connection must be strengthened.[9]

Magnet and Alternative Schools and Programs

The 1990s saw a rapid increase in the number of choices of school programs for students. Magnet schools and magnet programs, often used as a means of desegregation, were established to offer specialized programs in areas such as the arts, science, and technology. Alternative schools and programs offering new approaches to learning and discipline also have served to break the mold of traditional high school offerings.

Alternative education schools or programs usually offer smaller classes and work-at-your-own-pace incentives for students. Many of the students enrolled in these programs have had trouble conforming to traditional programs and classrooms. Computer software and curriculum packaging have made it possible for students to complete courses more quickly and reduce the time spent in high school. Alternative programs usually provide smaller classes, individualized learning, an emphasis on improving life skills, and close ties to the community. Alternative education takes the form of separate schools or separate school programs within traditional schools.

Advance Placement/International Baccalaureate Programs

Advance Placement (AP) allows high school students to attain college credit by passing a national examination in a content area. Many high schools offer such opportunities by providing AP courses to prepare students to pass such exams.

Since 1967 the International Baccalaureate (IB) program has uniquely prepared students for further study in colleges and universities both in the United States and around the world. As the United States attempts to raise the standards of secondary education, the growth of the International Baccalaureate diploma program, which originated in Europe, offers great hope to those who want the United States to have a "world-class" secondary program.

This global education program is an integrated form of study that offers a broad, liberal approach complemented by the opportunity to study a subject in depth. The IB founders' goal was to help students learn how to learn, how to analyze, and how to reach considered conclusions about people, their languages and literature, ways of society, and the scientific forces of their environment. The birth of the International Baccalaureate Office (IBO) in 1967 started from a concern for students who had attended many schools in the course of their educational experiences. The IBO was created to foster an examination system that could be used and recognized worldwide. After several years of preparation, the first diplomas were issued in 1971.

The IBO operates in four continents, including North America, and meets annually in Geneva, Switzerland. The founders of the IB desired a world-class curriculum that would emphasize internal coherence and maintain rigorous integrity. The two-year preparation stresses subjects that cover the many fields of human experience as well as academic pursuits. Almost all of the subjects offered have syllabi for two levels of achievement. The material included on the higher level requires two years of preparation for the examination, assuming five class hours per week, or a minimum of 240 teaching hours. The subsidiary level requires half as much time, which may extend over one or two years. During the last two years of secondary school, an IB candidate studies six subjects, three of which must be studied on the higher level and three on the subsidiary level. From the courses being offered, the candidate selects one from each of the following areas:

1. **Language A**   Study in the native language includes world literature in translation from at least two other language areas.
2. **Language B**   A second language at a level similar to that of Language A, but distinguished by not requiring the same depth and breadth of understanding of cultural and historical contexts.
3. **People**   A choice of one of the following courses, using a thematic, comparative, and intellectual approach: history, geography, economics, philosophy, psychology, social anthropology, or business studies.
4. **Experimental Sciences**   A choice of one of the following options: biology, chemistry, physics, physical science, or scientific studies.
5. **Mathematics**
6. **Electives**   A choice of one of the following: art, music; a classical language; a second language B; an additional option under 3, 4, or 5; computer studies; or special syllabi developed by the IB schools, including theater arts..

In addition to these six courses, the candidate takes a course developed for the IB on the philosophy of learning, known as the Theory of Knowledge. This course ensures that the students critically reflect on the knowledge and experience acquired. The student also prepares a four-thousand- to five-thousand-word research paper based on one of the subjects of the IB curriculum. In addition, the student must engage in 150 hours of extracurricular activities in the CAS Program (Creativity, Action, Service).

Assessment procedures include written examinations and oral examinations in languages. Grades awarded by the IB examiner are based on a scale of 1 through 7. A minimum of twenty-four grade points is necessary to be awarded a diploma.

Awareness of the IB program as an educational tool around the world and as a placement device in U.S. colleges and universities is increasing. The comprehensive nature of the program is commendable; its international approach to education is formidable. In this era of expanding global networks and a growing need for international understanding, the steady growth of an innovative contribution to world education is an inspiration and invaluable to American secondary education.

Comprehensive School Designs

A number of comprehensive school designs have affected K–12 schooling including Accelerated Schools, the Comer School Development Model, the Coalition of Essential Schools, the Modern Red School House, and Co-NECT, the Community for Learning (from Temple University).[10] The cost for training in the various designs varies. Some designs have no technology requirements, while others require substantial technology. Some of the designs require additional personnel such as "educational facilitators." All require substantial change and commitment on the part of the school staff to make the programs work. Whether these designs will result in better schools and better achievement on the part of students to justify the often heavy cost continues to be a source of debate in American education.

Promise of Technology at the Secondary Level

In the schools of the first eight decades of the twentieth century, shop classrooms were developed to train students in the vocational areas. The hands-on classroom of the twenty-first century is a technology studies laboratory. Students in these classrooms use computers and critical analysis to solve complex problems in all disciplines—solutions that they can apply to their daily lives. All students in the secondary school should have word processing skills and should be able to create papers using the libraries of the world.

The tie-in of home and school allows students to access data, review lessons, and interact with peers well beyond normal school hours. Education as practiced in the high school of the twentieth century will be centered in the home as much as, or more than, in a building called "high school."

Keeping abreast of the latest in technology will require constant evaluation of software and multimedia. The Association for Supervision and Curriculum Development (ASCD) publishes *Only the Best—Annual Guide to Highest-Rated Education Software/Multimedia for PreSchool–Grade Twelve*. Schools and school districts can negotiate site licenses for present- and past-year editions directly with ASCD.[11]

The promise of a World Wide Web in the classroom will continue to bring a global audience directly into classrooms. Using the World Wide Web, teachers can develop collaborative projects with international partners, compare data with classes in other parts of the world, share results on their own home pages, and get feedback from the global community on the Internet. Rural or urban schools now will have information that any school may obtain. The World Wide Web makes the virtual classroom a reality.[12]

ORGANIZATIONAL PRACTICES IN THE SECONDARY SCHOOL

The organizational structure of a secondary school is designed to carry out the instructional program. The dominant pattern of organization in most secondary schools is departmentalization, which operates under the assumption that the disciplinary construct is the purest form of organizing knowledge. The curriculum is organized around separate disciplines that are taught by teachers in a department, such as the mathematics or social studies departments.

Scheduling is fairly simple in a departmentalized school. Courses are taught in uniform lengths of time, for example, fifty-five-minute periods.

For years, most secondary schools have operated under the following assumptions:

1. The appropriate amount of time for learning a subject is the same uniform period of time, fifty to sixty minutes in length, six or seven periods a day, for thirty-six weeks out of the year.
2. A classroom group size of thirty to thirty-five students is the most appropriate for a wide variety of learning experiences.
3. All learners are capable of mastering the same subject matter in the same length of time. For example, everyone takes the same test on Chapter 5 on Friday. Everyone from level one of algebra passes to level two in June.
4. Once a group is formed, the same group composition is equally appropriate for a wide variety of learning activities.
5. The same classroom is equally appropriate for a wide variety of learning activities. Conference rooms are not provided for teacher–student conferences. Large-group facilities are not provided for mass dissemination of materials. Small-group rooms are unavailable for discussion activities.
6. All students require the same kind of supervision.
7. The same teacher is qualified to teach all aspects of his or her subject for one year.

Operating on these assumptions, we have locked students into an educational egg crate with thirty students to a cubicle from 8 A.M. to 3 P.M. five days a week. In short, schools operating under these assumptions have existed more for the convenience of teaching than for the facilitation of learning.

Secondary schools today are attempting to break this lockstep approach to instruction. Rigid class sizes, facilities, and fixed schedules are being challenged. Subject matter is being organized in terms of more than a single disciplinary instruction. Core or correlation of subjects, interdisciplinary instruction, and fusion (which provides for the merging of related subjects into a new subject) represent alternative patterns of curriculum organization.

The organizational structure in a secondary school must be flexible enough to allow for groups of different size to serve different functions. Scheduling in a secondary school should come after determining what kind of instrument is desired. For example, if departmentalization and interdisciplinary teaming are desired, a flexible schedule should be developed to accommodate those goals. Arrangements should be made to accommodate individual teaching, small groups, large groups, and laboratory study groups.

Teaming and variable grouping can be used to better serve student needs and draw on teacher talents. Interdisciplinary teaming can facilitate the correlation of subject matter. Common groups of students shared by common groups of teachers with common planning time is necessary for interdisciplinary teaching to succeed.

Year-Round Schooling

To help with the increasing numbers of students entering public schools each year and to make better use of school facilities, many school boards are adopting operating policies that provide for a year-round schedule. Using a year-round calendar, students attend the same kind of classes and receive the same amount of instruction as those attending schools with traditional nine-month calendars. From a national perspective, year-round education has proven to be more widely used than other reforms because each district must design their schedule to meet the needs of the community. Year-round education calendars include the following:

- **Block 45/15**   All students are placed on single track and attend the same nine-week instructional blocks and three-week vacation blocks.
- **Flexible 45/15**   Individualized instruction is used so that students may jump tracks for special reasons on four 9-week learning blocks and 3-week vacation blocks.
- **Staggered, block, flexible 90/20**   Similar to the 35/5 plan except that students rotate through three 60-day and three 20-day vacation periods, with one of the four groups always on vacation.
- **Concept 8**   Eight 6-week terms with students selecting or being assigned six of the eight terms.
- **Concept 16**   Sixteen 3-week terms (students select twelve of the sixteen terms).
- **Multiple access**   A partially individualized 45/15 plan in which students can enter or leave at any three-week interval, with the curriculum in three- or nine-week units.
- **Quarter plan**   Four 12-week terms with students selecting or being assigned three of the four terms.
- **Quinmester**   Five 9-week quinmesters with students selecting or being assigned four of the five quins.
- **Extended school year**   More than 180-day calendar with staggered blocks.
- **Summer term**   A conventional nine-month calendar but with full summer terms that offer continuous learning integrated with the nine-month curriculum rather than short, six-week, discontinuous summer school courses.
- **Flexible all year**   School is open 240 days with students selecting 180 days. The curriculum consists of small, self-paced packages to allow for interrupted learning blocks and differentiated vacation periods of one day to several weeks at any time.

Advantages of year-round schooling include the following:

- Students retain more and perform as well or better due to shorter vacations.
- Reduces time needed for postvacation review.

- ☐ Allows timely opportunities for intersession tutoring and special interest courses.
- ☐ Students exhibit better attitudes and less boredom.
- ☐ Better morale among teachers.
- ☐ Can reduce overcrowding.
- ☐ Dropout rate decreases.

Disadvantages of year-round schooling include the following:

- ☐ Disrupts friendships because friends are often scheduled for vacations at different times.
- ☐ Causes conflicts with summertime activities.
- ☐ Disrupts family vacations.
- ☐ Increases difficulty for students who are not time efficient.
- ☐ Causes frequent breaks in learning.
- ☐ Poses child-care problems.

Block Scheduling

The 1990s saw a major scheduling innovation implemented in secondary schools—the block schedule. As part of the restructuring movement, this scheduling innovation allowed secondary schools to make significant departures from conventional school organization and practice.

Different schools have had different reasons for considering block scheduling. Common reasons given are (1) to create larger blocks of time for instruction, (2) to permit students to enroll in one or more additional classes during the year, (3) to increase the time available for professional development, and (4) for teachers to teach fewer students for longer periods of time, thus getting to know them better.[13] The bottom line, though, in all considerations should be, What is best for students?

If "stand and deliver" did not work in a traditional schedule, it certainly can't in a longer block of time. Reorganizing instruction to include a variety of learning activities, using technology, and encouraging greater student participation in their own learning appear to be the greatest challenges of block scheduling.

Figures 9.5, 9.6, 9.7, 9.8, and 9.9 illustrate commonly used block scheduling models. Figure 9.5 allows eight credits over the school year and thirty-two possible credits during a four-year high school experience. Figure 9.6 allows classes to meet every other day for the school year, with Fridays being split as A week or B week. Figure 9.7 is a college-type schedule that features an interim four-week session, thus allowing nine credit hours a year instead of eight. Figure 9.8 works better with smaller schools. The "skinning" block can be placed anywhere in the school day, and more than one block can be divided. This schedule does reduce the benefit of having just four classes in a day. Figure 9.9 is a trimester model that adds about forty-five minutes to the school day and increases each class by about ten minutes. This model allows for twelve credit opportunities during a year and forty-eight credits over four years.[14]

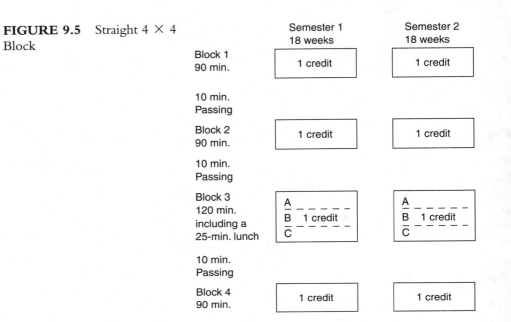

FIGURE 9.5 Straight 4 × 4 Block

	Semester 1 18 weeks	Semester 2 18 weeks
Block 1 90 min.	1 credit	1 credit
10 min. Passing		
Block 2 90 min.	1 credit	1 credit
10 min. Passing		
Block 3 120 min. including a 25-min. lunch	A B 1 credit C	A B 1 credit C
10 min. Passing		
Block 4 90 min.	1 credit	1 credit

FIGURE 9.6 Rotating A/B Block

	Monday 36 weeks	Tuesday 36 weeks
Block 1 90 min.	1 credit	1 credit
10 min. Passing		
Block 2 90 min.	1 credit	1 credit
10 min. Passing		
Block 3 120 min. including a 25-min. lunch	A B 1 credit C	A B 1 credit C
10 min. Passing		
Block 4 90 min.	1 credit	1 credit

FIGURE 9.7 $4 \times 1 \times 4$ Model

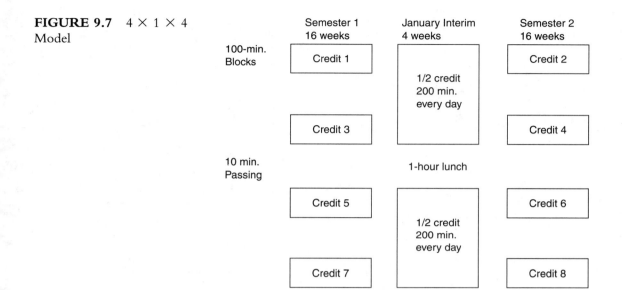

FIGURE 9.8 Modified Block with "Skinnies"

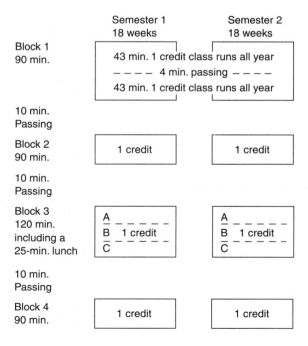

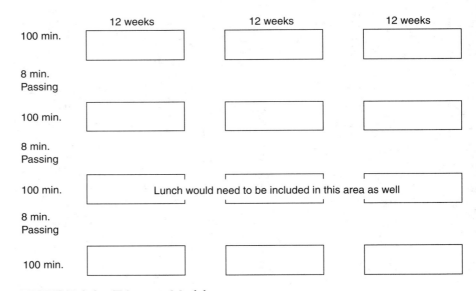

FIGURE 9.9   Trimester Model

FUTURE DIRECTIONS FOR THE SECONDARY SCHOOL

Many believe that the high school will disappear before it will change to the dynamic school that it should be to shape young people. Today, many districts are experimenting with block scheduling and alternative secondary schools such as magnet schools, academic and performing arts high schools, and charter schools. Also, special schools have been organized for students who have discipline problems. Athletic programs are also coming under increasing review by school officials who fear interscholastic sports have gotten out of hand.

Perhaps the greatest challenge facing the secondary school today is the attempt to establish its real role in American education. In the early years, the secondary school was viewed as an academic school designed to prepare students for college. Later, the high school assumed a greater function—that of preparing students for the immediate workforce. Fed by legislation after World War I, vocational programs were organized in school districts to train students who were not going on to higher education. By the 1950s, high schools assumed yet another function, which was to provide a comprehensive curriculum of academic and vocational courses for students under one roof.

By the mid-1980s, the functions of preparing students for college and training them for jobs came under attack by numerous groups in the United States. Reeling under pressure to provide better trained and better informed young people for high-tech jobs, colleges and secondary schools increased program requirements for their students. Because many vocational programs were training many young people for jobs that were rapidly becoming obsolete, the supporting public questioned the value of any vocational programs at the secondary level. Because over one half of our youth do not go on to higher education (of the 65 percent that even graduate), large numbers of our youth face the future with no marketable skills and may be unsuited for college or technical training. Our country can ill afford to write off two thirds of our young people entering society.

Compounding the problem is the increasing number of minority students found in large urban school districts who face language, cultural, family, and economic conditions that prevent them from learning. The experience of compensatory programs does not leave us with great optimism that more money and special programs will make a difference in the achievement of these youngsters.

We know that student achievement in secondary schools is higher when the following are in evidence:

- A high degree of parent involvement.
- Order and sequence in the curriculum.
- High expectations of teachers and the administrative staff.
- Maximum time spent on instruction time on task.
- A strong guidance program and opportunities for tutorial help from peers, parents, and other adults.
- A strong sense of structure and discipline.
- Positive reinforcement from both teachers and support staff.

A CHANGING COUNTRY AND A CHANGING WORLD

To understand the growing interdependence of the world that the secondary education graduate will enter, think about the number of multinational products produced and the military and economic partnerships within and outside the northern hemisphere.

If our world were a village of one thousand people, it would have

- 564 Asians
- 210 Europeans
- 86 Africans
- 80 South Americans
- 60 North Americans

The religious breakdown would be

- 300 Christians (183 Catholics, 84 Protestants, 33 Eastern Orthodox Christians)
- 175 Moslems
- 128 Hindus
- 55 Buddhists
- 47 Animists
- 85 other religions
- 210 without any religion or atheists

Of these people,

- ☐   60 would control half the total income
- ☐   500 would be hungry
- ☐   600 would live in shanty towns
- ☐   700 would be illiterate[15]

Of the new workers who came into the workforce between 1990 and 2000, 82 percent were a combination of female, nonwhite, and immigrant. Table 9.1 illustrates the most rapidly growing occupations.

Minority students are increasing in numbers while the nation's population under age 18 will actually decline between 1990 and 2010. Half of U.S. children live in only nine states. We will have an estimated 62,644,000 school-age students in the United States in 2010 of whom 32 million will live in our nine largest states. Of those 32 million school-age students, 15 million will be minority. Forty percent of students in thirteen states plus Washington, DC, will be from minority backgrounds. In 2000 the fastest growing minority groups were Asians and Pacific Islanders and Hispanics (see Figure 9.10).

The aging of the United States continues. Over 40 million Americans were identified in the 2000 census as being over 65 years of age. Fifty percent of children born today are first (and probably last) children; in 1950, only 25 percent of infants born were first children, and 75 percent were to families with more than one child.

TABLE 9.1   Most Rapidly Growing Occupations

Occupation	Percent Growth in Employment 1978–90	Number of New Jobs by 1990
All Occupations	22.5	21,980,000
Data processing machine mechanics	147.6	96,572
Paralegal personnel	132.4	39,310
Computer Systems Analysts	107.8	203,357
Computer operators	87.9	151,100
Office machine and cash register servicers	80.8	40,668
Computer programmers	73.6	153,051
Aero-astronautic engineers	70.4	41,315
Food preparation and service workers, Fast food restaurants	68.8	491,900
Employment interviewers	66.6	35,179
Tax preparers	64.5	19,997

Source: U.S. Department of Labor, *Monthly Labor Review,* 1996.

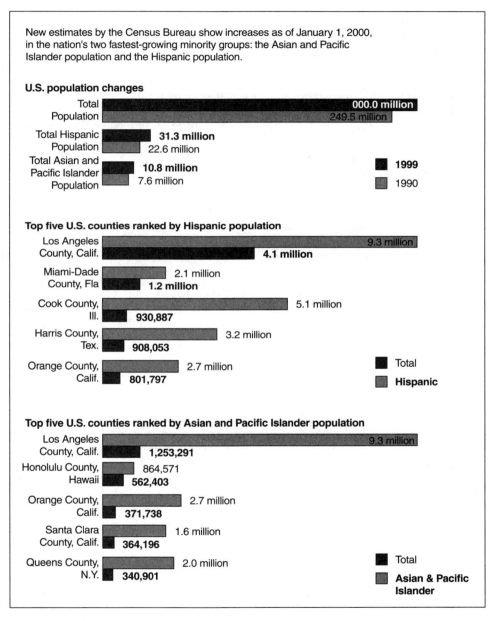

New estimates by the Census Bureau show increases as of January 1, 2000, in the nation's two fastest-growing minority groups: the Asian and Pacific Islander population and the Hispanic population.

U.S. population changes

Total Population	**000.0 million** / 249.5 million
Total Hispanic Population	**31.3 million** / 22.6 million
Total Asian and Pacific Islander Population	**10.8 million** / 7.6 million

■ **1999**
■ 1990

Top five U.S. counties ranked by Hispanic population

Los Angeles County, Calif.	9.3 million / **4.1 million**
Miami-Dade County, Fla	2.1 million / **1.2 million**
Cook County, Ill.	5.1 million / **930,887**
Harris County, Tex.	3.2 million / **908,053**
Orange County, Calif.	2.7 million / **801,797**

■ Total
■ **Hispanic**

Top five U.S. counties ranked by Asian and Pacific Islander population

Los Angeles County, Calif.	9.3 million / **1,253,291**
Honolulu County, Hawaii	864,571 / **562,403**
Orange County, Calif.	2.7 million / **371,738**
Santa Clara County, Calif.	1.6 million / **364,196**
Queens County, N.Y.	2.0 million / **340,901**

■ Total
■ **Asian & Pacific Islander**

FIGURE 9.10   Most Rapidly Growing Minority Groups

Source: U.S. Census Bureau.

Poverty continues to plague secondary students. Students who are poor continue to drop out of school in alarming numbers in spite of numerous programs to keep them in school. With new immigrants taking low-paying jobs and many non-skilled jobs going overseas, the need for more education and training is greater than ever. As a result of these trends as well as the increased use of technology in the workplace, the future is indeed bleak for students leaving school early.

The full-service school, offering health care and social programs along with academic programs, may well be the typical school of the future. Subsidized housing and free or reduced transportation for the poor to go to work, along with health and social services centered at school sites, may need to be increased greatly if we are to avoid a permanent underclass of citizens in the United States (see Table 9.2).

TABLE 9.2 Selected Characteristics of Persons under Age 18 Admitted to State Prison, 1985–97

| Characteristics | New commitments to state prison for persons under age 18 | | |
	1985	1990	1997
Gender			
Male	97%	98%	97%
Female	3	2	3
Race/Hispanic origin			
White*	32%	21%	25%
Black*	53	61	58
Hispanic	14	15	15
Other	1	1	2
Age at Admission			
14 or under	0%	0%	1%
15	2	3	4
16	18	17	21
17	80	80	74
Education			
8th grade or less	32%	28%	28%
9th to 11th grade	63	68	66
High school graduate	4	3	5
Some college	0	0	0
Other	1	1	1

NOTE: Figures may not add up to total because of rounding. Statistics include only those with a sentence of more than one year. High school graduate includes GED credential.

*Excludes Hispanics.

Source: Bureau of Justice Statistics, U.S. Department of Justice.

As we enter a truly international era in economic development, our country's pluralism will help us, but schools must work to eliminate poverty and develop new approaches to schooling.

The reform efforts of the 1980s and 1990s produced the following:

☐ Threshold exams for kids and teachers establishing minimum competence levels, which meant that the child was held back or the teacher did not get hired if their achievement level was too low.
☐ More difficult curricula.
☐ Choice plans, which assumed that parents would choose the "good" schools for their kids and shut down the "bad" ones.
☐ Restructured schools that gave the individual school more control over its destiny.

The results of such reforms included the following:

☐ No increase in high school or college graduation rates.
☐ No reduction in youth poverty.
☐ City schools that are as segregated for Hispanic students as they were for African Americans.
☐ No gain in scores of the lowest third.
☐ No increase in equity funding, which would provide the resources that would give every child a chance to actually attain the higher standards that some forty states have adopted.

In summary, the face of the United States is changing, and our secondary school curricula is forced to change as well. Our demographics suggest a growing underclass of citizens who will not have an opportunity to share in America's bounty unless the public school survives and adjusts to changing conditions. The term *at risk,* so popular in the 1990s, threatens to describe the majority of secondary pupils in the first decade of the twenty-first century.

IMPROVING TEACHER QUALITY

For the first time, we now have national standards of excellence for master teachers who demonstrate exceptional performance. The National Board for Professional Teaching Standards, an independent, nonpartisan group of teaching professionals, has developed standards for highly accomplished teachers. At the same time, quality concerns exist about teachers teaching out of their field and teachers not being given the training and time to acquire new skills to teach to high standards of excellence. Furthermore, the country needs a record 2 million teachers over the next ten years as a result of the increased enrollment and the retirement of teachers.

Partnerships in Education, a program of the U.S. Department of Education, offers the following checklist for helping schools improve teaching:

- ☐ Initiate programs that actively recruit talented young people and midcareer professionals to become teachers.
- ☐ Work with colleges to reinvent teacher preparation for beginning teachers including an "induction" period for their beginning years of teaching.
- ☐ Participate in efforts underway in many states to develop performance-based assessments for new teachers, such as those of the Interstate New Teacher Assessment and Support Consortium.
- ☐ Redesign professional development for the most experienced teachers so they get the training they need to help students master the basics and reach high standards in the core academic areas.
- ☐ Encourage master teachers to be Nationally Board Certified.
- ☐ Identify and provide peer assistance programs to improve the performance of burnt-out or low-performing teachers.
- ☐ Expand efforts to help teachers become more technologically literate and use technology to improve training available to teachers.
- ☐ Fund ways to get current information and hands-on help to teachers, addressing the isolation that is all too common in teaching.

A CLOSING NOTE

As curriculum persons, we are concerned about the trends of the early 2000s as they relate to the American high school. In the rush to return to the basics, raise achievement scores, and legislate quality control, we seem to have forgotten a purpose for secondary education that underpinned most planning prior to 1955: to foster democracy.

Democracy is a word that was used frequently by Dewey, Bode, Kilpatrick, and Rugg. These leaders spoke of democracy not as a system of government in which supreme power is vested in the people—although they understood these things—but rather as a way of life in which no single group could dominate others on the basis of class distinction, heredity, or privilege. These educators, whom we cherish and quote so often, perceived a danger in our way of life, which pitted social equality against economic competition. If capitalism and competition became dominant, they reasoned, basic human rights might be trampled. Schools, according to Dewey, "were the institution best organized to serve Democracy's cause."[16]

Education through the past century was the key response to repressive social relations. The education system, perhaps more than any other contemporary social institution, became the laboratory in which competing solutions to the problems of personal liberation and social equality were tested and the arena in which social struggles were fought out.

In short, democracy is *the* historic value or social ideal that has given direction to our educational aims. If education in public schools is our primary instrument to shape our destiny as a society, then should not our curriculum be planned with essentials first and refinements second?

What is the future of the secondary school? Perhaps the secondary school is destined to become less of a finishing school and more of a transitional school designed to send students on to higher education or to highly skilled technical jobs in a computer society. Redesigning a static curriculum to accomplish that task will be the greatest challenge facing curriculum workers in this new century.

SUMMARY

Because it is the exit school for many American youth, the secondary school is expected to find solutions for many of the problems of society by training individuals to make necessary changes to improve society.

The secondary school has experienced its share of reform movements in education. Over the course of its history, numerous committees and commissions were established to improve the curriculum.[17] Many of the reform movements, however, were aimed less at improving the high school than at preparing high school youth for college or specialized jobs.

Although most secondary schools are organized in a uniform pattern (departmentalization), some secondary schools have tried different scheduling patterns to allow for more flexibility in the instructional program.

The future of the public secondary school is threatened by many forces in the twenty-first century. The business of education is indeed big business. Schools for profit will earn 10 percent of the $360 billion now spent on K–12 education. Some question whether "public" education will continue. Educational leaders must begin to give direction to the secondary school. They must not leave decisions about that direction to politicians and special interest groups.

SUGGESTED LEARNING ACTIVITIES

1. Trace the development of the secondary school in the United States.
2. What are the major issues and problems facing secondary schools today? How do they compare with the issues and problems found in secondary schools in the past fifty years?
3. The curriculum for the secondary school has often been described as dull and irrelevant. How would you reorganize the present curriculum of the secondary school to fit the needs of a rapidly emerging high-tech society in the United States?
4. Develop a flexible one-block schedule for a medium-size high school that will include provisions for both departmentalization and team instruction.
5. Prepare a paper describing the high school as it exists in the first decade of the twenty-first century.

NOTES

1. Mortimer Adler, *The Paideia Proposal* (New York: Macmillan, 1982).
2. John Goodlad, *A Place Called School* (New York: McGraw-Hill, 1984), p. 94.
3. Goodlad, *A Place Called School,* p. 143.
4. Ted Sizer, *Horace's Compromise: The Dilemma of the American High School* (Boston: Houghton-Mifflin, 1984).
5. *America 2000,* U.S. Department of Education, 1989.
6. "What Work Requires of Schools: A SCANS Report for America 2000," U.S. Department of Labor, June 1991.
7. Maxwell Schauweker, "A Review of Standards of Reading and Writing," *Teaching K–8* (March/April 1995): 233–234.
8. Deborah L. Ball, "Teacher Learning and the Mathematics Reform—What We Think We Know and What We Need to Learn," *Phi Delta Kappan* 77, 7 (March 1996): 500–508.
9. Iuan Charner, et al., "Reforms of the School-to-Work Transition—Findings, Implications, and Challenges," *Phi Delta Kappan* 77, 1 (September 1995): 40–59.
10. Allan Odden, "The Costs of Sustaining Educational Change through Comprehensive School Reform," *Phi Delta Kappan,* 81, 6 (February 2000): 433–438.
11. Daniel Kinnaman, "ASCD Releases Only the Best," *Learning* 15, 5 (February 1995): 36.
12. Caroline McCullen, "World Wide Web in the Classroom: The Quintessential Collaboration," *Learning and Leading with Technology* 23, 3 (November 1995): 7–10.
13. Donald Hackman, "Ten Guidelines for Implementing Block Scheduling," *Educational Leadership* (November 1995): 24–27.
14. Robert Canady and Michael Rettig, "The Power of Innovative Scheduling," *Educational Leadership* (November 1995): 4–10.
15. World Development Forum, United Nations, April 1990.
16. John Dewey, *Democracy and Education* (New York: Macmillan, 1916).
17. Susan V. Sharvian-Gunk, "What's in a Name," *Phi Delta Kappan,* 81, 5 (January 2000): 345–355.

ADDITIONAL READING

Diaz, Carole, Byron Massinas, and John Xanthopoulous. *Global Perspectives for Educators.* Boston: Allyn and Bacon, 1999.

Fisher, Douglas. *Inclusive High Schools: Learning from Contemporary Classrooms.* Baltimore, MD: Brookes, 1999.

Gordon, Stephen P. "Ready? How Effective Schools Know It's Time to Take the Plunge." *Journal of Staff Development,* 20, 1 (Winter 1999): 48–53.

Helsby, Gill. *Changing Teachers' Work: The Reform of Secondary Schooling.* Philadelphia: Open University Press, 1999.

Hirsh, Stephanie. "Standards Guide Staff Development." *Journal of Staff Development,* 29, 2 (Spring 1999): 45.

Jenkins, John. *Banishing Anonymity: Middle and High School Advisement Programs.* Larchmont, NY: Eye on Education, 2000.

Koballa, Thomas, and Deborah Tippins. *Cases in Middle and Secondary Science Education: The Promise and Dilemmas.* Upper Saddle River, NJ: Merrill/Prentice Hall, 2000.

Marsh, David D. et al. *The New American High School.* Thousand Oaks, CA: Corwin Press, 1999.

Marshall, J. Dan, James Sears, and William Schuber. *Turning Points in Curriculum.* Upper Saddle River, NJ: Merrill/Prentice Hall, 2000.

McNeil, John D. Curriculum: *The Teacher's Initiative,* 2nd ed. Upper Saddle River, NJ: Merrill/Prentice Hall, 1999.

Rosad, Joan. *Multicultural Education in Middle and Secondary Classrooms: Meeting the Challenge of Diversity and Change.* Belmont, CA: Wadsworth, 2000.

Schmidt, John J. *Counseling in Schools: Essential Services and Comprehensive Programs.* Boston: Allyn and Bacon, 1999.

Sewell, Evelyn. *Curriculum: An Integrative Introduction,* 2nd ed. Upper Saddle River, NJ: Merrill/Prentice Hall, 2000.

Snodgrass, Diane M. *Collaborative Learning in Middle and Secondary Schools: Applications and Assessments.* Larchmont, NY: Eye on Education, 2000.

WEB SITES
Comprehensive School Reform Models

Accelerated Schools:
http://www.Ieland.stanford.edu/group.ASP
ATLAS Communities
http://www.edc.org/FSC/ATLAS
Coalition of Essential Schools:
http://www.essentialschools.org
Co-NECT Schools:
http://www.co-nect.bbn.com
Modern Red Schoolhouse (K–12):
http://www.mrsh.org
Paideia:
http://www.unc.edu/paideia
Roots & Wings/Success for All:
http://www.successforall.com
Assessment and Evaluation:
http://www.middleweb.com/contntassess.html
Teachers at Work:
http://www.middleweb.com/ContntsWork.html
Teacher Professional Development:
http://www.middleweb.com/ContntTchDev.html
Principal Professional Development:
http://www.middleweb.com/contntsPrin.html

Connecting with Other Teachers

Reading Online—The new International Reading Association electronic journal:
http://www.readingonline.org
Liszt Select:
http://www.liszt.com
Classroom Connect Jump Station:
http://www.classroom.net/classroom/edulinkds.html
Teachers Helping Teachers:
http://www.pacificnet_net/~mandel/
The Staff Room of Canada's SchoolNet:
http.www.schoolnet.ca/adm/staff/

Cross-Cultural Learning Experiences

Intercultural E-Mail Classroom Connections:
http://www.stolaf.edu/network/iecc/
Kid News:
http://www.vsa.cap.com/~pwers/Kidnews.html
International WWW Schools Registry:
http://web66.coled.umn.edu/schools.html

Africa Online: Kids Only:
http://www.africaonline.com/AfricaOnline/coverkids.html
Native American Indian resources:
http://indy4fdl.cc.mn.us/~isk/mainmenu.html

High School Scheduling

Definition of block scheduling:
http://www.nwrel.org/comm/monthly/clarify.html
Block scheduling questions and answers:
http://www.coled.umn.edu/CAREIwww/blocksch eduling/Q&A/q&a.htm
Tennessee High School Study:
http://www.coe.memphis.edu/coe/crep/news/briefs /scheduling.html
Current issues and ideas:
http://www.aasa.org/issues/block/block.htm
New School on Block:
http://www.phschool.com/profdev/bs/bsa04.html
Harnessing the Power of Scheduling:
http://www.ascd.org/pubs/el/canady/html

Professional Resources

Teaching Resources—Language-focused site that includes lists of language-related web sites and employment resources to help language teachers find jobs: http://www.tcom.hiou.edu/OU_Language/teachers.html
Busy Teachers—For K–12 instruction and learning:
http://www.gatech.edu/lcc.idt/Students/Cole/Proj/K-12/TOC.html
Webcrawler—Extensive children's Internet address that is an excellent resource for both teachers and students. Children also gain insights into traveling on the Internet: http://www.webcrawler.com/select/ed.kids.html
Bookwire—A subsite of the *Publishers Weekly* site, this is an excellent resource for best-selling and current writings: http://www.bookwire.com/pw/bsl/childrens/current.children
For software information:
http://www.epicent.com/
http://www.greatwave.com/thml/research.html
ASCD—Resources on technology and curriculum:
http://www.middleweb.com/currstregies.html

Safe Schools

Web Guide to Safe Schools:
http://www.air.org/cecp
Threats to Children:
http://www.aacap.org
Oregon School Safety Center:
http://www.nsscl.org
National Crime Prevention Council/National
    School Safety Center:
http://www.ncpc.org
Safe Schools: A Handbook for Practitioners:
http://www.nassp.org
Partnerships for a Drug-Free America:
http://www.drugfreeamerica.org
TV Free America:
http://www.tvfa.org

Skills- and Content-Based Reform Models

Breakthrough to Literacy:
http://www.wrightgroup.com
Carbo Reading Styles:
http://www.nrsi.com
First Steps:
http://www.heinemann.com/firststeps
Reading Recovery:
http://www.osu.edu/readingrecovery
Comprehensive School Mathematics:
http://www.mcrel.org/products/csmp
Math Connections:
http://www.mathconnections.com
Galaxy Classroom Science:
http://www.galaxy.org

Staff Development

National Staff Development Council—Over 35 top-
    ics relating to opportunities and techniques in
    staff development:
http://www.nsdc.org/library/
Santa Clara County, California, school district:
http://www.sccoe.k12.ca.us/edcstaff
Minneapolis Public Schools Staff Development
    Department—Standards are used to plan every
    event or course offered:
http://mplsk12.us/staffdev/stan/mplsesd.html

State Assessment Information

Idaho Department of Education:
http://www.sed.state.id.us/instruct/SchoolAccount/
    StateTesting.htm
Maryland: Queen Anne's County Public Schools:
http://boe.qacps.k12.md.us/boe/TESTS.HTM
New York: Montauk Public Schools:
http://www.516web.com/school/montauk/test.htm
Colorado: A Teacher's Guide to the Colorado Assess-
    ment Program:
http://connect.colorado.edu/connect/publications/
    teachers/index.html
North Carolina: The NC Testing Program under the
    ABC's Plan:
http://www.dpi.state.nc.us/account. . .y/testing/abcs
    _testing_program.html
Vermont Department of Education:
http://www.state.vt.us/educ/assmt2.htm

Others

Goals 2000—National education goals:
http://www.ed.gov/legislation/GOALS2000/
    TheACT/sec102.html
Content standards contracts: New Teacher's Guide:
    Raising Academic Standards:
http://www.ed.gov/pubs/TeachersGuide/raising/html
Steps for designing assessments: Select and/or Design
    Assessment that Elicit Established Outcomes:
http://www.ncrrel.org/sdrs/areas/issues/methods/
    assessment/as7sele2.htm
Parents for Public Schools:
http://www.parents4publicschools.com
Public Education Network:
http://www.publiceducation.org
Education Trust:
http://www.edtrust.org
Center for Education Reform:
http://www.edreform.com
U.S. Education Department:
http://www.ed.gov/offices/OVAE/nahs

chapter **10**

CURRICULUM DESIGN ALTERNATIVES

The new century has brought a substantial alteration to both the form and purpose of most public schools. While still not evident in many schools, the way learning occurs has been changed forever by the Internet and user-friendly search engines. After two centuries of a traditional delivery in the classroom, learning in the twenty-first century will be unique. Access to learning no longer is teacher dependent or print oriented, and schools in the future may well be operated by those outside of the public sector. Options for learning in the years to come will be numerous, and school sites may be only one of many places where young people can learn.

Curriculum development can be at the center of activity as these changes transform our schools. The questions that were asked at the turn of the last century, causing the formation of curriculum as a subspecialty in education, still remain. Being "high tech" doesn't remove the necessity of choosing from among many alternatives and organizing learning to achieve desired results in the teaching–learning process.

In a democratic society, opinions will differ about what schools should be doing. After all, the institution called "school" programs millions of Americans daily in thought, behavior, and feeling. Some 53 million children are being educated in public schools in the United States, and school districts range in size from tiny to New York City where 1.1 million pupils are enrolled.

American schools have faced major change constantly during the past fifty years, but the change being instigated by the Internet is structural and philosophical at the same time. Such change redefines the purpose of education and how an education will be acquired. We anticipate that the new century will bring a much increased effort by many publics to redirect American education, and curriculum workers should be ready to meet such challenges by being aware of the alternatives.

A HISTORY OF CHANGE

In the early years of the twentieth century, attempts to introduce changes in our schools came from professional educators who were concerned with broad philosophical issues about the role of education in society. Reform efforts, for the most part, had a philosophical base and evolved slowly over several decades. Only after considerable discussion and experimentation were educational reforms attempted.

Early attempts to reform the American school assumed a somewhat monolithic culture and were aimed at developing programs that would serve the entire society. In the latter half of the twentieth century, reform efforts became more frequent, arose from more diverse sources, and had less clear philosophical bases or records of controlled experimentation.

During the late 1950s and early 1960s, the American society experienced a cultural awakening. The diversity of the society, a pluralistic configuration of many subcultures, was revealed, and the historic pattern of the public school was called into question. If the public school was to serve all members of society, both the substance and the organization of the institution were open to review.

The frustrations and hopes of numerous groups became linked to the schools, which are the social institutions for instilling values. The divergent norms and values of the subcultures suggested new ideas about what schools should be. Some of these ideas and concepts were incorporated by the public schools, but many were not.

Related to these attempts to reform the school were numerous reformation efforts by external groups. The importance of public education as an influence for social change led industry, foundations, political action groups, and the federal agencies to introduce changes. The sponsorship of these many groups continues today, and these factions compete to influence the curriculum.

The implications of such trends for curriculum planners are multiple. First, those responsible for designing school programs must be able to view these forces of change with some degree of perspective. In our opinion, this may be the most important skill required of anyone involved in curriculum work. Innovations and educational trends need to be seen in terms of some overriding framework and in light of historical precedent where possible. An inability to categorize and order the multitude of curriculum changes found in today's public schools will result in short-range decision criteria and long-term chaos. This is especially true in the new technology age that is upon us.

Second, it must be recognized that public sophistication concerning curriculum development has grown considerably during the past several decades. Seeing schools as purposeful agents of change has led to the development of many restricting designs with little or no concern for long-term social implications. Such an educational focus has also led to the development of some relatively efficient public school programs. The "basic skills" focus and testing for minimal competencies has not been a bad thing for education.

Finally, recent changes in technology should suggest to curriculum leaders that schools are institutions with numerous possibilities. They no longer need to be contained between the covers of a book or the four walls of a classroom. In fact, the major costs of education—buildings, teacher salaries, textbooks, and buses—are no longer restrictive forces if we consider technological alternatives as a new form of schooling. To be influential in the educational environment, curriculum designers must break away from the familiar and begin to respond to the changing needs and conditions of society. If public schools do not offer imaginative curriculum options, their clients will go elsewhere.

This chapter addresses the many options in curriculum design and instructional delivery. Curriculum development, ultimately, means making wise choices from among alternatives.

MAJOR CURRICULUM DESIGNS

The many forms of schooling in the United States might be classified in numerous ways. Each social science perspective suggests a different set of variables and categorization. Perhaps the most useful existing classification available today is one developed by R. Freeman Butts.[1] In this classification, school forms are separated by function. Six major types of school design, and their rationale, are presented:

1. Conservative/liberal arts.
2. Educational technology.
3. Humanistic.
4. Vocational.
5. Social reconstruction.
6. Deschooling.

Conservative/Liberal Arts

In the vast majority of the schools in the United States, the pervasive form is one with roots leading back to Hellenistic Greece. This traditional form or design is based on the belief that a human being's unique and distinctive quality is intellect and that the quest for knowledge is the natural fulfillment of such an intellect. In short, the highest purpose in life is to engage in the process of inquiry—to move from ignorance to truth, from confusion to enlightenment.

Historically, this quest for knowledge was seen as a reflection of a world whose laws and physical order were fixed properties. The process of education was concerned simply with the pursuit of objective knowledge for its own sake. A liberal education was suitable to free people who possessed the legal opportunity and means to devote themselves to cultural attainment.

In later times, after scientific revolutions and the loss of a shared culture had diminished the concept of *paideia,* the cultured man, the liberal arts approach to educating became a perspective. Liberal arts was not so much a mastery of subject matter as it was a way of looking at things. The human mind was trained so that the individual might live fully.

As this notion of education was translated into a public education format during the early American experience, such knowing was seen as a means of producing an enlightened citizenry. In the words of R. Freeman Butts:

> the prime purpose of the public schools is to serve the general welfare of a democratic society by assuring the knowledge and understanding necessary to exercise the responsibilities of citizenship are not only made available but are inculcated.[2]

The curriculum of the conservative liberal arts is familiar to most of us as the curriculum we studied in high school and college. The curriculum was formally declared *permanent studies* or *great books* and included language, mathematics, sciences, history, and foreign languages.[3] Usually dominated by a standard text or set of materials, with a certain amount of time to master units, and leading to formal recognition of learning in a graduation from study, the liberal arts model is familiar to many people. In the late 1980s, Mortimer Adler's *Paideia Proposal* served as a guide to this form of learning in public schools.[4] In the 1990s, the lists of "things to know" by Hirsch were very influential.[5]

Educational Technology

Education in the new century is experiencing a technological "gold rush" atmosphere as relatively inexpensive and highly reliable products make major inroads to this nation's classrooms and school. These instruments are changing instructional delivery for many schools.

Technological instruments and personal learning systems offer the possibility of significant alterations in the teaching–learning act as we know it by offering individualized instruction for each student. Instruction, research, communication, and staff development are all targets of these novel machines and systems. In particular danger of becoming extinct is the print textbook, a relic of a time when information was contained and stored in a physical medium.

Driving this gold rush is the bare fact that schools represent the largest sales market in the United States. More important for planners, such technology also suggests a possible exit point for the spiraling costs of financing public education. An electronic delivery of instruction would significantly reduce the cost of facilities, teacher salaries, instructional materials, and the costs associated with transporting students to a learning place.

Most technological designs in the past century focused on process and technique (teaching machines) to the exclusion of goals and objectives. An early and nonelectric example can be found in the 1930s when the famous Winnetka Plan used mimeographed assignments to master essential skills. Self-instructive practice exercises were monitored through a diagnostic-practice-remediation format that was the forerunner of much of today's programmed instruction.[6]

Historically, technological designs stressed objectivity, precision, and efficiency. As major proponent B. F. Skinner stated:

> The traditional distinction comes down to this: when we know what we are doing, we are training . . . any behavior that can be specified can be programmed.[7]

Usually, in the past, learner behaviors were described overtly, infrequently lasting beyond the immediate treatment.

In the 1970s all of the objectivity of the technology of behaviorism began to break down as it was recognized that students were being influenced by unplanned effects of the technological delivery itself. Perhaps the best example of this occurred when millions of elementary students watching the launch of the *Challenger* spacecraft in science class were, instead, treated to a dramatic social studies lesson. Technology is powerful in that it allows the learner the new powers of direct access!

The impact of technology in the 1990s, however, was of a different scale than that of previous decades, even though each decade had seen its own miracle technology. Televisions in the 1950s; transistors and early computers in the 1960s; video cams and compact discs in the 1970s; facsimile machines and CD-ROMS in the 1980s; and the personal computer, World Wide Web, and Internet of the 1990s—all have greatly affected learning. However, the power of technology in this new century will be magnified significantly because of the integration of new digital systems capable of combining many media into one. ISDN, the integrated systems digital networks, can make computers, televisions, and communication instruments act as a single powerful multimedia delivery mechanism. Such a mechanism is not "place bound," with the result that the learner now possesses worldwide knowledge acquisition power from home or wherever he or she is located. Schools as we know them, if they are to survive in a viable form, will be hard-pressed to ignore these new technologies. Technology in the early years of the twenty-first century has the power to reform or destroy public education. The outcome will depend largely on what curriculum specialists in schools do with the new technologies.

In the 1980s and 1990s, the lack of meaningful use of technology depressed its impact on classroom learning. Our treatment of technology was 99 percent vocational and only 1 percent educational in nature. In many districts, little integration of hardware or software into traditional courses occurred, and true visions of how the new technologies could be used were nearly nonexistent. In addition to the computer, schools grappled with interactive television, various electronic networks, interactive cable and satellite-beamed video, CD-ROM technology, and other such tools.

In the new century, curriculum specialists must do better if they are to maintain control of the programming function. Not only is knowledge of how technology works (literacy) important, but also how technology can be used to improve communication and transmission of knowledge. Our eight curriculum designs and how they can shape technological applications represents one starting point in such a discussion of educational usage.

Five questions should focus this effort to regain control of education:

1. What are the implications of technology for learning?
2. How can schools receive and use technology in a meaningful way?
3. What technology is most effective for learning in a school (physical) setting?
4. How can we prevent technology from creating an intellectual elite in schools?
5. How can schools keep the home schooling trend from socially deschooling the learning process?

Curriculum leaders in the next years will play a very large role in defining technological designs by the answers given to these questions. Learning in public school settings will be redefined by technology; only the format remains to be determined. If educators are not aggressive students of the use of technology, the forces that control the new media will become the developers of the school curriculum.

Humanistic

A third curriculum design in the United States during the past century had as its main theme the humanizing of learning. Such designs generally feature student-oriented curricula, cooperative forms, and a decentralization of instructional organization.

Humane curriculum designs have deep roots in American education and have taken numerous forms in the past century. In such programs, there is a shift in atmosphere toward understanding, compassion, encouragement, and trust. Physical settings usually encourage freedom in the form of student mobility, increased choice of curricular activities, and a learning-by-doing format.

An early example of this design in the United States was the Dalton Plan, which was implemented in the Dalton, Massachusetts, schools in the 1920s. The program featured freedom of movement and choice of materials by students, cooperation and interaction of student group life through a house plan, and subject matter laboratories in the classrooms.

Another early version of a humanistic curriculum design was the organic method of education developed at the Fairhope, Alabama, school around 1910. This program held that children are best prepared for adult life by fully experiencing childhood. Children were led naturally into more traditional areas of schooling only after experiencing a curriculum of physical exercise, nature study, music, field geography, storytelling, fundamental conception of numbers, drama, and games. General development, rather than the amount of information mastered, controlled the classification of students.[8]

Contemporary versions of the humanistic design are found in open elementary schools, emerging middle schools, and student-centered programs such as

Outward Bound. In such programs, the instruction is humane, personalized, and individualized. Curriculum is geared to the maturational levels of students, and teachers serve as guides to learning rather than authority figures or purveyors of knowledge. The problem-solving process of the instructional format borrows heavily from another humanistic design, the core curriculum.

The core curriculum, developed in the 1930s in educational systems such as the Denver public schools, attempted to present learning from a humane and holistic perspective. The following excerpt from an evaluation report outlines the program objectives:

> It is so named because it represents an attack upon those problems which are relatively common to the young people in the school and because it carries the chief responsibility for guidance, for general testing, and for record keeping. It is that part of the total school program which is planned for the development in boys and girls of the ability to solve common problems and of the power to think together and to carry on the democratic process of discussion and group discussions.[9]

Core curricula used a ten-point plan in organizing for instruction:

1. Continuity of teacher–pupil relationships.
2. Greater teacher participation in formulating policies of the program.
3. Elimination of barriers to learning experiences through the attack on problems rather than through reliance on the logical organization of subject matter in isolated courses.
4. Development of core courses based on student concerns.
5. Relating school activities to the community.
6. Pupil–teacher planning, emphasizing choice and responsibility.
7. Guidance by a teacher who knows the student in an intimate classroom setting.
8. Using a wide variety of sources of information.
9. Using a wide variety of means of expression—words, art, music.
10. Teacher-to-teacher planning.

Humanistic designs generally are characterized by highly flexible instructional areas, high degrees of student involvement, and an emphasis on the process of learning as opposed to a product orientation or a *preparation for life* outlook.

Vocational

A fourth curriculum design present in the past century is concerned with vocation and economic aspects of living. Such programs generally go under either the traditional term *vocational education,* or the broader and newer term, career education. Most recently the phrase school-to-work has been widely used in the educational literature.

In the early years of the twentieth century, vocational programs were perceived as separate from the academic tracks and focused on the non-college-bound student. The curriculum consisted of crafts and labor skills. Such programs were strongest in areas with an industrial or agricultural community. More recently, educators have made efforts to connect or combine the vocational and technical areas into a structure called tech-prep.

Vocational education programs traditionally studied eight areas: (1) trade and industrial education, (2) business education, (3) agriculture, (4) home economics, (5) marketing education, (6) technical education, (7) technology education, and (8) health education. Vocational curriculum designs either try to integrate academics (interdisciplinary) and use vocational applications to illustrate the utilization of knowledge, or they create new tech-prep alternatives in which students branch off from the precollege curriculum while in high school.[10]

The tech-prep and school-to-work programs of the 1980s evolved into a new technical education curriculum for the college-bound in the 1990s. The Carl Perkins Vocational and Applied Technology Act of 1990 led to over one thousand tech-prep consortia. All states were represented in tech-prep consortia, and true partnerships were established between secondary and postsecondary schools, between academic and vocational/technical faculty, and between educators and business leaders. The 1994 School-to-Work Opportunities Act, which requires business involvement, extended the efforts of tech-prep.

Curriculum reform in the late 1990s became a central issue in tech-prep efforts with more attention being given to training teachers in applied learning and implementing applied academic courses. Many districts eliminated traditional vocational or general education programs and required all students to enroll in either a tech-prep program or a precollege program.[11]

Efforts to implement a comprehensive vocational design increased during the past two decades for a number of reasons. First, there has been a growing recognition that the schools are an essential piece of the national economic condition. Welfare, unemployment, large segments of the population without useful skills, and the fact that only 40 to 45 percent of all high school graduates attended college were given as reasons for an increased vocational emphasis in the schools.

Second, the relevancy movement of the 1990s revealed students who were bored and listless in senior high school and resentful of the holding pattern of formal schooling.

Third, vocational/career education has been promoted as a means of assisting minority groups and other disenchanted members of the society in breaking out of the cycle of poverty. Students experiencing such programs can escape the containment of impoverished environments and family backgrounds.

Finally, the whole concept of utilitarian education and no-frills curricula has increased the awareness and demand for vocational designs. The American public increasingly feels that insufficient attention has been paid to the hard social reality that everyone must eventually seek gainful employment. Technological and political conditions have demanded a change in the basic definition of an education.

Proponents of new vocational designs in the early twenty-first century picture them as a necessity: a means of serving all students in the public schools, a vehicle for making school useful and relevant, and a contributor to the well-being of American society in a new global economy.

More recently, American business has stressed technological and economic education as stimuli to the high school curriculum. Vocational designs are practical, say proponents. Critics of vocational designs, including career education, see them as static conceptions of life in American society and insufficient preparation for life in an unknown future.

There is little doubt that competing in the new global economy will force an even greater collaboration among business, labor, government, and education (public, private, postsecondary). Long-term industry–education collaboration will focus on staff development/in-service training, curriculum revision, upgrading, instructional materials and equipment, and improving educational management—all of which are central to an effective vocational education delivery system.[12]

Social Reconstruction

A fifth curriculum design found in the United States in the past century has as its main theme social reconstruction. The conception of the school as a vehicle for social improvement is not new. Arguments for this type of school were made in the 1930s by members of the social reconstruction wing of the Progressive Education Association (PEA), in the 1970s by those favoring deschooling, and in the 1990s by advocates of postmodernism. Harold Rugg of the PEA, for example, spoke of the changes impending in American society and encouraged the schools to influence social changes. He outlined characteristics of a needed curriculum in the twenty-sixth National Society for the Study of Education Yearbook:

> A curriculum which will not only inform but will constantly have as its ideal the development of an attitude of sympathetic tolerance and critical open-mindedness . . . a curriculum which is constructed on a problem-solving organization providing constant practice in choosing between alternatives, in making decisions, in drawing generalizations . . . a curriculum in which children will be influenced to put their ideas sanely into action.[13]

The social reconstruction designs seek to equip students with tools (skills) for dealing with the changes about them. So equipped, students can meet an unknown future with attitudes and habits of action. In the 1980s and early 1990s, special schools for minority youths illustrated this special kind of intellectual "arming" of the student.

More recently, the American curriculum has seen an increase in the teaching of thinking skills, skills that teach students how to use information, and skills in social interaction (cooperative learning). Advocates of the theory of multiple intelligences have focused attention on the idea that the way in which information is presented causes the student to use such information in certain ways. In other words, how we teach is how students learn.[14]

Another example of social reconstruction designs is the use of schooling to encourage certain social trends. For example, in the Duval County School district in Jacksonville, Florida, magnet programs are offered to encourage voluntary racial integration (see Table 10.1). Here, the curriculum offerings are multiple and

TABLE 10.1 Social Reconstruction Using Magnet Schools

Type of Program	Elementary Grades Pre–K–5		Middle 6–8	Senior 9–12
Academic Enrichment Learning Styles	Fort Caroline Oceanway Ortega	Sabal Palm San Jose Timucuan		
Aviation and Aerospace				Ribault
Business, Finance and Legal Professions			**Matthew Gilbert**	**Wolfson**
Careers	Greenfield		Stilwell	Baldwin
Citizenship	San Mateo West Riverside	Windy Hill		Lee
Communications	Beauclearc Lake Lucina **Norwood**	Ramona Whitehouse	**Eugene Butler**	Englewood
Computers/ Technology	**Bethune** **Central Riverside** Cedar Hills	Pine Estates **Carter G. Woodson**	**Ribault**	Paxon
Foreign Language	John E. Ford	Ruth Upson		
Fundamental	Crystal Springs Hendricks Avenue Holiday Hill	**Lackawanna** **S. P. Livingston** **John Love**		
Gifted and Talented	**R. L. Brown** **R. V. Daniels** **Jacksonville Beach**	**Martin L. King** **Rufus Payne** **Susie Tolbert**	**J. W. Johnson** **Pre-College** **Preparatory**	**Stanton** **College** **Preparatory**
Government and Public Service/ Community Outreach	Hogan-Spring Glen	Normandy		**Andrew Jackson**
International Studies/ Cultural Diversities	**G. W. Carver** Chimney Lakes Dinsmore	Oak Hill Reynolds Lane		Forrest **Mandarin**
Math/Science/ Pre-Engineering	Lone Star **Moncrief** Louis Sheffield	**Springfield** Stockton	**Kirby-Smith** Mayport Jeb Stuart	**Raines**
Medical Professionals and Health Care			**Darnell-Cookman**	
Modified School Calendar	Crown Point **John E. Ford**	Garden City Loretto		
Montessori	**J. Allen Axson**			
Performing Arts	**Brentwood** Fishweir **Lake Forest**	**Sallye B. Mathis** **Pine Forest**	**Landon**	Douglas Anderson
Physical and Academic Fitness	**S. A. Hull** Thomas Jefferson **Longbranch**	San Pablo Wesconnett **West Jacksonville**	Lake Shore Southside	**Ed White**
Schools for Success	**Sherwood Forest**	Mandarin Oaks		

Note: Bold type indicates magnet schools; nonbold type indicates select schools.

Source: Duval County Schools, Jacksonville, Florida, 1996.

secondary to the primary objective of meeting court-ordered compliance to desegregate under local initiative.

The major assumption of social reconstruction designs is that the future is not fixed, but rather is amenable to modification and improvement. The school, as an institution, cannot remain neutral in a changing world and can influence and direct social change.

Some recent applications of the social reconstruction design have used "futurism" to justify the necessity of social intervention. Since the future will not be like the present (it will be more multicultural and multilingual), it is necessary to be flexible and develop the ability to make value decisions.

Social reconstruction designs generally combine classroom learning with application in the outer world. Teachers and students are partners in inquiry, and instruction is usually carried on in a problem-solving, cooperative learning, or inquiry format.

Deschooling

As strange as it sounds, it is possible to design the "deschooling" of public schools. Through purposeful organization, or lack of it, it is possible to deemphasize or disestablish the public school programs and the formality of education by redirecting resources to alternatives. Although early efforts in such designs sought to free the learner from the bureaucratic control of the institution of the school, more recent attempts have focused on economic or political alternatives.

According to its chief intellectual forebearer, Ivan Illich, schools are social tools that actually operate to deprive individuals of an education and real learning. Schools are not the panacea for social ills, but rather are rigid, authoritarian institutions that perpetuate the social order through a number of functions. Illich saw deschooling as an alternative design:

> Will people continue to treat learning as a commodity—a commodity that could be more efficiently produced and consumed by greater numbers of people if new institutional arrangements were established? Or shall we set up only those institutional arrangements that protect the autonomy of the learner—his private initiative to decide what he will learn and his inalienable right to learn what he likes rather than what is useful to somebody else? We must choose between more efficient education of people fit for an increasingly efficient society and a new society in which education ceases to be the task of some special agency.[15]

Problems of institutionalized education revolve around questions of power, leadership, and structure. Schools, by dominating the values and focus of organization, control the leader. Such control is often racist and sexist and is always oppressive. Further, schools are undemocratic in their method of converting knowledge into power.

While opposition to formal schooling and its structure was a continuous phenomenon of the twentieth century in the United States, the free school movement of the late 1960s presented the best examples of the deschooling design. Allen Glatthorn outlined the emergence of the free school movement during that period:

> The period of the late sixties, then, was a time ripe for radical change. The curriculum reform movement had run out of steam. The innovations in scheduling and staffing were proving to be only superficial tinkering. And there was acute dissatisfaction with all the public schools. This dissatisfaction was most keenly sensed by militant blacks and by radicals of the New Left. Each of these groups responded by opening their own schools, and these schools were the progenitors of the public alternatives that followed.[16]

Glatthorn identified a number of ways in which free schools and alternative schools attempted to release the individual student from the institutional oppression of the school: travel-learn programs, work and apprenticeship programs, volunteer service, informal study in the community, and affective experiences. Collectively, these curriculum arrangements sought to define education as a personal act.

Another experiment of the 1970s was performance contracting, in which contractors were paid only for defined increases in test scores. The initial swell of enthusiasm for performance contracting was followed by disappointment in results. Factors that plagued performance contractors, such as abuses in testing and the instability of private firms attempting to turn a profit, may well plague the charter school movement.[17]

In the 1990s new forces entered the deschooling design. There was a significant home schooling movement in America in which parents refused to enroll their students in school and served as surrogate teachers at home. Although the variety of laws governing this phenomenon in the United States precludes any real generalization of motivation and practices, it can be stated that such parents do not support the concept of organized schooling for their children.[18]

A second force that affected public schools in the 1990s was the political push to give parents vouchers and the right to enroll their children in a school of choice. Although the voucher plan movement can be seen as a sincere effort to upgrade the public schools, it is probably more about privatizing formal education in the United States. Using either legislation or incentives, or both, proponents of this educational movement would eliminate foundational funding of public education.[19]

A third force that had an impact on the public schools of the 1990s was the charter school movement. First viewed as a move to privatize public schools by contracting them out to private groups, the movement in the mid-1990s turned to a more inventive approach. Groups both within and outside of the public school setting were encouraged to build innovative school programs using public funds. Even the National Education Association (NEA) joined the movement by developing NEA-run charter schools.[20]

Most recently, the accessibility of Internet resources has threatened to promote social deschooling in some districts. Using "virtual high school" offerings, students in Polk County, Florida, are able to take their senior year of school at home over the Internet. Similar schools exist in numerous states, demonstrating the possibility of no longer having to build $35 million high school buildings.[21]

Together, these six curriculum designs outline the diversity of educational programs in the United States during the early years of the twenty-first century. Curriculum leaders need to be aware that such diversity has always been present in American education and will continue to be present in the future.

CURRICULUM DESIGN IN THE FUTURE

Since curriculum leaders are actively concerned with a future in which school programs genuinely serve learners rather than handicap them, they should be aware of studies that project onrushing forces and events.

Futurism in education is a topic of concern to all educators and has been the subject of numerous commissioned studies and investigations by think tanks such as RAND Incorporated and the Hudson Institute. It is helpful to become familiar with resources such as those presented in the Additional Readings section at the end of this chapter.

In this chapter we hope to stimulate thinking about the many possibilities for education that the future might hold and to present the process of curriculum development as the vehicle by which schools might arrive at that unknown future. Following a theme found throughout this book, the future of educational programs is presented in a format that suggests a trend toward greater control in curriculum designs or greater flexibility in educational plans. It is entirely possible, of course, that other intellectual constructs may be more useful in addressing this highly complex topic.

A date of departure for this assessment is 1957, the date of the launch of *Sputnik I*. This event jarred American education into a purposefulness that had been absent in the past and opened fully the idea of using schools as an instrument of national policy. Although the space race of the late 1950s has evaporated in scale to that of "just another federal program," the question of what role the schools should play remains.

In the twenty-first century, American education is faced with a bewildering array of alternatives concerning what it might become. The question that must be faced by all leaders in the field of curriculum is the primary question of all educational planning: What is the role of education in our society? Failure to consider this critical question is to abdicate a basic responsibility and decide by indecision.

Specifically, some questions must be considered as we peer into the first years of the twenty-first century:

1. What directions seem to be most promising for the American society to pursue in planning for education?
2. Where and how do professional educators begin to assess educational alternatives?
3. Can the future be influenced by our actions, or is it largely predetermined?
4. Where do we as planners gain the value structure to plan for the future?
5. How can we most effectively involve others in our society in planning for the future?

These questions present a challenge to all who are involved in developing educational programs.

INSTRUCTIONAL OPTIONS

Along with curriculum designs, instructional options have multiplied significantly with the advent of new technologies. We have only a twenty-year experience with items such as VCRs, videocams, cell phones, and lasers. Our nation has had the Internet only since May of 1995. Yet, these technologies are pervasive in the United States, and our dependence on them grows daily.

In the classrooms, some teachers are making connections and using technology to enrich learning experiences for schoolchildren. These teachers are using television, telephones, computers, interactive video, and the Internet to expand the horizons of learning. Out of school, both teachers and students are growing wiser in the use of the new technologies.

Instructional strategies and designs are an important idea for all curriculum workers to understand. The medium does influence the message, as McLuhan told us thirty years ago. But, beyond the medium itself, the instructional design in which the medium is embedded also gives meaning to learning. Curriculum developers need to go this next step, to the classroom level, and design instructional episodes that highlight meaning in the curriculum.

In chapter 6, we introduced eight instructional designs: content, skills, inquiry and exploration, conceptual, interdisciplinary, cooperative, problem-solving, and critical and creative. These designs "form" the curriculum content by emphasizing some things at the expense of other things. These designs can be identified with Bloom's cognitive taxonomy and Krathwohl's affective taxonomy in the following manner:

Bloom's Cognitive	Krathwohl's Affective	Wiles's Instructional
		Critical and creative
		Problem-solving
Evaluating		Cooperative
Synthesizing	Characterizing	Interdisciplinary
Analyzing	Organizing	Conceptual
Applying	Valuing	Inquiry and exploration
Comprehending	Responding	Skills
Knowing	Receiving	Content

REFORM EFFORTS IN THE TWENTY-FIRST CENTURY

Slightly over one century ago, American education confronted the possibility that education could wear many faces and have many meanings. From an exploration of these ideas, the field of curriculum was born. During the first third of the twentieth century, the competing ideas of traditionalism and progressive thought flourished and found expression in both ideas and programs. The statements of the

Commisssion on the Reorganization of Secondary Education and the schools of the Eight-Year Study probably represent the high-water mark in such explorations of competing ideas. Following this period, sporadic manifestations of traditional and experimental views rose and fell with social forces in our nation.

The real and exciting differences of opinion about what education is and how it should be conducted are far from dormant in the twenty-first century. As the last century evolved to be one in which "process" in curriculum took the forefront, the twenty-first century may be a time in which the substantive dimension is fully explored. Change is upon us, and the educational choices of where to commit valuable and scarce resources are many. We no longer possess the wealth to carry all ideas forward without conviction or commitment to purpose.

Schooling in the twenty-first century continues to be highly political because the stakes are so high. Schools are the vehicle by which any nation renews itself and "programs" its youth to carry on values. Schools play a most significant role in determining access to work, providing social equity, and allowing understanding about our system of government and how it works. To control the curriculum is to steer the future of the United States.

Unlike a century ago, when the philosophical arguments of educators had been reduced to discussions of method and strategy, today we are witnessing a return to a more fundamental and primary argument about purpose in schooling. Should our schools proceed in an orderly fashion, an evolutionary fashion, to guide changes that we face in our society, or must there be an evolutionary alteration in the function and form of schools in America? Margaret Mead, America's most famous anthropologist, saw this as a moral issue:

> Our schools have long been torn between two moralities—the morality of individual success as measured by pecuniary gain in the private competitive system, and the morality of individual success as measured by socially useful work consciously directed to the welfare of the whole community. It is time that education made up its mind as to the kind of America it wants, and sought to educate the young on the basis of the integrated morality.[22]

The philosophical differences of American educators go beyond arguments about subject matter and methods, although there is even little agreement on these topics. In general, traditionalists argue that preparation for the future is primarily a process of preparing the mind through formal discipline, whereas more progressive educators see an immersion in true-life experiences as a superior preparation for a changing world. However, enter the extreme wings of American education and hear their pleas for "control" or lack of control in the educative process. Reform in the 1980s and 1990s witnessed parallel and unbending prescriptions for reforming schools. The assumptions of these extreme groups are divergent and uncompromising. Issues of "outcomes" or "inclusiveness" speak to different facets of the same system.

As we transition into a new era, and a time of hope, we look for increased competition among those interested in curriculum in schools. Curriculum workers, although sometimes pressed into the role of referee, must acknowledge a basic truth about the field: curriculum is a value-laden area of education. Neutrality, or simply burying professional activity in the development process, may not be possible in the years to come. With the movement to privatize public education may come an opportunity for creative expression in curriculum work. Knowing one's own values, and understanding that schools are about the promotion of values, will help the curriculum worker of the twenty-first century to be effective and maintain a crucial role.

We present, for your consideration, a contrasting set of images of education from the twentieth century that led us into the twenty-first century. Contemplation of these two apparently incompatible visions of schooling will help you become a thoughtful practitioner in the years to come.

Traditional View of Education

- ☐ Education is a process of changing the behavior patterns of people. *Ralph Tyler*[23]
- ☐ The ultimate goal of the educational process is to help human beings become educated persons. Schooling is the preparatory stage: it forms the habit of learning and provides the means for continuing to learn after the schooling process is completed. *Mortimer Adler*[24]
- ☐ The purpose of public education today is what it always has been: to raise the intellectual level of the American people as a whole. Certain intellectual disciplines are fundamental to the public school curriculum because they are fundamental to modern life. *Arthur Bestor*[25]

  Cultural literacy is the network of information that all competent readers possess. It is background information, stored in their minds, that enables them to take up a newspaper, and read it with an adequate level of comprehension.

  The failure of schools to create a literate society is sometimes excused on the grounds that the schools have been asked to do too much. There is a pressing need for clarity about our educational priorities.

  This author proposes for individuals to agree on the specific items of information that literate people currently share and on the necessity of communicating them in education. *E. Hirsch*[26]

Progressive, Radical, and Postmodern View of Education

- ☐ Traditional education consists of bodies of information (subjects) and of skills that have been worked out in the past. Progressive education cultivates individuality and acquiring skills to make the most of the opportunities of the present life. *John Dewey*[27]
- ☐ Capitalism, with its emphasis on individuality and competition, is incompatible with the morals of democracy . . . . America is the scene of an irreconcilable conflict between two opposing forces. On the one hand is the democratic tradition inherited from the past; on the other hand is a system of economic arrangements which increasingly partakes of the nature of industrial feudalism. Both of these forces cannot survive; one or the other must give way. Unless the democratic tradition is able to organize a successful attack on the economic system, its complete destruction is inevitable. *George Counts*[28]
- ☐ Reconstructionism evolved based on the premise that social change is inevitable. Since it is inevitable, social change is best when it is directed as

opposed to the result of natural drift. While many social groups are eager to direct social change, teachers should be the architects of the new social order as they are the most dedicated to democratic values, knowledgeable about social trends, and occupy the most strategic position to elicit change. *W. B. Stanley*[29]

☐ I believe a new sense of educational order will emerge, as well as a new relation between teachers and students, culminating in a new concept of curriculum. The linear, sequential, easily quantifiable ordering system dominating education today could easily give way to a more complex, pluralistic, unpredictable system or network. Such a complex network, like life itself, would always be in transition, in process. *William Doll, Jr.*[30]

☐ We should develop a system where students have the opportunity to experience the meanings of creating, love, knowing, and organizing; the components needed for the future. *Louise Berman*[31]

☐ Schools should be disestablished because they have a polarizing effect on society. Deschooling means an end to submission to an obligatory curriculum.

A primary alteration in the present educational system would entail the abolishment of the definition of school as an age-specific, instructor-related defined curriculum process that is mandatory for all for a specified period of time . . . we are taught in school that valuable learning is the result of attendance; that the value of learning increases with the amount of input; and that this value can be measured, and documented by grades and certificates. *Ivan Illich*[32]

☐ Curriculum is not neutral knowledge. The knowledge included in textbooks is the result of political, economic, and cultural activities, battles, and compromises . . . separation between education and politics is a myth.

The language of learning tends to be apolitical and ahistorical, thus hiding the complex political and economic resources that lies behind a considerable amount of curriculum organization and selection.

The study of educational knowledge is a study of ideology, the investigation of what is considered legitimate knowledge by specific groups and classes and specified institutions in specified historical moments . . . it is based on a de-integrative strategy which attempts to disenfranchise groups considered to be outside the mainstream (e.g., African Americans). *Michael Apple*[33]

☐ The educational system perpetuates the class structure. Education should be viewed as reproducing inequality by legitimizing the allocation of individuals to economic positions on the basis of ostensibly objective merit. *S. Bowles and H. Gintis*[34]

☐ Education is that terrain where power and politics are given fundamental expression, since it is where meaning, desire, language, and values engage and respond to the deeper beliefs about the very nature of what it means to be human.

Education represents a struggle for meaning and power. For the dominating class it becomes a political and social act that perpetuates a "culture of silence" among the masses and functions for the purpose of domestication . . . in the context of oppressive societies, education is dehumanizing and mechanistic and imparts the transference of knowledge. Schools have served as the mechanism for maintaining social control.

> The poor, voluntarily or involuntarily, knowingly or unknowingly, have been led by the rich and powerful to define themselves as naturally ignorant and inferior. Their minds have been invaded. They see reality with the outlook of the invaders rather than their own . . . and the more they mimic the invaders, the more stable the dominant position of the latter becomes . . . as long as the poor perceive themselves to be powerless, they will remain so. *Paulo Freire*[35]

☐ Curriculum, by its very nature, is a social and historical construction that links knowledge and power in very specific ways. Curriculum, along with its representative courses, is never value-free or objective. Its function is to name and privilege particular histories and experiences. In its current dominant form, it does so in such a way as to marginalize or silence the voices of subordinate groups.

> There is no agreed upon meaning for the term postmodern. It is certainly a rejection of grand narratives and any form of totalizing thought. It embraces diversity and locality. It creates a world where individuals must make their own way, where knowledge is constantly changing, and where meaning can no longer be anchored in history. *Stanley Aronowitz* and *Henry Giroux*[36]

☐ More advanced technology has hit the schools at about the same time as have ideas for school restructuring. *Howard Mehlinger*[37]

☐ Radical educational theory has brought to focus several relevant issues for the future: a) the political nature of schooling and the influence of the dominant culture, b) the potential for schools to serve as resistance to the dominant order, and c) the power of teachers to impact change. *P. G. Altbach*[38]

SUMMARY

Throughout the twentieth century, divergent opinions about education led to efforts to reform the American public school. Because these efforts continue today, curriculum leaders should be aware of the multiple curriculum designs in existence and be open to new thinking about how schools and educational programs are organized.

Six designs have been prominent in the American educational experience: conservatism, technological designs, humanistic designs, vocational designs, social reconstruction designs, and deschooling designs. Such diversity has unquestionably enriched the programs of the American public school. The future holds multiple possibilities for education in the United States. Curriculum development is the vehicle by which schools will approach the unknown future in planning education.

American society experienced enormous changes in the last quarter of the twentieth century. The rate and scale of these changes are continuing in the twenty-first century. The Internet and the new technological learning media present educators with a significant challenge.

Planning for the future of education is made difficult by impermanence in our society, by cultural lag in educational institutions, and by the inefficiency of traditional linear projections of the future. Educational futurists have responded to these conditions by using projection and prediction techniques to attempt to attract schools to preferred futures.

There are numerous conceptions of what education should be like in the future. Some educators favor decentralized programs focused on the individual or specific publics in the American society. Others favor highly centralized programs that serve the state. School districts throughout the United States have responded to these options during the past thirty years by pursuing diverse and multiple ends for education.

The exact nature of educational programs in the United States in the first decades of the twenty-first century will be heavily influenced by the thoughts and work of curriculum specialists. The challenge to all curriculum workers is to think about the meaning of education in our society and present viable alternatives to the sponsoring public.

SUGGESTED LEARNING ACTIVITIES

1. State in three sentences or fewer what you believe to be the purpose of formal education in the United States.
2. Brainstorm likely changes in our society during the coming decade. How will such changes affect public education? Which of your identified changes will have the greatest impact on educational planning?
3. Develop a list of ways in which the public schools might incorporate future thinking into their daily operations. How might curriculum specialists in public schools become more aware of alternatives in education?
4. Describe the purposes of tech-prep/school-to-work programs.
5. Compare at least two reform movements of the past with two recent reform movements (e.g., performance contracting of the 1970s versus charter schools of the 1990s).

NOTES

1. R. Freeman Butts, "Assault on a Great Idea," *The Nation* (April 30, 1973): 553–560.
2. Butts, "Assault on a Great Idea."
3. Robert M. Hutchins, *The Restoration of Learning* (New York: Alfred A. Knopf, 1955).
4. Mortimer Adler, *The Paideia Proposal: An Educational Manifesto* (New York: Macmillan, 1982).
5. E. D. Hirsch, *Cultural Literacy: What Every American Needs to Know* (New York: Random House, 1988).
6. J. Wayne Wrightstone, *Appraisal of Experimental Schools* (New York: Bureau of Publications, Teachers College, Columbia University, 1936).
7. B. F. Skinner, *Beyond Freedom and Dignity* (New York: Alfred A. Knopf, 1971), p. 169.
8. John and Evelyn Dewey, *Schools of Tomorrow* (New York: Dutton and Company, 1915).
9. The Progressive Education Association, *Thirty Schools Tell Their Story,* vol. 5 (New York: Harper and Brothers, 1943), p. 166.
10. Norman Grubb, "The New Vocationalism: What It Is, What It Can Be," *Phi Delta Kappan* 77, 8 (April 1996): 528–534.
11. Maurice Dulton, "Tech Prep/School-to-Work: Career Paths for All," *NASSD Bulletin* (January 1996): 61–63.
12. Donald M. Clark, "Industry-Education Collaboration That Works," *Youth Record* (January 1996): 60–63.
13. Harold Rugg, *The Foundation and Techniques of Curriculum Making,* 26th Yearbook (Bloomington, IN: National Society for the Study of Education, 1927), pp. 7–8.
14. Howard Garner, "Reflections on Multiple Intelligences: Myths and Messages," *Phi Delta Kappan* 77, 3 (November 1995): 201–209.
15. Ivan Illich, "After Deschooling, What?" in Alan Gartner et al., eds., *After Deschooling, What?* (New York: Perennial Library, 1973), p. 1.

16. Allen A. Glatthorn, *Alternatives in Education: Schools and Programs* (New York: Dodd, Mead, 1975), pp. 117–136.

17. Carol Ascher, "Performance Contracting: A Forgotten Experiment in School Privatization," *Phi Delta Kappan* 77, 9 (May 1996): 615–621.

18. Mary Moynatian, "Parents Opt for Home Schooling," *L. I. Business* (January 1995): 28.

19. Anne Lewis, "Public Schools, Choice, and Reform," *Phi Delta Kappan* 77, 3 (December 1995): 267–258.

20. James Goenner, "Charter Schools: The Revitalization of Public Education," *Phi Delta Kappan* 78, 1 (September 1996): 32–36.

21. As appearing in the Tampa Tribune, January 16, 2001, "On-Line in Polk District Schools," p. 15.

22. Margaret Mead, *The School in American Culture* (The Inglis Lecture, 1950) (Cambridge, MA: Harvard University Press, 1951), p. 236.

23. Ralph Tyler, *Basic Principles of Curriculum and Instruction* (Chicago: University of Chicago Press, 1949), p. 5.

24. Adler, *The Paideia Proposal*, p. 10.

25. Arthur Bestor, *The Restoration of Learning* (New York: Alfred A. Knopf, 1936), pp. 48–49.

26. E. D. Hirsch, *Cultural Literacy: What Every American Needs to Know* (Boston: Houghton-Mifflin, 1987), pp. 2, 26.

27. John Dewey, *Experience and Education* (New York: Macmillan, 1938).

28. George Counts, *Dare the Schools Create a New Social Order?* (New York: Day Company, 1932), p. 45.

29. W. B. Stanley, *Curriculum for Utopia* (Albany: State University of New York Press, 1992).

30. William Doll, Jr., *A Post-Modern Perspective of Curriculum* (New York: Teachers College Press, 1993).

31. Louise Berman, *New Priorities in the Curriculum* (Columbus, OH: Charles Merrill, 1968).

32. Ivan Illich, *Deschooling Society* (New York: Harper, 1970), pp. 38, 108, 112.

33. Michael Apple, *Ideology and Curriculum* (New York: Routledge, 1990), pp. 29, 45. *Official Knowledge: Democratic Education in a Conservative Age* (New York: Routledge, 1993), pp. 4, 46.

34. S. Bowles and H. Gintis, *Schooling in Capitalist America* (New York: Bantam Books, 1976).

35. Paulo Freire, *The Politics of Education* (South Hadley, MA: Bergin and Garvey, 1985), pp. 9, 116.

Pedagogy of the Oppressed (New York: Continuum, 1993), p. 33.

36. Stanley Aronowitz and Henry Giroux, *Postmodern Education* (Minneapolis: University of Minnesota Press, 1991), p. 96.

37. Howard Mehlinger, "School Reform in an Information Age," *Phi Delta Kappan,* (February 1996): 402.

38. P. G. Altbach, et al. *Textbooks in American Society* (Albany: State University of New York Press, 1991).

ADDITIONAL READING

Cruickshank, Donald. Preparing America's Teachers. Bloomington, IN: *Phi Delta Kappan* (February 1996): 376.

Guskev, Thomas, ed. *Communicating Student Learning.* Alexandria, VA: ASCD, 1996.

Henson, Kenneth T. *Curriculum Development for Education Reform.* New York: Addison Wesley Longman, 1999.

Johnson, Jean, et al. *Assignment Incomplete: The Unfinished Business of Education Reform.* New York: Public Agenda Foundation, 1995.

Joseph, Pamela Bolotin et al. *Cultures of Curriculum.* Mahwah, NJ: Lawrence Erlbaum, 2000.

Kent, Ashley. *School Subject Teaching: The History and Future of the Curriculum.* Herndon, VA: Stylus Publishing, LLC, 2000.

Medler, Alex, and Joe Nathan. *Charter-Schools—What Are They Up To?* Denver: Education Commission of the States, 1995.

Oldenquist, Andrew. *Can Democracy Be Taught?* Bloomington, IN: Phi Delta Kappa, 1996.

Parkay, Forest W., and Glen Hass. *Curriculum Planning: A Contemporary Approach.* Needham Heights, MA: Allyn and Bacon, 1999.

Philpot, Jan et al. *Partners in Learning and Growing: Linking the Home, School, and Community through Curriculum-Based Programs.* Nashville, TN: Incentive, 1999.

Pinar, William. *Understanding Curriculum: An Introduction to the Study of Historical and Contemporary Curriculum Discourses.* New York: P. Lang, 1995.

Tanner, Daniel, and Laurel Tanner. *Curriculum Development: Theory into Practice,* 5th ed. Upper Saddle River, NJ: Merrill/Prentice Hall, 1995.

Wishnietsky, Dan. *Brooks Global Studies Extended Year-Magnet School.* Bloomington, IN: Phi Delta Kappa, 1996.

~ ~

APPENDIXES

~ ~

appendix **A**

TRAINING PARADIGM FOR CURRICULUM DEVELOPERS

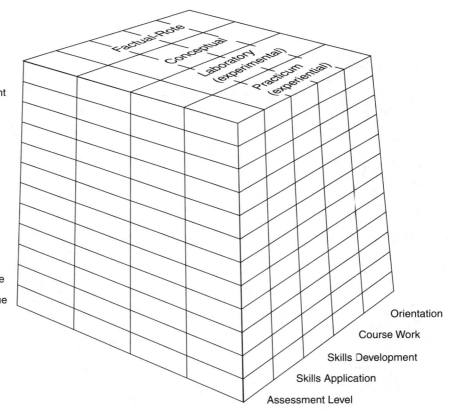

Learning
Human Development
Curriculum Theory
Psychology
Human Relations
Leadership
Change Theory
Instruction
Management
Systems/Commun.
Research Procedure
Evaluation Technique

Factual-Rote
Conceptual
Laboratory (experimental)
Practicum (experiential)

Orientation
Course Work
Skills Development
Skills Application
Assessment Level

appendix B

PARTIAL LIST OF ORGANIZATIONS AND ASSOCIATIONS AFFECTING AMERICAN EDUCATION

Citizens' Organizations
Council for Basic Education
1319 F Street, NW
Washington, DC 20004-1152
www.c-b-e.org

National Coalition for Children
6542 Hitt Street
McLean, VA 22101

National Congress of Parents and Teachers
1715 25th Street
Rock Island, IL 61201

Content Standards Organizations
Arts
Music Educators National Conference
1806 Robert Fulton Drive
Reston, VA 22091
800-350-4223

Civics and Government
Center for Civic Education
5146 Douglas Fir Road
Calabasas, CA 91302-1467
800-350-4223

Economics
Economics America
National Council on Economic Education
1140 Avenue of the Americas
New York, NY 10036
212-730-7007

English Language Arts
National Council of Teachers of English
Book Order Department
1111 West Kenyon Road
Urbana, IL 61801
800-369-6283

International Reading Association
Order Department
800 Barksdale Road
P.O. Box 8139
Newark, DE 19714-8139
800-336-7323 ext. 266

Foreign Languages
American Council on the Teaching of Foreign
Languages
6 Executive Plaza
Yonkers, NY 10701-6801
914-963-8830

Geography
National Council of Geographic Education
1145 17th Street, NW
Washington, DC 20036-4688
202-775-7832

History
University of California, Los Angeles
Associated Student
General Book Division
308 Westwood Plaza
Los Angeles, CA 90024-4108
310-206-0788

Mathematics
National Council of Teachers of Mathematics
1906 Association Drive
Reston, VA 22091
703-620-9840

Physical Education
National Association for Sport and Physical
Education
1900 Association Drive
Reston, VA 22091
703-476-3410

Science
National Science Education Standards
2101 Constitution Avenue, NW
HA 486
Washington, DC 20418
202-334-1368

Benchmarks for Science Literacy
American Association for the Advancement
of Science
1333 H Street, NW
Washington, DC 20005
202-326-6660

Skill Standards
U.S. Department of Labor
Office of Policy and Research
2090 Constitution Avenue, NW
Washington, DC 20210
202-208-7018

U.S. Department of Education
Office of Vocational and Adult Education
330 C Street, SW
Washington, DC 20202
202-260-9576

Social Studies
Expectations of Excellence: Curriculum Standards
for Social Studies
National Council for the Social Studies
3501 Newark Street, NW
Washington, DC 20016-3167
800-638-0812

General Information about Content
Standards
Office of Educational Research and Improvement
National Institute on Student Achievement,
Curriculum and Assessment
U.S. Department of Education
555 New Jersey Avenue, NW
Washington, DC 20208
202-219-2179

**Educationally Related Organizations
and Associations**
American Association for Higher Education
One Dupont Circle, NW
Washington, DC 20036
www.aahe.org

American Association of School Administrators
1800 North Moore Street
Arlington, VA 22209
www.aasa.org

American Council on Education
One Dupont Circle, NW
Washington, DC 20036
www.acenet.edu

American Educational Research Association
1230 17th Street, NW
Washington, DC 20036
www.area.net

American Vocational Association, Inc.
1510 H Street, NW
Washington, DC 20005

Association for Supervision and Curriculum
Development (ASCD)
1703 North Beauregard Street
Alexandria, VA 22311-1714
www.ascd.org

Children's Television Workshop
One Lincoln Plaza
New York, NY 10023
www.ctw.org

College Entrance Examination Board
888 7th Avenue
New York, NY 10019
www.collegeboard.org

Council for American Private Education
13017 Wisteria Dr. #457
Germantown, MD 20874
www.capenet.org

Council of Chief State School Officers
One Massachusetts Avenue, NW
Suite 700
Washington, DC 20001-1431
www.ccsso.org

International Reading Association
800 Barksdale Road
Newark, DE 19711-3269

Joint Council on Economic Education
1212 Avenue of the Americas
New York, NY 10036

National Art Education Association
1916 Association Drive
Reston, VA 20191-1590
www.naea-reston.org

National Association for Education of
Young Children
1509 16th Street, NW
Washington, DC 20036
www.naeyc.org

National Association of Elementary
School Principals
1615 Duke Street
Alexandria, VA 22314
www.naesp.org

National Association for Public Continuing
Adult Education
1201 16th Street, NW
Washington, DC 20036

National Association of Secondary
School Principals
1904 Association Drive
Reston, VA 22091-1537
www.nassp.org

National Council of Teachers of English
1111 Kenyon Road
Urbana, IL 61801-1096
www.ncte.org

National Council of Teachers of Mathematics
1906 Association Drive
Reston, VA 20191-9988
www.nctm.org

National Education Association
1201 16th Street, NW
Washington, DC 20036
www.nea.org

National Middle School Association
4151 Executive Parkway
Suite 300
Westerville, OH 43081
www.nmsa.org

National School Boards Association
1680 Duke Street
Alexandria, VA 22314
www.nsba.org

National Science Teachers Association
1840 Wilson Blvd.
Arlington, VA 22201-3000
www.nsta.org

Ethnic and Minority Organizations
Bilingual Education Service Center
500 South Dwyer
Arlington Heights, IL 60005

National Council of Negro Women, Inc.
633 Pennsylvania Avenue
Washington, DC 20004
www.ncnw.com

National Indian Education Association
700 North Fairfax Street
Suite 210
Alexandria, VA 22314
www.niea.org

National Organization for Women (NOW)
733 15th Street, NW
2nd Floor
Washington, DC 20005
www.now.org

Federal Bodies

House of Representatives
Washington, DC 20515
www.house.gov

National Institute of Education
555 New Jersey Avenue, NW
Washington, DC 20208

National Science Foundation
4201 Wilson Blvd.
Arlington, VA 22230
www.nsf.gov

U.S. Department of Education
400 Maryland Avenue, SW
Washington, DC 20202-0498
www.ed.gov

U.S. Senate
Washington, DC 20510
www.senate.gov

General Associations

Committee for Economic Development
477 Madison Avenue
New York, NY 10022

National Association of Manufacturers
Economic Development Department
1331 Pennsylvania Avenue, NW
Washington, DC 20004-1790
www.nam.org

National Urban League
120 Wall Street
New York, NY 10005
www.nul.org

Labor Organizations
American Federation of Teachers
555 New Jersey Avenue, NW
Washington, DC 20001
www.aft.org

Publishers

Association of American Publishers
71 Fifth Avenue
New York, NY 10003-3004
www.publishers.org

Association of Media Producers
1221 Avenue of the Americas
New York, NY 10020

GLOSSARY

Ability grouping   Organizing pupils into homogeneous groups according to intellectual ability for instruction.

Academic freedom   The right of instructors to decide the materials, methods, and content of instruction within legal and ethical parameters.

Accountability   Holding schools and teachers responsible for what students learn.

Accreditation   Recognition given to an educational institution that has met accepted standards applied to it by an outside agency.

Achievement test   Standardized test designed to measure how much has been learned from a particular subject.

Affective domain   Attitudinal and emotional areas of learning, such as values and feelings.

Aligned   A term used to indicate that a school curriculum is matched with state and national standards as well as with state and national tests.

Alternative education   Instructional programs that modify traditional approaches in one or more of the following areas: setting, structure, scheduling, instructional materials, curriculum development, and assessment.

Alternative school   A school—public or private—that provides alternatives to the regular public school.

Attribution training   Training that deals with the role of the individual's explanation for his or her own successes or failures.

Balanced curriculum   Incorporates all three areas: essential learning skills, subject content, and personal development.

Behavioral approach   An approach that focuses on observable behaviors instead of on internal events such as thinking and emotions.

Behavioral objective   Precise statement of what the learner must do to demonstrate mastery at the end of a prescribed learning task.

Bilingual education   Educational programs in which both English-speaking and non-English-speaking students participate in a bicultural curriculum using both languages.

Block scheduling   The reorganization of the daily or annual school schedule to allow students and teachers to have larger, more concentrated segments of time each day, week, or grading period on each subject. *See also* modular scheduling.

Career education   Instructional activities designed to provide students with the knowledge and skill necessary for selecting a vocation as well as for making decisions regarding educational and training options.

Categorical aid   Financial aid to local school districts from state or federal agencies for specific, limited purposes only.

Certification   The licensure of personnel through prescribed programs of training and education.

Cognition   Process of logical thinking.

Cognitive domain   In Bloom's taxonomy, memory and reasoning objectives.

Cognitive learning   Academic learning of subject matter.

Common planning time   A scheduling procedure that allows teachers to share the same period for instructional planning. The provision of common planning times facilitates collaborative efforts among teachers.

Competency   The demonstrated ability to perform specified acts at a particular level of skill or accuracy.

Competency-based instruction   Instructional programming that measures learning through the demonstration of predetermined outcomes. Mastery is assessed through an evaluation of the process as well as the product.

Conditioning   Reinforcing learning through repetitive response.

Continued learning   Refers to skills used in all disciplines, e.g., reading, writing, research skills.

Cooperative learning   Two or more students working together on a learning task.

Core (fused) curriculum   Integration of two or more subjects; for example, English and social studies. Problem and theme orientations often serve as the integrating design. *See also* interdisciplinary program.

Criterion-referenced evaluation   Evaluation that measures success by the attainment of established levels of performance. Individual success is based wholly on the performance of the individual without regard to the performance of others.

Criterion-referenced test   Measures of performance compared to predetermined standards or objectives.

Cultural diversity   The existence of several different cultures within a group encouraging each group to keep its individual qualities within the larger society.

Cultural pluralism   Cultural diversity; the existence of many different cultures within a group; encouraging different cultures to maintain their distinctive qualities within the larger society.

Curriculum   The total experiences planned for a school or students.

Curriculum alignment   Matching learning activities with desired outcomes, or matching what is taught to what is tested.

Curriculum compacting   Content development and delivery models that abbreviate the amount of time to cover a topic without compromising the depth and breadth of material taught.

Curriculum guide   A written statement of objectives, content, and activities to be used with a particular subject at specified grade levels; usually produced by state departments of education or local education agencies.

Curriculum management planning   A systematic method of planning for change (Wiles-Bondi Curriculum Management Plan Model).

Deductive learning   Instructional materials and activities that allow students to discover the specific attributes of a concept through an exploration that moves from the general to the particular.

Departmentalization   The division of instructional staff, resources, and classes by academic disciplines; service delivery models such as separate general and special education programming; or some other arbitrary structure for compartmentalization.

Developmental physical education   Instruction based on the physical development of the individual preadolescent learner, as opposed to a team sports approach.

Developmental tasks   Social, physical, maturational tasks regularly encountered by all individuals in our society as they progress from childhood to adolescence.

Discovery learning   A type of inquiry, emphasized especially in individualized instruction, in which a student moves through his or her own activities toward new learnings, usually expressed in generalizations and principles; typically involves inductive approaches. *See also* inductive learning.

Early adolescence   Stage of human development generally between age 10 and 14 when individuals begin to reach puberty.

Educational goals   A statement of expectations for students or a school program.

Environmental approach   An approach to learning that is concerned with the restructuring of the learning environment or the students' perceptions so they may be free to develop.

Epistemology   A branch of philosophy that examines (a) how knowledge is gained, (b) how much can be known, and (c) what justification there is for what is known.

Essential learning skills   Basic skills, such as reading, listening, and speaking, that are introduced in the elementary school and reinforced in the middle and high school.

Essentialism   A philosophy rooted in idealism and realism that began in the 1930s as a reaction to progressivism. Reading, writing, and arithmetic are the focus in elementary schools. English, mathematics, science, history, and foreign language comprise the secondary curriculum. Essentialism is subject centered like perennialism, but maintains a contemporary orientation. The arts and vocational education are rejected.

Exploration   Regularly scheduled curriculum experiences designed to help students discover and/or examine learnings related to their changing needs, aptitudes, and interests. Often referred to as the *wheel* or *miniclasses. See also* minicourses.

Extinction   Conditioning learning by withdrawing reinforcement.

Feedback   Evidence from student responses and reactions that indicates the degree of success being encountered in lesson objectives. Teachers seek feedback by way of discussion, student questions, written exercises, and test returns.

Flexible scheduling   Provisions in scheduling allowing for variance in length of time, order, or rotation of classes.

Formal operations   The last state in Piaget's theory of cognitive development characterized by an ability to manipulate concepts abstractly and apply logical methods in the solution of complex problems. Children are not generally expected to exhibit these abilities before 11 to 15 years of age.

Formative evaluation   A method of assessment that occurs before or during instruction to (a) guide teacher planning or (b) identify students' needs.

Gifted learner   The term most frequently applied to those with exceptional intellectual ability, but may also refer to learners with outstanding ability in athletics, leadership, music, creativity, and so forth.

Global education   Instructional strategies and curriculum frameworks that include multiple, diverse, and international resources through the use of technology.

Goals, educational   Desired learning outcomes stated for a group of students and requiring from several weeks to several years to attain.

Graded school system   A division of schools into groups of students according to the curriculum or the ages of pupils, as in the six elementary grades.

Heterogeneous grouping   Student grouping that does not divide learners on the basis of ability or academic achievement.

Homogeneous grouping   Student grouping that divides learners on the basis of specific levels of ability, achievement, or interest. Sometimes referred to as *tracking.*

House plan   Type of organization in which the school is divided into units ("houses"), with each having an identity and containing the various grades and, in large part, its own faculty. The purpose of a house plan is to achieve decentralization (closer student–faculty relationships) and easier and more flexible team-teaching arrangements.

Identification   A defense mechanism in which we identify a part of ourselves with another person.

Imitation   A process in which students learn by modeling the behavior of others.

Independent study   Work performed by students without the direct supervision of the teacher to develop self-study skills and to expand and deepen interests.

Individualized education program (IEP)   The mechanism through which a child's special needs are identified; goals, objectives, and services are outlined; and methods for evaluating progress are delineated.

Individualized instruction   Instruction that focuses on the interests, needs, and achievements of individual learners.

Inductive learning   Instructional materials and activities designed to assist students in the acquisition of knowledge through the mastery of specific subskills that lead to more general concepts and processes.

Innovations   New instructional strategies, organizational designs, building rearrangements, equipment utilizations, or materials from which improved learning results are anticipated.

In-service education   Continuing education for teachers who are actually teaching, or who are in service.

Integration of disciplines   The organization of objectives under an interdisciplinary topic that allows students to use skills and knowledge from more than one content area within a given instructional activity or unit of study.

Interdisciplinary program   Instruction that integrates and combines subject matter ordinarily taught separately into a single organizational structure.

Interdisciplinary team   Combination of teachers from different subject areas who plan and conduct coordinated lessons in those areas for particular groups of pupils. Common planning time, flexible scheduling, and cooperation and communication among team teachers is essential to interdisciplinary teaming.

Interscholastic program   Athletic activities or events whose primary purpose is to foster competition among schools and school districts. Participation usually is limited to students with exceptional athletic ability.

Intramural (intrascholastic) program   Athletic activities or events held during the school day, or shortly thereafter, whose primary purpose is to encourage all students to participate regardless of athletic ability.

Learning   A change of behavior as a result of experience.

Learning center   Usually a large multimedia area designed to influence learning and teaching styles and to foster independent study; also called a *learning station*.

Least restrictive environment   The program best suited to meet the special needs of a child with a disability while keeping the child as close as possible to the regular educational program.

Magnet program   A specialized school program usually designed to draw minority students to schools that historically have been racially segregated. School-based programs are developed around a common theme, discipline, theory, or philosophy. Performing arts, mathematics, and medical fields are representative of the curriculum and instructional components on which magnet programs have been built.

Mainstreaming   A plan by which exceptional children receive special education in the regular classroom as much of the time as possible.

Metacognition   The process by which individuals examine their own thinking processes.

Middle school   A school between elementary and high school, housed separately, ideally in a building designed for its purpose, and covering usually three of the middle school years, beginning with grade 5 or 6.

Minicourses   Special interest (enrichment) activities of short duration that provide learning opportunities based on student interest, faculty expertise, and community involvement; also called *exploratory courses, short-interest-centered courses,* or *electives.*

Minimum competency testing   Exit-level tests designed to ascertain whether students have achieved basic levels of performance in such areas as reading, writing, and computation.

Mission statement   A statement of the goals or intent of a school.

Model   A written or drawn description used to improve the understanding.

Modeling   Demonstrating a behavior, lesson, or teaching style.

Modular scheduling   The division of the school day into modules, typically fifteen or twenty minutes long, with the number of modules used for various activities and experiences flexibly arranged.

Multicultural education   Educational goals and methods that teach students the value of cultural diversity.

Need-structured approach   A learning theory concerned with the needs and drives of students that seeks to use such natural motivational energy to promote learning.

Nongraded school   A type of school organization in which grade lines are eliminated for a sequence of two or more years.

Nonverbal communication   The act of transmitting and/or receiving messages through any means not having to do with oral or written language, such as eye contact, facial expressions, or body language.

Norm-referenced grading   Evaluating a student's performance by comparing it to the performance of others.

Normal learning curve   The expected progress of the average student in a class.

Normal school   Historically, the first American institution devoted exclusively to teacher training.

Paraprofessional   A person employed by a school, program, or district to assist a certified professional and extend the services provided to the students. The paraprofessional may have entry-level training but is not a fully licensed educator or therapist.

Performance objective   Targeted outcome measures for evaluating the learning of particular process-based skills and knowledge.

Personal development   Designed to foster the intellectual, social, emotional, and moral growth of students through such programs as advisor/advisee, developmental physical education, and minicourses.

Portfolio, learner's   A diversified combination of samples of a student's quantitative and qualitative work.

Process–pattern learning   A learning design that focuses on each student's experience rather than on a predetermined body of information.

Progressive education   An educational philosophy emphasizing democracy, the importance of creative and meaningful activity, the real needs of students, and the relationship between school and community.

Readiness   The point at which a student is intellectually, physically, or socially able to learn a concept or exhibit a particular behavior.

Reinforcement   Strengthening behavior through supportive action.

Restructuring   Changing a school's entire program and procedure as opposed to changing only one part of the curriculum.

Scaffolding   Providing a context for student learning, such as an outline or question stem (Vygotsky).

Schema theory   In cognitive learning, large basic units for organizing information. Schemata serve as guides describing what to expect in a given situation.

Scope   The parameters of learning; for example, a subject-matter discipline sets its own scope, often by grade level.

Self-contained classroom   A form of classroom organization in which the same teacher conducts all or nearly all of the instruction in all or most subjects in the same classroom for all or most of the school day.

Semantic mapping   Organizing meanings in language.

Sequence   The organization of an area of study. Frequently the organization is chronological, moving from simple to complex. Some sequences are spiraled, using structure, themes, or concept development as guidelines. A few schools use persistent life situations to shape sequence.

Social competence   The ability to interact positively with persons and groups.

Special learning center   A designated area of a classroom, media center, or some other setting on the school campus with materials and activities designed to (a) enrich the existing educational program or (b) provide students with additional drill and practice in a targeted skill.

Staff development   A body of activities designed to improve the proficiencies of the educator-practitioner.

Subject content   A type of curriculum that stresses the mastery of subject matter, with all other outcomes considered subsidiary. Also called *subject-matter curriculum. See also* homogeneous grouping.

Support personnel   Ancillary personnel such as guidance, media, custodial, clerical, and social services persons who help facilitate the instructional program.

Teacher empowerment   Policies and procedures that enlarge the scope of decisions that educators are allowed to make individually as well as in collaboration with others. Curriculum, instructional materials, budget, scheduling, and pupil assignments in particular classes are a few of the areas that practitioners are increasingly called on to address.

Teachers Training Teachers (TTT) An in-service process by which teachers receive instruction from peers, usually at the school level.

Team teaching A plan by which several teachers, organized into a team with a leader, provide the instruction for a larger group of children than would usually be found in a self-contained classroom.

Tracking The method of grouping students according to their ability level in homogeneous classes or learning experiences.

Transfer In learning, shaping the student to a predetermined form by connecting behavior with response.

Unified arts All nonacademic subjects such as the fine arts, vocational education, and physical education.

Unified studies Also known as integrated or interdisciplinary studies; combines subjects around themes or problems.

Unstructured time Periods of time during the school day that have not been designated for a specific purpose and that present students with less supervision. The time between finishing lunch and the bell to return to the classroom is an example of unstructured time.

Voucher plan Governmental funding programs that allow students and their parents to select among options for schooling by providing predetermined tuition allotments that can be applied to private or public institutions.

Work-study program Collaborative efforts between the schools and community-based employers that allow students to earn course credit for time spent working. Students attend school for a designated number of periods per day and work a predetermined number of hours per week. Grades for work in the community are assigned based on the number of hours worked and the evaluation of the employer.

AUTHOR INDEX

SUBJECT INDEX

ISBN 0-13-089347-1

90000>